Melville Weston Fuller

CHIEF JUSTICE
OF THE UNITED STATES
1888-1910

THE COURT AND THE CONSTITUTION

A SERIES EDITED BY
Philip B. Kurland

MELVILLE WESTON FULLER

Melville Weston Fuller

CHIEF JUSTICE OF THE UNITED STATES
1888-1910

WILLARD L. KING

With an Introduction by PHIL C. NEAL

PHOENIX BOOKS
The University of Chicago Press
CHICAGO AND LONDON

Library of Congress Catalog Card Number: 67-12152
THE UNIVERSITY OF CHICAGO PRESS, CHICAGO & LONDON
The University of Toronto Press, Toronto 5, Canada
© *1950 by Willard L. King*
Introduction © *1967 by The University of Chicago*
All rights reserved
Originally published 1950 by The Macmillan Company
Reissued 1967 by The University of Chicago Press
Phoenix Edition 1967
Printed in the United States of America

To my two Margarets

If the law is respected in part because of its impersonality, it is interesting in part because of its personalities. This is especially true of the men who have sat on the Supreme Court of the United States. Their biographies are worth writing and reading, and not merely because as a group they have been men of attainments beyond the ordinary, but also because the history of the Supreme Court and its influence on the American scene is in a special way a history of men more than events or ideas. To a degree not true of law in general, the law shaped by the Supreme Court bears the indentifiable imprint of the experience, outlook, prejudices, and style of individuals who have been its members. The reading of opinions is only one of the trails that must be followed for a full appreciation of this history. As with statutes, the bare words of legal text are not the whole story. It is necessary, among other things, that we try to see the legal problems of another day as they appeared to those who judged them and to know something of the intellectual equipment with which they addressed their task.

Perspectives of this kind are not easily come by. Our judges have been less accustomed than other public figures to leave memoirs or other self-revelations, witting or unwitting, that might disclose the inner forces of judgment. Whether because of the weight of their official literary burdens, or a sense of the proprieties of judicial office, or the ingrained habit of lawyers to preserve the seal of confidentiality on their professional work, we have been left few extramural accounts of their labors by members of the Supreme Court. Still rarer are the materials for pursuing one of the most fascinating aspects of the history of the Court, the contests of the conference room and the interplay of judicial personalities. The Court itself has provided no record of tentative votes, memoranda and early drafts of opinions, or similar materials that might illuminate the process of decision. Such interior views of the Court's work must be built up from the fragmentary glimpses afforded in the personal papers of individual justices to the extent that they have been preserved. The materials are less rich than one might expect. Not many justices have left for scholars the kind of collection of work papers which enabled Alexander Bickel to reconstruct the process of development of some of Mr. Justice Brandeis' positions.[1] There is some reason to believe that the Justices of a later day have acquired a greater sensitivity to the needs of historians and that such materials may hereafter be more abundant. But one has the impression that the earlier members of the Court were by and large content to let the United States Reports speak for them, an attitude that may tell something about their conception of the nature of law and the role of the Supreme Court.

For an adequate biography of the institution—which is to say, an understanding of one important slice of American history—we are forced to depend on the accretion of familiarity and of insights that individual biographies can bring us. Happily this is a process that is now well under way. The biography of Melville W. Fuller by Willard L. King, Esq., of the Chicago bar, first published in 1950, added an interesting and substantial piece to the mosaic, as did Mr. King's subsequent work on David Davis, the only other Illinois member of the Supreme Court until recent times.[2]

The rise of Fuller to the nation's highest judicial office is a story of the rewards of professional competence in ordinary affairs and also an illustration of the role of chance in the selection of American judges. As such, it holds interest for any lawyer, although the career is one not likely to be repeated in our day. But the special interest of Fuller's biography lies chiefly in its refracted views of the personalities that comprised the Court during his tenure and of the historical events that projected themselves into the Court's field of vision. Those who expect of biography an account of dramatic conflict, striking achievement, or powerful influence are unlikely to find in Fuller himself a satisfactory subject. An admirable but un-

---

[1] Alexander Bickel, *The Unpublished Opinions of Mr. Justice Brandeis: The Supreme Court At Work* (Cambridge: Harvard University Press, 1957).

[2] Willard L. King, *Lincoln's Manager, David Davis* (Cambridge: Harvard University Press, 1960).

exciting figure among the ranks of Supreme Court Justices, Fuller is an important object of attention mainly because, as the eighth Chief Justice, he presided over the Supreme Court for twenty-two terms, beginning in October, 1888, and ending with his death on the Fourth of July, 1910, a period of steward-ship exceeded only by the tenures of Marshall and Taney.

It is dangerous to epitomize so lengthy an interval in the life of an institution, especialy by a figure of speech. But if one thinks of peaks and valleys, the Fuller period appears pre-dominantly flat, perhaps even a trough, from the viewpoint of half a century later. The landscape is more interesting on closer view, however, which is one of the justifications for a biography such as this. Then, as now, the Court was from time to time at the center of great public issues and heated contro-versy, as in the Income Tax Case, the Debs Case, and the In-sular Cases. Then, as now, the greater part of its work was in areas of the law that to the layman appear dry and technical. There is no reason to suppose that the Fuller Court's output was less significant, volume for volume, in the development of American law in its own time than that of the Court at other periods, or that the average competence of its members was lower. But the fact remains that the lasting imprint of the Fuller Court seems faint by today's light and in comparison with the work of the Court at both earlier and later periods.

It would be possible, indeed, to view the Court's record during these years as a chronicle of futile efforts and wrong turnings with respect to central problems. Its attempt to bar the way to a federal income tax was rejected by constitutional amendment. Its unrealistic view of federal powers produced a startling frustration of the Sherman Act in the Sugar Trust case, a position from which the Court was steadily forced to retreat. It failed signally in efforts to erect viable doctrines for fencing off the respective spheres of federal and state powers to regu-late and tax interstate commerce. It embarked on a theory of judicial supervision of public utility rate regulation that led only to confusion and eventual repudiation. It dealt with the issues of the great Pullman strike in a way that hastened the crippling of the courts in the field of labor disputes. Its decision in *Lochner v. New York* brought the entire doctrine of judicial review of statutes into disrepute, along with the concept of substantive due process and the idea of liberty of contract. It was responsible for the "separate but equal" doctrine of *Plessy v. Ferguson,* a decision that survived longer than some of its other work, but only to become one of the most infamous in the Court's history. It rejected crucial opportunities to redress blatant discrimination against the Negro in both the field of education and that of voting rights.

To account for such an impressive record of failures is among the reasons that make study of Chief Justice Fuller and his colleagues interesting. It would be a mistake to hold the Chief Justice primarily responsible for these unfortunate (as they now seem) directions taken by his Court. He spoke as one of nine; in some of the decisions cited above he did speak for the Court, while in most of the others he acquiesced. He was not visibly a dominant influence on the outlook of his Court. But neither was he dominated. If his Court's contributions were ephemeral to an unusual degree, it is reasonable to look for one important key in the stock of experience and ideas that the Chief Justice brought to the bench. Critics of the process of judicial selection have often deplored the frequency with which a political career has been the path to the Court. On the other hand, academic or philosophical concern with problems of public law has also been depreciated as preparation for judicial office. The case of Fuller, who had neither set of qualifications, is worth examining not only to try to distill his constitutional points of view but to see what other sources in his education and prior career might have been expected to give him an outlook adequate to the task of shaping a living Constitution.

It must also be remembered, however, that the Supreme Court of Fuller's period was in important respects a very different institution than it is today. The almost wholly obligatory jurisdiction of the Court, including large classes of private-law cases, brought the docket to its historic peak in the early years of Fuller's administration. None of his predecessors or successors has carried a burden of opinion-writing like that discharged by Fuller in the first decade and more of his service (see Appendix I). The Judiciary Act of 1892 began the process of change, but it was many years before the Court acquired the control over its docket that has enabled it today to concentrate its attention on cases deemed to be of general importance. Accompanying that change, no doubt, has been an increased sensitivity on the part of the Court to the social and political implications of its work. It is a fair question whether the prerequisites for distinguished service on the Court and the criteria for judging accomplishment remain the same today as for Fuller's time.

It is unlikely that further scholarship will produce a portrait of Chief Justice Fuller markedly different from the result of Mr. King's gleanings, the product of long and scholarly investigation of the scattered source materials. Differences in estimates of his rank will persist. Mr. King's account refutes the harsh appraisal given us earlier by Umbreit,[3] for example, partly because Mr. King has taken a stronger interest in appreciating Fuller the man. Fuller emerges in these pages as, among other things, an attractive human being. Faithful to the record, Mr. King does not attempt to make of him a giant in the history of the Supreme Court. But we are fortunate indeed that the art of biography does not attract talent and labor such as Mr. King's only for the study of heroic figures. Our understanding of a major era of the Supreme Court is the richer for this work.

PHIL C. NEAL

[3] Kenneth Bernard Umbreit, *Our Eleven Chief Justices* (Harper, 1938), chap. 8.

ACKNOWLEDGMENTS

∘‿∘

No biography of Chief Justice Fuller has ever before been written. The material for this book was gathered over a long period of time as a lawyer's hobby. For many years, with the obstinacy of a hobbyist, I have haunted people having documents or memories of the Chief Justice.

My principal debt is to his granddaughter, Mrs. Rivers Genet, of Tarrytown, New York, who graciously granted me access to thousands of letters in her possession, none of which had previously been published. I am indebted, too, to Mr. Charles Robinson and Mr. G. F. Edelman of the Tarrytown National Bank and Trust Company for making microfilms of Mrs. Genet's papers.

Other descendants and relatives of the Chief Justice have generously furnished me with many intimate family papers and pictures. These include:

Dr. B. A. G. Fuller, a second cousin;

Miss Dorothy Fuller, a grandniece;

Mrs. G. M. Fuller, the widow of a cousin;

Henry M. Fuller, Esq., a third cousin;

Miss Cony Moore, a granddaughter;

Mr. Hugh Campbell Wallace, III, a great-grandson;

Mr. Melville Weston Fuller Wallace, a great-grandson;

R. D. Weston, Esq., a second cousin.

Descendants of his partners and close friends have given me hundreds of letters from him, as well as many pictures, some of which appear in this book. These persons include:

Mr. Robert Catherwood;

J. Spalding Flannery, Esq.;

Mr. Uri Grannis;

Tappan Gregory, Esq.;

Mrs. Edwin Hawley;

Mrs. Aimee B. Lane,

John S. Miller, Jr., Esq.;

Mrs. Philip Moon;

Henry C. Morris, Esq.;

Mr. Perry M. Shepard.

I am deeply indebted to President Kenneth C. M. Sills and to Bursar Glenn R. McIntire of Bowdoin College for access to many Bowdoin College manuscripts. Professor Mark De Wolfe Howe has given me copies of the Chief Justice's letters to Justice Oliver Wendell Holmes; and Eben Winthrop Freeman, Esq., of Portland, Maine, has furnished me with the letters of the Chief Justice to Judge William L. Putnam.

To the Library of Congress I am indebted for copies from the Cleveland, Gresham, Bancroft Davis, Olney, and Taft manuscripts; to the National Archives of the United States for the large number of papers relating to Fuller's confirmation; to the Widener Library at Harvard University for manuscript letters; to the Maine State Library for manuscript poems; to the University of California Library for the Field manuscripts; to the University of Louisville Library for the Harlan manuscripts; to the Wisconsin Historical Society for the Vilas and Doolittle manuscripts; to the University of Chicago Library for the Douglas manuscripts; to the Illinois Historical Society Library for the Breese and Browning manuscripts; to the Chicago Historical Society for the Henry C. Morris manuscripts; to the McCormick Historical Association for Fuller's letters to Cyrus McCormick; and to the Library of the Supreme Court for the Horace Gray manuscripts.

Many people who knew the Chief Justice have given me their recollections of him. These include:

Colley W. Bell, Esq., of New York;

Professor Zechariah Chafee of Cambridge, Massachusetts;

Mr. Charles Elmore Cropley of Washington, D. C.;

Mrs. James E. Freeman of Washington, D. C.,

Roland Gray, Esq., of Boston, Massachusetts;

Henry C. Morris, Esq., of Chicago, Illinois;

Lessing Rosenthal, Esq., of Chicago, Illinois;

William P. Sidley, Esq., of Chicago, Illinois;

Edgar Bronson Tolman, Esq., of Chicago, Illinois;

Mr. Nathan Weston of Augusta, Maine;

R. D. Weston, Esq., of Boston, Massachusetts;

Russell Whitman, Esq., of Chicago, Illinois;

Professor Samuel Williston of Cambridge, Massachusetts.

Many libraries have given me aid far beyond their duty. These include:

Chicago Public Library;
John Crerar Library, Chicago;
The Newberry Library, Chicago;
Library of International Relations, Chicago;
Chicago Historical Society Library;
Illinois Historical Society Library;
University of Chicago Library;
Chicago Law Institute Library;
Chicago Bar Association Library;
Library of the University Club of Chicago;
Library of Congress;
New York Public Library;
Harvard Law School Library;
Portland Public Library at Portland, Maine;
Bowdoin College Library;
Library of the Maine Historical Society at Portland, Maine;
Lithgow Library at Augusta, Maine;
Maine State Library at Augusta, Maine;
Library of the Supreme Court of the United States.

Senator Robert A. Taft gave me free access to his father's letters and kindly granted me permission to quote them, as I have done. William P. Thompson, Esq., of Boston, sent me a particularly valuable letter of President Cleveland's. Thomas E. Waggaman, the Marshal of the Supreme Court, has aided me in ways too numerous to mention.

The most delightful privilege of the amateur biographer is to submit drafts of his chapters to professionals and receive their criticisms and suggestions. I cringe at the errors I should have committed had it not been for the watchful eyes and penetrating criticisms of Justice Felix Frankfurter and Professors Allan Nevins, Zechariah Chafee, Mark De Wolfe Howe, Carl Brent Swisher, Charles Fairman, Samuel Williston, Albert T. Volwiler, William W. Crosskey, and Wayne E. Stevens, each of whom has read portions of the manuscript. In Chicago, Messrs. Paul M. Angle and Stanley Pargellis, Leon Stolz, Honorable William H. Holly, and the late Henry Crittenden Morris, Esq., must be added to this list; in Boston, Roland Gray, Esq., and R. D. Weston, Esq.; in Washington, Charles Warren, Esq., and Richard W. Flournoy, Esq.; and in California, Professor B. A. G. Fuller.

To all who have helped me, I give my sincere thanks. Many merits of this book are theirs; any error in it is mine.

W. L. K.

CONTENTS

。◡。

ILLUSTRATIONS

○‿○

CHAPTER I

◦‿◦

LIFE IN MAINE

On May 21, 1830, the *Kennebec Journal*, a weekly of Augusta, Maine, carried this item:

> "Married . . . In this town on Monday morning last by the Rev. Mr. Tappan, Frederick A. Fuller, Esq. to Miss Catharine M. Weston, daughter of Nathan Weston, Jr."

It was not then customary for a newspaper to print the local news. This journal is full of Federalist vitriol against President Andrew Jackson, but it says no more about this wedding, which is a pity, for a Chief Justice of the United States—the highest judicial office on earth—was a child of the marriage.

Melville Weston Fuller was born in Augusta, Maine, in 1833. His life divides naturally into three periods: He lived in Maine until he was twenty-three, when he went West to Chicago. He practiced law there from 1856 to 1888, when he was appointed Chief Justice. He served in that position for twenty-two years, a longer term than any Chief Justice except Marshall or Taney.

Like most of our Chief Justices, his background was New England. This fact compels some mention of his ancestry—a peril to a biographer, lest he lose his readers when they strike the "begats."

But the story of this wedding can be quickly told. The bride, Catharine Weston, twenty years old, was given in marriage by her father, Nathan Weston, Jr., then one of the three justices of the Supreme Court of Maine. He was afterward for many years Chief Justice, and received honorary degrees from Dartmouth, Bowdoin, and Waterville (now Colby) colleges.

Although the first Weston had come to Salem, Massachusetts, in 1644, the judge was no witch-killer. He was a gentle, kindly, considerate man. He told, in his later years, with obvious horror how a poor woman in Augusta had once been sentenced to sit on the gallows with a rope around her neck. But the sheriff, together with Weston, then a lad, inflicted the punishment in the early hours of the morning and in a remote part of the town, so that no unkindly eye could see it.

He had once condemned a man named Hager to be hanged, and every now and then he read over his notes of the trial—just to reassure himself. One day he came home white and trembling, and when his daughters asked him why, he said: "I was introduced to young Hager and I almost said to him, 'I knew your father.'" But the judge took comfort in the manner of Hager's hanging, which illustrates the grimness of the New England character as well as its spirit of accommodation. A great crowd had gathered for the event and it was raining. The sheriff went to Hager in midmorning and said: "It isn't customary to have a hanging till noon, but all these people are here to see you hanged and it is raining. Don't you think it would be all right to go ahead with it now?" Hager said Yes, and the hanging proceeded.

Like his father before him, Judge Weston was a Democrat. When the boy wrote to his father from Dartmouth College in 1801 that he had decided to become a lawyer, the elder Weston replied: "Lawyers have heretofore occupied a high position in society. They have reaped where they have not sown. They have reaped where others have sown. But all that is changed now that Jefferson is President."

Judge Weston was originally appointed to the bench by Governor Gerry of Massachusetts after a redistricting which Gilbert Stuart, the famous artist, said made one district that looked like a salamander. "Salamander!" snorted a Federalist. "Better say a Gerrymander"; and the name stuck. Gerry went out; but such was the esteem in which Judge Weston was held that he was continued in office through all of the changes of administration. He first went on the bench when he was twenty-nine and served continuously for thirty-four years. Not even a caucus call from the Democrats in the legislature to accept the nomination for governor would tempt him. His opinions, in the first twenty volumes of the Maine reports, are still cited with respect. He was a scholarly man (a Phi Beta Kappa at Dartmouth) of fine appearance and had a ready flow of speech.

Judge Weston had one virtue that would have been a vice in other times and places. He was thrifty. His letters to his grandchildren invariably contained a homily on saving. He neither smoked nor drank. "Smoking," he wrote one of his grandsons, "is a filthy, disgusting and offensive practice, is the occasion of not a little expense, and sooner or later leads to drink." He never would allow any of his children or grandchildren to have an overnight guest in his home. But there was some excuse for this attitude: he had strained himself to the breaking point to put his four boys through college on the meager salary of a Supreme Court judge. When Chase was appointed Chief Justice of the United States, Judge Weston said: "I hear that Chase is a man of independent property and, if that is so, I don't understand how he can bear to sit there and be talked at by a parcel of d——d lawyers."

Judge Weston's mother, the bride's grandmother, who lived in Augusta at the time of the wedding, was the sister of the Reverend Aaron Bancroft of Worcester, the author of the well known *Life of Washington*. She had a nephew, Dr. George Bancroft, who had graduated with honors at Harvard and taken a doctor's degree at Göttingen in Germany. Dr. Bancroft was then writing articles for the *North American Review*. He was yet to write a *History of the United States* in ten volumes and become a cabinet member, minister to England and Germany, and political boss of Massachusetts.

Judge Weston's wife, the bride's mother, was one of the four beautiful Cony sisters, daughters of the Honorable Daniel Cony. Their father had sent each of the girls down to Boston to spend the winter and make her debut at the great mansion

THE WEDDING

<table>
<tr><td>

First Weston
Salem
1640

</td><td>

First Fuller
The Mayflower
1620

</td></tr>
</table>

Hon. Daniel Cony, the bride's
maternal grandfather

Sarah Bancroft Weston, the bride's
paternal grandmother

The four beautiful Cony Sisters:

Benjamin Apthorp Gould
the groom's maternal uncl

Abigail (m. Rev. John H.
Ingraham), the bride's
maternal aunt

Sarah (m. Reuel Williams,
U.S. Senator), the bride's
maternal aunt

Hannah Flagg Gould, (the poetes
the groom's maternal aunt

Susan (m. Gen. Samuel Cony),
the bride's maternal aunt

Paulina,
the bride's mother

Esther Gould Fuller,
the groom's mother

C. J. Nathan Weston, Jr.,
the bride's father

Col. Henry Weld Fuller,
the groom's father

Louise Weston (Emerson's friend),
the bride's sister

Louisa Fuller (m. Gov. Sam
Smith), the groom's sist

Catharine Martin
Weston (the bride)

Frederick Augustus
Fuller (the groom)

4

of Governor Bowdoin. Each of them had repaid the effort by a
handsome marriage. Paulina had married Judge Weston; Susan
had married her cousin, General Samuel Cony (thus preserving
the Cony name); Sarah had married the Honorable Reuel
Williams, afterward United States senator from Maine; and
Abigail had married the Reverend John H. Ingraham. A talent
for marriage ran in the family; and Paulina's daughter, Catharine, was carrying on the family tradition at this wedding.

The bride's grandfather, the Honorable Daniel Cony, was
an austere old Federalist who added dignity, if that were possible, to the nuptials. As a lieutenant in Washington's army, he
had worn a cocked hat and knee breeches, but in the last few
years he had belatedly donned pantaloons. (Ministers had
preached sermons against that change!) Daniel Cony had been
a practicing physician in Augusta and also judge of the Court
of Common Pleas and judge of probate of Kennebec County
prior to the separation of Maine from Massachusetts. Each
year he celebrated the surrender of General Burgoyne, at which
he had been present. He had been a presidential elector on
Washington's second election. Electors were then supposed to
exercise their own discretion in electing the President, but it
could not have taken much judgment to vote for Washington.
Daniel Cony had also been temporary chairman of the constitutional convention that framed the first constitution for
Maine in 1820. Two of his grandsons were to be governors of
Maine, and a great grandson, Chief Justice of the United
States.

The bride's little sister, Louise, doubtless watched the ceremony with solemn eyes. She grew up to be a serious girl whom
Ralph Waldo Emerson, in a letter to Margaret Fuller, called
"mine & your Louise of Augusta." Tradition in the family
claims that Aunt Louise was "half crazy—she was a transcen-
dentalist."

The groom, Frederick A. Fuller, then twenty-four, also came
from a distinguished family. His first American forebear was
Edward Fuller, whose name appears in the Mayflower Com-

pact. The groom's father was Colonel Henry Weld Fuller, who had graduated from Dartmouth in 1801, where he was a classmate and intimate friend of Daniel Webster.

The colonel's letters from "Black Dan," who later became the "Godlike Daniel," tend to confirm the family tradition that the colonel was a gay dog. Writing to Fuller of a trip to Dartmouth in 1803, Webster said: "Really, Weld, bad as you are, I should have been glad to see you there, merely because it would have been more like old times. On retiring, the possessor of my arm was so preposterous as to say 'Weld is truly very sprightly and amiable!' With all the rhetoric I had, I could not beat her out of this foolish idea, and I believe in my soul she will carry it to the grave with her. Alas, Alas, the perversity of female minds!"

Again reporting to Fuller on a party at Concord, Webster wrote: "I asked Miss Lucy if she wished to see Mr. Fuller very much. She said that—that—that—, the Lord knows what she did say. I could not tell. There was a No, and a Yes, and a blush, and a smile, and a laugh, and so you may make what you can of them."

The colonel's father and maternal grandfather had graduated from Yale. Colonel Fuller had been county attorney for Kennebec County and was, at the time of the wedding, judge of probate. He was a sweet and amiable man who had made a fortune by the purchase in 1818 of the acreage on which a principal part of Augusta was to be built. He had none of Judge Weston's lack of conviviality. Fuller and Weston had attended Dartmouth together and were then the leading Democrats of Augusta. Doubtless they had had something to do with arranging the match. Colonel Fuller had built and sold to Judge Weston the mansion house on Pleasant Street at the head of Oak Street in which the wedding was held.

Colonel Fuller's wife, the groom's mother, was Esther Gould. Her sister, Hannah Flagg Gould, was the author of many popular volumes of verse; her brother, Benjamin Apthorp Gould, was the famous principal of the Boston Public Latin School and the author of the standard annotated school editions of Ovid, Horace, and Virgil. She had a nephew, then only five, also named Benjamin Apthorp Gould, who was to become one of America's great astronomers. The groom's sister Louisa was undoubtedly present at the wedding. Two years later she was to marry Samuel E. Smith, the governor of Maine.

From the Westons, Chief Justice Fuller inherited his sensitivity and conscientiousness, his gentleness and kindliness, and his capacity for methodical work and monklike study; from the Fullers, his passionate and romantic traits, his independence of judgment and his genius for friendship.

It is not surprising that the Chief Justice always took a New England pride in his ancestry. Though he had lived for several decades in Illinois (where the culture is ruggedly equalitarian, an interest in genealogy is usually frowned upon as undemocratic, and it is a common statement that only unsuccessful people are interested in their ancestors), he was able to speak in his later years of the "continuity" of life in Augusta—and "without continuity," he said, "men would become like flies in summer."

The date of the wedding, 1830, was the year after the inauguration of Andrew Jackson, probably the sharpest change that ever took place in American history. To the Democratic fundamentalists it is the true American revolution, surpassing in importance the Revolution of 1776. Their opponents retort that hitherto our Presidents had been notable men who had rendered outstanding service to their country, and that hereafter (with rare exceptions) they were to be little men who had antagonized no one but had caught the popular fancy. As Henry Adams ruefully intimates, the opportunities for a man of culture with "continuity" in his family to render important public service were far less after Jackson than before. But both the Fullers and the Westons were Jacksonian Democrats in a period when people took their politics seriously. Sometimes there were two celebrations of the 4th of July in Augusta because the members of neither party would admit that the adherents of the other were sufficiently patriotic to be entitled to celebrate such a day.

But Jacksonian Democrats fared better in the elections in Maine than elsewhere in New England. Frederick Jackson Turner, in his study *The Frontier in American History,* has pointed out that the American frontier for many years ran along the coast of Maine, and that Maine's culture has always, as a result, had a frontier, or Western, savor. In 1830 Maine was only a seacoast and a forest. Its people, spread along the coast, built and sailed the Yankee clippers at a time when they covered the seas. Augusta, the State capital, though well inland on the map, was the head of the tide on the Kennebec. In 1834, two hundred and sixty-five ocean sailing vessels arrived there, and in the same year a steam packet line started from Augusta to Boston. The railroad did not reach Augusta until 1851. Before that, transportation—except for the river—was by stage. A man could take the stage in Augusta after dinner and be in Boston the next day at night, the third day in New York, the fourth day in Philadelphia, and the fifth day in Washington.

Augusta had a population of about 4,000 in 1830, and about twice that in 1850. Even then the population was 97 per cent native born. Augusta had a dam, several sawmills, a quarry, a cotton mill, a state house, an insane asylum, and a United States arsenal, whose morning and evening gun, heard so many times in his youth, was later to arouse poignant feelings in a Chief Justice of the United States when it sounded seventeen times in midday. Life was raw and crude, but the people were remarkably cultured: Augusta had bookstores, circulating libraries, a privately owned high school, and lyceum lectures as early as the thirties. But the men consumed great quantities of rum; Fuller liked to tell of his great-grandfather, who could lift a barrel of rum with his hands and drink from the bunghole.

The New England character is a peculiar blend of contradictions. The people of Augusta in 1830 were a sensible, conscientious, law-abiding folk, and yet they were quixotic nonconformists. "Whoso would be a man," said Emerson, "must be a nonconformist." All his life Fuller wore his hair long. They were reserved, reticent, restrained, and undemonstrative; yet the writing of poetry was well nigh universal among them. The Chief Justice wrote a great deal of it in his younger days. They were shrewd, calculating, and thrifty individualists, and yet had a profound sense of social responsibility. They held to the puritan ideal that to justify existence one must serve one's fellow men in some way. They were passionate reformers. But they adhered to what was tried unless a proposed reform convinced their reason. They were against unthinking experiments and had no ear for those resting on an emotional appeal. Years later the Chief Justice was to say in a speech at Bowdoin College: "It was said of Turgot [the French Economist] that he was filled with an 'astonished, awful, oppressive sense of the immoral thoughtlessness of men; of the heedless, hazardous way in which they dealt with things of the greatest moment to them; of the immense, incalculable misery which is due to this cause.' "

The period from 1830 to 1850 is the time of the flowering of New England, the age of transcendentalism, the Romantic era in American history, the period of the rise of the common man, the period of manifest destiny. In New England it is a time comparable to the Elizabethan era in England when, at one time, Shakespeare, Marlowe, and Ben Jonson were all living in London, then a town of only 100,000. New England had Emerson, Melville, Longfellow, Thoreau, Hawthorne, Whittier, Holmes, and Lowell. (Melville Fuller read all of these except Thoreau and Lowell as they came from the press.) A wave of optimism spread over the land. Three cheerful ideas dominated the thinking of the people: First, that not the few elect (as Calvinism had it) but everybody—at least almost everybody—would be saved for the life hereafter; second, that the possibilities of man's intellectual development were unlimited; and third, that the United States was destined to become the greatest nation on earth.

Few boys in New England in that day escaped being told that, with hard study, they might become President of the United States. Such youthful fantasies were akin to religious and patriotic fantasies, and it was equally sinful not to cherish them. Melville Fuller, half jestingly, once told his cousin Paulina (who was raised in the same household) that he would some day be Chief Justice of the United States.

After the wedding Frederick and Catharine Fuller settled down in Augusta, where the groom had been admitted to the bar. In 1831 a son, Henry Weld Fuller, was born, and on February 11, 1833, a second son, Melville Weston Fuller. Three months after he was born, his mother filed a suit for divorce against his father in the Supreme Court of Kennebec County. Divorces were rare in 1833. Catharine Fuller alleged that her husband had committed adultery with persons unknown to her on the first day of July, 1830 (less than two months after their marriage), and at divers times between that day and the first day of February, 1833. Frederick Fuller was served with summons in Penobscot County and answered, denying the charge "in the form alleged" and demanding a jury trial. But the court denied a jury trial and decreed a divorce.

Divorces were then so new that lawyers were not sure that the guilty party could remarry. A year later Frederick Fuller filed a petition in the same court, reciting the divorce granted to his wife and praying that a like divorce be given him. This prayer was allowed; and it was decreed that the infant children, Henry Weld Fuller and Melville Weston Fuller, should remain in the custody of their mother, but if she should place them in the custody of Colonel Fuller (their grandfather) he gave bond that he would maintain and educate them to the age of twenty-one years. Five years later Frederick A. Fuller remarried in Orono, Maine, and had five children before his death in 1849. He practiced law and was once Chairman of the

Board of County Commissioners of Penobscot County. He had no part in his son Melville's life except to transmit to him the family characteristics.

Children of divorced parents are usually pitied. But, as Henry James has pointed out so graphically in his novel *What Maisie Knew,* such a child sometimes gains an early education in diplomacy which is valuable to him all through life. This result is even more likely to occur where the divorced parents marry again and where there are large groups of relatives on both sides to be propitiated by the child. Certainly this influence can be traced in the life of Melville Fuller. Everyone who knew him comments on his urbanity and his diplomacy. He was always careful of what he said. He never took sides unnecessarily. He had a passion for conciliation rather than dispute.

For several years after her divorce, Catharine Fuller, with her two small boys, lived with her father, Chief Justice Weston, in Augusta. She made her living by giving piano lessons. She bought her sheet music in Boston from a young man named Oliver Ditson. Ditson took more than a commercial or musical interest in his Augusta customer. He mentioned in his letters his tender regard for her son "Mellie," and the Fuller library at Bowdoin College contains a book given by Ditson to Melville W. Fuller when the boy was seven.

Catharine Fuller was a tiny woman of intense verve. Against the parsimony of her father she fought like a tigress to secure an education for her sons. Every penny that she could save from her piano lessons went into their schooling.

As boys, Henry and Melville Fuller slept in a below-zero bedroom. There were no furnaces, no stoves, no storm windows in those days; houses were warmed by open fires. There were no matches, no lamps, no plumbing; in fact, as Senator Hoar said, no new household comforts or conveniences for everyday living had come into use since the time of the Romans two thousand years before. The twenty years, from 1830 to 1850, were to see great advances in these respects.

Melville and Henry sledded and fished and played crack-the-whip and one old cat. But books soon became Melville's chief interest in life. Judge Weston had a fine library, and the boys soon started to build their own. Many of the books in Fuller's library contain inscriptions in a child's hand, such as, "Library of H. W. and M. W. Fuller, shelf 7 book 82." He was a methodical little boy—a merit that did not abate as he grew older. He was also fussy—"persnickety" is the New England term. One of his early books contains this inscription in his childish handwriting, "Whoever reads this book let him not think I bent the leafs as I did not. M. W. Fuller." This methodical turn and painstaking attitude—rare in a person of his brilliance and facile speech—was one of the secrets of his professional and judicial success.

The most vivid impression of Melville's boyhood (and one which had a profound effect upon his life) was the trial, when he was seven, of his mother, his grandparents, and his Uncle Daniel before the South Parish Church for permitting children to dance square dances in their home.

In the early 1800's such dances had taken place in the presence of the minister, with no restraining frown, but in the 1830's qualms began to arise. Dances to music seemed "pleasure loving" and inconsistent with true piety. A committee of the South Church was appointed to consider the question. It reported that dancing encouraged an undue love of dress, display, and admiration; and nourished levity, vanity, pride, and envy; it "increased the natural aversion to the duties of religion." The report was adopted by the church.

The Westons did not agree with it. More important, they did not concede that the church could control their conduct in such things. Soon thereafter, when a group of young people were attending a party at the Weston home, they danced; Melville's mother played the piano and his Uncle Daniel, the violin. A month later Daniel Weston, who was then a young lawyer in Augusta, published a vindication of the minority view of dancing. A secret caucus of selected church members was then called by the pastor, the Reverend Benjamin Tappan, a stern puritan, to consider "what should be done with Judge Weston's family." A long, painful church trial ensued and, though Chief Justice Weston conducted it with consummate skill, it went against the Westons. As soon as the charges were made, all of the accused were by vote requested to abstain from the communion.

After several harrowing hearings Judge Weston pressed for a decision. The pastor's party indicated that such proceedings sometimes took two years. At this Melville's mother fainted; and Judge Weston, turning to the pastor, said: "This affair must be brought to a close. You will kill my wife and daughter. I don't know but what you have killed my daughter." It was only by the greatest efforts of Judge Weston's friends that the excommunication was softened by a resolution to the effect that the "oversight of the Church" over Chief Justice Weston and his wife should cease. Daniel Weston was excommunicated outright. Mrs. Fuller, on her own request, was dismissed and recommended to the St. Marks Episcopal Church, which the family thereafter attended.

These are the bare facts, but there is more in the atmosphere of the case.

One of the complaints of the South Parish Church against Daniel Weston was that, in his argument on behalf of his mother, he had stated that the church had tolerated an "outrageous crime" by one of its members. Daniel Weston's basis for this charge was that the Reverend Thomas Adams, editor of the *Temperance Gazette,* had published a gross libel upon Daniel's brother, George Melville Weston, who was then the Democratic county attorney of Kennebec County.

The puritan Church was Federalist and Whig. Its Democratic members were at first regarded as harmless, even charming, eccentrics. There is no country where originals are more valued than in the back country of New England. But in the reign of Jackson this eccentricity had lost its charm. Democrats were made uncomfortable in the Congregational Church and many of them joined the Episcopal—perhaps the least democratic in spirit of the Churches. But it offered the best hope of a union of all minorities against the dominant religion and politics.

Melville Fuller, although baptized in the Congregational Church, was a lifelong Episcopalian. He was reared in an atmosphere of resentment against Calvinism. In later life he sometimes ironically referred to his hero, President Cleveland, as "the Presbyterian young man." And Fuller's adherence to the Democratic party never wavered until the days of Bryan; Fuller voted against Lincoln in 1864. There is no stronger party man than one who has suffered social ostracism for his politics.

In December, 1844, eleven years after her divorce, Catharine Fuller was married to Ira Wadleigh, who was engaged in the logging business at Old Town, near Bangor, on the Penobscot River. Melville, who was a very emotional and sensitive child, was desolated by his mother's remarriage. Her letters to his grandmother describe his jealousy and tears. "Melly knows," she wrote, "that I love him best but he argues and argues till I am half dead. . . . The poor baby is in a perfect agony and says he will try to overcome his jealousy." After his mother's marriage, Melville lived much of the time with his grandparents in Augusta.

The year after her marriage, Catharine Fuller took a trip with her husband to the "Far" West—Wisconsin—to see about logging prospects there. They went to Boston by coastal ship, visiting there Oliver Ditson, who had a baby boy, four days old; thence to Stonington, Connecticut, by the "cars" (the engine broke down on the way); then to New York by ship; thence up the Hudson to Albany by river boat, and then on the cars and by horse and wagon to Buffalo. From there they took a lake steamer to "Milwaukie," Wisconsin—a five-day trip on the Great Lakes. From Milwaukee Mrs. Wadleigh wrote to her mother: "This country is settled by N. England people & you can feel more at home than in any place between here and

Maine. Tell Pa he is well known here and spoken of with great respect. Mr. W. [Wadleigh] says, if Pa would come out here, in 2 years he would be king of all he surveyed. . . . I am perfectly willing to come out here if it is best for the boys."

The next year, when he was thirteen, Melville was taken on a visit to Duanesburg, New York, by his Uncle Daniel. A letter dated "Satteday," May, 1846, describes the journey: "We had a very smooth night coming to Boston. We went to the United States Hotel. After breakfast, we visited for awhile. Went into Ditson's store. He was out. Uncle Daniel had a little business to do so he left me for a little while. By and by he [Ditson] came in. He didn't recognize me. I did him though. I asked him if he knew me. He said he didn't know that he did. Then I told him and he shook hands and talked. He appeared glad to see me. I saw the Old South Meeting House and Brattle Street Church with the cannon ball in it and I saw the Temple and the Tremont House and walked in the Common. I saw Quincy Hall, a description of which I have seen in the Age." The letter continues with similar details of the sights in New York, where his uncle left him on his own and Melville went to the theater: "I went to the Pit. Price was 50 cts. The play was The Beggar on Horseback, a Comedy. It was not very good but there were some pretty fair things said in it. I thought they didn't pronounce so well as they might. They pronounced Worse, Wus, &C, &C."

The boy's affectionate nature is shown by his fascination with pets. In one letter from the farm in New York he mentions the hens and little chickens, turkeys and little turkeys, pigeons, sheep, and lambs, cats and kittens, a pony and a pet turtle. Already he had apparently read much of Dickens: he named the turkeys "Oliver Twist," "Barnaby Rudge," and "Nicholas Nickleby," and the turtle, "Quilp." He wrote: "I have been reading a novel by Dumas called 'Marguerite du Valois' and I think Grandpa would like it as well or better than Matilda. Give my love to him. I am glad he has so great a case to attend to. Write me all about it."

When he was thirteen, war with Mexico occurred. As frequently happens, his memory of the war centered around an almost irrelevant incident. His Aunt Abby's husband, the Reverend John H. Ingraham, was chaplain of the State Senate, and every day he prayed that the enemies of the Republic might be "smitten hip and thigh." The literal picture raised in the boy's mind of this rear attack upon the Mexicans tickled him, and he remembered it all his life. His sense of the ridiculous was always one of his most endearing traits.

In 1847, when Melville was fourteen, President Polk visited Augusta with James Buchanan, Secretary of State, and Nathan Clifford, then Attorney General. The President stayed all night at Aunt Sarah Williams's house. Her husband, Reuel Williams, had known the President when Williams was in the United States Senate and Polk was Speaker of the House.

As Melville listened to the President's speech, he heard perhaps for the first time the vibrations of a coming conflict. Ours was the noblest structure of human government ever devised by the wisdom of man, said the President; but it was founded on compromise and mutual concession, and whoever should disturb those sacred compromises would "destroy this fairest fabric of human wisdom and inflict an irreparable evil upon mankind." "Sir," said the President, "how shall the local jealousies that disturb us compare with the great object of binding and continuing this free and happy people." Melville was impressed.

In May, 1849, the Dialectic Club of Augusta was organized, with Melville Weston Fuller as President. He was then sixteen. Many such clubs were organized in New England in this period at the suggestion of lyceum speakers. Education and self-improvement were then the passion of the people. According to the printed catalogue of this club, it was "founded for mutual improvement" but it was particularly devoted to "exercises in discussion and composition." It had a library of ninety volumes. Among them was *Scenes in a Vestry,* which Melville's Uncle Daniel (who had become an Episcopal clergyman) had written to tell the story of the Weston expulsion from the puritan church. There was also in this library a long poem called "Philo," written by Sylvester Judd, Jr., the Unitarian minister in Augusta who had married one of Uncle Reuel Williams's daughters. Sylvester Judd was a good friend of Emerson, and Judd's novels *Margaret* and *Richard Edney* (descriptive of the Augusta scene in the 1840's and before) were much read, and *Margaret* was praised in print by James Russell Lowell. The Dialectic Club also had a mineralogical cabinet with two hundred specimens collected by the members. The printed programs of the club show M. W. Fuller as taking the parts of Macbeth and Brutus, Mr. Blushington in scenes from *The Bashful Man,* Sir Anthony Absolute in scenes from *The Rivals,* and Samson Slasher in the "laughable farce, Slasher & Crasher." In June, 1849, he was the lecturer at the annual exhibition of the club; in 1850 he was the orator at its anniversary, and, in the same year, he was elected its poet.

◦◡◦

CHAPTER II

BOWDOIN AND HARVARD

Iɴ September, 1849, Melville Fuller, aged sixteen, took the stage at Augusta for Brunswick, Maine, where he entered Bowdoin College. Bowdoin was then more than fifty years old and was already famous. It was a family school; most of his uncles had gone there; his great-grandfather, Daniel Cony, was one of the founders and overseers, and Judge Nathan Weston and former Senator Reuel Williams were trustees.

Three forces molded the boy at Bowdoin: his family, the faculty and his fellow students.

For a time it had seemed that he would not go to college, for his grandfather refused to send him. His mother and his grandmother finally shared the cost, his grandmother contributing $100 each year and his mother the remainder. A year's education at Bowdoin then cost about $150. Mr. Wadleigh, his mother's second husband, had failed in business, and his wife's only source of income was her music. She wrote to Melville: "Now listen soberly—it is your Grandmother & not yr grandfather that allows you $100 per year. She will do it because she loves you so—Now this amount must not be exceeded and whatever else is necessary must come from me. . . . Your grandpa may ask you if you need money & let you have it but he will charge it [against the $100]."

His mother and his grandmother wrote to him every week. Grandma Weston's letters had a twinkling wit. "Louisa" [his unmarried aunt], she wrote, "sends you one of her knit dish cloths. I suppose you will use that for your Company dish cloth." She reveled in New England understatement: "Uncle Nathan was very pleased with his visit to you—said your room

18

looked complete." She could even laugh at her own oversolicitude, thus: "Uncle Charles [who had just visited Brunswick] is very pleased with you and thinks you will be something great. Don't let the students inveigle you into any mischief. If there is anything disorderly going on—go directly to your room. Suppose the College gets on fire, is there any way for you to escape? Couldn't you have a rope in your room to let yourself down from your window? . . . But you would tear the skin off your hands and you must put on mittens—now don't laugh and if you do I shan't know it—but I *know* you *will*."

But chiefly she urged him on and corrected him. "Stick to your studies like a tick and you will never be sorry," she wrote. "The word you should use for hollered is hallowed—look in your dictionary." "Don't say Jim Bates, but James. . . . Any endearing name in the family you can use but it is more well bred to speak everyone's name as it is. Grandy wishes you to be as near perfection as possible."

She was anxious to have Melville gain the approval of his grandfather. "Your G.pa will go to Brunswick next Wednesday. . . . I suppose in the stage. . . . You must plan to see him all you can & think before of what you will say to him. You may need some advice about something or other." When the lad made a good impression on his grandfather, she purred with pleasure: "Your G.pa received your letter & was highly pleased with it. He thinks you are considerable of a boy. He expressed himself more elegantly than I have & you are at liberty to imagine as many fine speeches as your good sense will allow you to. I don't know when I have seen your G.pa more pleased."

His grandmother and his mother warned him never to touch liquor. Judge Weston was more judicious. "Avoid periodicity in your drinking," he counseled.

Melville's mother's letters were full of fond admonitions but lacked his grandmother's humor. "I am busy all the time with my scholars," his mother wrote, "and I hope you are reaping the benefit of my labors so that you may be a man by & by & a right smart one." "Your career opens bright before you & it depends upon yourself alone how great and useful you may become—it is a great privilege for you to receive an education. I hope you will not waste one cent or one moment of time."

She implored him to avoid liquor, tobacco, and debt. "I wish you would not have one single debt," she wrote. "It is horrible and debasing to the character." When he sent her the newspapers with the story of the trial of Professor Webster of Harvard who had murdered a man to whom the professor was indebted, she responded: "I got the papers about that unhappy Prof. Webster, . . . the moral of his life is that extravagance leads to vice direct."

The boy was a great satisfaction to her. He was studious; he was orderly; he was thrifty. When she came to see him, she found that his room was neat and his "barrel of kindlings" not used up. Uncle Reuel Williams visited the college and reported that Melville's "character" stood high and that he guessed Melville "took after" Grandpa Cony. "This is very gratifying," his mother wrote, to one "whose heart is all bound up in your welfare."

It is a pity that these women did not live to see their boy become Chief Justice of the United States. He carefully preserved their letters, marked them "sacred", and sometimes reread them in later years.

College professors in that era usually had only A.M. degrees. But the Bowdoin faculty was not to be scorned. For example, there was Thomas Cogswell Upham, a tall figure with a scholar's stoop. He was professor of mental and moral philosophy, and had been brought to Bowdoin to combat the pernicious philosophical doctrines of Immanuel Kant. Upham published sixty books during his lifetime, including one book of verse. The professor of Chemistry and Mineralogy was Parker Cleaveland, with a strong face like that of Bismarck. His text on the minerals of America had at one time gained an international acclaim. The president was Leonard Woods, a classical and theological scholar of renown, noted for his feats in the composition of Greek iambics and hexameters, for having dined with Louis Philippe in Paris in 1840 and conversed with Pope Gregory for some hours in Latin.

The curriculum was classical and theological. To be well versed in Latin and Greek was an entrance requirement. Advanced Latin and Greek, with courses in French, Spanish, German, Italian, and Hebrew were obligatory; there were no optional courses. Weekly exercises in elocution were demanded of all students. The freshmen were required to study Paley's *Natural Theology* and the seniors his *Evidences of Christianity.* Compulsory chapel was held twice a day, at dawn and evening. In Hawthorne's famous line, the college inculcated in its students "a deep and awful sense of religion which seldom deserted them through life."

Contacts with classmates were perhaps more educational than attendance at classes. One small class at Bowdoin in 1825 included Longfellow and Hawthorne, and President Franklin Pierce was in the prior class. There were twenty-five in Fuller's class, all from New England, and all but four from Maine. They were serious-minded boys: seven of them became ministers; five, lawyers; four, doctors; and two, editors.

College athletics were yet unknown; their place was filled by the literary societies and the Greek-letter fraternities. Fuller was initiated into the Chi Psi Fraternity. Almost immediately he was elected to a minor office in the chapter; and thereafter, until his graduation, he took an active part. In his senior year he was treasurer and acting president, and half of the meetings were held in his room. The minutes refer to his eloquence, to his facility in composition, and to his constant activity in campus politics; they also show the affection in which he was held by his fraternity brothers.

Fuller roomed at Winthrop Hall and Maine Hall, the college dormitories; his roommate during his last two years was his cousin, Joseph E. Smith, son of the former governor of Maine, and later Fuller's law partner in Chicago. The long vacation was in the winter instead of summer, so that the students might make a little money by teaching school, but Fuller worked during the vacations for a newspaper in Augusta called the *Age*. There are many traces of his activities as a campus politician: at one place his record is marked "11 times whisp. chap.", which, being interpreted, means that on eleven occasions the future Chief Justice of the United States was guilty of whispering in chapel.

He joined the Athenaean Society, one of the two literary and debating societies to which practically all of the students belonged. The society was then forty-four years old and had a library of about 5,000 volumes. Fuller's withdrawals of books from the library indicate that he educated himself in spite of the college curriculum: he withdrew more books than any other member. The records of the society show that he gave frequent dissertations before it. The library of the Chief Justice at the time of his death contained five sets of books given him during his college days by President Woods as declamation prizes. Fuller also took part in many debates. He was assigned the negative of the proposition: "Resolved that dueling is never excusable," and lost by a vote of eleven to four. Years later, friends in Washington wondered where he acquired his extensive knowledge of the history of dueling in America. But he won easily on the affirmative of the question: "Resolved that the bar offers a wider field for eloquence than the pulpit." In his junior year, through a political combination of the Chi Psis and Psi U's, he was elected president of the society. The minutes thereafter refer to his "eloquent and impressive" addresses.

A college theme, written when he was a junior, contains the key to his career. The subject was: "Are great intellectual powers preferable to energy and decision of character?" His answer was No. "The world furnishes many examples of the superiority of the truly earnest and laborious mind over the merely intellectual." He concluded that it was far better to have a firm and indomitable will than to have brilliant talents. His life was to be a demonstration of this thesis. He did not

MELVILLE W. FULLER ON HIS GRADUATION
FROM BOWDOIN COLLEGE IN 1853

lack talents, but his character surpassed his intellect in significance.

His speech on the installation of his successor as president of the Athenaean Society is also prophetic of qualities that marked his Chief Justiceship. Know your parliamentary law, he enjoined, but apply it with restraint and discretion. Parliamentary forms, he declared, are to serve the will of the assembly rather than restrain it. Some of his colleagues on the Court thought that, because of his tact and diplomacy, he was the best presiding officer that they had ever known.

He warned his successor in the chair at the Athenaean against partisanship and partiality. "You are the representative of no particular party," Fuller reminded him, "but of each and every individual of this fraternity." Fuller was appointed Chief Justice as a Democrat, but even the most bitter opponent of his party conceded that as Chief Justice he had been absolutely free from partisanship.

He told the new president of the Athenaean that, as the head of the society, he would be looked to by its members "to uphold its character and represent its dignity." It was agreed when Fuller died that none of his great predecessors as Chief Justice had surpassed him in upholding the dignity of the Court.

Fuller's most engaging quality as Chief Justice was his extreme modesty. The boy concluded his farewell remarks at the Athenaean: "And remember, Sir, that however much he who is about to retire from this chair may have failed in all these respects, there is no advice so precious—none likely to prove as profitable, as that coming from one whose experience has been bitterly gained."

A daguerreotype taken in this period shows a very serious youth. The face is intense and poetic, with a great mop of hair covering his ears and curled on one side to expose a high forehead. A Spanish cape is raised on the other side to compensate the imbalance of his hair. The boy looks as much like Lord Byron as the Chief Justice resembled Mark Twain, for whom he was often mistaken. Fuller stood only 5½ feet high when he left college, and weighed only 130 pounds.[1] His hair was light and his eyes gray. He was a slight, frail, sensitive boy, with the spiritual and intellectual factors predominating in his personality.

Of his poetry in college the less said the better, although some of his later poems had more merit. Most of his college poems were odes written for class dinners at the end of the year. The theme is "Thank the Lord, we're thru with that." He spent the rest of his life trying to live down the reputation as a poet that he thus gained among his classmates. One of these poems in Latin is a little better than the rest, perhaps because commonplace thoughts are more palatable in Latin. It starts:

> O Charta Mathematica!
> Vale! Vale, ad te!
> Cantamus nunc cum gratia,
> Non vexati esse.

One line of his ode at the end of the Freshman year is: "We'll Stowe our Paleys on the shelf." Paley refers to Paley's *Natural Theology,* and Stowe to Calvin E. Stowe, Professor of Natural and Revealed Religion. Professor Stowe's wife was the daughter of the Reverend Lyman Beecher, the sister of the Reverend Henry Ward Beecher, and her name was Harriet Beecher Stowe. While Fuller was a student in Brunswick, she had a vision, while praying one Sunday in the Congregational Church, of a harmless old negro being beaten to death by a cruel overseer. This apparition appeared later in a book completed by her in 1851 in Brunswick. It was called *Uncle Tom's Cabin,* and was afterward translated into thirty-seven languages.

Fuller was no abolitionist but he abhorred slavery. He wrote a college theme on the "Effect of Slavery on the Southern Character." "A passionate temper," he declared, "and a hard hearted insensibility to suffering are consequences inevitably ensuing from slavery." He spoke of its "tyrannical cruelties."

[1] In 1866, and for many years thereafter, he weighed only 114 pounds.

Furthermore, he said, "the Planters constantly indulge in their lustful propensities [toward their slaves] and hence the brutish and sensual is predominant in their characters. He concluded that "to expect any other result than evil from so revolting a wickedness is as absurd as to suppose we can gather 'grapes from thorns or figs from thistles.'"

In his senior year his Grandfather Fuller's old friend Daniel Webster died, and at the request of the students Professor Hitchcock and Fuller attended the famous funeral in the yard at Marshfield as the representatives of Bowdoin College. A month later President Woods presented him with a six-volume set of the *Works* of Daniel Webster. Perhaps these books were given in the same spirit with which a minister might give a Bible to an atheist who had lost his mother. President Woods was of staunch puritan background and it may be assumed that he did not entirely approve of Fuller's Democratic leanings. If it was Woods's purpose, however, in selecting the gift to win Fuller from his Democracy, the effort was without avail. But both Woods and Fuller, while detesting slavery, were opposed to the Civil War and both suffered an eclipse of their careers from their opposition. It is possible that by this gift Woods meant to commend to Fuller the example of Webster in temporizing with slavery until time could destroy it. If such was the president's purpose, the gift may have had some effect.

But Fuller was a Democrat in every fiber. In 1852 he organized the Granite Club at Bowdoin to work for Franklin Pierce, a Bowdoin graduate, who was then the Democratic candidate for President. The Granite Club held a mammoth rally for Pierce at Augusta. Among the guest speakers were Governor Hubbard and Senator Hamlin of Maine, John A. Dix of New York, and Pierre Soulé of Louisiana. The temporary chairman, whose speech was reported in full in the Boston *Post*, was a young Bowdoin junior then only nineteen. He declared, "There is that in the noble and chivalric character of our candidate, particularly calculated to animate and interest youth as affording them a shining example of what earnest and honorable effort will accomplish for itself—as teaching them ever to be, as he has been, true to themselves, true to their country, true to the best and purest instincts of their nature in order to fit themselves for eminent positions by distinguished worth."

As the orator finished, a man in the front row turned to George Pillsbury, the station agent, and said, "Who's that?"

"Name's Fuller," Pillsbury responded, loud enough to be heard by the speaker. "Smarter 'n hell, ain't he."

Life has so few supremely happy moments! And when they do come they frequently have disagreeable aftermaths. The next visiting committee at Bowdoin condemned the Granite Club. They said that political activities by students not only engendered ill will but "seriously interfered with the appropriate duties of the College." But his grandmother wrote him: "had a nice letter from your mother. . . . She says the Judge may as well open his eyes to the fact that you are a very smart young man."

A college theme entitled "The Supernatural in Fiction," written when Fuller was a senior, indicates his growth in sophistication. It also shows his indebtedness to transcendentalism. Man has, he said, "an innate consciousness of a capacity for the highest and noblest actions, higher and nobler far than fall within the realities of life." He did not find that idea in Paley or his catechism. But he manifested his abiding attachment to the religion of his time when he concluded, "We might well consider ourselves but as the beasts that perish did we feel no sympathy with the unseen world" of the supernatural.

Fuller graduated A.B. at Bowdoin in September, 1853. Though not at the head of his class, he was one of eight elected to Phi Beta Kappa. He immediately started to study law in the offices of his uncles, Nathan Weston and George Melville Weston, in Bangor. Nathan was Clerk of the Supreme Court in Bangor and George Melville was a practicing lawyer. A letter from Fuller's mother a few months before his graduation is typical of many such letters and shows her plans for his law studies:

"Sunday, OLD TOWN, March 15, 1853

"MY DEAREST MELLY

"I was very much pleased to receive your letter dated March 6th & it is now before me—it does me so much good to get one from you, if it only contains one line. Coming events seem to be casting their shadows before with you—we shall have time enough to talk every thing over together respecting your future course. I shall endeavor to ascertain somewhat about the expediency of your settling in Bangor between this and then. I think exactly as you do about your studying where you will locate. I am inclined to think your Uncle Nathan's office will be a good place to learn law in. He says you will have time for as many hours study as you ought to devote to that purpose, besides helping him,—and helping him you cannot fail to acquire knowledge of forms and practical matters. Then his office is in the Court house & with ease you can hear all the pleading &C that is interesting. I shall try fully to inform myself of all these matters. Above all your salary must be definite. I think well of a 6 months at Cambridge—yr Uncle says 'he will give you enough to board, clothe & pocket money you' Now we must have a definite sum. I shall clothe you and board you at Henry's—that is, I shall pay Henry exactly what it costs & I do this to help him as he at present has to walk a crack. Thus if you can learn your profession & in the meantime save enough to go to Cambridge it will do very well. I shall make every inquiry & you and I will plan mightily together. If you use proper diligence and prudence I should think you might be married in two years—now certainly that is worth trying for. Keep yourself unspotted from the world and deserve to have a wife—you know very well what I mean—you may safely follow my advice, for your happiness has been my desire ever since you breathed the Breath of life—the *vicious* don't enjoy a wife as the virtuous do & the path of virtue is the path of happiness in this life. You must let me know about yr money in due season. . . . Don't worry yourself about your future—

the way will open as we go along—take care of your health.
. . . Yr Grandpa & Uncle Dan[1] are both going to Brunswick
in May—next time you write let me know exactly when your
May Exhibition is—the day of the month—Dear Melly

"I am ever & ever yr

affec mother

C. M. WADLEIGH"

She wrote many times that as soon as he was through college, she would be ready to die—to "go down" into her "little
short grave," as she put it. She lived only four months after his
graduation. Soon afterward he wrote a poem called "Remorse."

> I may not flee it; in the crowded street
>   Or in the solitude but all forgot
> Tis ever there, a visitant unmeet
>   Deep in my heart the worm that dieth not.
>
> There is no consolation in the thought
>   That from her lips no chiding words were spoken
> That her great soul on earth for nothing sought
>   Toiling for me until its chords were broken.
>
> Too late the knowledge of that deep devotion
>   Too late belief of what I should have done
> Chained to my fate to suffer the corrosion
>   Of my worn heart until life's sands are run.
>
> Why should I weep? Why raise the voice of wailing?
>   Why name the pangs that keep me on the rack
> Or prayers or tears alike were unavailing
>   She has gone home. I cannot call her back.
>
> And I alone must wander here forsaken
>   In crowded streets or in secluded spot
> From that sad dream, oh, never more to waken
>   Or cease to feel the worms that dieth not.

In the fall of 1854 Fuller entered Harvard Law School,
rooming at Mrs. Swan's on Everett Street with his Bowdoin
classmate Henry Downes. The law school faculty then con-

sisted only of Joel Parker, Theophilus Parsons, and Edward G. Loring. Joseph H. Choate and James Bradley Thayer, afterward Fuller's friends, were students in the law school while he was there. Fuller always belittled his Harvard experience: he said that he only attended lectures for six months. No grades of the students were kept at that time, but the records of the Harvard College Library show that he was still a hearty reader.

In 1855 he was admitted to the bar in Maine and clerked for a few months in the office of his Uncle Nathan at Bangor. In June of that year he delivered an oration before the convention of the Chi Psi Society at Springfield, Massachusetts. The fraternity thought enough of it to print it in pamphlet form. Here a lad of twenty-two sets forth his philosophy of life. He described at first in flaming words the Crusades, when a "universal frenzy seemed to seize upon all the people." "High and low, rich and poor, infirm and strong, men, women and even children, rose as with one simultaneous movement and demanded to be led against the infidel." But the orator said that he wished to speak of a later crusade—the crusade on behalf of the great cause of "Human Rights and Human Progress" by those who have the "good of mankind" as their object.

He cited Dante and Petrarch, Tasso and Galileo, Shakespeare and Cervantes, Spencer and Schiller, Wordsworth and Burns, and, finally, Columbus, as examples of modern crusaders. It was, he said, "through the wounds and sufferings of men like these that we pass on through the breaches they have won to certain victory." He emphasized their "chivalric spirit" and their "religious sentiment." The pursuit of truth and the contemplation of the infinite, he suggested, was essentially religious in its character; the desire to perform acts for the everlasting good of humanity was an instinct implanted by divinity. "Ours is no age" of "fervent religious zeal," he admitted. "It is perhaps only an age of invention and contrivance, of dollars and cents, of subjection to public opinion and popular sovereignty," yet "it steadily advances on the sure road of progress and reform." "Let us aid," he concluded, "insofar as in us lies, the onward movement of the New Crusade, and let our blows fall thick and fast upon the side of Truth and Justice and in behalf of all Humanity."

In the summer of 1855 Fuller moved back to Augusta to assume the editorship of the Augusta *Age* in partnership with another uncle (this time on the Fuller side), Benjamin Apthorp Gould Fuller, sometimes called "Bag" Fuller. Sketches of Melville Fuller commonly state that he practiced law in Augusta in this period, but Bowdoin College has a letter from him in which—with his usual scrupulousness—he corrects this statement. He says that his principal occupation was editing the *Age,* although he may have tried one or two small cases on the side.

Until January, 1855, the *Age* had been a very prosperous paper. As the principal Democratic paper in Maine, it had held for thirteen years a lucrative contract as State printer. But the long Democratic lease of power in Maine was ending. In 1854 Senator Stephen A. Douglas had sponsored in the United States Senate an Act forming two territories to be known as Kansas and Nebraska and permitting the people in each to determine for themselves the question of slavery by "popular sovereignty." The Northern people were not pleased with this law, for it repealed the provision of the Missouri Compromise that the area north of Missouri should be forever free. President Pierce supported the bill, and Senator Hamlin of Maine said that Pierce had a secret understanding with the slavery group before Pierce was nominated. Senator Fessenden of Maine also spoke and voted against the bill. And when it passed in June, 1854, and was signed by the President, the anti-abolitionist Augusta *Age* was so disgusted as to exclaim "What next." The Republican party was being born and Maine was to be among the first Republican states. A Republican state administration was elected in September, 1854, and in January, 1855, the Augusta *Age* lost its contract as State printer.

The *Kennebec Journal,* which became the State paper, was

edited by a young man named Blaine. Fuller was to meet Blaine again thirty-five years later, when, as Chief Justice, he administered the oath of office to President Harrison, whose Secretary of State was James G. Blaine. Blaine liked to reminisce in later years that as State printer he made $4,000 a year and spent $600—a ratio between outlay and income which he said he had never since been able to maintain.

The *Age* and the *Kennebec Journal* were not respectful to each other in their columns. In fact, neither Fuller nor Blaine gave promise of their future eminence in the pages of those papers. But Fuller still read books. He recommended in the *Age* volumes III and IV of Macaulay's *History of England*. They would be read, he said, with a "delight equal to the anxiety with which their advent has been anticipated." He suggested that those who had read Herman Melville's *Typee* and *Omoo* would want to read his *Piazza Tales* just published. And there are frequent references in the *Age* to Chicago: its sudden growth, its politics, its murders, the great rise in the price of its real estate.

On March 13, 1856, under the caption "Augusta Redeemed," the *Age* reported: "Our city election came off yesterday and has resulted in the utter overthrow of the combined forces of the 'Dark Lantern Order' [the Know-Nothing, or antiforeigner, party] and black republicanism although they have been desperately at work for many days previously." Melville W. Fuller is shown to have been elected as one of the three aldermen for the Sixth Ward. The next week the *Age* reported the organization of the common council with Melville W. Fuller as president and also as city solicitor. But only two months later, a resolution was passed tendering the thanks of the council to Mr. Fuller, and wishing him success "in his adopted home." He was leaving for the West.

Some have speculated on why he moved to Chicago since he had done so well in Augusta. But in that period there was some mysterious compulsion that moved hundreds of thousands of New England people to the West, like a flight of

lemmings to the sea. As Horace Bushnell said, "To stay here
. . . among the snows and rocks and worn out old fields . . . is
supposed to indicate a want of manly determination." Augusta,
after gaining in population for many years, had become static.
The political group to which Fuller belonged was disintegrat-
ing under the impact of the Maine liquor law and the rising
tide of antislavery sentiment. There is a strong tradition in the
Weston family that his uncle, Nathan Weston, loaned him the
money to go to Chicago; it is clear that the Westons disliked
his partnership with B. A. G. Fuller in Augusta.

But the real reason for his sudden departure was a broken
engagement. In 1852, while a junior at Bowdoin, he had become engaged to Susan Robinson of Augusta. Susan was seventeen and he was nineteen, but he was attractive to women and
had already had one or two youthful entanglements. One of
these had ended in successful negotiations by his brother Henry
for the return of Melville's letters. The affair with Susan pursued a stormy course over the next four years. His mother and
Susan's mother favored the match; Susan's stepfather, Judge
R. D. Rice, of the Supreme Court of Maine, opposed it. Under
this pressure Susan was continually breaking the engagement.
During his mother's lifetime, Melville shared with her his distress on these occasions. "I am thankful," she wrote him on the
first break-up of the engagement, "that you wrote me all about
it. I will not let your Grandma nor Mrs. Rice know that you
have done so. I would cultivate good feelings toward Mrs. Rice
for she is very much your friend."

After his triumph in 1852 as temporary chairman of the
Franklin Pierce rally in Augusta, the engagement was renewed.
"I am very glad that you had a good time at the Rice's," his
mother wrote, "and that your matters there look favorable."
His grandmother took another view: "I want to say something
about your being at Judge R's so much. . . . Let things rest
for the present. You are both too young to make an irrevocable
engagement fraught with such appalling consequences. . . .
You wont be affronted with poor Grandy, I know, who loves

you as the apple of her eye." But the engagement was broken off again in 1854, as shown by the following poem which he wrote at that time:

Dost Thou Remember!

Dost thou remember, when, the sweet words spoken
Thy little hand lay lovingly in mine
And vows were uttered, never to be broken?
(Vows I have kept, would it were so with thine!)
How gazed I then, half doubting and yet daring,
Into the liquid depths of thy dark eyes,
To catch that rich and burning glance declaring
The strength of passion that the soul supplies.

Dost thou remember in those fond caresses,
The tender secret of thy heart confessed,
How thy dear head with all its wealth of tresses
So timidly was pillowed on my breast?
Ah, blessed hour, beyond imagination
To feel thus bent thy matchless form above
Our twain hearts throbbing with but one pulsation
Responsive beating to a single love.

Dost thou remember, by the quiet river,
While down the path our wandring footsteps strayed
We saw the mellow moonlight flash and quiver
As on the ripples tremblingly it played;
Thine eyes were full of tears, yet tears of gladness
And in thy tone so tremulously low
Mingled with joy there came a certain sadness
As fearing too great happiness to know.

Thou hast forgotten! but though we are parted
Though the bright dream, so dear, so short, be o'er,
Mem'ry, consoler of the broken hearted,
To me brings back the golden days of yore
In whose sweet Past, despite the sad farewell
Still at thy shrine a worshipper I bow,
While in thy heart, Affection's potent spell
Preserves, as then, its olden powers now.

After his election as president of the common council, the engagement was again restored only to be broken again—and then he left for the West. It is notable, however, that he took with him to Chicago a letter of recommendation from Judge Rice, for it was Fuller's lifelong habit to cultivate a known enemy. Soon after he arrived in Chicago, he received a letter from his cousin Benjamin Smith, reporting several talks with Susan: "I think there is not the slightest doubt," Ben wrote, "of her love for you and constancy to you but between her love for you and what she considers her duty to the 'elder party' she is placed in rather an unpleasant position." Susan was married to a Mr. Goodwin in 1857, and Fuller's marriage in Chicago followed in a few months. Goodwin became governor of Arizona and later representative in Congress from that Territory. He died in 1887, the year before Fuller was appointed Chief Justice. Mrs. Goodwin lived in Augusta thereafter and was one of the *grande dames* of the city. In later years the Chief Justice of the United States never failed to call on her on his annual visit to Augusta.

CHAPTER III

•◡•

CHICAGO

1856–1858

Fuller's train pulled into Chicago on pilings over Lake Michigan and into the station just south of the river and east of Michigan Avenue. In later years he was to devote a good part of his professional life to the legal tangle made by these railroad tracks out in the lake in front of the city—the famous Lake Front case. His train was crowded: the rail connection between Chicago and the East had been open only three years; and Chicago, on the outskirts of civilization, was daily receiving a great influx to its population. Among those who arrived that year—1856—was a Yankee store clerk named Marshall Field. George M. Pullman and Richard T. Crane had arrived only the year before. As Fuller came out of the depot, he saw the historic landmark, Fort Dearborn, which was torn down only that summer. It stood at what is now the south approach to the Michigan Avenue Bridge. With some trouble, he secured a bed in a hotel. Chicago was then justly proud of its hostelries; but all of them reserved the right, unless an unusual rate was paid, to give a guest a bedmate. Fuller had a new one almost every night.

His first impressions of Chicago are preserved in a series of letters which he wrote to the Augusta *Age*. His first letter is dated "Chicago, May 27, 1856," only a few days after his arrival. It starts: "In the midst of the whirling, active, busy life of this great city, it is difficult to know where to commence." All the people in Chicago, he says, are telling fabulous stories about the real estate that they have for sale. But "the joke is" that "the facts stated are literally true." "It is impossible to rub out that fixed fact, a soil fertile beyond imagination. Plough or spade cannot enter the earth without a rich harvest, provided you accidentally sow after you have broken the ground."

Then he indulges in a fantastic prophecy: "With a population of over 100,000, this city is steadily increasing. . . . Probably no other city in the Union will surpass it in size, with the exception of New York. Anyone who will take the trouble to examine the map, will see that this must result from its situation. Anyone who has noticed the immense shipping of the Lakes centering here, the numberless railroads tapping the Mississippi at every available point, and tesselating the whole country with an iron net work, having its fastening at this place, and this alone, the countless myriads who pour in day and night seeking their fortunes here, . . . must be satisfied that this is the second great business point of the country."

This prediction shows rare judgment for a boy of twenty-three. But already the West was affecting him: he exaggerates the population of Chicago, which in 1856 was nearer 85,000 than 100,000. The census figures are: 1840, 4,470; 1850, 28,269; 1860, 109,263. In 1850 Illinois had only 100 miles of railroad, but by the end of 1856 it had 2,235 miles, more than any other state in the Union. In 1856 thirteen railroads with 104 daily trains entered the city.

Shortly before he left Augusta, the *Age* had begun to carry a large advertisement for through tickets from Augusta to Chicago and beyond, with a stopover, if desired, at Niagara Falls. His letters indicate that he stopped there. Fuller's ticket to Chicago was perhaps received by him in exchange for this advertising in the Augusta *Age*. Apparently the journey to Chicago did not use up his ticket; for a few days after his arrival, he took a trip to Clinton, Iowa, which he found had "the sweetest location on the Mississippi." "Last year a cornfield," he said, "it now contains 800 inhabitants." From Clinton he took a river boat to Dubuque, Iowa, where (as everywhere in the West) he found many former residents of Maine. "The depopulation of Maine," he declared, "seems inevitable."

Lake Street was then the principal retail street of Chicago. There, at Lake and Dearborn, stood the Tremont House, five stories high—so high that it "scraped acquaintance with the skies," as the Chicago *Democrat* said. But when it rained, the streets were knee-deep in mud, with an occasional pig or cow roaming in them. Millions of rats scurried under the wooden sidewalks. Fuller reported, however: "All the stories of water in the streets, marshy ground, epidemics, etc., are founded on nothing save the disadvantage of the original site and the ordinary diseases of any large city." Boston's mortality in one week, he declared, equaled the deaths of a month in Chicago. He grew almost lyrical in his enthusiasm: "It is a 'great place,' . . . great in size, great in projects, great in its possibilities, great in its realities."

A few days after his arrival, he received a letter from his Grandmother Weston. She addressed him as "My dearest darling baby," but said, "You write like a man of 40." "Oh how I hope you will prosper," she wrote. "For pity's sake don't spend a cent you can possibly help. . . . Wear a nightgown when you possibly can as it saves your shirts more than you have any idea of." His Grandfather Weston wrote to him: "Extravagance is constantly ruining thousands in cities who are driven away to perish prematurely or pine in hopeless poverty. A wise man will save. . . . The world does not sympathize much with saving, but it acknowledges and at length does homage to its fruits." This thought impressed the boy, and twenty years later he included these words in a famous speech.

On his first Sunday in Chicago Fuller went to church. Like any young man in a new habitat, he was curious about the appearance of the girls. He reported that a first-class church with a packed congregation "gives about one lady to each forty of the other gender, and even that one female though rather scraggy contrives to afford a glimpse of about 40 times as many articles of feminine apparel as are ever dreamed of in a northern city." Although the census shows that there were substantially as many women in the city as men, other visitors to Chicago in this era also mention the absence of women in the churches. Apparently some Chicago ladies were not church-goers.

Fuller concluded, however, that the city was "sparsely populated with women." But, he said, "what is lacking in numbers on the part of the ladies is made up in the tremendous determination of those who are here to place before the public in as large a measure and as fashionable a style all the latest importations, the ribbons, laces, satins, etc., as their minority enables to. Such inconceivable bonnets! Such variegated shawls! Such terrific hoops! . . . Such multitudes of flounces, tucks, [and] stripes."

The desecration of the Sabbath in Chicago shocked him. "Sundays, as days devoted to the worship of God," he said, "are decidedly at a discount, but as days of nothing-to-do-but-to-spree-it-ness, are above par." His views on this subject were to become more liberal in the next fifty years.

When he came to Chicago, he was not certain whether he would go into law or newspaper work. The Westons hoped it would be law. His grandmother wrote him: "A newspaper might do for *6* months but you would have to work so hard." As thousands of young lawyers have done since, he made the rounds of the Chicago law offices, looking for a connection. His grandmother wrote: "The Judge says 'the moment people find out your industry and business habits, they will demand your services.' " Chicago then had a large bar, and its numbers were fast increasing. By the end of 1857, 360 lawyers were practicing in Chicago, an extraordinary number for a town of less than 100,000.

Fuller secured a position at $50 a month with the firm of Pearson & Dow, and by September, 1856, the Augusta *Age* carried a half-column announcement of the firm of Pearson, Dow & Fuller, located at No. 4 Exchange Building, corner of Clark and Lake streets, Chicago. The firm stated that they were prepared to give personal attention to legal business of importance in Michigan, Wisconsin, Iowa, and Illinois, and were in correspondence with the most reliable attorneys in every city and county in the northwest. Judge Weston was so pleased that he sent Melville all of his Maine and Massachusetts law reports, a magnificent gift. Grandma wrote: "The Judge quite opened his heart in sending you so many law books. I was quite surprised as he holds on to everything with great tenacity."

"Who are Pearson & Dow," his grandmother wrote, "where did they come from and what sort of men are they—I hope they don't drink, smoke or swear." The good lady's fears were perhaps well founded. Pearson soon vanished from the firm. In 1857 he was sued for a board bill by Emily Chapman. His defense was that he lived with her at her request and for her "accommodation, edification, entertainment and benefit." Emily's lawyer was Pearson's former partner, Melville W. Fuller, who secured a judgment for $947 against him. Pearson was shot and killed in a brawl by a policeman in Springfield a few years later.

In 1857 Dow & Fuller moved their office to the Methodist Church block at the corner of Clark and Washington streets. The church was on the two top floors of the building; there were stores on the ground floor and offices on the second. Fuller unsuccessfully litigated in the Supreme Court of Illinois the claim that the entire building was exempt from taxation because of its religious use and ownership.

He soon found a boardinghouse on Wabash Avenue, then a principal residential street of Chicago. Grandma Weston wrote: "I have never dared to ask you what you pay for your board." "You have so much expense that I enclose $3. for you to use for anything you need. Don't mention the $3. in your letter. If you get my letter, you will of course get what it contained." He wrote to the *Age* that "many thousands" of people in Chicago lived in boardinghouses. There was no better way, he said, to "see the elephant." This last is a slang expression of the forties and fifties meaning "to see the world, to gain worldly experience." He described his room as seven by nine, with two shaky chairs, an unstable table, a cracked pitcher and washbowl and a bed which seems to be filled with shavings from "the hard side of a bird's eye maple board." The bed had a "spread" compared to which factory cloth, that is, unbleached cotton, would be a buffalo robe.

The food was even worse. The soup, he said, was like the refuse from a tanyard; the roast beef was like a side of sole leather; the potatoes, like a dozen boiled cobblestones; and the mince pie, like steeped tea leaves between two sheets of blotting paper.

Tall tales from the West! How many New England boys must have written such letters? How many prim New England girls must have shuddered as they read them? Fuller's letters, though written anonymously for publication, are clearly intended for the eye of Susan Robinson in Augusta. He reports that one of the landlady's daughters is very attractive. "She wears pretty boots, neat hats and exhibits some considerable taste in her toilet generally." She has glossy, luxuriant hair. The "Western Correspondent" writes her a sonnet occasionally and gets "a pleasant payment therefor in a contact with lips that *are* soft in the hall."

A year later, in June, 1858, Fuller married Calista Ophelia Reynolds. She was a beautiful girl, judging by her picture. That she was the young lady mentioned in his letter to the *Age* is indicated by many details and is proved by the Chicago Directory of 1857 (the year before his marriage), which lists Mrs. Jane Reynolds, his future wife's stepmother, as residing at 297 Wabash Avenue, the same address as Fuller's. Long before his marriage, he had written to the *Age* that his description of life in boardinghouses was partly imaginative and had caused him considerable embarrassment.

Ophelia's father was Eri Reynolds, who had been a leading Chicago butcher and packer in the forties, but had died in 1851. At his death Eri Reynolds had a packing plant on the Chicago

River, where he employed about thirty hands and slaughtered ninety cattle a day. Eri Reynolds also owned the land at the corner of Madison and Dearborn streets, in the heart of what was to be Chicago's Loop.

Fuller was deep in politics from the moment of his arrival in Chicago. The national political conventions took place in June, 1856. In the first week after his arrival, he reported that he had slept in his hotel with many delegates who were en route to the Democratic convention at Cincinnati. Buchanan was nominated by the Democrats and Frémont by the Republicans. This last nomination was a source of some worry to Fuller, because Frémont had married Senator Benton's daughter Jessie; and Benton was always one of Fuller's heroes. He liked to call himself a "Benton Democrat." A copy of Benton's *Thirty Years' View* is in Fuller's library inscribed to him by Benton. The *Age* was jubilant when Benton stated that he would not vote for his son-in-law.

The campaign of 1856 gave birth to the Republican party, which was formed to fight the extension of slavery in the territories. The occasion was the passage of the Kansas-Nebraska Act of 1854, which allowed the people of those territories to determine for themselves the question of slavery and declared "inoperative and void" that section of the Missouri Act which prohibited slavery north of 36° 30′, the southern boundary of Missouri. To the Republicans this repeal was the violation of a sacred compact.

Fuller must have spent a great deal of time in his early months in Chicago in a study of the Kansas-Nebraska Act. His detailed analysis of this law was published in early October, 1856, as the *Address of the Young Men's Democratic Union Club of Chicago*. He made it clear that he regarded slavery as an evil. But it was a domestic institution in certain states, and the national government under the Constitution had no power to interfere with it. The Kansas-Nebraska Act seemed right to him. It would effectually prevent the spread of slavery in the territories by allowing the people there to forbid it. The North was growing in population far faster than the South, and Northern people would populate the territories and make them free states. The North gained in population each year 350,000 more than the South. The value of its real estate by the census of 1850 was three times that of the South. Fuller said that it was well known that emigrants move from an area of high-priced land to a part of the country where land is cheap.

The Missouri Act was no solemn compact, he declared, but a mere congressional compromise repealable like any other law. And it had been abandoned by both sides. The abolitionists, he charged, were dragging the country into civil war by raising great sums to send armed settlers into Kansas. His address closed with an appeal to all "reasonable men against this systematic scheme to engender sectional conflict."

He wrote to the *Age* that to the Republicans "the recent troubles in Kansas have given unmitigated delight. Every shot fired on the border is another gun for their nominee; every fresh outrage they can provoke is so much contributed to the cause—the cause not of freedom, not of liberty and union, but of private aggrandisement and the gratification of political ambition."

"The feeling on the subject of Kansas is wrong," he asserted. "It is based on the naturally honest sentiments of the masses North, but it is fanned into a blaze by the machinations of disappointed and reckless politicians. I am testifying to what I have seen and speaking of what I know. The rascality of the Missourians would have had no opportunity to be displayed had it not been for the fanatical and hot-headed course of the abolition madmen."

His Grandma Weston rebuked him for these hot words. "In these party times," she wrote, "men express themselves too freely about their opponents—it does no good but harm—have your own opinion but don't advise those who differ with you." And when his political fury continued, she wrote him: "You will be just as likely to be chosen President if you don't knock everybody down who presumes to differ from you." But never was advice more sharply spurned; never was retribution more complete; never was a lesson better learned. The youthful Fuller came to grief as a violent partisan in politics, and his administration as Chief Justice was marked by scrupulous political impartiality. He was confirmed in that office only through Republican votes. He had finally learned to disagree without being disagreeable.

His grandmother gave him other advice that he might well have heeded. "Don't come forward too soon," she said. "Get knowledge and experience to stand upon like a rock—then if the winds beat upon you you won't fall." She was puzzled, she complained, by the campaign of 1856 because she had sons and grandsons on both sides. Her son George Melville became a Republican; her son Nathan remained a Democrat. But she wrote Melville in Chicago: "Don't go against Freedom." Apologizing to him, however, for her delay in sending him a box of books, she said: "We have been so taken up with speeches, processions, bonfires, flags, talking and telling what this one said, what that one thought, what another guessed, etc. etc. that we could not attend to anything short of *'preserving the Union.'* "

The next year Fuller apparently went to Kansas for two months as a reporter for the New York *Herald.* He had always wanted to see the situation there at first hand. Soon after he arrived in Chicago his grandmother had written him, "Don't get killed going to Kansas." Recently there have come to light among Fuller's effects ten bound volumes of the New York *Herald* for the period between 1857 and 1861. Marks on these papers show that they were received by him at the time they were issued. An 1860 dispatch in them can be proved to have been written by him. His first bound volume starts and ends at odd dates: December 22, 1857, to February 27, 1858. These dates are contemporaneous with a series of articles from Kansas by a special correspondent. Some of these articles are in Fuller's style. They use legal phrases, Latin and French words (to which he was much addicted), references to Dickens and

Shakespeare, and contain ideas, arguments, and peculiar phrases which he had used in his letters to the Augusta *Age*. There is strong evidence, but not conclusive proof, that these articles were written by him.

Their purport is that the possibility of slavery ever existing in Kansas has completely vanished; and that the Kansas agitation is being kept up for political purposes, for "self aggrandisement" by candidates for office. "I have no desire," he said, "to do injustice to the free state men whose professed aim I concur with." But he noted that the Free-State men "for two years at least have had a decided majority." "To say they could not have secured entire control is absurd." They had stayed away from the polls, he declared, not because they were intimidated but because they had followed the advice of corrupt and fanatical Republican leaders from abroad who wished to prolong the Kansas imbroglio.

"That free state men have been outraged," another article states, "no one will deny; but that they should, when the sectional parties in our Union are standing in such a dangerously hostile position . . . throw themselves into rebellion against the United States to irrupt said sectional parties, should be deprecated." "Reason should teach them that human Governments and laws are but a compact, a compromise. . . . And history should teach them devotion to this prodigy of human government, [and] contempt for little local passions and interests." This argument is, of course, a repetition of certain portions of President Polk's speech which Fuller had heard in Augusta in 1847.

Soon after these articles were published, the famous Lincoln-Douglas senatorial campaign took place in Illinois. The Buchanan administration was trying to "purge" itself of Douglas because of his opposition to the admission of Kansas under the Lecompton constitution (which guaranteed existing property rights in slaves) without submitting that constitution to a vote of the people of Kansas. Douglas's patronage in Illinois and elsewhere was taken from him. A new party in Illinois, called the Nationals, composed largely of postmasters and other Buchanan officeholders, was formed and nominated a state ticket with Sidney Breese as its candidate for senator. Douglas, who had a national reputation and an immense personal following in Illinois, had rather preempted the Republican position regarding Kansas. It was therefore largely through the split in the Democratic ranks that Lincoln hoped to win the senatorship. It was necessary for Douglas to build a new organization to supplant the old, which had gone over to the administration.

Two of his new lieutenants, who made more speeches for him than anyone in Chicago, except the candidates for office, were Melville W. Fuller and Sidney Smith. Both of them were young Eastern college men who had been in Chicago only two years. They were both slight in figure and personally attractive. They spoke with an Eastern accent. Fuller said "bean" for "been" to the end of his days. The Chicago *Herald,* which was the organ of the Buchanan party, published an editorial commenting on their youth and inexperience. It did not mention them by name, but it obviously referred to them.

"It is instructive and amusing," the editorial said, "to observe the class of man whom Mr. Douglas has appointed to the vacancies left by his lost lieutenants." The editor then speaks of their *"au fait* attire," "delicate attainments," "gentle innocence of ability," "maidenly timidity," "courteous curving of the neck," and "polite weakness of the knees." They speak the "merest extraction of language" and are "harmless aromatic ornaments of society." "They 'shine so brisk and smell so sweet and talk so like waiting gentlemen,' of platforms and principles and convictions that we should not wonder if half the young misses of the city were pouting soft orisons for the welfare of the 'Little Giant.' "

"It is a refreshing sight to see one of these pretty Othos in his perfumed armour of spotless linen, attacking the lager beer in the saloon of some sturdy German, or tapping coquettishly, with his lavender kids, some truculent Hibernian. And then to see one of them standing on his 'light, fantastic toe' upon a stump, addressing with 'many holiday and lady terms' the broad-shouldered and double fisted yeoman of the democracy, the least of whom has a right arm bigger than the waist of his orator! Bless their dear little valorous hearts,they are worth their weight in rose water. . . . Buckle on your armour, Nationals; the day is rapidly approaching when you will be called upon to 'break a butterfly upon the wheel.' " Far from being broken, one of the two butterflies became Chief Justice of the Superior Court of Cook County, and the other, Chief Justice of the United States.

Although the opposition forces received the larger popular vote, Douglas won the senatorship, and Fuller went back to his law practice. But Lincoln, in the debates, had so ably phrased the half-formed sentiments of the North that he became at once a national figure.

CHAPTER IV

 ∘↩∘

POLITICS AND THE WAR

1860–1865

THE Civil War high-lighted Fuller's independence and courage. He remained a militant moderate at a time when there was no room for moderation, when not to be a radical was almost to be a traitor. But the war also forced him to admit mistakes and curbed his overconfidence in his own judgments. Thereafter he often referred to the importance of a "sober second thought" and he never again assailed an adversary's motives.

When Lincoln was nominated for President in 1860, Fuller wrote to the New York *Herald* that he was "a gentleman of unblemished moral character, and an amiable and agreeable member of society." "But as a politician," Fuller declared, "little can be said in his praise."

Fuller was selected to make the address of welcome when Douglas came to Chicago in the ensuing campaign. This assignment was a great honor for a young man of twenty-seven who had been in Chicago only four years. Fortunately, perhaps, that speech has not been preserved. Years later Congressman "Sunset" Cox of Ohio, who heard it, said of it, "He was not wanting then in a species of invective, which time has toned down."

But soon after Douglas arrived in Chicago, he was convinced by the October elections in Pennsylvania and Indiana that Lincoln was to be the next President. Douglas then abandoned his Illinois campaign and went south in a supreme effort to dissuade the Southern states from secession. Cox, whose state-

ments must be slightly discounted—his nickname of "Sunset"
came from his journalistic flamboyance in describing a setting
sun—said that there were many men, including himself, who
then tried to take Douglas's place in the Illinois campaign;
"but no one came so near filling it as the eloquent young
lawyer from Maine."

A few days before Lincoln's inauguration Fuller was a
speaker at the Washington's birthday celebration in Chicago.
He was assigned the conventional toast to the ladies, perhaps
to prevent him from suggesting concessions to the South. But
he phrased his toast: *"The Ladies*—Ever devoted to Union,—
their legitimate relation to man: a compact depending for its
harmonious endurance upon mutual concessions." The Chicago
Tribune said: "Mr. Fuller's remarks we are unable to report.
They were undoubtedly gallant, chaste and vigorous judging
alone from the reputation of their author." Thomas Dent noted
in his diary of this occasion: "The speeches many of them were
full of patriotism."

But Douglas made himself conspicuous at Lincoln's inaugural and, when Fort Sumter was fired upon, fervidly supported the Union. His war speeches in Springfield and Chicago
in 1861 made Illinois perhaps the strongest pro-Union State in
the country. "There are only two sides to the question," he declared. "Every man must be for the United States or against
it. There can be no neutrals in this war,—only patriots or
traitors." Douglas died a few weeks later, and Fuller wrote to
his grandfather: "The war in this section will be prosecuted
with vigor. The death of Judge Douglas is a sore loss to me and
I believe to the country. He was our strongest man and I regard
his death almost in the light of an omen of defeat to our cause."

In November, 1861, Fuller was elected one of four delegates
to represent Chicago in the convention which met at Springfield in the following January to frame a new constitution for
Illinois. He was elected on the Regular Union Ticket, supported by both parties. He wrote exultantly to Judge Weston:
"There are but 75 delegates in the whole state & they are to

make a constitution for a million & a half (or more) population. So you see it is a great honor. I shall probably be the youngest man in the convention. I am the only Democrat from this city and County which sends *four* delegates. The Democracy has the convention however having elected 52 out of 75. This will eventually lead to the ascendancy of the party."

Fuller's colleague in the convention was Long John Wentworth, who had been a congressman, newspaper editor, and mayor of Chicago. Originally a Democrat, he had joined the Republicans on the repeal of the Missouri Compromise. Almost twenty years before, John Quincy Adams had stepped across the aisle in Congress to ask Wentworth, "How do you pronounce the name of that town of yours?" Although Fuller had earlier spoken disparagingly of Wentworth in his letters to the *Age,* they made their campaign together for the constitutional convention. In fact the Chicago *Tribune* said after the election that although Wentworth had been denounced by the Democrats during the campaign as a "John Brown Abolitionist," he had not only been elected but had "carried Mr. Fuller, a Democrat, in with him on the presumption that Fuller must be a pretty good Abolitionist to be running on the ticket with Long John." This taunt stung Fuller; it was not intended to please him.

The other delegates from Chicago were Elliot Anthony and John W. Muhlke. Muhlke, a Republican running on the People's Union Ticket, had defeated Fuller's mentor, W. C. Goudy. Goudy was afterward for many years a leading attorney and Democratic boss of Chicago. To a degree Fuller was a protégé of Goudy. But Fuller was also a protégé of Wentworth and sometimes of the arch-Republican Chicago *Tribune.*

The youngest delegate immediately took a leading part in the convention. He moved a memorial resolution for Senator Douglas and delivered the principal memorial address. "When war came," Fuller said, "Judge Douglas threw the whole weight of his influence in behalf of the government, and 'in thoughts that breathe and words that burn' rallied the nation to a vigorous prosecution of the war, in a manner and with a success that would have followed the words of no other man." This effort, Fuller declared, was the "crowning act" of Douglas's life.

Fuller quickly earned the esteem of the convention. He urged that greater efficiency in the dispatch of business be required of the courts and that the judges be given larger salaries. He made a proposal to expand the bonding power of the State to aid the federal government "in suppressing insurrection or rebellion." He did effective work in fixing adequate pay for the members of the legislature and limiting their allowances for mileage and other perquisites which had been a great scandal in the past. He was one of the vice presidents at the meeting held at the State House to celebrate the Union victory in the capture of Fort Donelson. On one occasion the convention voted to give the use of the convention hall on a certain evening "to Mr. Fuller, a delegate, to deliver a poem for the benefit of a blind girl."

Two constitutional arguments made during this session demonstrated his skill in that field. Fuller was a disciple of Senator Benton, who was commonly called "Old Bullion," because of his fanatical stand for hard money. At that time, Illinois permitted banks to issue paper currency against state or national bonds deposited by a bank with the State auditor. When the war came, it was found that the deposited securities were largely bonds of Southern states and that the Illinois currency, as a result, had depreciated. It was proposed by the new constitution to stop the issuance of any more currency of this sort. In opposition, a prominent delegate argued that the adoption of this proposal would impair the charter contract of the State with the banks and would thus violate the rule of the Dartmouth College case. Not so, said Fuller: the constitutional provision against laws impairing the obligations of contracts does not protect "hopes" but only vested rights. The right to issue currency in the future, he said, is not now "vested" in any bank. It would become "vested" only when a bank made the proper certificate and deposit with the State auditor. Fuller read from the decisions of the Supreme Court of the United States to support this argument. His contentions prevailed, and the convention adopted provisions to prevent the further issuance of paper money by banks.

Fuller's second constitutional argument related to the power of the convention to make a congressional reapportionment. The State had been divided into thirteen congressional districts, but fourteen congressmen had been awarded it, thus necessitating fourteen districts instead of thirteen. But it was argued that only the legislature could divide the State into these districts since the federal Constitution provided: "The times, places and manner of holding elections for . . . representatives shall be prescribed in each State by the legislature thereof."

The phrase "manner of *holding* elections," Fuller argued, had no application to redistricting. "Holding elections," he said, does not mean a "condition of things but a transaction." "It refers not to the division of a state into districts . . . but to whether the voting should be by ballot or *viva voce*—what officers should preside," and so forth. He pointed out that another provision of the federal Constitution provided that representatives shall be "chosen . . . by the *people* of the several states." The people through this convention, he argued, could obviously adopt a constitution limiting the manner in which the legislature could divide the State into these districts. To say that *only* the legislature could form these districts would be inconsistent because it would bestow upon the legislature, a body owing its existence to the people, a power denied to the people.

In the midst of this speech, Fuller was stopped by the ten-minute rule of the convention and unanimous consent was denied him to continue. But Wentworth moved to suspend the rules to permit him to proceed; and this motion was carried by a vote of 44 to 8, Fuller voting in the negative. The convention made a congressional reapportionment, in accordance with his argument.

But Fuller's final victory in the convention had a part in defeating the proposed new constitution. As a Democrat, he was the only member from Chicago on the legislative apportionment committee. When this apportionment was brought before the convention, his colleagues from Chicago asked twenty-four hours' postponement to discuss it with him. He opposed this motion on the ground that the apportionment was correct and that delay would only force him to differ from his colleagues outside of the convention. Wentworth then charged that Fuller had made one district expressly for his friend Goudy, but Fuller, while admitting their friendship, denied that he had talked to Goudy on the subject. The apportionment was, however, a shameless gerrymander, doubtless imposed by a Democratic caucus.

Anthony said—with some exaggeration—that the apportionment made a district around every "Democratic grocery." Fuller was taunted with having been elected as a nonpartisan Union delegate, but he responded: "I deny it. No convention on God's foot-stool can, or has a right to, run me and make anything but a Democrat out of me. . . . If I got any votes on the hypothesis that I would forswear my principles, then the voters were very much mistaken, and I regret it."

Fuller handled this debate with Wentworth, Anthony, and Muhlke with great skill. His extemporaneous style far surpassed his prepared speeches in effectiveness. His written style had been spoiled as a medium of communication by overindulgence in the classics and Carlyle. And Anthony afterward stated that Fuller was never offensive in his partisanship, as were many Democrats in the convention.

But it would have been better for Fuller and the convention if he had lost this battle. Largely because of this apportionment, the Republicans rose against the constitution, characterizing it as a "secesh" document, and it was defeated at the polls. There was ample material for the Republican charge that the Democrats in the convention had been lacking in enthusiasm for the war. The vote by counties on the adoption of the constitution was almost identical with the Lincoln-Douglas vote in 1860.

This result was a disappointment to the young Chicago lawyer. But he wrote to Judge Weston: "So far as my own constituency is concerned the result was highly flattering as the constitution gained 400 in Cook County. We were beaten however in the State. I shall take no more active participation in such matters until I am out of debt and have a better business than I have here. I have no cause to regret my action in the premises as it has made me known in the State & if there be any future for this unhappy country I shall be able to make something out of it. . . . Have you any hopes for the country?"

While the debate on the new constitution was going on, the Chicago *Morning Post* editorially suggested Fuller for mayor. He was no officeseeker, the *Post* said. He was a modest man who would never be selected for any office by his own "obtrusiveness." He was a "Democrat . . . who would vote as cheerfully to enable Mr. Lincoln to crush the rebellious secessionists, as he would to entrust the same measure to a democratic President."

In August, 1862, Fuller, as president of the Democratic Invincible Club of Chicago, presided at a meeting of the club which was held to encourage enlistments. "Whatever might have been our opinions," Fuller said, "concerning the inception of the war, the time has come when we are all willing to agree that there can be but one result." But a few days later he wrote his grandfather: "I trust the country will come out but I am full of fears. It seems to me that our leading men are pigmies. The spirit of party is not abated as it ought to be. . . . It is useless to cry out 'no party' when . . . all that is meant is that a man shall become a Republican. But nevertheless it would seem that God should and will protect our cause which to human understanding seems so just."

Before the year was over, Fuller was again a candidate for office—this time for the State legislature. "I was compelled to run," he wrote his grandfather, "as being the only candidate on our ticket likely to succeed." He was elected by a close vote from the legislative district which comprised the south side of Chicago. But it took a mandate of the Supreme Court to seat him. The vote of one precinct in which he had a majority was thrown out by the election commissioners, with the result that John Lyle King, then corporation counsel, was elected instead of Fuller. But, with Goudy as his counsel, Fuller filed a petition for mandamus in the Supreme Court of Illinois and was declared elected.

When the legislature met in January, 1863, Fuller, although a "first termer," immediately became a leader and, before the end of the session, was practically *the* leader of the House. This success was the greatest misfortune of his career. In 1863 the Democratic party in the Northwest (now the Midwest) opposed the war—an error from the effects of which the party did not recover for more than a generation.

Douglas had originally secured the support of the Democrats in Illinois for the war; but Douglas had died, and the North had suffered a long series of humiliating defeats on the battlefields. Then Lincoln had announced in September, 1862, that on January 1 he would issue the Emancipation Proclamation. Many men had pressed Lincoln to take that step. He had resisted largely through fear of losing the support of the War Democrats. The result in Illinois and throughout the Middle West shows how right Lincoln was in that fear. In fact, Goudy told Senator Browning that when the Democrats nominated their ticket in the fall of 1862 they expected to be beaten and had no intention of making a contest until Lincoln's preliminary proclamation was issued. Thereafter the Democrats won the State election by large majorities. Since Fuller was elected by such a small margin, his election was apparently a direct result of the proclamation.

Governor Yates, a Republican, in his address to the legislature scraped the raw wounds. He congratulated the country on the prolongation of the war since it had resulted in the Emancipation Proclamation. The House at first refused to print this message except with "a solemn protest against its revolutionary and unconstitutional doctrines."

The first task of the legislature was the election of a United States senator. There were several candidates who, according to the Chicago *Tribune,* "vied with each other in their expressions of disloyalty." One of the candidates was Fuller's sponsor Goudy. Goudy declared that "in the event of the President's refusing to withdraw the Proclamation he was in favor of marching an army to Washington and hurling the officers of the present administration from their positions." "A Union man," the *Tribune* reported, "is in as much danger in some localities here as if he were in Richmond." Goudy was afterward proved to have been active in the Knights of the Golden Circle, the secret Copperhead or pro-South organization. But everyone who knew Fuller agreed that he was no Copperhead. William A. Richardson was elected senator, Goudy receiving only eight votes in the Democratic caucus.

Both the Illinois and Indiana legislatures were Democratic in 1863, while the governors of both states were Republicans. The legislative sessions were similar. In each state the House of Representatives as a strict party measure passed resolutions protesting against further prosecution of the war unless the Emancipation Proclamation were withdrawn. In Illinois this resolution denounced "the flagrant and monstrous usurpations" of the administration, demanded an immediate armistice, and appointed several prominent Democrats (Goudy among them) as commissioners to secure the cooperation of other states for a peace convention at Louisville, Kentucky.

Fuller made one of the principal speeches in support of this resolution. He was a man of rare courage but here his daring approached rashness. He knew, he said, what a tremendous risk he was taking in opposing an administration involved in a civil war. But the War Democrats felt that they had been induced to support the war by false pretenses. They had been assured that it was a war to save the Union. Now it appeared to be a war to establish abolitionism. It was said that slavery was the *cause* of the war. "But," Fuller asked, "if slavery is the cause of the war, is not abolitionism? Supposing slavery to be as explosive and destructive as gunpowder, where does the guilt lie of the catastrophe following its ignition—on the inert material, or on him who applies the lighted brand thereto?"

"The Emancipation Proclamation," he protested, "is predicated upon the idea that the President may so annul the constitutions and laws of sovereign states, overthrow their domestic relations, deprive loyal men of their property, and disloyal as well, without trial or condemnation." The only possible course, he insisted, was a return to the Constitution.

In Indiana this Resolution for the Peace Convention barely failed of passage in the State Senate; in Illinois its passage in the Senate was prevented only by the Republicans absenting themselves to break a quorum. The session was ended in Indiana when Governor Morton advised the Republican members to withdraw. In Illinois, Governor Yates, taking advantage of a technical disagreement between the two Houses as to the date of an adjournment, prorogued them. Under the Constitution the governor had the right to fix the date of an adjournment if the two Houses disagreed on it.

Fuller presented the formal protest of the legislature against the governor's action. It recited the alleged crimes of Governor Yates in the form that George III's delinquencies are detailed in the Declaration of Independence and concluded that these "usurpations" would "receive the condemnation they deserve from an outraged people." Fuller was counsel in the subsequent litigation on the legality of the governor's action, but the Supreme Court held that regardless of its validity, the legislature had acquiesced in it. And Governor Yates was elected by the next legislature to the United States Senate.

Fuller returned to his law practice and was never again a candidate for an elective office. He had been a member of a constitutional convention whose work had been rejected by the people and of a legislature that had been prorogued by the

governor. But he was perhaps the only prominent Democrat
in these sessions who retained the respect of the Republicans.
No one doubted his courage or sincerity, and he was fair and
conciliatory. When the Republicans were demanding that
10,000 copies of the governor's message be printed, and the
Democrats were insisting that 2,500 copies would suffice, it
was Fuller who moved to amend the motion and print 5,000
copies. Similarly, when the Republicans were fighting the bill
to prevent the immigration of free negroes to the State and
were demanding a long postponement, it was Fuller who
moved a short postponement as a compromise. He presented
on the floor of the House many of the reports of the important
judiciary and finance committees. His name was mentioned
nearly every day during the session in both the Republican
and Democratic papers in Chicago. The *Tribune* called him
"Little Fuller" or "the darling of the Times," but grudgingly
admitted that he made a good speech. The *Times* boasted that
Fuller, as a debater, had no superior in the House.

He fought for higher pay for the page boys and strenuously
but unsuccessfully resisted a bill to give gold pens to each member of the House. When the legislature officially visited Chicago, the twenty-five carriages stopped at Fuller's home on
Eldridge Court, where "hospitality was generously dispensed
by Mr. Fuller and his lady." He appealed directly to his Republican colleagues for support of his bill to appropriate $50,-
000 for a Douglas monument at the site of Douglas's grave.
When this bill failed to pass, Governor Yates went to the floor
in an unavailing effort to secure reconsideration, since Mrs.
Douglas was threatening to remove the senator's body from
the State. Fuller's resolution condemning General Burnside's
suppression of the Chicago *Times* for disloyalty was approved
by the leading Republicans in Illinois, and President Lincoln
the next day revoked Burnside's order. Obviously, Fuller's in-
telligence and moderation under these trying circumstances
impressed his adversaries.

But there was another threatened blot on Fuller's career in

this session. A down-state senator introduced a bill to incorporate the Wabash Railway Company. This bill authorized the company to build and operate street railways on Wabash Avenue and on all of the other streets of Chicago. It was claimed that the bill had been passed through the legislature by deception since its sponsor did not explain its purpose and bills were then read only by title. This title would be understood to refer to a railroad on the Wabash River rather than one in Chicago. Fuller had charge of this bill in the House of Representatives and conducted the subsequent litigation on the alleged invalidity of the governor's veto of it. The veto was sustained.

The Chicago *Tribune* said that the bill had been "stolen" through the Senate and "bribed" through the House and was the "greatest swindle of the session." No evidence was offered to sustain these charges, and the *Tribune* afterward printed a letter from a Republican member of the House pointing out that the bill had been correctly explained and had passed the House with only five dissenting votes. The correspondent stated that money was rumored to have been spent against the bill by the existing street-car interests. The attorneys for the old horse-railroad lines defended the litigation brought by Fuller. The principal sponsor of the bill was Charles Hitchcock, a leading lawyer of Chicago, noted all his life for his scrupulous rectitude. Hitchcock was elected president of the Illinois constitutional convention a few years later.

As the campaign of 1864 approached, Fuller was full of hopes and fears. The radical peace advocates under the leadership of Vallandigham of Ohio were threatening to dominate the Democratic party. In December, 1863, Fuller reported to Sidney Breese a conference of leading Democrats in which the thought had been expressed "that the defeats we sustained this fall were perhaps providential." "Had Vallandigham been elected our leaders would have proven so defiantly radical that we could have done nothing with them—all conservative men would have been driven off."

On April 7, 1864, however, he wrote from Memphis to the Democratic Invincible Club of Chicago, of which he was president: "Of the result of the momentous political contest approaching, I have not permitted myself to indulge in a doubt for to do so seems to me well nigh equivalent to the abandonment of my convictions of the capacity of man for self-government. . . . I believe that the position of Democracy today to be that of devotion to the Union, without an 'if or a but'; devotion to the country whether right or wrong (though when wrong to be put right). . . ."

Fuller condemned the administration's disregard of constitutional rights, its unlawful arrests, its suspension of the writ of habeas corpus, its issuance of the Emancipation Proclamation, and its unconstitutional admission of West Virginia as a state. He deplored its lack of military success. "We have only to be wise to be triumphant," he said, "and that wisdom is to be found in the avoidance of extremes and the practice of that moderation which is strength."

He was a delegate to the Democratic national convention which met in Chicago in August. Lambert Tree, a distinguished Chicagoan and a lifelong friend, was his alternate; Fuller's cousin and college roommate, Joseph Emerson Smith, was a delegate from Maine. The convention nominated General George B. McClellan, and even President Lincoln was convinced that McClellan would be elected. But the convention under the leadership of Vallandigham adopted a resolution that the war was a failure and demanded a peace convention. Never were words more thunderously denied by events: Farragut had won the battle of Mobile Bay in August and Sherman captured Atlanta the week after the convention adjourned. McClellan's first duty as a candidate was to repudiate the principal plank in his party's platform. Fuller, who in the convention had done what he could to minimize Vallandigham, never ceased to criticize himself for allowing the war-failure resolution to be adopted. He had been so intent, he said, on securing a platform declaration for the Monroe Doctrine and condemning European usurpation in Mexico that he had failed to protest sufficiently the declaration that the war had been a failure.

But he fought on to the end of the campaign. He denounced abolitionism and secessionism and said that the Democratic party occupied the middle ground between them. "The administration regards the people of the south as a nation to be conquered," he said, while "the democracy looks upon them as brethren to be restored. . . ." Military victories, he insisted, belong to the people, not the administration. "Under the leadership of McClellan, we may hope that the blood that has been shed, and the treasure which has been expended will not have been entirely in vain."

But in November, McClellan carried only Kentucky, Delaware, and New Jersey; and Lincoln was reelected by a popular vote of 2,203,831 to 1,797,019.

When a few months later Lincoln was assassinated, the Chicago City Council appointed a committee of one hundred of the most prominent citizens, who were to "proceed to Michigan City, receive the remains of President Lincoln, escort them to Chicago and accompany them to Springfield." Fuller was a member of this committee. His pigmy had become a giant; the genius of Lincoln had won him.

CHAPTER V

 ◦‿◦

LAW AND LIFE

1856–1877

FULLER went through a cruel starvation period in his law practice. It was due not so much to lack of clients as to their lack of money with which to pay him. But the story of this torturous struggle reveals his resourcefulness and his industry. In his early years in Chicago he apparently supplemented his legal earnings by writing for the New York newspapers. And after his marriage in 1858 his family income was increased by the small rents from the little stores (hardly more than shacks) that he had built on his wife's real estate.

Despite this extra income and a rapidly growing law practice, he had trouble keeping his head above water. He borrowed sums ranging from $100 to $300 from his grandfather and his uncles, Daniel Weston, B. A. G. Fuller, and General Cony. Renewals of these loans required constant importunities, and B. A. G. Fuller finally sued the firm of Dow & Fuller on their note for $100 and took judgment against them.

On May 1, 1860, Dow & Fuller dissolved their partnership. Fuller wrote to his grandfather that the firm had $6,000 due them which they were unable to collect. Most of the firm's clients, he said, were his. He was even being employed, he reported, as senior counsel in cases where older lawyers were to act as his juniors.

The next year—1861—was a frantic one in Fuller's life. The war commenced, the Illinois currency collapsed, his law practice expanded, and the few clients who could pay him could do so only in the depreciated currency. But in that year he had eight cases in the Supreme Court of Illinois, delivered three speeches and lectures which were reported in the local newspapers and campaigned for the constitutional convention. "I am going almost mad," he wrote to his grandfather. "Every lawyer here is flat on his back." "But," he said, "I still preserve my courage which is a great mercy."

In January, 1862, he wrote: "I have given up housekeeping, sold a part of my furniture, got rid of my lease and gone to board at Mrs. Fuller's stepmother's." But in 1863 the currency situation began to be relieved. "I am in better spirits than I have been for some time," he wrote. "Real estate is going up rapidly by reason of the volume of paper emitted by the Govt." The city was condemning part of his wife's property for the widening of Dearborn Street and this windfall promised some financial relief.

In 1861 Fuller had moved his office to 84 Dearborn Street,[1] where he took as a partner Charles H. Ham, under the style of Fuller & Ham. From 1862 to 1864 inclusive, the firm won nine cases consecutively in the Supreme Court of Illinois, and the senior partner lost only the two cases involving Governor Yates's proroguing of the legislature.

One of these victories was a criminal case. Fuller defended a junkman who had bought from a thief several brass car couplings that had been stolen from a railroad. The question was whether the defendant knew that these brass parts had been stolen. They were brought to him in a bag, weighed as old brass, paid for as such, and thrown into a barrel standing in the room. All this was done openly and publicly, in broad daylight, in the usual course of business. The thief had not told the junk dealer that the couplings were stolen. Nevertheless the defendant was convicted.

Fuller's appeal was delayed by the absence from Chicago of Judge Beckwith of the Supreme Court. Finally, however, Fuller perfected his appeal. "My client," he wrote, "had been sent to the penitentiary but by letter and telegram I prevented

[1] Now 124 North Dearborn Street, between Randolph and Washington streets.

the shaving of his head which would certainly have been a contempt of court & by *habeas corpus* I got him back and discharged" pending the appeal.

In the Supreme Court Fuller secured a reversal of the conviction because the trial court had excluded the testimony of two witnesses offered by him. They were machinists and brass finishers of large experience and were called to prove that by common observation and without close inspection it could not be told whether these were perfect couplings or junk.

So many victories in the Supreme Court increased Fuller's employment by other lawyers. In 1864 he reported that he was overwhelmed with legal work but that his income from his profession was still not sufficient to support his family. Stark tragedy fell upon him in this year. His second daughter, Maude, was born in January, and Mrs. Fuller never recovered from the ordeal. In March, at the doctor's suggestion, he took her to Memphis and in July, to Minnesota. But he finally realized that she was dying of tuberculosis. "I should break down," he wrote his grandfather, ."were it not for the flow of spirits I inherited from my mother." A few days after his great disappointment in the national election of 1864, his wife died, leaving him with two small children.

He had then been in Chicago eight years and his life could hardly be called a success. Although he had worked hard at his profession and had come to be recognized as a rising lawyer, he had never made as much as $2,000 a year. In fact, he said he would be satisfied with an income of $100 a month from his profession. He was in debt to everyone from whom he could borrow. His best efforts had gone into politics and, though his ability had been recognized, his labors, through the ruthlessness of war, had been worse than wasted. He now turned his back deliberately on public life and plunged into his law practice.

In 1864 the law firm of Fuller & Ham became Fuller, Ham & Shepard. Henry M. Shepard had come to Chicago from New York only three years before and had met Fuller in the Young

Men's Association, of which both were officers. Fuller wrote his grandfather that Shepard was a young man of "standing, wealth and legal ability." When the new partnership was formed, Fuller expressed what he called the "modest hope" that his "bread, at least," might thereafter be earned in his profession. "It is about time," he declared, "for I know of no man at this bar who gives to his clients more for their money than I do."

But the next year he was able to write that his "period of starvation" had finally ended. "I permit no lawyer in the city," he wrote Judge Weston, "to surpass me in attention to . . . the cases of my clients. . . . It seems as if God had finally, after demonstrating the worthlessness of these earthly treasures, permitted me to enter on the successful pursuit of them."

In 1865 Fuller & Shepard (Ham had retired from the firm) moved their offices to Nos. 1 and 2 Reynolds Building, one of the largest office buildings in the city. Fuller had built this structure in the same year. It covered not only the land on Dearborn Street inherited from his wife, but also an adjacent lot which he had bought, and his wife's sister's adjoining property. He borrowed $55,000 for the purpose by a mortgage on his property. His office remained there until the building was destroyed by the Chicago fire six years later.

Early in 1866 he moved his home from 9 Eldridge Court, where he had lived for some time, to 473 South Wabash Avenue, then a fashionable residential neighborhood. Franklin MacVeagh, later Secretary of the Treasury, lived across the street and William F. Coolbaugh, president of the city's largest bank, next door. Coolbaugh and Fuller soon became close friends. They had a poignant memory in common—each had been a staunch lieutenant of Stephen A. Douglas. Coolbaugh, until a few years before, had been a merchant and banker at Waterloo, Iowa, where he was also Douglas's representative for the State of Iowa. Coolbaugh was president of the Union National Bank of Chicago, of the Chicago Clearing House, and of the National Bankers' Association for the West and Southwest. He was the leading banker in the West.

He had a daughter, Mary Ellen, usually called "Mollie," a charming, vivacious girl of twenty-one. It was a case of love at first sight between her and the young lawyer, although some of her friends thought she was throwing herself away on a widower of thirty-three with two children: "she could have had so many fine, younger men." But, as Fuller wrote to Justice Holmes, many years later: "This was a love match. . . . I was introduced to her on a Saturday, with her the next Saturday, engaged the Wednesday after." They were married in May, 1866, at Grace Church in Chicago. The groom's uncle, the Reverend Daniel Weston, came from Connecticut to officiate. Henry M. Shepard later confessed that as he marched down the aisle at the wedding it did not occur to him that he was walking with a future Chief Justice of the United States.

They went abroad on their honeymoon. Fuller kept a diary of the trip which is still among his papers. They landed at Liverpool and went thence by rail to Edinburgh, where he showed an almost incredible familiarity with Scotch history and the works of Sir Walter Scott. Then to Glasgow and Ayr, where he wrote in his diary the following punning doggerel:

To Burns
Warm *burns* my heart as by the *burns* I roam,
That wander frequent near a *Burns'* home
The *air* I breathe, what *e'er* my eyes may see
All things at *Ayr, are* redolent of thee.

His inveterate punning, his inexhaustible knowledge, his eager energy must have been a trial to the youthful Mollie. He records at one point, "Mollie was so tired, and so mad that she was tired, that she got into the bottom of the carriage, covered herself with her silk umbrella and refused to be comforted."

In London they attended the July 4th reception of the American minister. Charles Francis Adams was then a great hero, both in England and the United States, because of his exceptionally able conduct of affairs between the two countries during the Civil War. Fuller wrote: "Mrs. Adams assured me that the English thought everything of Mr. Adams—thought he saved the two countries from a war, etc. In vain (she said) she strove to explain it was Mr. Seward's policy, etc. They persisted it was Mr. Adams. 'I am willing,' said Mrs. A., 'to admit that my husband is a great Statesman & all that, but he is not entitled to the credit for the policy pursued wh. tho' it was really Mr. A's, was initiated by . . . the Sec'y of State.'" Mrs. Adams was apparently as polished a diplomat as her husband. If Fuller met the minister's son, Henry Adams, he made no mention of it. Colonel Oliver Wendell Holmes, Jr., of Boston, was making his first trip abroad that summer, but his path and that of the Fullers did not cross.

In Westminster Abbey the honeymooners made irreverent jokes in the usual manner of American visitors. They saw the tomb of one of the Cecils with the recumbent effigy of his first wife on his right and a slab with only an inscription for his second wife at his left. "She refused," Fuller wrote, "to be buried or at least have her effigy on his left. Mollie says she was right. I should say it was a case of first come, first served."

F. H. Morse, the American consul, who remembered Fuller from their Maine days, gave him a ticket to the House of Lords. "This evening," Fuller wrote, "I got a place & listened to Lord Derby's opening speech explanatory of the formation of his administration. . . . He was very fluent—for an Englishman remarkably so—exceed'ly *adroit* & said as little in an apparently candid, open & frank exposé as ever I heard." Fuller thought that his lordship's speech would have been "no discredit" to an American politician.

In his diary Fuller displays a prodigious knowledge of English history and literature, as well as a considerable acquaintance with the paintings that they saw. But on the whole they did not like England—Mollie became ill—and they were glad to escape to Brussels. From Brussels, after doing the palaces, galleries, and the field of Waterloo, they went to Bonn and

MELVILLE W. FULLER

1867

thence up the Rhine to Baden-Baden. Then to Lucerne and Berne, where the diary records: "Bot a paper & read dispatches via Atlantic cable dated N. York, July 29 & Aug. 1. Harlan out of the cabinet & Browning in." The Atlantic cable was opened that summer. Browning was Fuller's friend, Orville H. Browning of Quincy, Illinois, who had become Secretary of the Interior in President Johnson's cabinet.

The forthrightness of the diary entries indicates a development in Fuller and also a change in the times. He says: "Stambach Fall is very fine but Lord Byron's comparison of it with the tail of the horse that Death rode on is farfetched and full of hoakus like a monkey or a conundrum. Great men are always trying to keep themselves up to concert pitch wh. is ridiculous and not to be respected." Fuller's early style was florid: his writings were full of poetic quotations. It is significant that he remembered this simile from Byron but that he no longer liked it. The times, too, had changed. Lincoln's laconic sentences at Gettysburg in contrast to Edward Everett's classical oration perhaps marked as sharp a turning point in American literature as the Battle of Gettysburg in American history. From that date the embellished style was doomed. Even Fuller, in his speeches, began to quote Lincoln.

They returned to Chicago about October 1, and the groom plunged into his law practice. Just before his return, an accident had occurred on the premises of his old client John J. Schwartz. The resulting litigation lasted for ten years and involved four appeals to the Supreme Court of Illinois. Schwartz was building a four-story brick store at the corner of State and Madison streets in Chicago. The building was 120 feet long but only 25 feet wide. After the side walls were built, they were observed to be leaning slightly. The owner notified the architect, who instructed the mason contractor to brace them. The next day a high wind—no novelty in Chicago—blew them down, smashing the adjoining residence and killing a lady who lived there. Her husband sued Schwartz, the owner, for negligence and secured a judgment in the trial court; but Fuller reversed it in the Supreme Court of Illinois. The trial court's instructions to the jury had imposed liability on Schwartz without requiring the jury to find that the condition of the building before its fall was such as to excite the apprehension of a reasonable and prudent man.

But the carpenter contractor secured a judgment against Schwartz for the work done before the walls fell. Fuller was not successful in reversing this judgment, although he cited cases from New York, Massachusetts, Connecticut, New Jersey, and England to the effect that the risk of loss in such a case was on the contractor. The court held that the risk of destruction of the building might be on the contractor where he was to be paid only on completion; but here payment was to be made on architect's certificates as the work progressed.

Schwartz then sued the mason contractor for his failure to shore up the walls when the architect requested him to do so. The first trial resulted in a verdict for the defendant, but Fuller secured a reversal for failure of the trial court to give the jury an instruction on the duty of the contractor to obey the architect's directions. On the next trial the verdict was for plaintiff, and Fuller sustained it in the Supreme Court.

These cases illustrate the litigation of the period. Clients stood up for their rights and lawyers fought their cases to the end. The law was not yet settled so that there was a field for such battles. Today lawyers would make strenuous efforts to compromise and adjust such a series of cases and would probably be successful in doing so. Fuller apparently tried every case that came to him and appealed every case that he lost. There is no record that he ever settled a case.

He now began to appear in the courts on behalf of the Union National Bank and Coolbaugh, its president. He also represented Franklin MacVeagh and at times the First National Bank. He took part in establishing the early law of Illinois on banking transactions. His income increased proportionately. In 1861 the federal government had imposed an income tax, and each taxpayer's annual income was published in the Chicago papers. Fuller's name was not included in these reports for 1862–1865, indicating that his income did not exceed $2,000; but for 1866 he reported an income of $10,913 and for 1867, gross income of $23,161 and net of $18,275. Of course a portion of this money represented receipts from the Reynolds Building, which had been completed in 1865.

Real estate in Chicago was booming in the postwar period. If any visitor from the East pitied his Chicago friends for the crudity of their society, they, in turn, pitied him because he did not own a corner lot in Chicago. "You might as well," James Parton said in the *Atlantic Monthly*, "pity the Prince of Wales because he is not yet King." Men who had invested in Chicago real estate only seven years before were now independently wealthy. In 1868 Henry M. Shepard, who had come to Chicago in 1861, retired from the firm of Fuller & Shepard to look after his real estate; but he remained one of the most important clients of the office and later became a judge and a leading citizen of Chicago.

Fuller's cousin and roommate at Bowdoin, Joseph Emerson Smith, who had been practicing law in Wiscasset, Maine, then came to Chicago, and the firm name was Fuller & Smith until Smith's death thirteen years later. He was the son of Governor Samuel Smith of Maine; he had buried two wives in Wiscasset and his mother (the governor's widow and Fuller's Aunt Louisa) kept house for him in Chicago until his third marriage. Like Fuller, Smith had political and literary tastes: he was a member of the State legislature and the author of a novel called *Oakridge*.

In 1869 Fuller was retained in his most famous case: the Church trial of the Reverend Charles E. Cheney. Cheney, who was rector of Christ Church in Chicago, was Low Church, or evangelical; his bishop, Henry J. Whitehouse, was High Church, or sacerdotal. The Low Church group held a meeting in Chicago in the summer of 1869 at which Cheney discussed the question of whether they should continue to use a Prayer Book which many thought, if taken literally, contained almost

false doctrines. In England, twenty years before, the Bishop
of Exeter had refused to install a vicar named Gorham nominated by the queen to a vacant parish because Gorham doubted
that the sacrament of baptism conferred spiritual regeneration
unconditionally on an infant. The ecclesiastical courts sustained the bishop, but on appeal the Judicial Committee of the
Privy Council reversed this decision and the vicar was duly in-
stalled. High-churchmen were outraged that a lay court should
thus establish Church doctrine, and some of them—notably
Henry Edward Manning, afterward Cardinal Manning—left
the Church of England and became Roman Catholics.

But the Prayer Book in the infant baptismal liturgy still
contained the declaration that the child after baptism was "regenerate." Low-churchmen sometimes omitted the word or inserted after it the words "we fondly hope." Somebody called
Bishop Whitehouse's attention to this omission by Cheney and
the bishop questioned him about it. Upon his refusal to desist
from the alteration of the liturgy, the bishop brought him to
trial for violation of his ordination vow. Fuller, although himself a High-churchman, was retained as Cheney's counsel and
undertook the defense, grasping at any straw that he could
find. The outcome of the Church trial was a foregone conclusion, since the bishop appointed only High-churchmen to the
group from which the court was to be chosen and there was no
appeal.

Fuller therefore filed a bill for an injunction in the Superior
Court, and on sundry technicalities the Church court was enjoined from proceeding. But this injunction was reversed by
the Supreme Court of Illinois with W. C. Goudy and S. Corn-
ing Judd representing the bishop. The court said that whether
Cheney's omission of the word "regenerate" constituted an
offense against the law of the Church was peculiarly a matter
for ecclesiastical decision. However, the court referred to
Fuller's "earnest, able and elaborate" argument and disposed
of each of his technical points. The depth of his researches into
ecclesiastical law had astounded his adversaries and the court.

Cheney was deposed, but he then organized the Reformed Episcopal Church and his congregation stood by him. Years of litigation ensued over the Church property but Fuller won. The Supreme Court held that the property belonged to the trustees of Christ Church and was not in any way subject to the bishop's control.

All of the doctrinal points, however, were reargued in this second case. Fuller wrote to his wife during the argument in the trial court: "Judd is boring away commencing with 'Numbers' & ending with 'Revelations' & so on down through Ignatius & Cyprean to Whitehouse." And the next day: "He [Judd] is trying to convince Judge Williams who is a Presbyterian that he ought to be a High Church Episcopalian. . . . I am heavily engaged every night on ecclesiastical history." After arguing two days in reply, Fuller wrote: "I am 'going in' with Gibbon, Hume, Macaulay, Froude, Morheim & Milman,—reading much more amusing than any which Judd furnished the Court with. . . . He has not got an Ecc[lesiastical] court to deal with. . . . Still of course I may be beaten." The next day, he wrote: "Sam Smith [his law clerk] turned up in Coleridge the following lines On An Infant who Died before Baptism which I . . . intend to quote on Williams:

> Be rather than be called, a child of God
> Death whispered—with assenting nod
> Its head upon its mother's breast
> The baby bowed, without demur
> Of the Kingdom of the Blest
> Possessor, not inheritor.

Two days later: "I have spoken three days & expect to go on at least one & perhaps two days more. . . . I am frightfully tired and shall be heartily glad when it is over." Before the case was decided, Bishop Whitehouse died. Fuller wrote: "Peace to his ashes. He was a good fighter." But Fuller's rare ability to retain the respect of his adversaries is shown by the fact that he was one of the bishop's pallbearers. The day after the funeral he wrote his wife: "The Cheney case is to be decided tomorrow P.M. It was to have been—singular coincidence— yesterday, at the very time we were bearing the body of my great antagonist to the grave."

By this time Fuller had acquired a reputation as an orator; courtrooms began to be crowded when he spoke. He was losing his early flamboyance; Governor Palmer said that while Fuller's arguments were "bright and sparkling" he did not deal out "tropes and figures and imagery" but always spoke directly, "like Melville W. Fuller of Augusta, Maine."

In 1874 he was elected president of the Chicago Law Institute, succeeding W. C. Goudy. The institute had been organized several years before by the principal lawyers of Chicago and had built a fine law library for its members, only to have it destroyed by the Chicago fire. After the fire Fuller had taken a leading part in restoring the library. Illinois lawyers in that era cited cases from other states much more than they do now, since the local law was not yet settled; some of Fuller's briefs cite cases from as many as twenty states. A good library was therefore a necessity to the bar.

In 1870 Fuller had his first case in the Supreme Court of the United States. It was, however, submitted on briefs without oral argument. He was not admitted to practice there until 1872, when he argued a bankruptcy case before the Court. While waiting for his case to come up, he wrote to his wife from the "Supreme Court Room." "It is a singular thing," he said, "that this city which bores me so, seems to delight others to such an extent that they wish to spend their lives here." Chase was then Chief Justice but was succeeded two years later by Morrison R. Waite.

Fuller argued the first case in which Waite delivered an opinion as Chief Justice. It was Fuller's third in the Supreme Court, while Waite, prior to his appointment, had never argued there. This case attracted some attention because more than eighty pending cases in Illinois turned on its decision. It involved the taxation of national bank stock under a federal statute which was, to a degree, inconsistent with the Illinois constitution. Fuller represented the Merchants National Bank; and although he lost, his employment as sole counsel in so important a cause enhanced his prestige in his profession.

In these years Fuller's family life was idyllic. In 1869 Coolbaugh gave Mrs. Fuller a fine residence on Lake Avenue, a block south of the Douglas monument.[1] Here the Fullers raised a large family. Mrs. Fuller was a real mother to the two daughters by his first marriage. Their own first child, Mary, commonly called Mamie, was born in 1867; their second, Mildred, in 1869; Paulina in 1870; Melville, the day after the Chicago fire in 1871; Catherine, commonly called Cassie, in 1873; Jane Brown in 1875; Fanny in 1879, and Weston in 1880. The only tragedy was the death of the first son, Melville, in 1874. The poor child fell against a hot stove and was so burned that he died a few days later.

Each year Mrs. Fuller spent March and April in the South, at Aiken, Jacksonville, or San Antonio. His letters to her when she was away suggest the rare felicity of his domestic life. A typical letter runs: "The children are all well. Catherine is wearing out her new dress—she is in high fettle. Pauline was indignant last night because I entered the house before she could come down and get behind the front door. . . . The *he* mouse is getting very tame—the she has several small red children. . . . The hens lay—the ducks are expected to." His emotional nature, his tenderness and compassion, are shown by the part that pets always played in his life.

His relations with Coolbaugh continued to be intimate. A letter to Mrs. Fuller in 1874 reads in part: "Today I called on your father at the bank & went out to lunch with him. . . . He inquired particularly concerning you and finally said he thought the last of April he'd go down there, i.e. to Jacksonville. 'Well,' I said, 'I'll go with you.' Whereupon he suggested that we'd better go to Washington, Charleston, Savannah, & c. I rather shrank from that & told him that when I started for

[1] Now 3600 Lake Park Avenue.

you I generally went straight through. But he insisted that the better way was to stop over. . . . I thought he suggested that he'd pay the bills. This wild & romantic idea threw a cloud of doubt on his previous statements but I do believe that he'll come."

By the census of 1870 Chicago had a population of 334,270 and was the fifth largest city in the country; the next year it passed St. Louis and became the fourth largest. It had 1,149 factories with an annual production of over $89,000,000. More vessels in number (though not in tonnage) arrived at its port in one year than at New York, Philadelphia, Charleston, San Francisco, and Mobile combined. But from October 8 to 10, 1871, Chicago's soaring career was brought suddenly to earth by the most disastrous fire in American history. Fuller's building, the Reynolds block, vanished, together with practically every building in an area of three and a third square miles in the heart of the city. All of the books and papers in his law office were destroyed; 90,000 people were left homeless, and the property loss was $200,000,000. Since Fuller's home was on the far south side, well out of the range of the fire, he perhaps did not know of his loss until he awoke the next morning. But he then found that almost all of the property he had amassed in the past fifteen years had been devoured. Before the ashes were cold, however, Fuller & Smith reopened their law office in the bedroom of a residence at 543 Wabash Avenue, just south of the burned area. The Union National Bank, as well as the National Bank of Commerce, was in the same house, and the First National and several other banks were only a few doors away. In a few months Fuller & Smith moved their office to the Central Union Block on Market Street. The next year Fuller borrowed $80,000 on a mortgage of the lot where his part of the Reynolds building had stood and built the Fuller Building, a four-story store and office building.[1] His office re-

---

[1] This building was torn down in 1910 and the Hamilton Club erected on the site. It is now (1950) the location of the Hamilton Hotel, 20 South Dearborn Street.

mained in this building until his appointment as Chief Justice sixteen years later.

But Fuller felt "wiped out" by the fire, just as he had been eliminated from public life by the war. In 1873 his class at Bowdoin sang a song written by him containing these lines:

> What dreams have vanished as the sun ascended;
> What hopes have withered in the noontide blaze!
> What bitter disappointments have attended
> The keen ambitions of those early days.

> Yet, though these fond illusions have departed,
> And glittering dreams and buoyant hopes have fled,
> Faith, courage, strength, remain to the true hearted,
> To wage life's battle until life be sped.

However, Chicago recovered from the fire with a rush. Four days after the holocaust the Chicago *Tribune* said that there had been wild, visionary schemes for the federal and State governments to advance $100,000,000 to rebuild the city. The *Tribune* snorted at such an idea: "It must be built by its own people on their own credit and with that self-reliant energy that has already erected one of the noblest cities of modern times." This was exactly what happened and sooner than expected. Railroad construction boomed; the Chicago grain market increased its activity in swift spurts; real estate continued to rise in value.

But credit became overextended. Panic came. It started in 1873 with the failure in New York of Jay Cooke & Company. Several Chicago banks, including Coolbaugh's bank, the Union National, closed their doors. However, the Union National was solvent; and Coolbaugh, with the other directors, at once issued a statement that they would be responsible as individuals for the payment of all deposits. Coolbaugh thought that it was suicidal for the Chicago banks to stay open and pay out currency after suspension had occurred in all other important cities in the country. But the situation improved in a short time; and the Union National reopened on the written request of most of the leading Chicago banks, who stated that they had complete faith in its solvency. Its directors voted their confidence in Coolbaugh and a few weeks later increased his salary from $10,000 to $15,000. But the public trust in the bank was shaken because it remained closed longer than the other banks, and it never regained its leading position.

By 1877, twenty-one years after his arrival in Chicago, Fuller, despite many vicissitudes, had attained success and happiness. His years of starvation, the war, his first wife's death, and the fire were only dim memories. He was highly respected in his profession, his income was adequate to his needs, and his domestic life was blissful. He had no ambitions for public position.

CHAPTER VI

°॒∽॒°

POLITICS

1868–1880

Although Fuller had been a delegate to the Democratic National Convention in 1864, he did not sit in the convention of 1868. He was, however, a member of the conventions of 1872, 1876, and 1880.

His absence from the convention of 1868 was doubtless due to his strong stand for hard money. As a Benton Democrat, he had opposed paper currency. All his life he fought inflation. In the Illinois legislature he had even voted against receiving the wartime greenbacks in payment of State taxes.

In 1867 George Pendleton, a prominent Democrat of Ohio, called attention to the fact that certain war bonds of the government were not by their terms payable in gold. He suggested that these bonds should be paid in greenbacks, which were much depreciated. Most of the bonds were held in the East, and Pendleton became, in the West, the leading Democratic candidate for President.

As soon as Pendleton's plan was proposed, Fuller condemned it. It was repudiation, he said, since the bonds could not be "paid" by tendering another promise to pay. It would destroy the "credit" of the government. It would result, he argued, in the most "fearful rise in prices." He tried to suggest Judge Sidney Breese, another Benton hard-money Democrat, as Illinois' "favorite son" candidate for the Presidency. But at the State convention the Illinois delegates were instructed to vote for Pendleton. The Pendleton plan to pay the bonds in greenbacks was adopted in the Democratic national platform; but

Horatio Seymour, a sound-money man from New York, was the nominee against Grant.

In the campaign Seymour put more emphasis on taxing the bonds than on paying them in paper currency. Fuller concurred that the bonds should be taxed and made several speeches for Seymour. The radical Republicans—who had failed that year in the impeachment charges against President Johnson—planned to maintain themselves in power, Fuller charged, by negro suffrage and white disfranchisement. Such, he argued, was the purpose—candidly confessed by its sponsors—of the proposed Fourteenth Amendment to the Constitution.

He wrote four campaign songs which were published anonymously in the Chicago *Times*. Grant, the silent "man on horseback," did not please him:

> Hurrah for that glorious hero, Grant!
> The bondholder's choice is he;
> He'd speak if he could, but he luckily can't
> And the masses won't know what a regular plant
> A "glorious hero" can be.

The next year—1869—another constitutional convention was called in Illinois. Since Fuller had been a member of the last convention in 1862, he might well have wished to attend this one. But he deferred to his father-in-law, who with Fuller's support was elected a delegate. Thus started the potent political combination of Coolbaugh and Fuller which endured for eight years, until Coolbaugh's death.

Fuller tried to persuade Coolbaugh to run for president of the constitutional convention but he refused. When the convention met, Fuller wrote his wife from the State capital: "Darling Mollie: I arrived here last night. Your father doesn't want it [the presidency] and we are concentrating on Hitchcock and shall elect him." A few days later Coolbaugh nominated for president of the convention Charles Hitchcock, a Republican lawyer of Chicago, who was elected. The constitution framed by this convention is still in force in Illinois eighty years later.

In the year that the constitution was adopted (1870), Fuller was chairman of the platform committee of the Democratic State convention. The convention declared for free trade on principle, conceded the legality of a tariff for revenue only, but denounced a protective tariff as "enriching the few at the expense of the many." It condemned the Grant administration as "extravagant, wasteful and corrupt" and declared that it was destitute of principle and was held together only by "the cohesive power of public plunder." Time was to make these words less empty than they then seemed, but Fuller later came to recognize that even Grant had some merits.

The next year Fuller was pleased by the growing split in the Republican party between the Grant forces, or radical Republicans, and the liberals led by Carl Schurz. The situation demanded the union of the Democrats and liberal Republicans in a bipartisan campaign against Grant. In Illinois a leading anti-Grant Republican was Orville H. Browning of Quincy, an able lawyer who had drafted the original Republican platform in Illinois in 1856 and had been a close friend of Lincoln and Secretary of the Interior in President Johnson's cabinet. In June, 1871, Browning recorded in his diary a discussion with another intimate friend of Lincoln, Justice David Davis of the Supreme Court of the United States. They agreed, Browning said, that Grant was "weak, vain, ignorant, mercenary, selfish and malignant"; that he was surrounded by corrupt and unprincipled men and that his reelection would be a great calamity to the country. Browning told Davis that if the Democrats would nominate Davis for the Presidency, Browning would support him.

A month later Browning received a letter from Fuller urging him to become a candidate for congressman-at-large against the radical party. "It is a duty," Fuller wrote, "arising upon conviction to endeavor to impress the conviction upon others, the State & the Nation. Why should you entertain well settled views of public affairs & not assist in impressing them upon the popular mind & bringing the government into harmony with them?" Browning noted the receipt of this letter in his diary, but replied that he could not run.

As the election year of 1872 dawned, politics were in ferment. Justice Davis had come to be regarded as a possible nominee for President by both the liberal Republicans and the Democrats—a possibility not discouraged by Judge Davis. Fuller was in Washington in February, arguing his first case before the Supreme Court. On his arrival he wrote to Mrs. Fuller: "I saw Judge Davis & [intend to] call on him tonight. *He is the coming man.*" And the next day: "The excitement is intense over politics. Davis is the man as it looks now. I had a long talk with him last night & he is exceedingly frank & communicative."

Fuller was doubtless attracted to Davis by his famous opinion in *Ex parte Milligan,*[1] sustaining the constitutional guaranties of civil rights in wartime. But the liberal Republican convention at Cincinnati in May, 1872, was stampeded into the nomination of Horace Greeley over Charles Francis Adams, David Davis, and Lyman Trumbull. The Democrats were thus forced to accept Greeley as their candidate, and the ensuing campaign enriched the American language by the expression "to eat crow." No one had vilified the Democrats as Greeley had. Furthermore, he was the arch-apostle of a protective tariff, and Protection in Fuller's eyes was not only wrong but unconstitutional. To make things worse, Fuller became involved in a humiliating quarrel with Cyrus McCormick over the management of the Illinois campaign.

A few weeks after the liberal Republicans had nominated Greeley, the Illinois Democrats and liberal Republicans held their conventions on the same day in Springfield. Fuller was a member of the Democratic convention. Among the liberal Republicans were Governor John M. Palmer, ex-Senator Lyman Trumbull, and Horace White, editor of the Chicago *Tribune.*

[1] 1866, 71 U.S. 2.

Each convention appointed a conference committee, with the result that each endorsed the platform and candidate of the Cincinnati convention and each nominated Gustave Koerner for governor. He had been a close friend of Lincoln, who had appointed him Minister to Spain. It was thought that Koerner would secure the German vote already weakened in its Republican attachment by the leadership of Carl Schurz in the liberal Republican movement. Fuller and Coolbaugh were elected delegates to the Democratic National Convention at Baltimore and, with some repugnance, voted for Greeley.

Cyrus McCormick, who had come to Chicago from Virginia before the war, had always been a staunch Democrat and, as his reaper business prospered, he became the financial angel of the Democratic party in Illinois. He was an old friend and early supporter of Greeley. He was elected Chairman of the State Central Committee in 1872 and was disappointed because he was named as an alternate instead of a delegate to the national convention at Baltimore. He refused to accept the position of alternate and attributed this slight to Fuller, whose lack of enthusiasm for Greeley was well known.

After the nomination of Greeley, McCormick was elected to the national committee and pledged $10,000 to its campaign fund, stipulating that it be spent in Illinois. A bipartisan State campaign committee, of which Governor Palmer was chairman and Fuller a member, was selected in Illinois. McCormick demanded, as a condition of furnishing this money, that Palmer and Fuller resign and that he be made chairman. Fuller acceded, though not very cheerfully. "If the fact that I am on the Finance Committee interferes with McCormick's liberality, it is better to sacrifice me," he wrote. "Consider my head in the basket. . . . 'The blood of the martyrs is the seed of the Church.' "

Greeley was defeated as never a man had been beaten before, and Fuller was rueful all his life for his part in the nomination. But his lack of rancor and his pliable mind are well shown by this campaign. In an effort to end oppression in the South and venality in Washington, he supported a candidate whom he abhorred and who represented economic principles that he despised. And he sacrificed his own position in the campaign for the prosperity of the cause. It was characteristic that he at once started to cultivate Cyrus McCormick. A few years later Fuller was writing McCormick deferential and friendly letters and they became good friends.

In the middle seventies Fuller wrote to his wife: "I'm pretty thoroughly sick of politics. I have too much to attend to." But early in 1876 he became interested in Governor Thomas A. Hendricks of Indiana as a presidential candidate. He was disappointed because Coolbaugh preferred another candidate, Samuel J. Tilden of New York. But Fuller wrote his wife that he had little hope for any Democratic nominee, even though Grant's Secretary of War, Belknap, had been caught red-handed in accepting a bribe. Belknap had resigned to escape conviction on impeachment. "The moral perceptions of the whole country are so blunted," Fuller declared, "that the Belknap business won't be 'much of a show.'" In April, however, he presided at the Democratic County Convention and wrote to Mrs. Fuller, "I did it upon reflection and deliberately & don't regret it."

Fuller was selected to make the argument before the Democratic National Committee in favor of Chicago for the national convention, but he was not successful and it was held at St. Louis. There Fuller made the greatest public speech of his career in seconding the nomination of Hendricks for President. This address was published widely in the newspapers. Like most of his formal discourses, it started with a long, rambling sentence: "Mr. President and Gentlemen of the Convention: Depressed under the weight of debt and taxation, universal corruption, general demoralization, and all the evils that inevitably flow from a persistent disregard of fundamental law and the long and uninterrupted retention of power in the same hands, the country demands a return to the principles and practices of the fathers of the Republic in this the hundredth year of its existence, and the restoration of a wise and frugal government, that shall leave to every man the freest pursuit of his avocation or his pleasures, consistent with the rights of his neighbors, and shall not take from the mouth of labor the bread it has earned."

The "nominee," Fuller asserted, "must be intrinsically honest that he may inspire honesty in others [an oblique reference to the proved dishonesty of men close to Grant]; capable himself, that he may be quick to discern and to appropriate the capacity of others [Grant had chosen many incompetents] . . . and pure in spirit that . . . he may . . . bring governmental administration from the depths into which it has descended and elevate and purify the moral tone of the nation." Fuller said that Hendricks had these qualities and would deserve success; "and, if deserved, what better leader to insure it?"

This speech was apparently not prearranged for any length of time. Governor Hendricks wrote Fuller a few days later: "I beg that you will allow me to express my high appreciation of the honor you did me at the convention. I did not know that you would second my nomination until I received the dispatch that you were speaking. . . . I was glad because you were from Illinois, because you were a relative of Mr. Coolbaugh, my friend, and because you are an ornament to the profession of which I am proud."

The convention, however, nominated Tilden for President and Hendricks for Vice President. Fuller and, even more so, Coolbaugh (who was said to be slated for Secretary of the Treasury) were well satisfied with the nomination of Tilden. But again disappointment was their lot—and this time after the prize was almost in their hands. Tilden received the popular majority but lacked one vote of an electoral college majority, after an electoral commission, by a strict party vote, had decided the contests against him. Again Fuller went back to his law practice.

Again he vowed that his retirement was permanent. The

next year he wrote his wife: "I am entirely 'out of politics'—
My ambition is to make you happy and our children." He was
not even tempted by a suggestion made by Samuel J. Tilden
when he met Coolbaugh in Europe that Fuller should go to
the United States Senate. "I always supposed," he wrote Coolbaugh, that "Sammy had 1880 on the brain. . . . Tilden's
mention of me was political. He not only knew our relations
but he knew you knew he knew & that shows his ingenuity.
The Senatorship is a great way off and in the clouds. To accept
the office is almost to change one's life and I am growing too
'set' in my groove, I sometimes think." And he added slyly:
"If you run into Governor Hendricks remember me most
cordially."

But in 1878 Fuller campaigned for his friend Judge Lambert
Tree, who was running for Congress. Fuller's speeches in this
campaign present his political philosophy. He was against the
concentration of power in Washington and in favor of maintaining authority in the states. He was opposed to governmental paternalism: government is best, he asserted, when it
governs least. He decried the lavish governmental expenditures which, he said, always followed from the retention of
power in the same hands for long periods. "It is with parties as
with individuals," he declared. "Years of unlimited power
and the collection and distribution of enormous sums of money
unfit for the application of the methods of economy."

At the Democratic National Convention of 1880 in Cincinnati, Fuller was again a delegate from Illinois and almost was
elected chairman of the delegation. He wrote Mrs. Fuller from
Cincinnati: "There was terrific trading against me for chairman. . . . Nevertheless I got a good vote—19 out of 41. . . .
Then Green, my Cairo friend who had been obliged to vote
against me nominated me for the Committee on Resolutions
[the Platform Committee]. . . . I was elected unanimously."
General Winfield Scott Hancock was the nominee of this convention and was defeated in the election by James A. Garfield.
According to the Chicago *Tribune,* Mayor Carter Harrison

blamed Fuller for the defeat of Hancock. The Democratic platform had contained a plank for a tariff for revenue only. Many Democratic areas were in favor of a protective tariff, and Hancock repudiated this platform declaration. "The tariff question," he declared, "is a local question." When the result of the November election was foreshadowed by a Republican victory in October in Indiana (where the Republican campaign had emphasized the tariff issue), the *Tribune* said: "The model Mayor declares that he cannot tell a lie and 'Mel' Fuller did it. . . . It was Melville Fuller, who put that 'for revenue only' free trade plank in the Cincinnati platform."

Sound money, free trade, states' rights, no paternalism, governmental economy, and the preservation of the civil rights of the individual: these were the keys to Fuller's political philosophy as evidenced by his career prior to his appointment as Chief Justice.

CHAPTER VII

•◡•

LITERATURE AND LAW

1877–1888

Eʌʀʟʏ on the morning of November 14, 1877, the body of William F. Coolbaugh was found at the foot of the Douglas monument with a bullet in his brain. He had been missing since the day before, and his son-in-law had searched all night for him. Because of Coolbaugh's prominence, Fuller had not notified the police but had engaged Allan Pinkerton to help find him.

There were many speculations on why he had killed himself. He was only fifty-six years old; his bank was in good condition, and his private fortune was more than adequate to his needs. He had a young wife and his home life was not unhappy, though a son and daughter by his first marriage preferred to live with the Fullers rather than in the Coolbaugh home. But for some time he had been subject to spells of depression.

The Chicago papers quoted a gentleman intimately connected with the family whose name was withheld: "Mr. Coolbaugh was a very ambitious man and a very sensitive one. He was ambitious of political honors. There had been a time during his residence in Iowa when he was on the verge of going to the United States Senate. . . . He never abandoned those aspirations which he held in his younger years. It was, perhaps, during the latter part of his life a sort of morbid craving which was, looking at it calmly, beyond his reach. He began to see latterly that these dreams were hopeless. He had also been very proud . . . of being considered the leading banker in the

Northwest, of being the man whom everybody consulted and whom everybody looked up to. . . . Of late years he had been losing his high standing and he knew it. . . . It was a source of intense mortification to him . . . that another institution [The First National Bank] had got ahead of his. . . . I attribute his suicide wholly to the conviction that his days of prominence were over and to the fear that he was going to break down physically and mentally."

Coolbaugh's death, under these circumstances, could not have failed to confirm Fuller in his growing aversion to public life and his seclusion in his library and his law office. His literary life began soon after Coolbaugh's death. Within a few weeks thereafter, Fuller was nominated for membership in the Chicago Literary Club. This club met every Monday night; the members ate and drank together, and one member read a paper on a subject of his own selection. Fuller attended these meetings for the next ten years. The club, therefore, had some influence in the education of the man who became Chief Justice.

The Chicago Literary Club—then only four years old—was both puny and magnificent. It cast a feeble literary light in the crude and roaring Chicago. Its members were clergymen, architects, lawyers, doctors, journalists, and a few literary businessmen. Yet, of the 148 essayists at the club during Fuller's time, 66 are now enshrined either in *Who Was Who* or in the *Dictionary of American Biography;* of these, 31 appear in the latter work. These include Senator Lyman Trumbull; Isaac N. Arnold, biographer of Lincoln; Joseph Kirkland, novelist and inspirer of Hamlin Garland; William Frederick Poole, librarian and founder of *Poole's Index;* Henry Demarest Lloyd, journalist and Socialist; as well as Bishops Cheney and Fallows; Rabbi Emil G. Hirsch; and Secretaries of the Treasury Gage and MacVeagh.

Cabinet members, ambassadors, governors, and judges of the Supreme Court of Illinois have been chosen from the ranks of this small club. But such honors are fortuitous; Fuller, until his selection as Chief Justice, was among the members not so honored, many of whom deserved more renown than some of those who achieved it. He was notable for being eminently "clubable"—a word coined by Dr. Samuel Johnson. The members called him "Mel" and loved his shining face as much as they admired his brilliant speech. He had a genius for friendship—intensive rather than sporadic. He had no careless friendships, for he was too reserved and too intellectual. But all his life he was surrounded by men who idolized him.

His faithful attendance at the Literary Club expanded his circle among diverse people and perhaps made him more tolerant of otherwise offensive ideas. There were atheists in the club—and Roman Catholics. There were Socialists and Republicans. There were Jews and (most deplored of all by Fuller in his youth) Presbyterians. Controversial papers were frequent and the club early adopted a rule—found to be necessary—forbidding adverse discussion of them.

Fuller's first literary effort in the club was on Thomas Jefferson, from whom he derived his political philosophy. To Fuller the Bill of Rights was the most important part of the Constitution. His opposition to Lincoln in the Civil War was based on Lincoln's wartime transgressions of those rights. With Jefferson, Fuller believed that "that is the best government which governs least." And he was firmly convinced of the necessity of preserving the rights of the states against the centripetal force of the central government.

But Fuller was soon enjoying a literary reputation that extended beyond the Chicago Literary Club. In January, 1879, he was invited to deliver the memorial address on Justice Sidney Breese before the Illinois State Bar Association. Fuller spoke for more than three hours. Yet Orville Browning's diary notes: "to the State House to hear the address of Melville Fuller on the life and services of Judge Breese . . . a good and interesting performance."

Fuller had argued many cases before Justice Breese, who, in one of his opinions, had gone out of his way to speak well of

Fuller's grandfather, Chief Justice Weston. Fuller and Breese had corresponded regarding politics, literature, and professional affairs; they had given each other books; Fuller had proposed Breese as a candidate for President of the United States, and they had discussed the project of Fuller's writing the judge's biography. Immediately on Breese's death, Fuller had expressed his deep sense of personal loss. Next to Stephen A. Douglas, Fuller probably admired Breese above all the men whom he had met up to that time. This speech, therefore, contains Fuller's unconscious portrait of the model for his own service as Chief Justice.

Breese, born in 1800 in New York, had graduated from Union College and had come to Illinois in 1818. He had been a United States senator in the forties and a justice of the Supreme Court of Illinois for twenty-three years. His "dignity" and "majestic aspect," Fuller said in the memorial, "drew audience and attention." Yet he had a courtesy that was "the subtle essence of good breeding and refinement." He was naturally "imperious," but that quality was never displayed toward youth or inexperience. He was severe yet he was catholic in his sympathies and never uncharitable.

He had large "experience in affairs," a "wide and varied culture," and great "familiarity with the [law] books." He had a "retentive memory," a "strong grasp of general principles," and "indomitable industry." But justice was to him a cardinal virtue, and his powers of analysis were so acute that he could always find relief from "technical decisions or rules when, in his judgment, they were invoked to defeat the claims of justice."

His judicial style was "graceful, easy and flowing," though sometimes "too ornate." His opinions had "vigor, clearness and precision," and "fervid, imaginative force"; they were "enlivened by his wit" and his quotations were usually brief. He was tenacious of his judgments, when once arrived at, and his "native combativeness" and "aggressive force" in the conference room are displayed in his dissenting opinions.

This speech also forecasts the great development of the police power (or the power of a state to invade the constitutional rights of the individual for the public health, welfare, or safety) which was to come from the Supreme Court during Fuller's regime. He praised Breese's decision in the case of *Munn* v. *People* [1] that the state had the power to regulate the practices and rates of grain warehouses. This decision had been affirmed by the Supreme Court of the United States in a landmark opinion by Chief Justice Waite. The decision was anathema to many businessmen who foresaw in it the beginning of an era of regulation that would stifle free enterprise.

Fuller's literary efforts soon multiplied. He became a regular contributor to the *Dial,* a monthly review of current literature, which had recently been launched in Chicago. John Greenleaf Whittier said a few years later that the Chicago *Dial* was the "best and ablest literary paper in the country."

Fuller's first contribution to this review was in part political. In October, 1880, the *Dial* published a review by him of three current biographies of General Winfield Scott Hancock, then the Democratic candidate for President against James A. Garfield. It is significant that this time Fuller's political contribution took a literary form rather than a purely political one. Recalling, perhaps, his suggestion twelve years before that it was not safe to assume that a military hero like Grant would be a great President, he wrote with restraint of the heroism and generalship of Hancock.

Fuller made it clear that Hancock, if elected, would be no radical. "Paternalism," he said, "with its constant intermeddling with individual freedom, has no place in a system which rests for its strength upon the self-reliant energies of the people." Most Chicagoans of that era would have subscribed to this statement. The miracle of Chicago's growth and prosperity rested squarely on self-reliance. This background was to find expression in some of Fuller's opinions as Chief Justice. Just as Marshall's bitter winter at Valley Forge, caused by a weak and

[1] 1873, 69 Ill. 80; *Munn* v. *Illinois,* 1876, 94 U.S. 113.

improvident government, led him to favor a strong national government, so Fuller's life in Chicago during the time of its prodigious growth gave him an aversion toward governmental interference with individual enterprise.

His next review was of Disraeli's *Endymion*, which was then having an enormous commercial success. Fuller was an inveterate novel reader (in later years he turned to detective stories), and this review shows that he had read most, if not all, of Disraeli's fiction. "Upon the whole," he said, "the Earl of Beaconsfield must depend for his posthumous fame upon something else than his novels." Fuller was an admirer of Disraeli's rival, Gladstone, about whom he had written a paper for the Chicago Literary Club. But it was Disraeli rather than Gladstone, Fuller pointed out, who foresaw the outcome of our Civil War. He concluded that Disraeli's speech upon the death of President Lincoln placed Disraeli "in a far better light . . . than anything . . . that can be written of his literary efforts."

As they were published in the next few years, Fuller reviewed in the *Dial* five biographies in the American Statesmen Series. He showed that he was well acquainted with the classics in biography such as Boswell's life of Johnson, Lockhart's Scott, Southey's Nelson, Twiss's Eldon, Forster's Dickens, and Trevelyan's Macaulay and Fox.

He complained that Morse, in his life of John Quincy Adams, had obtruded his own opinion of General Jackson: it should suffice to give Adams's opinion of the General. But Fuller praised Adams for his "great pluck" and said that "if he had been less rancorous and more cordial he might have been one of the most popular men that the country has ever seen." After his Civil War experience, Fuller was never again rancorous or malignant; indeed, he was amiable almost to a fault.

His reviews of the life of Thomas Jefferson by John T. Morse, Jr. and that of Alexander Hamilton by Henry Cabot Lodge start with a succinct statement of Fuller's analysis of our political history: "Two great parties have always divided the people of this country. . . . The doctrine of the one is that all power, not expressly and clearly delegated to the general government, remains with the states and with the people; of the other, that the efficacy of the general government should be strengthened by a free construction of its powers. The one believes that that is the best government that governs least; the other, that government should exercise the functions belonging to Divine Providence, and should regulate the profits of labor and the value of property by direct legislation. The leader and type of one school of thought and politics was Thomas Jefferson; and Alexander Hamilton was the leader and type of the other."

If Fuller had lived until the present day, he might have detected some lack of historical continuity in the positions of both parties. In fact, he began to note in a few years that the Democratic party was no longer the party of strict construction. But he continued to prefer the governmental philosophy of Jefferson to that of Hamilton.

His most scholarly review was of Allan B. Magruder's *Life of John Marshall*. Fuller compared Marshall favorably with his contemporaries Kenyon, Ellenborough, Tenterden, and Denman, who were Chief Justices of England, and with Eldon, Erskine, Lyndhurst, and Brougham, who were Lord Chancellors during the same period. He noted that the Justices of the Supreme Court had usually been prominent in politics before their elevation but that "freedom from partisanship" had always characterized their official conduct thereafter. Fuller said, however, that the political philosophies of the Justices were expressed in their opinions, as witness Marshall's broad extension of the federal power. The result of Marshall's opinions, Fuller declared, was that any law that Congress deemed necessary to carry a granted power into effect was constitutional, regardless of whether such law was "actually necessary." But he ended with a tribute to Marshall: "In mere judicial learning, he has been surpassed by some but in the power of pure reason by none."

His review of Theodore Roosevelt's *Life of Thomas H. Benton* furnished a real test of Fuller's amiability. But he passed it easily. He quoted without comment young Roosevelt's hostile opinions of Jefferson and Jackson and, as Roosevelt called them, the "little men" who were Presidents between Jackson and Lincoln. Fuller then remarked: "It will thus be seen that Mr. Roosevelt holds the pen of a ready writer." Fuller was addicted to dry, New England understatement. He concluded his review with a summary of the life of his own hero, Benton. But it is probably just as well that the reviewer did not have a prevision of himself administering the oath that made the author President of the United States.

Whenever possible, Fuller spent his evenings in his library. He read among other things the Greville papers, Pepys's and Evelyn's diaries, Froude's life of Carlyle, and many books by Walter Bagehot. But his evenings were frequently interrupted by visitors. He wrote Mrs. Fuller in 1878 about a fantastic story told him one night by James F. Wilson, formerly a representative and later United States senator from Iowa. The tale related to a new invention called the phonograph. "It is difficult to realize," Fuller wrote, "that talk can be put on a cylinder & then unwound years afterwards & thousands of miles away. He [Wilson] says that the inventor will bring the machine to such perfection that the songs of Kellogg & Cary—i.e. the actual singing will be phonografted, then stereotyped & sold in the music stores & by having the machine you can put the sheet on the cylinder & sound out Kellogg & Cary or any other. This beats the horn of Munchausen. It is in fact the same thing."

During these years, his law practice became one of the largest in Chicago. He sometimes turned clients away because he was too busy to serve them—to the consternation of young lawyers who overheard the conversations. His partner, Joseph E. Smith, died suddenly in 1881, and thereafter Fuller practiced alone. The era of big law firms had not yet arrived.

His office was on the second floor at the front of the Fuller Building on Dearborn Street. The lawyers on his floor often came in to chat and smoke with him; Fuller smoked a big meerschaum pipe in those days. Robert T. Lincoln, son of the President, at one time had his office next door, and they became fast friends. John Morris, who like many other lawyers frequently employed Fuller to try cases for him, also had his office on the same floor. Morris had been a physician before he studied law, and Fuller, in turn, sometimes employed him in cases with a medical aspect.

Typewriters had not arrived, and he did not have a telephone until 1882. Fuller paid his office boy $3 a week, and his law clerk, Henry M. Booth, $125 a month, a princely wage for a law clerk in Chicago at that time. Law students served without compensation. From 1884 to 1888 James S. Harlan, son of Justice John M. Harlan, was a student in the office.

Practically all lawyers in those days spent their principal efforts in the courts; the day of the office lawyer did not come in Chicago until about twenty-five years later. Fuller defended many personal-injury cases for the Chicago, Burlington & Quincy and Illinois Central railroads. He also tried cases for the Union National Bank and the Merchants Loan & Trust Company. He was attorney for the South Park Board and conducted many condemnation cases for it. Two of Fuller's most valued clients were John W. Doane, President of the Merchants Loan & Trust Company, and Erskine M. Phelps, merchant and capitalist.

Fuller also represented Chicago's great merchant, Marshall Field, in a famous party-wall controversy with Field's former partner, Levi Z. Leiter. Fuller was friendly with both litigants, and the party-wall agreement was submitted to him for an opinion before the suit started. In asking for his opinion, Field and Leiter concealed from him their respective positions so that he would not know which one his opinion favored. They owned adjoining buildings in Chicago with a party wall between, that is, one wall on the division line. Field wanted to use the party wall in erecting a much larger building on his property to the east. Leiter, while conceding that Field had the right to use the wall, denied that Field could strengthen the foundation on Leiter's west half of it. Unless Leiter's half of the foundation was strengthened, it would not bear the weight of Field's new wall. But the contract between them provided that Field in using the wall should strengthen the "wall, and the foundations thereof, by making such additions thereto *on the east side thereof*" as might be required to prevent all injury to Leiter's building.

It was Fuller's view that, since the agreement had no effectual meaning if Leiter's interpretation should be adopted, Field had the right to strengthen the foundation on Leiter's property. The decision was adverse to Fuller's opinion in the Circuit Court and the Appellate Court, but Field won in the Supreme Court of Illinois. Fuller was counsel for Field in the last court but always remained on very friendly terms with both litigants.

Undoubtedly his most important case, both in value of the property involved and intricacy of the issues, was the famous Lake Front case. In 1883 the State of Illinois brought a suit to reclaim the entire lake front which was occupied by the Illinois Central and other railroads under certain statutes and ordinances. The land involved was over a mile in length, extended for a mile into the lake, and had been partially filled in. The city of Chicago was made a defendant and at first took a rather desultory part. But when Fuller was employed as the city's attorney, he evolved theories under which the city claimed that it, rather than the State, was the owner of all this property. He claimed that the statutory grants to the railroad were void or had been repealed by a subsequent act and that the city had acquired this land by virtue of its riparian rights as the owner of Michigan Avenue along the lake shore. His position was almost entirely sustained in an opinion of Mr. Justice Harlan sitting in the United States Circuit Court. This decision was finally affirmed in substance by the Supreme Court after Fuller's appointment as Chief Justice. He, of course, took no part in the decision there.

Another famous case in which he was engaged at the time of his appointment was the divorce case of *Carter* v. *Carter*.[1] The complainant was Mrs. Leslie Carter, a tall, titian-haired sylph, who deserves a place among the famous courtesans of history. She became a stage star after her divorce. Fuller was senior counsel for Carter, a wealthy Chicago lawyer. Carter's cross bill for divorce was first prepared by his junior counsel, who had made an investigation of the facts. The cross bill charged adultery with four specific men, giving places and dates in each case. None of these men was a resident of Chicago. A conference of Carter's counsel was then called to consider whether the cross bill should be amended to charge adultery with two additional men. These men were Chicagoans. Conclusive proof to sustain all of the charges had been unearthed. But Fuller vetoed this project with a quip: "All my life, I've been a Democrat," he said, "but in this case I'm a Republican. I'm for the protection of home industry. Let's leave out the Chicago men." On the trial, a jury found Mrs. Carter guilty on all four counts, but before that time Fuller had become Chief Justice of the United States.

The extent and variety of his practice in this period is almost incredible. He tried (to name only a few) mandamus cases, quo warranto cases, personal-injury cases, trade-mark cases, and tax cases. Perhaps the only field of litigation in which he did not practice was criminal law, and in his younger days he had been quite successful in that branch. As *Harper's Weekly* stated on his appointment as Chief Justice, he had had a wider experience in all branches of the law than any member of the Court.

In 1886 he spoke by invitation at the annual meeting of the Illinois State Bar Association. His subject was the recent decision of the Supreme Court of the United States in *Juilliard* v. *Greenman* [2] sustaining the power of Congress to issue in peacetime legal tender United States notes. He was critical of the decision. His relative, Dr. George Bancroft, the historian, had

[1] 1894, 152 Ill. 434. [2] 1884, 110 U.S. 421.

issued a pamphlet on this case entitled *A Plea for the Constitution of the United States Wounded in the House of Its Guardians*. But Fuller did not refer to this pamphlet and was temperate in his criticism. Perhaps he remembered his grandmother's advice about his political fulminations in 1856. On the currency question he was beginning to doubt that the Democratic party was the party of strict construction of the Constitution.

A few hours after this speech, he was elected president of the State Bar Association. In his presidential address the next year, he called attention to the excessive number of cases encumbering the docket of the Supreme Court of the United States. "From less than 300 cases in 1858," he said, "there are [now] over 1,300 on the calendar." He recommended that the association support legislation to relieve this situation, such as the bill for the creation of intermediate Appellate Courts proposed by the late senator and former Justice David Davis. Bar associations throughout the State responded favorably to Fuller's appeal and petitioned Congress for the passage of this Act. But it was not until three years after he became Chief Justice that he succeeded in securing the enactment of the Circuit Court of Appeals Act.

CHAPTER VIII

◦◡◦

APPOINTMENT

THE appointment of Fuller, who was unknown outside of Illinois, as Chief Justice of the United States was so unusual that, like Lincoln's election as President, it has given rise to many speculations—even myths.

Many Easterners persist in regarding Fuller's appointment to this high office as somewhat comparable to the selection of a Dalai Lama, the great religious ruler in Tibet. When the Great Lama dies, the Buddhist authorities select his successor from the children in the country born at the time of his death, into one of whom his spirit has supposedly entered. A child of an obscure family from a remote part of Tibet is thus likely to be elevated to the most exalted office in the country.

But there have been many efforts to explain Fuller's selection. Judge John Barton Payne, a distinguished Chicago lawyer, said, years later, that President Cleveland had been charmed by Fuller's urbanity when the President visited Chicago in 1887, a few months before the appointment. Judge Edward Osgood Brown added that the appointment was acutely accidental since Fuller had almost not been named as a member of the reception committee for the President's visit.

A story that still circulates in Democratic circles in Chicago is that Fuller "went down to Washington to get the appointment for Goudy and came back with the appointment for himself." It is a tradition in the Goudy family that *he* would have been appointed except for the fact that he was a corporation lawyer; and that, since he was not eligible himself, "he had the right of putting Melville Fuller's name forward in his place."

Senator Farwell of Illinois sometimes claimed credit for the appointment. He said that Mrs. Melville Fuller had suggested it to him at a dinner party at the Fuller home; she asked who the new Chief Justice would be and they discussed various persons whose names had been suggested for the position, including Mr. Goudy. Senator Farwell said that he did not believe Goudy could be confirmed by the Senate. She then said: "Why not my husband?" and this suggestion, according to Farwell, ultimately led to Fuller's appointment.

Carter H. Harrison, in his *Growing Up with Chicago,* wrote of Fuller as a friend of his father, the mayor, but said that Fuller's friendship was of slight political value because he was an "avowed candidate" for Chief Justice and "leaned over backward from any action that smacked ever so little of politics."

George F. Parker in his *Recollections of Grover Cleveland* quotes the President to the effect that the Supreme Court was about three years behind with its work and the Associate Justices suggested to him that he appoint a Chief Justice who would not only have high legal ability but would be an efficient business manager. After a long search, Cleveland, according to Parker, found such a man in "Melville W. Fuller, then almost a stranger."

Some of these stories may have traces of truth—doubtless their authors sincerely believed them to be true—but in the main they are refuted by Fuller's and Cleveland's letters. Fuller never sought the position, and he and the President were intimate friends long before his appointment.

Fuller was not, however, a delegate to the convention that nominated Cleveland. Although he had been a member of four previous national conventions, he was defeated as a delegate in 1884 by Joe Mackin, who, a few years later, was sent to the penitentiary for perjury in connection with election frauds. Cleveland's Republican opponent was Fuller's old acquaintance of his newspaper days in Augusta, James G. Blaine; but Fuller supported Cleveland in this famous "mugwump" campaign.

In a letter to Cleveland written at the time of the inaugural, Fuller applauded the President's forthright stand for the repeal of the Silver Purchase Act and quoted a line from Tennyson, "the wisdom of doing right in scorn of consequence." This phrase touched the right spot. Courage was the core of Cleveland's character; his dying words were, "I have tried so hard to do right." The example of his stalwart rectitude in a corrupt age is now, by general agreement, one of the great heritages of the American people.

After Cleveland became President, Fuller was frequently in Washington, where he usually had a case or two pending in the Supreme Court. Whenever he was in the Capital, he dropped in at the White House and saw the President or Colonel Lamont, the President's secretary, with whom he formed a strong friendship. Fuller was a marked man among the President's visitors because he never asked for anything. And he had a faculty of endearing himself to his intimates; Cleveland was drawn to him.

In a few months he was asked to report to the President on various candidates who had been suggested for federal positions in Chicago, such as postmaster and district attorney, and he made these reports for the next three years. According to the newspapers, Goudy was the President's "right-hand man" in Chicago; but actually Fuller was in much closer touch with the White House. In fact, he usually transmitted to the President Goudy's recommendations on the patronage. Fuller tried hard in his reports to the President to be objective; he ordinarily supported one person for a position but he was generous in his judgments of other candidates and praised them when possible.

Eight months after Cleveland's inauguration, he suddenly asked Fuller to accept the position of Chairman of the Civil Service Commission. This chairmanship was one of the most critical places in Cleveland's administration; he almost owed his election to his advocacy of civil service reform; but he was the first Democratic President since Buchanan, and the demands for office were overwhelming.

Fuller apologetically declined. He said that acceptance would entail a sacrifice of $20,000 a year. He explained, however, that money would not stand in the way if he could adjust his private affairs so as to enable him to come to Washington. "But," he continued, "I have nine children . . . and one of them is an invalid. Her mother is obliged to take her away in the winter and when one bird is off the nest, the other has to go on." He concluded: "I regretted being compelled to leave Washington so soon the other day and would have stayed, had I known you wished to speak with me. You were so terribly beset that I thought it more considerate not to seek an interview. . . ."

The next June, Cleveland was married; in the same month Fuller was at the White House with his daughter Mildred, then at Wells College, and the President introduced them to Mrs. Cleveland, who was a recent Wells graduate.

A month later, Cleveland pressed Fuller to come to Washington as solicitor general. "Candidates are already presented by partial friends; but I have my own ideas. . . . I want *you*," said the President. "The salary is $7,000—the office is quite an independent one, as you will see by looking at the law. You've got money enough (you don't want too much) and you've got a lot of old Snags on hand in your profession that it would be a comfort to turn your back on and forget. . . . This is a very unofficial letter but I have the subject matter very much at heart."

Again Fuller refused. "I am so thoroughly in accord with the administration," he wrote, "and so strongly attached to you personally that it gives me sincere regret that circumstances render it impossible for me to accept . . . in view of the claims of my home circle upon me. But I hope you won't think that I love money for its own sake and therefore would not accept an office that paid less than I earn." A few weeks later, Fuller wrote Colonel Lamont that he hardly dared write the President. "I feel," Fuller said regretfully, "like a snail who declines to go off his own grass plot."

The President then asked Fuller to be one of three United States Pacific Railway Commissioners authorized by Congress to investigate the great scandals in the manipulation of the finances of the Western railroads to which the government had advanced many millions. Fuller was requested to secure the acceptance also of his old Bowdoin college friend, William L. Putnam of Portland, Maine. Fuller faithfully executed this mission, going to New York to meet Putnam; although he deplored to the President the proposed appointment, as their co-commissioner, of David Littler of Illinois, who, according to Fuller, was "a politician pure and simple, of the aggravated Republican type." Fuller wrote the President: "But for personal attachment to you, I would not think of this thing for a moment and, as it is, I hope you will not insist upon it." He wrote to Lamont that he would like to be let off because of his "profound disinclination to be thrown or brought into prominence." He had taken the veil and had no thought of apostasy.

Cleveland excused both Putnam and Fuller and appointed ex-Governor Pattison of Pennsylvania, E. Ellery Anderson, a New York railroad lawyer, and David Littler. Fuller lectured the President on the last appointment: "I congratulate you on the appointment of Governor Pattison and Mr. Anderson," he wrote. "I can't on Littler's—he is a Republican partisan thoroughly devoted to Cullom and if the latter is playing for high stakes, Mr. Littler will bear considerable attention from his colleagues." Senator Cullom of Illinois had recently achieved the greatest triumph of his career—the passage of the Interstate Commerce Act—and Fuller was apparently afraid that he had his eye on the Presidency.

About this time (1887) Fuller was consulted by the administration on the appointment of a United States District Judge for the Southern District of Illinois. He strongly recommended Judge John Scholfield, an able young judge of the Supreme Court of Illinois. When Scholfield, to Fuller's great regret, declined the position, Fuller recommended either of two candidates. He wrote the President that, after Judge Scholfield's refusal, "one of these two was the best choice and the other the next best." As usual, the President followed his recommendation for the judgeship.

By 1887 Cleveland had gained his reputation as a veto President and, in that year, Fuller read an erudite essay on "The President's Vetoes" at the Iroquois Club (the Chicago Democratic Club) and also at the Chicago Literary Club, which, Fuller wrote, was "full of Mugwumps," or Republicans who had voted for Cleveland. In the paper he reviewed Cleveland's forthright veto messages to the great glorification of the President.

In May, 1887, Fuller wrote to Lamont acknowledging a note from the "Presbyterian young man" [Cleveland] and suggesting that the President and Mrs. Cleveland should visit Chicago sometime soon, preferably in September or October. "Mrs. Fuller and myself," he wrote, "would be delighted to invite Mrs. Cleveland and the President to visit us and, as we are not in practical politics, there couldn't be any heartburnings." Thereafter, when the President's proposed visit was announced, Fuller wrote to him repeating the invitation but saying that of course questions of policy must be considered and the Fullers would not feel at all hurt if the President decided to go somewhere else.

Fuller's arrangements, at Lamont's request, of hotel accommodations and other details of Cleveland's visit to Chicago were interrupted by a hasty trip to Europe in August. On his return he wrote Lamont that Mayor Roche had read to Fuller the mayor's speech for the President's visit and it was being forwarded. Remember, Fuller said, that Chicago's first charter was issued in 1837 "so it is now only 50 years old." "I have been here 31 years and the population is about *ten* times as large as when I arrived. October 5th [the date of the President's visit] will be the 16th anniversary of the great fire (October 9, 1871) which licked up three hundred millions and

compelled us to start again. I know of no better illustration
of the enterprise of the west and the indomitable energy of this
people." He concluded: "Command me in any way that will
promote the success of the President's trip and his and Mrs.
Cleveland's convenience while here."

The President's visit to Chicago was a triumph. Doubtless
he was charmed by Fuller's urbanity, but they were hardly
strangers at that time. Fuller's letters to Lamont usually closed
with "affectionate regards" to the President. Once he wrote,
"Give my love to the President and through him to Mrs. Cleveland."

On March 23, 1888, Chief Justice Waite died suddenly at
the age of seventy-two and President Cleveland had to select
his successor. Only five of the twenty-one Presidents before
him had made such an appointment: Washington had appointed Jay, Rutledge, and Ellsworth; John Adams in 1801
had appointed Marshall, who had served thirty-four years;
Jackson had appointed Taney, who had served twenty-nine
years; Lincoln had appointed Chase, who had served nine
years; and Grant had appointed Waite, who had served fourteen years.

The newspapers noted that to secure such long service the
President must appoint a young man. Furthermore, it was a
rule of the judiciary committee of the Senate that, to be confirmed, a nominee for the Supreme Court must not be over
sixty years of age. This canon is sometimes slightly relaxed,
but any other rule would be inconsistent with the law which
permits a Justice to retire on full pay at seventy after he has
served ten years. Only a few months before, Cleveland had
nominated Justice Lamar, who was sixty-two. He had been
confirmed after a heated wrangle at which his friends had produced the family Bible to prove that he was not sixty-six,
as claimed by his opponents. Even at sixty-two, it was pointed
out in the Senate, he was the oldest man ever nominated for
the Supreme Court. One thing was certain: Cleveland's nominee for Chief Justice would be under sixty, and the younger,

the better. The Chicago *Times* suggested that this appointee might well serve until that mythical year, A.D. 1920.

Geography was another important factor to be considered in the selection. It is important that the Justices be from different parts of the country, because sectional issues frequently come before the Court. Fuller had protested in 1877 when Harlan from Kentucky was appointed to succeed David Davis of Illinois. There were then nine federal court circuits, and one Justice of the Supreme Court was assigned to each circuit. The appointment of Harlan left the seventh circuit, consisting of Illinois, Indiana, and Wisconsin, without any representation on the Court. Illinois alone furnished more litigation in the Supreme Court than any other state except New York. Furthermore, the Democrats of Illinois had long endured the taunt that they were wholly unrepresented in Cleveland's cabinet, although such men as Senator Trumbull, Governor Palmer, William R. Morrison, and William C. Goudy were thought well worthy of portfolios.

But other sections of the country also claimed the appointment. Senator Blackburn of Kentucky called on the President and suggested Speaker Carlisle for Chief Justice. The South, however, had just received a place on the Court in the appointment of Justice Lamar. And the President (who regarded persons suggesting an improper appointment as thieves caught in the act) growled at Blackburn: "You know why I won't appoint him. I won't appoint a man to be Chief Justice of the United States who might be picked up in the street some morning."

The New York bar—and particularly Cleveland's intimate, Francis Lynde Stetson—strongly recommended for the position their most distinguished member, James C. Carter. But Carter was sixty, and Justice Blatchford came from New York.

New England had a candidate in Edward J. Phelps of Vermont, then Cleveland's Ambassador to Great Britain. His claims were pressed by Senator Edmunds of Vermont, the Republican Chairman of the Judiciary Committee of the Senate. However, the Irish protested that Phelps was an Anglo-phile, the newspapers pointed out that New England already had Justice Horace Gray, and Cleveland afterward wrote that Edmunds represented Phelps' age to be sixty-one or sixty-two when in fact he was sixty-six. A younger New England candidate who was considered was Fuller's old friend, William L. Putnam of Portland, Maine.

A likely candidate was Senator George Gray of Delaware, who had the supreme merits of being only forty-eight and of having more national prominence than any other candidate. Cleveland seriously considered him. There are two versions of why Gray was not appointed. One is that twenty-seven of his Democratic colleagues in the Senate petitioned for his appointment and that Cleveland was outraged by this attempt to dictate to him. The other is that Cleveland would have appointed Gray but that the President could not arrange to have Gray succeeded in the Senate by Thomas F. Bayard, Cleveland's Secretary of State. The Republicans had a majority of two in the Senate, and Gray, or some one of equal strength, was needed there by the administration.

Some of the Justices of the Supreme Court recommended that one of their own number, such as Justice Field or Justice Miller, be advanced to Chief Justice. But Cleveland at once rejected this suggestion. The tradition was then against advancing an Associate Justice.

But it was necessary for the President to act promptly. An election was only a few months away; and the longer he delayed, the greater would be the Republican inclination to hold up the appointment in the Senate until the possible new Republican President could make it. Cleveland therefore quickly decided that the new Chief Justice should be from Illinois. Since Fuller had been emphatically urging upon the President the merits of Judge John Scholfield of the Supreme Court of Illinois for appointment as District Judge and Scholfield had declined that appointment, it was natural that he should have been the President's first choice for Chief Justice. Scholfield was fifty-four years old. The President consulted Fuller, who heartily recommended Scholfield for the position. The President then authorized Congressman Townshend to feel out Scholfield and see if he would accept. Scholfield again refused. The published reason for his refusal was that he had a large family of children and that Washington was a bad place to raise children. He told some of his intimates, however, with tears in his eyes, that he would give his good right arm to be Chief Justice of the United States, but that he couldn't take his wife to Washington. She was a woman of sterling worth but of frontier habits; she went barefoot in the summer. Scholfield's friends sympathized but agreed with him.

Fuller had no part in the spontaneous efforts of his friends to have him appointed. His hesitation and embarrassment, as the movement gathered force, are almost amusing.

The day after Waite's death the Chicago *Times* said that the names of Goudy and Fuller were being suggested for the position by many Chicago judges and lawyers. Goudy was then in Washington, and the President bluntly told him that he was not eligible on account of his age, which was sixty-four. There were other things that would have prevented Goudy's confirmation: his Civil War record and the fact that he was general counsel of the Chicago & Northwestern Railroad. But he was embittered by his rejection and did nothing to further Fuller's candidacy until after the President had practically determined on the appointment a month later. Then Goudy wrote the President, endorsing Fuller.

As early as April 3, Fuller's friend, Erskine M. Phelps, had written Colonel Lamont from New York, strongly recommending Fuller for the position. "I have been absent from Chicago two or three weeks," he wrote, "and Mr. Fuller has not the remotest idea I am writing this letter." On the same date, however, Senator Farwell, Republican United States senator from Illinois, wrote Fuller that he had received an inquiry about Fuller's age from Senator Payne, father-in-law of Secretary of the Treasury Whitney. "I told him," Farwell said, "that you were about fifty." (He was actually fifty-five.) "I told him," Farwell continued, "that you stood at the head of your profession in Ill. and that you were in good health."

Four days later, Francis Lynde Stetson wrote to the President, reporting on his investigation (made at the President's request) of Carter, Scholfield, and Fuller. He strongly recommended Carter; and as between Scholfield and Fuller, he suggested Scholfield as the younger man and as having had judicial experience. He said that he knew little about Fuller.

That week Fuller took his wife and infant son to Old Point Comfort. He wrote Mrs. Fuller on April 14 from Baltimore, on his way home, that he had seen General Hyde from Maine, who told him that the Eastern papers had been full of discussion of the Chief Justiceship. "He said," Fuller wrote, "it was the general judgment that if the appointment went West it would be tendered me and if East to Putnam. So Maine would get it anyway. I do not believe in this. I am more and more satisfied it will be someone more prominent."

On Fuller's arrival in Chicago he found that Robert T. Lincoln, son of President Lincoln, had written to Cleveland recommending Fuller for the position. Shepard and Doane had suggested this letter. They had also secured a ringing editorial in the Chicago *Tribune* written by Joseph Medill in support of Fuller's appointment. In addition, Fuller found that United States Circuit Judge Walter Q. Gresham, then the *Tribune's* candidate for the Republican nomination for President, had written President Cleveland recommending Fuller for Chief Justice. This support, it will be noted, was entirely from Republican sources. The Chicago *Times* said that the *Tribune* was indeed becoming an independent newspaper when it supported Fuller, the *Times's* candidate for Chief Justice. Fuller sent these newspapers to his wife with the comment, "I don't think I shall be appointed to the place and I really don't wish for it."

He wrote to Judge Gresham: "I cannot bring myself to believe that the appointment will be tendered to me or that I ought to accept if it were, and yet . . . I cannot help being flattered by the action of my friends." Gresham responded: "You must permit me to say that should you be appointed, you will make a blunder not to be excused if you decline the position. Modesty is a good thing but it should not be carried too far. . . . In a conversation with Judge Drummond [1] yesterday I told him what I had done and he remarked that he would write a similar letter should you desire it. I told him I did not think you would ask him to do so and that he should write the letter unasked as I had."

The next day Fuller wrote the President a rather stammering letter. He did not refer to his candidacy, but he advanced the strongest reason that could be brought against it—his lack of national prominence—and he praised his old friend Putnam as a candidate:

"DEAR MR. PRESIDENT:

"I expected to be in Washington early last week to settle a decree before Mr. Justice Harlan and then to be able to express myself more fully about Judge Scholfield and I think I so wrote. . . . But I don't know but that I sufficiently expressed myself as it was and I regret to notice that Judge S. would probably not accept the appointment if tendered—My view is that when satisfied of the fitness then the effect ought to be considered, and that a certain prominence is desirable.

"In the instance of Judge S. whoever wished to know him, could turn to the Illinois reports and fifteen years on the bench of the highest tribunal of a State renders a man prominent, more or less, but somewhat so, anyway. Thus members of your cabinet, Mr. Phelps, Judge Peckham, Gov. Hoadly, Mr. Putnam (admirable lawyer & man) are all publicly known to a greater or less extent and I am sure this is an element not to be disregarded.

[1] Thomas Drummond, retired U.S. Circuit Judge in Chicago, whom Fuller had urged for a position on the Supreme Court in 1877, when Harlan was appointed.

"If Judge Thurman were ten years younger or Judge Trumbull either would be what is wanted. But seventy-three or seventy-five is too old. Lord Bacon truthfully says: 'A hale old man is a tower undermined.'

"I write because I wished to explain why I did not put in an appearance as I expected to do, and as I think I said I should."

A few days later Putnam received a letter from Fuller to the effect that he was surprised at the suggestions that the President would appoint him Chief Justice and that he thought someone "already in the public eye" would receive the place. He said that he had heard Putnam's name mentioned for it. Putnam had just rendered a great public service in the negotiation of the treaty with Great Britain over the rights of American fishermen in Canadian waters. "The President," Fuller wrote, "knows my opinion of you."

Apparently Mrs. Fuller also berated her spouse for his excessive modesty. Like Mary Lincoln, she wanted her husband to be President. The day after his letter to Cleveland, Fuller wrote her: "The papers are full of Phelps this morning and that is where I think it will land. You will remember that was my original judgment. Judge Drummond wrote a beautiful letter in favor of my appointment. It was very fine. I shall certainly get the benefit of it through advertisement and some say will be offered a high position. If Phelps is affirmed that leaves the ministry to England vacant & I hardly know where the President will turn. To my mind Paris is far the most attractive mission but I never had an inclination that way. There is really nothing but U.S. Senator that has a strong attraction to me and to get that involves very disagreeable labor."

A few days later Fuller received a letter from his old friend Congressman Springer reporting a call on the President with Congressman Townshend to recommend Fuller for Chief Justice. "The President heard us with interest," Springer wrote, "and spoke very kindly of you. He said he had received a great many letters urging your appointment and some from you recommending some one else. I said you were too modest to recommend yourself or even to ask others to recommend you and that we had called at our own insistence, etc."

Fuller's confidence that he would not be appointed was shaken by a letter from Justice Harlan on April 23. Fuller had an important appointment with Harlan in Washington on May 14, and Harlan wrote him not to come because his presence in Washington would be misunderstood. It is traditional that a candidate for judicial office must stay away from Washington. Fuller was perturbed. He wrote to Mrs. Fuller: "It is quite clear the President is exercised and I am one of the persons he is seriously considering. I can not contemplate such a thing without serious misgiving. It would be an entire change of life and at my age not to be contemplated as a matter of course. I had far better go out for the Presidency in 1892. I hope he will not tender the appointment to me."

And a few days later he wrote her: "I still think it will be Phelps. I am quite contented as I am but if you will help me I will select something & go in for it. My heart is not in this appointment for I really believe another would be better & I do not feel loyal to my friend the President in not writing him my exact judgment in the premises."

In the meantime Cleveland had determined on Fuller. The basis of the President's choice was Fuller's age and location, professional eminence and reputation for integrity. Fuller's political philosophy and his stand for sound money and against a protective tariff were strong additional reasons. Attorney General Garland had written the President that the vacancy offered an opportunity to impose their political views on the Court. Garland said the Chief Justice amounted in weight to two-thirds of the Court. That the President was very fond of Fuller did not, of course, militate against the appointment. Harlan afterward wrote him that Cleveland had said that he had prayed over the appointment. Justice Lamar had then remarked: "The Lord is very kind to Cleveland—He always tells him to do the thing he wants to do."

The President immediately moved to assure Fuller's confirmation. For this purpose Republican votes were necessary. Shelby M. Cullom, Republican senator from Illinois, tells the story in his memoirs. He was seeing the President on a personal errand early one morning when Cleveland suddenly asked him what Democratic lawyers in Illinois would be worthy of the position. Before Cullom could answer, the President asked him what he thought of Melville W. Fuller. Cullom answered that Mr. Goudy was the ablest lawyer among Democrats in Illinois but was probably not eligible because he was a railroad lawyer. Cullom had seen the newspaper suggestions of Goudy and had doubtless been gloating over his vulnerability on confirmation. Pressed as to Fuller, Cullom answered guardedly that if he were asked to name the five ablest Democratic lawyers in Illinois, Fuller would be among them and that Fuller was a scholarly lawyer who would grace the position.

On April 29, Colonel Lamont wired Fuller at Chicago: "The President has determined on you and will act tomorrow unless you object." To this Fuller responded on the same date: "I object unless I may have one day to consider." But Cleveland answered gruffly that an immediate nomination was so important that he had sent Fuller's name to the Senate, leaving the question of acceptance to be determined by him.

Fuller thought it over for five days and then wrote the President:

"CHICAGO, May 5th, 1888

"MY DEAR SIR:

"I believe it to be impossible that the idea can have occurred to you of want of appreciation on my part of the magnitude of the position tendered me and of the personal confidence in me which the appointment demonstrates you must have felt.

"Words are entirely inadequate upon such a subject and I

assume entirely needless. I was taken by surprise for the reason already given you and I have been kept in a state of astonishment since by the response which the nomination has evoked —you have afforded me the opportunity to discover an amount of personal regard for me which I did not know existed, and the expression of which will be a precious heritage for my family, irrespective of the occupancy of this great place.

"My grounds of hesitation were many & some difficult to explain, and their strength was unimpeded by any personal wish for prominence.

"I do not give expression to any misgivings I may entertain as to the extent of my ability to fill the place as I approve of what Dr. Johnson told to Boswell in reference to certain compliments the King had paid him, that it was not for him to deny what the King said.

"But my home ties are so strong, my personal ambition so slight, and the conservation of my business interests so very important to my large family, that I hope you will not misconceive me and think me ungracious if I say that I would be glad still to remain in what has been a very happy retirement. This, however, would disappoint, perhaps embarrass you, and would occasion pain to a multitude of friends and it might be a censurable avoidance of public duty, although this could hardly be in view of the excellence at your command.

"I shall therefore accept the position, trusting that the country will never have cause to regret your calling me to it, and earnestly hoping that God will give me strength equal to the exalted responsibilities imposed.

"I am,

> Your obedient servant
> M. W. FULLER

The President"

CHAPTER IX

∘〰∘

CONFIRMATION

CHICAGO was jubilant on the news of Fuller's appointment: no resident of that city had ever achieved so important a position. Lawyers and businessmen flocked to his office to congratulate him. Even Marshall Field—never an effusive man—called there that afternoon. Telegrams and letters of congratulation poured in: according to the newspapers, 1,318 such messages were received. Press comments were generally favorable, but the New York *Herald* observed that Fuller was so unknown that his name did not appear in the latest standard works of contemporary biography; the New York *World* asked whether it was necessary to fill such an important office with a comparatively unknown man; and the Philadelphia *Press* remarked that he was the most obscure man ever appointed Chief Justice.

This last statement is probably true, as appears from the table of the public services of the Chief Justices which is printed on the opposite page. But Fuller's professional career compared favorably with that of any of his predecessors. Chief Justice Waite, for example, had never argued a case before the Supreme Court when he was appointed to head it. Fuller had had one or more cases there each term for sixteen years.

But his prior public services were pitifully small. He had never served in any federal position. Years before, he had been a member of a state constitutional convention and of a state legislature. But the constitution proposed by this convention had been rejected by the people and the legislature of which he was a member had been accused of disloyalty and prorogued by the governor. It had taken Fuller twenty-five years to live down his part in the Illinois legislature of 1863. Now he was to hear of it again.

The nomination was referred as usual to the judiciary committee of the Senate, of which Senator George F. Edmunds of Vermont was chairman. Soon thereafter, Fuller's kinsman, J. C. Bancroft Davis, the Reporter of the Supreme Court, wrote him from Washington: "Yesterday for the first time . . . I had an opportunity to talk in confidence with Edmunds. The interview was short but decisive. There is no doubt where he will stand when the question of your confirmation comes up. Unless he changes, his own vote will be given against it; and unless I misinterpret his manner, his active efforts against you are to be feared." Edmunds had personal as well as political grounds for his opposition. He had recently been Fuller's adversary in a hotly contested case in the Supreme Court. Besides, Edmunds claimed that President Cleveland had practically assured him that the position would go to Edmunds's friend Edward J. Phelps. Moreover, it was dubious politics for

| | PRIOR FEDERAL POSTS | | | PRIOR STATE POSTS | | |
Chief Justice	Legislative	Executive	Judicial	Legislative	Executive	Judicial
Jay	Yes	Yes	No	Yes	Yes	Yes
Rutledge	Yes	No	Yes	Yes	Yes	Yes
Ellsworth	Yes	No	No	Yes	Yes	Yes
Marshall	Yes	Yes	No	Yes	Yes	No
Taney	No	Yes	No	Yes	Yes	No
Chase	Yes	Yes	No	No	Yes	No
Waite	No	Yes	No	Yes	No	No
Fuller	No	No	No	Yes	No	No
White	Yes	No	Yes	Yes	No	Yes
Taft	No	Yes	Yes	No	Yes	Yes
Hughes	No	Yes	Yes	No	Yes	No
Stone	No	Yes	Yes	No	No	No
Vinson	Yes	Yes	Yes	No	No	Yes *

* From an article by Arthur Krock in The New York *Times* of Aug. 6, 1946.

the Republican Senate to confirm a Democratic Chief Justice with a national election only four months away.

The opponents of Fuller's confirmation soon discovered the records of the Illinois legislature of 1863 and issued a printed pamphlet entitled *The War Record of Melville W. Fuller*. After the Emancipation Proclamation he had introduced a bill to ratify the Corwin amendment to the federal Constitution. This amendment, which prohibited interference with slavery, had been proposed by Congress before Lincoln's inauguration. Furthermore, Fuller had voted for a resolution denouncing Lincoln's banishment of Vallandigham; he had voted against permitting soldiers in the field to vote; he had spoken in support of the resolution for the peace convention at Louisville.

The pamphlet concluded: "The records of the Illinois legislature of 1863 are black with Mr. Fuller's unworthy and unpatriotic conduct. . . . They cannot be answered by fond exclamations about 'Mel Fuller' or that he was a Douglas man or that 'Maine cannot produce copperheads.' . . . Let us hope that no Senator . . . whether he calls himself a Democrat or Republican will tolerate a copperhead as Chief Justice of the United States."

The conclusion from this evidence that Fuller was a Copperhead or a Southern sympathizer during the war was unfair. He had abhorred slavery and had despised the secessionists as well as the abolitionists. But this attack on Fuller's loyalty was fully met by the character of his sponsors: Joseph Medill, Lyman Trumbull, Leonard Swett, Robert T. Lincoln—the war President's closest friends and his son. Who could suggest that a man for whom they vouched had been disloyal?

Medill in the Chicago *Tribune* said at once that Fuller's war record would endure the closest scrutiny. "Some foolish things he undoubtedly did," Medill admitted. But he "was never a traitor; never worked in the dark; was never an offensive partisan." "He was an exception to the vast majority of leading Democrats in that he would have nothing whatever to do with the secret societies that flourished in those days and emphatically declined all invitations to join them."

After the question of Fuller's loyalty was raised, Lyman Trumbull, senator from Illinois during the war, sent to Senator Edmunds an endorsement of Fuller signed by all of the judges in Cook County, state and federal, and by all living ex-judges for the past thirty-five years. It was also signed by Judge Magruder, the only judge of the Supreme Court of Illinois residing in Chicago.

But the research into Fuller's war record also turned up the story of the Wabash Horse Railway bill in the Illinois legislature of 1863. "Fuller's Fulsome Record" the St. Louis *Globe-Democrat* screamed in headlines. "More documentary evidence showing his redolent legislative acts—Monopolist and Corruptionist." The files of the Judiciary Committee of the Senate, now in the National Archives, are full of memoranda of minute investigations of this bill. But Judge Shepard and W. C. Goudy quickly pointed out that the controversy about this bill was a war between competing streetcar companies; that the bill had been printed, fully explained, and passed in the House of Representatives on Fuller's sponsorship with only five dissenting votes; and that the president of the Wabash Horse Railway had been Charles Hitchcock, later president of the Illinois Constitutional Convention of 1870, whose name was a symbol of probity in Chicago. The Chicago *Tribune,* which had shouted loudest in 1863 against the Wabash bill—for a year or so it had referred to Fuller as "Wabash Fuller"—made no comment on this subject in 1888 except to say that all of the charges against him were "trivial."

The Judiciary Committee of the Senate received certain letters making vague charges of unprofessional conduct against him. The Chicago *Tribune* said: "Nearly every crank in the country seems to be taking an interest in the nomination. Many of these people write to Senators Farwell and Cullom, but as the Illinois Senators know the character of their correspondents the rubbish goes in the waste basket. Others write directly to the judiciary committee whose members do not know the writers and have to take the time to do something about them."

Edmunds made the error of confronting Fuller by letter with these charges without divulging the name of the accuser. Edmunds said that the Senate rules forbade such disclosure. These charges were:

1. That in the case of *Lay* v. *West Chicago Park Board* Fuller had taken from the funds of the Park Board $103,000 in payment for a piece of land for which the owner was willing to accept $30,000 and that Fuller had received $5,000 or $10,000 of the difference.

2. That in the case of *Kerr* v. *South Park Commissioners* Fuller had, by his influence as Jury Commissioner of the United States, had the jurymen put in charge of a bailiff who had improperly influenced them.

3. That in the case of *Doolittle* v. *Forsyth* he had asked the attorney for Forsyth not to include in the record the fact that Fuller, who was attorney for Doolittle, had been the Jury Commissioner at the time the jury was drawn.

Edmunds concluded his letter to Fuller: "Any statement you may think proper to make in reference to these subjects the Committee will be glad to receive."

Fuller replied to Edmunds by telegram: "While assuring the committee that I intend no disrespect to them, I cannot consent to reply to anonymous aspersions of the character referred to in yours of the 11th. With your permission I will publish your letter with this reply. Please answer by telegraph."

Edmunds, caught off balance, answered: "Unable to consult committee but think you can, so far as the committee is concerned, do what you think proper."

To this telegram Fuller responded: "Thank you. In my judgment publication will dispose of these fabrications without subjecting me to the humiliation of having to notice them."

However, the files of the Judiciary Committee contain complete refutations of all these charges. Attorneys on both sides of the *Lay* case wrote that Fuller had nothing whatever to do with that case. In the *Kerr* case, affidavits were submitted showing that he had no part in selecting the bailiff in charge of the jury. In the *Doolittle* case it turned out that it was Doolittle and not Fuller who had asked the attorney for Forsyth not to include in the record the fact that Fuller had been Jury Commissioner. Fuller had accepted this position at the request of the court, which had always appointed an outstanding attorney, trying cases in the court, as such commissioner.

The first two of these charges were made by former Judge John C. Dunlevy. In interviews published in the Chicago *Tribune*, Dunlevy said that Fuller had not treated him with due respect "in caucuses where we have figured" and that "revenge is sweeter than money." The charges in the last case were made by Jacob Forsyth. His own attorney, William H. King, wrote the Judiciary Committee that the charges were untrue and that Fuller stood too high in the estimation of the people who knew him to be injuriously affected by the statements of "semi-irresponsible" persons.

But the greatest bar to Fuller's confirmation yet remained. There was a strong feeling among the Republican senators that party loyalty required them to refuse to confirm a Democratic Chief Justice with a national election only a few months away. For a time Senator Cullom weakened in his demand for confirmation and said that he did not know how he would vote. Consideration in the Senate was delayed by the national party conventions in June. But with the nominations of Cleveland and Harrison it was clear that the election would be close and would depend on the attitude of the independent voters. Many Republicans in Illinois and elsewhere, as well as some newspapers, thought that unless the Republicans could state real grounds for rejecting Fuller it would hurt the party in the election to delay or refuse confirmation. This attitude was reinforced by the consideration that the Supreme Court and the other federal courts were already heavily Republican. Political partisanship to correct an inequality on the bench might be justifiable, but partisanship to increase an inequality might react unfavorably. Independent voters usually believed in an independent judiciary.

Fuller wrote the President in July that if the Senate should delay the confirmation further or refuse to confirm, such action would strengthen the strong Democratic hopes of carrying Illinois in the approaching election. "I . . . rather secretly prefer," he said, "that they should commit this blunder." He reported that he had just returned from Maine, where he had attended the Bowdoin commencement, and concluded: "As far as I could judge from a pretty thorough investigation of the Eastern newspapers, Mr. Edmunds' conduct has met with universal condemnation."

The Judiciary Committee decided to report the nomination to the Senate without recommendation, and Cullom finally concluded to support confirmation. Edmunds's opposition was based in part on his advocacy of Phelps for the position; and someone gave Cullom a printed copy of a speech delivered by Phelps during the war in which, as Cullom said, he attacked Mr. Lincoln "in a most outrageous and undignified manner." Cullom put the speech in his pocket and bided his time. Three weeks later, when the nomination came before an executive session of the Senate, Edmunds took the floor and launched an attack on Fuller. "How long," Edmunds inquired, "will the results of the Civil War be safe, if the President may fill up the Supreme Court with disloyalists?"

Cullom followed and suggested that Edmunds's attack on Fuller was based on pique because Phelps had not been appointed. Cullom then read Phelps's anti-Lincoln speech, "much to the chagrin and mortification," as Cullom put it, "of Senator Edmunds." "Twenty-five years ago," Cullom said, "Mr. Fuller was wrong—just as many a man was then wrong who has been conspicuously right ever since."

Cullom reported in his autobiography that the Democrats laughed heartily over the spectacle of two Republicans quarreling over a Democrat. They sat silent and took no part in the debate. But Fuller was confirmed by a vote of 41 to 20. As soon as he arrived in Washington, he began to cultivate Senator Edmunds, and they exchanged New Year's greetings by letter or telegram for the rest of their lives.

The day after his confirmation, Fuller wrote Senator Cullom:

"CHICAGO, July 21, 1888.

"MY DEAR SENATOR:

"I cannot refrain from expressing to you my intense appreciation at the vigorous way in which you secured my confirmation. I use the word 'vigorous' because, though it was more than that, that was the quality that struck me most forcibly when I saw the newspapers this morning. When we meet, as I hope we will soon, I would very much like to talk this matter over with you. I hope you will never have cause to regret your action. I can't tell you how pleased I am that Maine and Illinois, both so dear to me, stood by me. But because I love them, I do not love my country any the less, as you know.

"And so I am to be called 'Judge' after all! This is between ourselves.

"Faithfully yours,
M. W. FULLER."

Some twenty-five years before, when Fuller was a very young member of the Illinois legislature, his demeanor had been so solemn as to attract the nickname of Judge; and Cullom, doubtless ironically, sometimes called him that. Fuller finally remonstrated that he never had been a judge and probably never would be. Now he had become one partly through Cullom's efforts.

The bench and bar and the citizens of Chicago united in a banquet to honor Fuller on his departure for Washington. Among the judges present were Thomas Drummond, Walter Q. Gresham, and John P. Altgeld, soon to be governor of Illinois. The bar included Robert T. Lincoln, S. S. Gregory, and John Barton Payne. Marshall Field, Joseph Medill, and George

M. Pullman were among the businessmen who were there.

Judge Gresham was a principal speaker. He described the immense powers of the Supreme Court of the United States and the veneration in which it had always been held. "Power and responsibilities so great," he said, "should be intrusted only to men of commanding ability, great learning and worth. . . . Our fellow-townsman and honored guest was recently exalted to the position of Chief Justice of this august tribunal. Knowing him as we do, we entertain no misgivings as to his ability to vindicate the wisdom of his appointment."

Similar expressions were given by Judge Drummond, Judge Thomas A. Moran, James L. High, Lyman Trumbull, and Charles L. Hutchinson, president of the Board of Trade. They spoke of their affection for Fuller as well as their admiration of him.

Fuller answered characteristically: "Whatever the vicissitudes of these thirty-two years, they have never been marred by personal estrangement from my brethren and they have been happy years. Personally unambitious, I have not thought myself selfish in indulging my preference for the sweet habit of life rather than the struggle involved in prominent position. . . . But I also know, of course, that the performance of duty is the true end of life and I find consolation in the thought . . . that I shall be sustained by the sympathy, the friendship and the good will of those with whom I have dwelt so long, and my affection for whom no office, however exalted, no eminence, however great, can impede or diminish."

There was only one slight breach in the paean of praise and affection. W. C. Goudy, responding to the toast, "The Bar," lectured the lawyers for encouraging litigation. Instead, he said, they should settle their cases, for "it is far better to practice in the office than in the court room." Goudy must have known that the only criticism that could be made against Fuller as a lawyer was that he had carried an unusual number of cases to the courts of last resort. It was his practice to litigate cases to the end rather than settle them. Goudy was bitterly disappointed by Fuller's appointment, but they remained good friends until Goudy's death in 1893.

President Cleveland had urged that Fuller take the oath of office as soon as he was confirmed. But he held off for reasons that were typical of him. He thought that his associates would prefer that he take the oath in open court as all of his predecessors except Taney had done—and Taney, he pointed out, had qualified in Baltimore and at once held Circuit Court. Furthermore, Fuller said, if he took the oath, he would immediately be required to reassign the circuits and give himself a circuit. He preferred the Chicago circuit rather than the Richmond one, which Chief Justice Waite had held. But it would obviously be more diplomatic toward his associates to consult them before taking any such action.

Mrs. Fuller and seven of their nine children saw him take the oath on October 8. A crippled Bowdoin classmate, William P. Drew, then a national bank examiner in Washington, has left a record of the event. "I was hobbling away on my crutches toward the main entrance of the [Capitol] building . . . when I observed that a carriage had driven up . . . and that its occupants were alighting. Then I heard the clear ringing call of a voice I once knew so well.

" 'Hello, Bill!'

" 'Well, Fuller!'

". . . He placed me at once under the charge of Justice Harlan of Kentucky, who kindly afforded me all the facilities required."

They went into the courtroom, and Drew describes the oath-taking: "A small white-walled room . . . a long massive desk, behind which, seated in their massive chairs ranged side by side, sit eight figures . . . clothed to their feet in flowing robes of 'solemn black,' apparently unmovable with stern fixed gaze, and seemingly almost as emotionless as effigies of departed greatness which are clustered in 'Statuary Hall' not far distant. . . .

"Then from the 'robing room' at one side of the court room,

a small lithe and graceful figure, which his rich bench robe rather accentuates than conceals, steps lightly and quickly forth unattended and stands for a moment, as if in prayerful invocation just below and in front of the bench. . . .

"Then holding raised before him the Holy Bible in his right hand he administers to himself . . . in a voice clear and steady at first, but toward the close somewhat shaken, as if by overmastering emotion that simple yet comprehensive 'oath of office' which completes and sanctifies this great office to which he thus consecrates himself."

"I, Melville Weston Fuller, do solemnly swear that I will administer justice without respect to persons, and do equal right to the poor and to the rich, and that I will faithfully and impartially discharge and perform all the duties incumbent on me as Chief Justice of the Supreme Court of the United States, according to the best of my abilities and understanding, agreeably to the Constitution and laws of the United States, so help me God."

The ceremony over, Drew says that Chief Justice Fuller, with unaffected dignity, retired behind the long desk and took his place in the center of the line of his associates. He looked at the papers before him and broke the heavy silence with his first official utterance: " 'Motions are now in order for nominations of attorneys to practice before the Supreme Court of the United States. The clerk will read the names.'

"A tremor as of reviving consciousness seems to pass through the other justices, who during the entire ceremony have sat unmoved, and more than one of them is seen to cast an almost startled look upon their new chief, as though some new 'force' had suddenly invaded their quiet ranks."

CHAPTER X

·‿·

WINNING THE COURT

Oh, but there were Giants on the Court in those days,"
Fuller sometimes said in his later years. He referred first of all
to Samuel F. Miller and Stephen J. Field, who, in accordance
with their seniority, sat on his right and left. They were the
last survivors of the appointees of President Lincoln.

Miller had originally studied medicine in Kentucky and
practiced there as a physician. Then he had taken up law and,
because he detested slavery, had moved to Iowa. Like Lincoln,
he was a typical American country lawyer. Such a man by long
experience in thinking out his own problems without preconceptions often surpasses the more sophisticated city lawyer.
The law reserves its richest prizes for the inductive mentality
rather than the deductive; for the man who formulates his own
major premises from his experience rather than remembers
them from books. Miller illustrated Justice Holmes's famous
dictum: "The life of the law has not been logic: it has been
experience."

He was a big man—blunt as a hippopotamus and candid as
sunlight; even his rival, Field, admired his "backbone." Miller
had been on the Court twenty-six years when Fuller became
Chief Justice and had written more than his share of important
constitutional opinions; he was sometimes referred to as the
greatest figure in constitutional law since Marshall. His colleague, the Boston intellectual, Justice Horace Gray, said of
him: "In a rough and tumble frontier community Miller was a
type to gain advancement—but if he had had a legal education,
he would have been second only to Marshall." Chief Justice

Chase had declared that Miller was beyond question "the dominant personality" on the Court.

Fuller set out to win Miller's good will—no easy task for a well-to-do city man and a Democrat. "It is from some western prairie town," Miller had asserted, "rather than some metropolis that future Marshalls . . . shall arise." And he himself died poor. Furthermore, he had been disappointed when his strong claims to the Chief Justiceship had been ignored at the time Chief Justice Waite was appointed. And he had also been mentioned for the place prior to Fuller's appointment. But Miller never held a grudge: even Chief Justice Taney, who was odious to all Republicans because of the Dred Scott decision, had won Miller's affection in 1863. And Fuller's powers to convert hostility into friendship were remarkable, though for more than a year he felt that he was making no progress with Justice Miller.

Fuller's efforts to achieve a friendly basis with his colleagues are shown by a story that he told them soon after he came on the Court. He said that when he went to Augusta after his appointment he rode in the bus from the railroad depot to the Augusta House. The bus driver was a boyhood acquaintance, and the following colloquy took place:

FULLER: Have the boys heard that I have been appointed Chief Justice?

BUS DRIVER: Oh, yes.

FULLER: What did they say?

BUS DRIVER: Oh—they laughed.

Fuller's personal humility was inexhaustible and in sharp contrast to his fierce pride in the Court and his position on it.

His success in winning Miller's respect and affection is shown by an incident that occurred the following year. Fuller had been invited to speak before the joint session of Congress on the centennial of Washington's inaugural as President. He did his best in this address and it was well received. Shortly thereafter, Bancroft Davis, the Reporter of the Supreme Court,

THE COURT WHEN FULLER WAS APPOINTED, 1888

Top row: Justice Mathews, Justice Gray, Justice Harlan, Justice Blatchford
Bottom row: Justice Bradley, Justice Miller, Chief Justice Fuller, Justice Field, Justice Lamar

wrote him that, at the suggestion of Justice Miller, the Justices had decided to publish this speech in the Supreme Court reports—a most unusual compliment. Fuller replied: "Your note yesterday took me by surprise—a pleasant one. . . . I am deeply gratified that the suggestion came from Mr. Justice Miller. . . . I think you will understand—No rising sun for me with these old luminaries blazing away with all their ancient fires."

But Fuller's complete capture of Miller is recorded by Senator Cullom in his memoirs: "Justice Miller told me on one occasion that Fuller was the best presiding judge that the Supreme Court had had within his time; and in addition he was a most lovable, congenial man."

Another titan on the Court was Justice Stephen J. Field, who, as the second member in point of seniority, sat on the Chief Justice's left. Field was one of the famous sons of a New England Congregational minister. Justice Field's brother Cyrus Field had laid the Atlantic cable; his brother David Dudley Field was the author of the New York Code and a leading New York lawyer; his brother Henry Martyn Field (hero of the novel *All This and Heaven Too*) was a prominent clergyman; and a sister's son, David J. Brewer, later became Field's colleague on the Court.

Stephen Field, after high honors in college, a trip abroad, and several years of law practice with his brother David in New York, had gone to California during the gold rush. His career there had been turbulent, involving near-duels, disbarments, and reinstatements; election to the legislature, where he secured the adoption of the Field codes; and, finally, brilliant service as a judge of the Supreme Court of California. Although, like all the Fields, he was a Democrat, he had been appointed to the Supreme Court by President Lincoln in 1863. He had a keen mind and a capacity for sharp precision of statement; he was methodical and untiring in his industry; his distinction as a Judge lay in his iron character, earnestness, intensity, and persistent force. But he was self-confident almost to the point of being offensive; and he was sometimes hot-tempered and vindictive.

He differed from Justice Miller as the doctrinaire differs from the empiricist. Field's approach to any problem was likely to be in terms of fundamental principles, of natural or inalienable rights; he took his major premises from his preconceptions rather than formulated them from his experience; he sought governing principles rather than an expedient course. As Professor Swisher puts it, "He tended to overemphasize the importance of selected principles, and to disregard too much the determining influence of the whole welter of human experience."

If such generalizations were not so dangerous, it might be suggested that this antithesis between Field and Miller marks a difference between the historical Democratic approach and the usual Republican reaction to problems. Jefferson was more doctrinaire than Hamilton, Hamilton more empirical than Jefferson; and similar examples could be cited. But the categories of doctrinaire and empirical are as dangerous as those of liberal and conservative; such classifications lead to naïve conceptualism. Too much depends upon the vantage point. Fuller claimed to despise doctrinaires, but his political adversaries so classified him on the issues of the protective tariff, state's rights, and hard money.

When Fuller's appointment was announced in Chicago, Wirt Dexter, a prominent lawyer, referring to Field's intensity and Fuller's diminutive size, said, "Field will eat him in one bite." As the outstanding Democrat on the Court, Field had wanted the place for himself; but there is no evidence that President Cleveland considered him for it. Fuller, however, quickly established cordial relations with Field based upon their New England backgrounds, fundamental Democracy and deep attachment to the Bill of Rights.

About a year after Fuller's accession, the centennial celebration of the organization of the federal judiciary was held in New York. The Chief Justice felicitously introduced Justice Field, a former member of the New York bar, as the speaker for the Court. Thereafter in acknowledging a copy of this introduction and Field's address, Fuller said: "I am more pleased with your . . . [speech] than ever. I can't exactly define what the particular charm is but I think it is the ease with which a good deal of weighty thought is conveyed without fatigue to the reader." Field, as a result of his early years of code-drafting, had a succinct, compressed style which Fuller, whose style was less concise, sincerely envied.

Fuller's winning of Field is indicated by a letter from the Chief Justice to his wife a year later. "Field told me on the bench this morning," Fuller wrote, "that in the conferences I was almost invariably right. He said I was remarkably quick in seizing the best point. He has never said as much before."

The Justice Holmes of that Court was Joseph P. Bradley, who sat at Miller's right. He was the son of a poor New York farmer, and his early education had been in the rural schools. At the age of twenty, in 1833 (the year in which Fuller was born), Bradley had entered Rutgers College. After his graduation he had studied law in a Newark, New Jersey, law office and practiced there with high success until his appointment to the Court in 1870. He was a man of prodigious industry and breadth of learning. He had the ascetic, intellectual face of an Italian cardinal; his avocations were mathematics, genealogy, and Arabic; but the qualities that made him an outstanding judge were his mental muscularity and his extreme open-mindedness. Despite his life-long record as a Whig and a Republican, the Democrats had chosen him as the best odd-man or umpire, under the circumstances, on the electoral commission in the Hayes-Tilden contest for the Presidency in 1876 and had accepted (though not without sharp complaint) his adverse decision.

When Fuller was appointed, Bradley had wished to have the

Chief Justice appointed from the Court; he preferred Miller or Field to an outsider and wrote Field expressing his regret that he was not appointed.

Fuller submitted to Bradley the draft of his address on the Washington Centennial and carefully preserved Bradley's letter of criticism. "I must say that I think it admirable in conception and execution," Bradley wrote. "One man's style is not another's, any more than his voice. Yours is more florid, more dipt in poetical dyes than mine for example (if I have any); but I am not sure that I should not come to prefer it by greater familiarity." Who could resist so tactful a criticism? The address, which established Fuller's reputation, was not too florid when it was delivered.

In another criticism of this address Bradley was more direct. " 'Destructive giant of paper currency by government fiat,' " he wrote, "is a strong expression and might be thought to hint a rebuke to the final decision of the court on that subject— though I am sure not so intended." This last was a polite judicial fiction. The final decision of the Court on this subject was *Juilliard* v. *Greenman*,[1] which Fuller's relative, Dr. George Bancroft, had railed against in his *Plea for the Constitution of the United States Wounded in the House of its Guardians*. This was the case which Fuller had criticized in his presidential address before the Illinois State Bar Association in the year preceding his appointment. Bradley was one of the judges who was said to have been put on the Court by President Grant to reverse the first legal-tender decision,[2] but this charge was unjust to Bradley in the light of the evidence since produced. However, the decision was reversed [3] as a result of the appointment of Justices Bradley and Strong, so Bradley's sensitivity on this subject is understandable. On his suggestion Fuller struck out the objectionable words, but his speech still indicated that the public credit (which Washington commended

[1] 1884, 110 U.S. 421.   [2] *Hepburn* v. *Griswold,* 1870, 8 Wallace, 603.
[3] *Knox* v. *Lee,* 1871, 12 Wallace, 457.

to be cherished) had been saved by the abandonment by Congress of paper currency.

Fuller won Bradley by asking his aid on this address much as Benjamin Franklin reported that he gained a man's good will by borrowing a book from him. The spirit of helpfulness is strong and easily aroused in intellectual people. Bradley took the new Chief Justice under his care and constantly counseled him. Fuller was closer to Bradley than to any other Justice during the three years of their joint service.

Bradley's opposite number on the left of the Chief Justice and Justice Field was John Marshall Harlan of Kentucky. Born in 1833, the same year as Fuller, he had been a member of the Supreme Court for eleven years when Fuller was appointed and he was to serve until one year after his death. Originally a Whig, Harlan had not supported Lincoln for President in either 1860 or 1864, but he was a colonel of a Kentucky regiment in active service on the Union side during the war. He was elected Attorney General of Kentucky in 1863 on the Union ticket, but after the war he at first opposed and later supported the Thirteenth Amendment and became a stalwart Republican. He was twice an unsuccessful candidate for Governor of Kentucky, and was appointed to the Court by President Hayes in 1877 after honorable service as a member of the President's Louisiana Commission to determine the claims of the rival governments there.

He was a tall, aggressive, courageous man who made up his own mind regardless of the opinions of others. His dissents were frequent and vehement. Next to his religion he revered the Constitution, but he believed that it should be interpreted by common sense as a layman would read it. He was averse to the subtle refinements on which many legal questions ultimately turn. This attitude did not always gain for him the respect of his colleagues. Thus Holmes wrote to Pollock that Harlan's mind was "a powerful vise the jaws of which couldn't be got nearer than two inches to each other." Holmes said that

Harlan, "although a man of real power, did not shine either in analysis or generalization."

Harlan loved political maneuvering. Justice Miller once wrote that Harlan had "secured more favors at the hands of the President than any man I know." Although Fuller had opposed Harlan's confirmation, they had become great friends by the time of Fuller's appointment. Fuller had argued many cases before Harlan on circuit, and Harlan's son James was a law student in Fuller's office. Before his appointment, the Fullers frequently stayed at the Harlan home when they went to Washington. Harlan took charge of the efforts to secure Fuller's confirmation. When he was confirmed, James Harlan accompanied him to Washington and became his secretary, but he returned to Chicago in a few weeks on the organization of the law firm of Gregory, Booth & Harlan, which took over Fuller's practice in Chicago. Fuller made his headquarters in the office of this firm during his summer visits to Chicago.

On the occasion of Fuller's Washington Centennial address, Justice Harlan wrote Mrs. Fuller: "After the crowd dispersed today, I happened to meet quite a number of Senators and Representatives. The commendation of the Chief Justice's name was general and hearty. The address has *fixed* the position of the Chief Justice before the country and will add greatly to the power and prestige of the court in the popular mind." Fuller and Harlan remained close friends for the rest of their lives, although they frequently disagreed in their opinions.

The next seat on the Court was vacant, because of the illness of Justice Stanley Matthews, when Fuller took the oath. Matthews never returned to the Court and died a few months later.

Perhaps the greatest legal scholar on the Court was Justice Horace Gray. He came from a distinguished Massachusetts family; his half-brother was John Chipman Gray, the Harvard Law School professor and Boston lawyer, whose reputation still stands preeminent as the authority on the law of real property.

Horace Gray had graduated from Harvard College at sixteen; had been appointed Reporter of the Supreme Court of Massachusetts at twenty-six and a justice of the court at thirty-six. Nine years later he became chief justice. He had served on that court for seventeen years when, in 1881, he was appointed (by almost universal demand) to the Supreme Court of the United States.

Gray's forte was historical legal research: he loved to cite the Year Books. He had a prodigious and accurate memory of the thousands of cases that he had read, reported, or decided. It was suggested that his relation to Justice Miller was like that of Story to Marshall; that is, Gray found a basis in legal history for Miller's intuitive decisions. Gray was an indefatigable worker; his devotion to the law was like that of "a holy priest to his religion." He had a great capacity to synthesize the ideas of others: in his seventeen years on the Supreme Court of Massachusetts, he had written only one dissent. He was the first Justice of the Supreme Court of the United States to employ a legal secretary, and a new secretary joined him in October, 1888, as Fuller took the oath. This young man, Samuel Williston, has since become the great authority on the law of contracts. In his autobiography Professor Williston says: "Judge Gray was more than tolerant. He invited the frankest expression of any fresh idea of his secretary . . . and welcomed any doubt or criticism of his own views." But Williston was not successful in his efforts to get Gray to dissent in Fuller's first important case.

Gray was six feet four in height and had a serious but boyish face. A few months after Fuller became Chief Justice, Gray was married, for the first time and at the age of sixty-one, to the daughter of his colleague Justice Stanley Matthews, who had died a short time before. Williston tells a story which portrays the judicial mind in love. The secretary was also engaged to be married, and one day the Justice showed him a ring and said: "You, being if I may say so, *in consimili casu* can perhaps tell me whether this would be likely to please a young lady." Gray's marriage (inside the Court family, so to speak) was a great success, to the delight of all of his colleagues, including the Chief Justice.

Fuller's skill in avoiding acrimony in the conference room immediately aroused Gray's admiration. He sometimes told Williston after returning from a Saturday conference that the discussion had been heated but that the Chief had kept the Court from flying apart. Since Gray had been a chief justice in Massachusetts, he could appreciate Fuller's diplomacy. The Court then consisted of highly individualistic men of great pride of opinion, and Fuller's capacities as a conciliator were much needed. He inaugurated a custom, which has prevailed on the Court to this day, of requiring each Justice to greet and shake hands with every other Justice each morning. This practice tends to prevent rifts from forming.

Fuller came to rely heavily on Gray's scholarship, and Gray in turn recognized Fuller as a resourceful lawyer of vast practical experience.

The work horse of the Court when Fuller came to it was Justice Samuel Blatchford. Born in New York in 1820, he had graduated at the head of his class from Columbia College in New York and had been secretary to Governor Seward and later the governor's law partner at Auburn. Then he had formed his own law firm in New York with Seward's nephew as his partner. In 1867 he had been appointed District Judge for the Southern District of New York, and five years later, Circuit Judge. He was also the Reporter of Blatchford's Circuit Court Reports, which contained, among others, his own opinions, by which he came to be held in high esteem, especially in maritime and bankruptcy cases. He was appointed to the Supreme Court in 1882. His specialties were admiralty and patent law, and his reputation was for industry rather than brilliance. In the first three years of the Fuller regime he wrote more opinions than any other Justice—even more than the Chief Justice. He was the only Justice during that period who wrote no dissenting opinion.

Fuller and Blatchford had a focus of interest in their mutual regard for Governor Seward. Fuller had apparently reported for the New York *Herald* portions of Seward's campaign trip to the West in 1860. At any rate he had collected many books by, and about, Seward. Fuller early took occasion to write Blatchford about Seward's reference to the Justice in Seward's published letters. Blatchford responded: "Seward refers to me several times in his letters. The occasion you refer to was when I resigned, in Sept. 1841, my place as his Secretary after having been with him since January, 1839. Thanks for your kind words. Your friendship is highly valued and reciprocated." Soon the Chief Justice and Justice Blatchford were attending dinners at each other's homes, inquiring about each other's families, and Blatchford was calling for the Chief Justice in a T cart to drive him to the country club.

Lucius Q. C. Lamar of Mississippi, who as the junior member of the Court sat on the extreme left, was of French Huguenot ancestry. He had lived a more checkered life before coming to the Court than any of his colleagues. Before the war he had been Professor of Mathematics at the University of Mississippi and a member of Congress from that state. He had drafted the Mississippi ordinance of secession and served in the Confederate Congress and as the Confederate Envoy to Russia. He had surrendered at Appomattox as a colonel in the Confederate Army. Returning to Mississippi, he had practiced law and had been Professor of Ethics and Metaphysics and later of Law in the State University. He was elected to Congress in 1873 and won national renown when he seized the occasion of the memorial proceedings for Senator Sumner to deliver an address showing how completely the South accepted the war's verdict and suggesting the same humanity toward the prostrate South as Sumner had shown toward the slaves and later toward the vanquished.

In the Senate, to which he was elected a few years later, he had earned the respect of the Northern senators as a dangerous adversary in debate. While he was senator, he became the intimate friend of Henry Adams. Lamar is spoken of in ecstatic praise in the *Education of Henry Adams*, the author of which was not prone to careless friendships nor to overgenerous judgments—even of his friends. Before Lamar was appointed to the Court, he was Secretary of the Interior in President Cleveland's Cabinet. He and Fuller were the only Justices appointed by Cleveland in his first term; Lamar had only been on the Court a few months when Fuller was appointed.

He was perhaps the Court's most thoughtful member—almost dreamy in his preoccupation. But he had an extraordinary memory of a lifetime of diligent reading. Fuller said of him, "His was the most suggestive mind that I ever knew, and not one of us but has drawn from its inexhaustible store." Like Fuller and Field, Lamar was a Democrat and was not inclined to yield principle to expediency.

He was anxious that Fuller's appointment as Chief Justice should command popular approval. A few days after Fuller's accession, Lamar wrote him suggesting that the Chief Justice himself should write the opinion in the Bell Telephone case. "It is a very important and notable case," he wrote, "to which public attention has been directed and the opinion delivered will certainly attract attention. . . . The case is one on which you will have a good opportunity to make your first exposition of national law in your character as Chief Justice. I do not think you should give it away." Fuller, however, assigned the case to Justice Miller.

Lamar was jubilant when Fuller's centennial speech on Washington was so well received. A week later, Grover Cleveland (now retired to private life) wrote Fuller that he had not read the address but that everyone was praising it as a fresh approach in an overworked field. "Mr. Weston [1] was here today," Cleveland wrote, "and . . . I enjoyed his description of it all and especially the joy and triumph of that grand character, Lamar. . . . It was so like Lamar to rush in to your house and tell you all the good things he had heard." A week

[1] Probably Fuller's cousin, Melville Weston, Esq., of Boston.

later Cleveland wrote Fuller that he had read the address. "I cannot refrain from telling you," he said, "how well in my opinion it and its author deserve all the grand things said about them. . . . Lamar wrote me on the 6th of December: 'The Chief Justice has read me his address on Washington. It is admirable even for a Chief Justice.' "

The Court, of which Fuller became the head, thus consisted of extremely forceful, able men. But they were highly diverse in their backgrounds and philosophies. They were not likely to be unanimous in any case where there was room for difference of opinion. They required a Chief Justice who would command their respect and keep their differences within the bounds of propriety.

Since Fuller was so small in stature, it was thought necessary to elevate his chair on the bench and give him a hassock to keep his feet from swinging in the air. Most of the pictures of the Court taken during his regime show this arrangement. But a granddaughter of Justice Miller recently wrote: "You speak of Justice Fuller being a 'tiny man.' I never heard any reference whatever to his size. His position on the bench gave him the necessary stature and he was always invariably 'The Chief.' "

CHAPTER XI

◦◡◦

EARLY CASES, RELATIONS WITH GRAY
AND BRADLEY AND THE
CIRCUIT COURT OF APPEALS ACT

1888–1891

Fuller's first important case displayed the warmth of his humanity. An insolvent man had taken out life-insurance policies payable to his wife and children but, upon his death, his creditors claimed the proceeds. The legal principal was clear: "A man must be just before he is generous"; he cannot give away his creditors' money. Samuel Williston, Justice Gray's secretary, was able to prove conclusively that, under a statute enacted in the thirteenth year of Queen Elizabeth, such payment of premiums was constructively in fraud of creditors and must inure to their benefit. Williston convinced Justice Gray, but the Chief Justice persuaded the Court to the contrary. He pointed out that an insolvent man had a right during his life to make reasonable expenditures for the support of his wife and children. The same public policy, he said, except in case of actual fraud, should be extended to protect them from destitution after the debtor's death.

Williston was surprised when Justice Gray failed to dissent, but the opinion was unanimous and the young secretary afterward wrote a law review article to criticize it. He records that many opinions without a dissent in Fuller's first year were unanimous only in the published reports; strong dissents at the conference table never appeared in print. Fuller had a remarkable capacity for mediation; he liked to "tinker a com-

138

promise," as Justice Holmes put it. But the almost complete absence of dissents was a phenomenon only of Fuller's first year; thereafter, despite his efforts, the Court gradually became notable for the number of its dissents. There were to be more five to four decisions in the twenty-two years of Fuller's regime than in the twenty-two years after his death. Even the Chief Justice frequently "withheld" his "consent" to an opinion, but he insisted that dissenting opinions be respectful toward the majority.

Fuller's first great dissent required some fortitude. Alone with Lamar, he protested against releasing without trial one Neagle, a United States deputy marshal who, in defense of Justice Field, had killed a man. The case attracted national attention, for it involved a beautiful woman, her affair with a United States senator, and the killing of her husband, an eminent California judge.

Senator William Sharon of Nevada had a young, dark-haired, lustrous-eyed mistress named Sarah Althea Hill. He grew tired of her and cast her off. She claimed a wife's share of his large estate under a written contract of marriage which, if not forged, made her his wife under California law. The California courts held that the contract was valid; the federal courts condemned it as a forgery. One basis for this adverse decision was that Miss Hill, during the period when she claimed to be Sharon's wife, had told her friends how she had hid in his hotel room and gleefully described his intimacies with another woman. The federal courts thought that such glee was unwifely.

After Senator Sharon's death, but while the litigation was proceeding, she married her lawyer, Judge David S. Terry, a man of great physical prowess, who had killed Senator Broderick of California in a duel. Terry had been a colleague of Justice Field on the Supreme Court of California.

While Field, on circuit in California, was reading an opinion condemning the Sharon-Hill contract as void, Mrs. Terry suddenly shrieked, "You have been paid for this decision." Field calmly ordered the Marshal to remove her. Terry sprang to her aid and in the melee that followed drew a bowie knife which was taken from him with great difficulty by the marshals, one of whom was David Neagle. Field sentenced Judge and Mrs. Terry to jail for contempt. Terry filed an original petition for *habeas corpus* in the Supreme Court of the United States which was awaiting argument when Fuller took his seat on the bench. It was denied in a unanimous opinion written by Justice Harlan. At the same term the Supreme Court affirmed the decision against the Terrys which Field was delivering when the contempt occurred. Justice Field took no part in either of these decisions.

While Terry and his wife were in jail, they made many threats against Field, should he return to California, and the Attorney General instructed the Marshal to protect the Justice when he again went on circuit there. Although Field protested that he needed no protection, David Neagle was assigned to him as a bodyguard. While Field and Neagle were eating breakfast in the railroad dining room at Lathrop, California, the Terrys entered the room. Field did not see them; but when they saw him, Mrs. Terry at once went back to the train to get her valise containing a revolver. Terry came up behind Field and struck him a blow on each side of the face. Neagle rose and shouted: "Stop! Stop! I am an officer." Terry turned to Neagle, seemed to recognize him, and at once turned his hand to thrust it in his bosom to draw, as Neagle felt sure, a bowie knife. Neagle instantly shot him dead.

Neagle was charged with murder under the California law but was at once released on *habeas corpus* by the federal courts there. The appeal from this decision posed a question of the boundaries between state and federal jurisdictions. A federal statute provided that federal courts should not issue a writ of *habeas corpus* for a state prisoner "unless he is in custody for an act done . . . in pursuance of a law of the United States." There was no such law in any literal sense, as the Attorney General of California was quick to point out. However, the Attorney General of the United States and Joseph H. Choate, who had been specially retained in the case, argued that the power to protect a federal judge in the discharge of his duties was inherent in the national government.

The majority opinion sustaining this view was written by Justice Miller. He said that Neagle was acting in pursuance of the President's constitutional power to take care that the laws be faithfully executed. Neagle was set free, without trial.

In a vigorous dissent, Lamar and Fuller defended California's jurisdiction against federal encroachment. They quoted a prior opinion of the Court that a state prisoner could not be released on *habeas corpus* by a federal court simply because he was not guilty. They pointed out that the word "law" was used forty-two times in the Constitution, and that each time the context indicated that it meant an Act of Congress. If Terry had killed Field, they asked, could Terry have been prosecuted under any federal law? Obviously not. The United States was powerless to try Neagle for murder for lack of a law authorizing such trial. It should not, therefore, discharge him without trial.

Fuller wrote to Morris that "it was very painful to dissent but it was simply duty." The country was almost unanimous in its approval of Neagle's act. Although Field took no part in the decision, he displayed to all his brethren his deep concern over the outcome. He had given Neagle a gold watch inscribed, "Stephen J. Field to David Neagle, as a token of appreciation of his courage and fidelity to duty under circumstances of great peril at Lathrop, Cal., on the fourteenth day of August, 1889." But it is almost certain that if Field had not been personally involved in the case, he would have joined his two Democratic colleagues in protesting against the federal invasion of the jurisdiction of California.

Two days after the decision, the Chief Justice received a letter from Grover Cleveland, now a New York lawyer:

"MY DEAR CHIEF JUSTICE:

"It was very kind of you to give me the exceedingly welcome assurance that our dear Lamar had done himself credit in the

Neagle case. . . . It must have taken a little back bone—
speaking after the manner of men, in view of the modern
standard of courage.

"Mr. Choate asked me to look over his brief though I told
him I was instinctively against him. After reading it, I said to
him that if there was anything in his position, it grew out of
the fact that the Judge on his way to hold an appointed term of
Court was under Federal protection under the same theory as
when actually holding Court. I am very submissive to your
Court but I don't believe in that doctrine either."

But time has dealt well with the dissent in the *Neagle* case.
The Court was soon forced to the position that state prisoners,
unless they were held in violation of the Constitution, could
not be released on *habeas corpus* in the federal courts except in
cases of "peculiar urgency," such as existed in that case. And
in 1916 the statute was amended to provide for removal to a
federal court *"for trial"* of any state prosecution of a federal
officer for an act done under color of his office.

A quality that Fuller early manifested on the Court was his
capacity for taking pains in small matters. He had often told
how Count Cavour remarked to a gentleman at whist: "I perceive, Sir, that you do not pay enough attention to your small
cards." Fuller regarded them with scrupulous intentness. Soon
Bancroft Davis, the Court Reporter, was receiving letters from
the Chief Justice such as this:

"In Mendenez v. Holt [128 U.S. 514] the initials of the
name of the English reporter, Johnson, are given V.C.—3rd
line from top of page 522. I think but am not sure that they
are H.V.C. P.S. They are H.R.V."

He wrote many letters to correct punctuation and capitaliza-
tion. Frequently he wrote out head notes for his own opinions
and sent them to Bancroft Davis, thus doing the main part of
the Reporter's work for him.

Fuller's modesty was immediately shown by his assignments

of cases among the Justices. He did not reserve for himself historic opinions or those that might reflect glory on the author. Thus in his first year, in addition to the Bell Telephone Patent case, which he assigned to Justice Miller despite Lamar's urging that he keep it for himself, he assigned to Justice Field the important Chinese Exclusion case. He usually assigned patent and admiralty cases to Justice Blatchford, mining cases to Justice Field, and difficult real property cases to Justice Gray. The cases that he kept for himself were the commercial cases with intricate, complicated factual situations to be untangled. Such cases are sometimes referred to among judges as a "barrel of fishhooks." Writing opinions in these cases involved many days of hard, grinding work with no prospect of inspiring admiration.

An opinion delivered by him in his second year did, however, arouse favorable comment. Jacob Baiz, an American citizen, was consul general for Guatemala in New York. The Minister of Guatemala asked the Secretary of State that Baiz be allowed, in the impending absence of the minister, to communicate emergency matters to the Secretary. The Secretary acceded and certain minor communications passed between them. When Baiz was later sued for libel in the United States District Court in New York, his counsel, Joseph H. Choate, asked for a writ of prohibition in the Supreme Court, claiming that Baiz as a public minister was immune from suit except in the Supreme Court. Choate argued that, since Baiz was addressed by the State Department in its letters as "in charge of the legations of Guatemala, Salvador and Honduras," he became *chargé d'affaires*, a recognized diplomatic position. "Can it be said," Choate asked, "that the use of the literal English translation of the French title of office deprived the petitioner of the position which, under all the authorities, he occupied?"

The State Department was disturbed. Alvey A. Adee, the Assistant Secretary, afterward wrote the Chief Justice: "I was on trial." After the argument of the case, James G. Blaine, the Secretary of State, wrote to Fuller:

"MY DEAR CHIEF JUSTICE:

"Pray regard this note as quite confidential and if it is proper advise me what I should do.

"I see in the last answer made by the attorneys of Consul General Baiz that the comment is made that Secy. Bayard & myself have both recognized his Diplomatic character.

"This is flatly and absolutely the reverse of the truth and the reverse of the official record. I have no desire to meddle in the matter and have sought to keep aloof from it—but I cannot allow my position to be made to appear before the Supreme Court the exact reverse of what it is.

"I do not know what I should do before the Court but I am very reluctant to make any public declaration if it can be avoided. Pray advise me at my home before the case is decided.

"Very Resfy & truly
JAMES G. BLAINE"

Fuller wrote a beautifully erudite opinion denying Choate's contentions. He secured certain books on international law from the State Department library which were not in the Congressional library. These were in French and he made his own translations, asking Davis, the Reporter, to verify them because—the Chief Justice said—he couldn't find his dictionary. He was always proud of his facility in French. He also secured from the files of the State Department records of similar cases which had arisen in prior years. Baiz was not *chargé d'affaires*, Fuller held, but a mere medium of communication. Furthermore, Baiz had previously been appointed *chargé d'affaires* for Honduras; and Secretary Bayard had expressly declined to receive him as a diplomatic representative of that country because of Baiz's American citizenship. In any event, Fuller held, the Supreme Court should accept as final the certificate of the State Department as to whether a person was a public minister.

Years later, after Gray's death, Judge Putnam wrote to Fuller: "I asked him [at the time] what he thought of your opinion in In re Baiz, and he expressed himself about it in the highest terms of admiration and added that Chief Justice Waite had had one or two occasions when he might have done as well but did not accomplish this." Putnam concluded: "Indeed he developed for you a very striking affection."

Another colleague who quickly acquired a strong regard for Fuller was Justice Bradley. Bradley's power on the Court in this period, Fuller's deference to him but his lusty dissent when he believed Bradley to be wrong, are strikingly shown by four cases decided in 1890.

Bradley's influence on the Court is indicated by a case where, after a five to four decision in conference, Bradley changed his vote and carried his four colleagues with him to join the original four dissenters. This feat is demonstrated by a letter from Bradley to Fuller found among the Chief Justice's papers. It related to the famous Virginia coupon cases. The State of Virginia had issued bonds, the coupons on which were receivable for taxes. The State afterward placed certain conditions upon accepting these coupons in payment of taxes. These restrictions were held void, as impairing the obligation of the State's contract, in a unanimous decision delivered by Justice Bradley.

However, among the Chief Justice's papers is a letter from Justice Bradley dated February 2, 1890, ten days after the cases were argued and five months before the decision:

"DEAR CHIEF JUSTICE:

"I was not in reality prepared yesterday as I should have been to vote on the Va. Coupon cases. . . . Under other circumstances, I should have asked a week's delay. I have carefully re-examined them and shall ask to change my vote in 1055, 1056, 1057 and 1142 which will change the decision from affirmance to reversal in those cases."

The ultimate decision delivered by Bradley was unanimous for reversal.

Another letter of Bradley showing his weight with the Chief

Justice relates to the cases of *Cole* v. *Cunningham* [1] and *Reynolds* v. *Adden*.[2]

The *Cole* case was an opinion by Fuller holding that a Massachusetts court could enjoin a resident of that State from prosecuting an attachment suit in New York. Before the National Bankruptcy Act of 1898, Massachusetts had worked out an elaborate system of insolvency laws designed to secure equality of distribution among the creditors of a bankrupt. In this case the Massachusetts court enjoined a Massachusetts creditor from prosecuting a suit in New York to gain a preference by attaching a debt due the insolvent there. The New York attachment had been started after the Massachusetts creditor knew of the insolvency. The question was whether this injunction violated the duty of the Massachusetts court to give full faith to the judicial proceedings in New York. Fuller and a majority of the Court held that the injunction did not violate the Constitution. The dissent was by Justices Miller, Field, and Harlan. They argued that, except for the injunction, the creditor would have secured a judgment in New York which Massachusetts would have been bound by the Constitution to respect. Massachusetts should be equally bound under the Constitution, they said, to respect the lien created by the attachment.

The decision has been sharply critized, but the intellectual weight of the Court (Bradley, Gray, Blatchford, and Lamar) was with Fuller. The gist of his argument was that the lien of the attachment in New York was only potential or inchoate. The lien would fail by reason of a discharge of the debtor in the Massachusetts insolvency proceedings. The right of a state, he said, to enjoin its own citizens from litigating elsewhere questions rightfully pending in its own courts had always been recognized.

Reynolds v. *Adden* [2] involved the question whether a citizen of New Hampshire could prosecute an attachment in Louisiana

[1] 1890, 133 U.S. 107.　　　　[2] 1890, 136 U.S. 348.

against a Massachusetts bankrupt. The Court in a unanimous decision by Justice Bradley held that he could.

In the *Cole* case, Fuller had pointed out that under the early cases of *Sturges* v. *Crowninshield* [1] and *Ogden* v. *Saunders* [2] courts in state bankruptcy proceedings had no jurisdiction over citizens of other states unless such nonresidents had become parties to the bankruptcy proceedings in some way. In Bradley's case of *Reynolds* v. *Adden* the New Hampshire citizen had signed as surety the bond of one of the assignees in bankruptcy in Massachusetts. Fuller raised the question whether he had not thereby become bound by those proceedings. Bradley wrote the Chief Justice:

"Dear Ch. Justice:

"Sturges v. Crowninshield and Ogden v. Saunders are old friends of mine. In my early practice, away back in the forties, I had a case that involved them, and made an elaborate study of them which is somewhere in my garret now I presume. They fit well in your opinion, but I hardly think that the fact of 'voluntarily becoming a party to the proceeding' in the sense of those cases, arises upon a man going surety for an assignee (as in my case of Reynolds v. Adden) after having sued out an attachment in another State or even before. I am afraid that would be carrying the estoppel too far. Sincerely yours,

Joseph P. Bradley"

Fuller deferred to Bradley's diplomatic suggestion that he was familiar with these cases when Fuller was a schoolboy.

But one of the greatest glories of Fuller's career was his short and devastating dissent from Bradley's opinion holding valid the Act of Congress forfeiting the property of the Mormon Church. Bradley argued that this property had been amassed to propagate a religion, one of the tenets of which was unlawful polygamy. Since the charter of the Church had been issued by the Territory of Utah and Congress had plenary power over

[1] 1819, 4 Wheat. 122.   [2] 1827, 12 Wheat. 213.

the Territories, it had the right to seize this property and devote it to legitimate religious and charitable purposes.

Fuller answered: "Congress has the power to extirpate polygamy in any of the territories by the enactment of a criminal code . . . but it is not authorized to seize and confiscate the property of persons . . . because they may have been guilty of criminal practices." Congress, he insisted, had only such power as was delegated to it by the Constitution, and no power such as this could be found in that instrument. He was joined in this dissent by his two Democratic colleagues Field and Lamar, so that the decision was on strict party lines. The moral force of Fuller's dissent was eventually recognized by a joint resolution of Congress returning the forfeited property to the Mormon Church.

The condition of the Court's calendar when Fuller came to the bench was desperate: the Court was more than three years behind with its work and the arrears were constantly increasing. In 1888 there were 1,571 cases on the docket; in 1889, 1,648, and by 1890, 1,816. Not more than 450 cases could be disposed of by the Court in any one year. The Court was like a man with a shovel trying to empty a grain elevator with the new grain flowing in and engulfing him. A year before his appointment, Fuller as president of the Illinois State Bar Association had rallied the bar to an attack upon this disgraceful situation. Now he found himself in the middle of the mire.

Desperately he struggled in the morass, and all of the Justices bent their backs to help him. The Chief Justice's burden, however, was the heaviest. Justice Miller had written in 1885: "In consequence of the illness of the Chief Justice [Waite] I have had to be acting Chief Justice in his place. I always knew that he did a great deal more work than I, and had many apparently unimportant matters to look after to which the other judges gave no time and very little attention. I find now that what I have suspected hardly came up to the draft on his time as he performed these duties. Disposition of practice cases, motions to dismiss for want of jurisdiction, reading carefully and . . . answering letters or telling the Clerk how to answer them constituted in his way of doing it a heavy load on his time and on his mind."

Fuller had additional burdens. Friends from Chicago, Augusta, or elsewhere called on him whenever they came to Washington, and he was too kind to discourage them. They wrote him, soliciting personal favors, and no such letter was ignored. Despite all these annoyances, however, he wrote more than his share of the opinions. But he complained of being constantly "driven." "And all of the time a hundred other things intervene to take the precious minutes," he wrote his old friend Morris. "I am so weary I can hardly sit up," he confessed to Bancroft Davis near the end of the 1889 term.

A by-product of the overcrowded docket was the dismissal of many appeals on technical grounds. The Court doubtless at this time acquired the habit which has persisted to this day of asking in each case: "How does this case come up to us?" Twice blessed by his colleagues was the Justice who could discover some basis for denying jurisdiction in a particular case. He not only summarily disposed of that case but restricted the cases that could be brought to the Court in the future.

One cause of the docket congestion was the large number of patent, copyright, and trade-mark cases then arising. It was the heyday of patents, many of which were held void for want of novelty. To the end of his days, Fuller told of the patent which came before the Court at this time for a triangular piece of cloth to be sewed in the crotch of men's drawers or pantaloons to reinforce them. "Not a man on the bench," said the Chief Justice, "but had seen his mother sew that kind of a patch in his drawers." The principal cause of the overcrowded docket, however, was the immense number of cases, not involving any federal law, arising between citizens of different states: the so-called "diversity of citizenship" cases.

For more than ten years various bills for the relief of the Supreme Court had been pending in Congress. A bill for a

Court of Patent Appeals had been proposed in 1878 and was now again offered. Former Justice David Davis of Illinois had introduced in the Senate a bill for a device which had been found successful in his State: the insertion of an intermediate Court of Appeals between the trial courts and the Supreme Court. An alternative proposal was the division of the Supreme Court into three panels of three Justices each; but this was attacked as degrading to the Court if not violative of the integrity demanded by the constitutional provision for "one Supreme Court." There were many variations of these plans.

Fuller quickly moved to bring some order out of these chaotic proposals. In January, 1890, he gave a dinner at his home in honor of a new Justice, David J. Brewer, who had been appointed to succeed Justice Stanley Matthews. The guests were the Justices of the Court and Senators Edmunds, Evarts, George, Ingalls, Hoar, Vest and Pugh—all members of the powerful Judiciary Committee of the Senate, where the bills for the relief of the Supreme Court were pending. Fuller's cultivation of Senator Edmunds was about to bear fruit.

A few weeks later the Senate Committee on the Judiciary ordered that copies of all pending bills for the relief of the Supreme Court be sent to the Chief Justice with the suggestion that it would "be agreeable to the Committee to receive . . . the views of the Justices." Shortly thereafter the Justices responded in a printed report giving unanimous approval to eleven features of these bills. The Chief Justice had assigned Justice Gray to prepare this report, which is a model of precision. The first three recommendations of the Justices were the establishment of a Court of Patent Appeals, restriction of patent appeals in the Supreme Court to questions of law, and the transfer of pending patent appeals to the new court. Six of their recommendations were for the establishment of intermediate Circuit Courts of Appeal, the judgments of which on questions of fact should be final in all diversity-of-citizenship cases. They recommended transfer of the appropriate pending cases on their docket to the new courts.

The Court of Patent Appeals was never established; but, under pressure from the bar, as well as the public, the Circuit Court of Appeals Act, substantially as requested by the Justices, was finally passed early in 1891. It created nine intermediate courts and routed the diversity and patent appeals and certain other cases to them. It did not, however, transfer to the new courts the appropriate pending cases on the Supreme Court calendar and it actually increased the jurisdiction of the Supreme Court in criminal cases. But the relief to the Court was immediate. Whereas in 1890 the new cases were 623, in 1891 they were 383 and by 1892, 290. The new Chief Justice had met and mastered his first great difficulty on the Court.

CHAPTER XII

❦

LIFE OFF THE BENCH
THE HARRISON ADMINISTRATION

1888–1893

At first the Chief Justice lived in a turreted stone house called "Belmont," in northwest Washington, near the end of the 14th Street car line. In a few months, however, he bought the great brick mansion at 1800 Massachusetts Avenue, just off Dupont Circle, where he lived for the next seven years. Every morning, with his three youngest daughters, he took what Sir Julian Pauncefote, the British minister, called the "tram": the girls went to school and their father went to Court. On the street car, as elsewhere, his small figure, his massive head, his long white hair, his bright and scholarly face, and his courtly manners caught the attention of everyone. "I am as much of a curiosity as Jumbo," he complained to Morris.

The courtroom was the historic old Senate Chamber in the south wing of the Capitol. There was no adequate conference room, and the Saturday conferences were sometimes held around a table in the bookstacks of the Supreme Court library. In a few years, however, it became quite usual to have these conferences at the Fuller home.

The Justices assembled for their daily sessions in the robing room. Then the Marshal of the Court led them in their robes across the corridor to the courtroom. This procession at twelve o'clock noon each court day was witnessed by a cluster of sightseers who were kept at bay by silk ropes stretched across the corridor. Justice Holmes often told how, one day as this parade passed, he heard a country visitor whisper in awe: "Ker-riist, what Dignity!"

Fuller looked forward with dread to his first social season—and well he might. It was rumored that his predecessor, Chief Justice Waite, had been killed by excessive dining out—no rare thing in those days when to speak of a man as "a good thick-waisted fellow" was a compliment. The Justices were not then socially secluded; each of them made a formal call on all Justices senior to him and on all members of the Cabinet, and these calls were reciprocated by dinner invitations. Mondays were set aside for receptions by the wives of the Justices. "I don't know how I was so stupid," Mrs. Cleveland wrote to Mrs. Fuller, "as to ask you to come to me on Monday for I ought to have remembered that it would be impossible." If Mrs. Fuller was out of the city on Monday, the Chief Justice called on the wives of all of the Associate Justices. Since the days of Kate Chase Sprague, the daughter and hostess of Chief Justice Chase, the wife of the Chief Justice had held a high position in Washington official society.

Socially, Mrs. Fuller was as gracious as her husband was benign. Years later, when she died, Justice Brewer wrote: "She was always so kind to me—she seemed to think as much of me as she would of her own brother—I felt at home in her presence." And Secretary of War William Howard Taft wrote the Chief Justice: "We shall never forget the kindly interest which Mrs. Fuller took in Mrs. Taft and me when we first came to Washington and became as it were a part of her official family.[1] We were very lonely then and quite unfamiliar with Washington society and she aided us and encouraged us much. . . . Her successful efforts to shield you from interruptions when under the stress of your great labors were known to all of us. . . . I hope my dear Mr. Chief Justice it is not improper or inappropriate in this letter of condolence for me to express my life long gratitude for the uniform courtesy and great kindness you have shown to me since our acquaintance began."

[1] Taft became Solicitor General in 1890.

But Fuller loved his slippers and his books, and he came from a family with a profound aversion to promiscuous society. Besides, the strain of these social duties combined with his Court work was overwhelming. He struggled to restrict his engagements off the Court. "I shall not go to the Department reception tonight," he wrote to Mrs. Fuller. "I intend tomorrow if in strength enough to make the Cabinet calls." And again: "I went to the Stanford dinner last night. . . . The Pres. & wife & V.P. & wife were there—Old Stanford is interesting—very. Although I did not drink much of anything I do not feel well this morning—quite jaded—I can't stand these dinners." And a few days later he wrote to her: "I enter upon this week with a kind of shrinking. Dinners at Gen. Scholfield's, Mr. Evarts and the Judiciary reception on Friday of all nights in the week." (The Saturday conference of the Court was the most important business of the week.)

But the next year he was able to write: "I have refused all invitations, including one to Blaine's . . . to meet the President. I declined to go to Washburn's [1] but have accepted a second invitation for Jan. 30. I had not time to explain & feared they might be hurt." It is perhaps not too much to say that this social withdrawal by Fuller started the trend which has resulted in the seclusion of the Supreme Court from formal Washington society.

But this retirement did not cut off the dinners which the Chief Justice gave for each new Justice. President Harrison appointed four Associate Justices to the Court.

In January, 1890, Fuller gave a dinner in honor of Justice David J. Brewer, a new Justice on the Court. Four years younger than Fuller, Brewer had graduated with honors from Yale in 1856, studied law for two years in the office of his uncle, David Dudley Field, in New York, and then settled in Leavenworth, Kansas. Almost immediately, he became a Judge, first in the lower State courts, then, at the age of thirty-

---

[1] William D. Washburn, senator from Minnesota and a friend since Bowdoin College days.

three, in the Supreme Court of Kansas, where he served for fourteen years, until his appointment as United States Circuit Judge. He had filled that position for five years when he was appointed to the Supreme Court.

Brewer was a tall, sturdy man noted for his jovial wit (he once declared that Harlan went to bed every night with his Bible and the Constitution clasped in his hands), his indefatigable industry (he rose at five every morning and, fortified by strong coffee, went to work in his library), and his desire to preserve the freedom of enterprise which had made Kansas what it was. "The paternal theory of government," he declared in an early dissent, "is to me odious." He was a man of sharp independence of judgment, and his advent ended the nondissenting era of Fuller's first year. Brewer's length of service on the Court was almost the same as Fuller's: he died in the same year, 1910. In that period he was surpassed in the number of his dissents only by Justice Harlan.[1]

To the Brewer dinner the Chief Justice invited the Justices of the Court and, as previously mentioned, the members of the Senate Judiciary Committee, where the bills for the relief of the Supreme Court were pending. The success of the dinner is testified to, not only by the passage of the Circuit Court of Appeals Act (which passed the Senate Judiciary Committee by only one vote), but, more strikingly, by a letter from Fuller to his wife in the following year: "Brewer . . . spoke out . . . this morning in the Conference Room in laudation of you & myself in our treatment of him and his wife when they came here. He said he was rather prejudiced against me (which I did not know) when he came but he became at once one of the warmest friends and then [he said] a variety of complimentary things. . . . I was amused and rather pleased. Brewer is a great favorite with me. He is a genuine man."

President Harrison's second choice when Brewer was appointed was Brewer's Yale classmate Henry Billings Brown, of Michigan. Brown had been pressed upon the President by

[1] Dissents for the period: Harlan, 283; Brewer, 219.

his old colleague in the Senate, Howell E. Jackson, who was then a fellow federal judge with Brown in the Sixth Circuit. A year later, in December, 1890, after Justice Miller's death, the President appointed Brown to the Court. He was born in Massachusetts of well-to-do parents and graduated from Yale in 1856. He then spent a year abroad and, on his return, attended law school at both Yale and Harvard. After a successful career at the bar in Detroit, President Grant appointed him Judge of the United States District Court in Michigan, where he served until his appointment to the Supreme Court. His fields of special competence were admiralty and extradition cases.

A candid estimate of Justice Brown is contained in his official biography by his close friend Charles A. Kent. The biographer said that he had never talked with any lawyer who did not think Brown a good judge. But Kent asked: "Was he a great judge, superior to his associates on the Supreme Bench?" "I doubt it," Kent answered, "I do not think he thought himself such." Kent concluded that Brown's life showed how a man, "without perhaps extraordinary abilities," might "attain and honor the highest judicial position by industry, by good character, pleasant manners and some aid from fortune."

Fuller's relations with Brown were excellent. When Brewer confessed that he was originally rather prejudiced against Fuller, Brown spoke up and said that "*he* knew better than to have any prejudice" against the Chief Justice. "Brown really warmed up," Fuller reported to his wife.

Brown was rather ponderous in his utterances—a fault which annoyed Gray and amused Fuller. (In his own short biography Brown records that Gray was "somewhat brusque.") When Brown, at the age of sixty-eight, was married for the second time, a newspaper reported that Mr. Justice Brown, when interviewed, said that his marriage "partook of the nature of an elopement." Fuller commented: "Justice Brown can not deny the accuracy of that report. It is too judicial not to be correct."

George Shiras, Jr., of Pittsburgh, was appointed by President Harrison to succeed Justice Bradley on his death in 1892. Shiras was born in Pittsburgh in 1832 (he was a year older than Fuller), graduated with honors from Yale in 1853, and had become one of the most successful lawyers in western Pennsylvania. His near to six-foot stature and his open countenance with side whiskers or "muttonchops" made him perhaps the most dignified and imposing Justice on a Court that did not lack for either austerity or stature.

His amiability and sprightliness, however, belied his austere face. "Greet the brethren with a holy kiss," he wrote the Chief Justice in asking to be excused for illness. "I could sustain this patent," he said from the bench in a patent case involving a collar button, "if this hump in the shank would prevent the button from rolling under the bureau."

Fuller's contacts with Shiras were always pleasant. Both were devotees of Dickens and each used this bond to cultivate the other. On the bench they frequently exchanged notes to designate the lawyer who was arguing as Micawber, Uriah Heep, or other Dickens characters. Shiras occasionally gave Fuller a new book about Dickens. After Shiras retired in 1903, they carried on a bantering correspondence until Fuller's death seven years later.

When Fuller was appointed, each of the Justices was assigned to a circuit where he was to sit whenever possible as a trial judge and thus keep in touch with local conditions. Since the days of John Marshall, the Chief Justice had been assigned to the circuit in which Richmond was—then the Fourth Circuit. Fuller was extremely anxious to have the Seventh [Chicago] Circuit. He owned buildings there that frequently demanded his attention. His salary of $10,500 a year was entirely inadequate to support his large family without the income from his Chicago real estate. Before accepting the appointment as Chief Justice, he asked Justice Harlan whether he would be willing to relinquish the Chicago circuit. Harlan's answer was a reluctant Yes. "In reference to my taking another circuit," he wrote, "the usage has been for the Chief Justice to take the Va. circuit. After a little while the Chief Justice must be settled here and he is convenient to the Va. Circuit. There is very little there to do. . . . As my boys are to be at Chicago, my present assignment is agreeable. . . . If your comfort as Chief Justice is to depend *in any degree* upon your having the Chicago Circuit, you shall have no difficulty about it so far as I am concerned."

Fuller's desire for the Seventh Circuit was almost pathetic. In August, 1888, he wrote to President Cleveland: "I am perfectly certain apart from all other considerations that it will delight my people and help the cause [in the approaching election] to some extent on rather slight but definite grounds if I can get this Circuit." He suggested that it would be a compliment to the West to give the Chief Justice a Western circuit instead of a Southern one.

The circuit assignments were not made by the Court until December 17; and Fuller, despite his desire for the Seventh Circuit, was given the Virginia, or Fourth, Circuit, which he held for the remainder of his life. Harlan's suggestion that the Virginia circuit was easiest because it was closest was probably not correct. The circuit Judges of a distant circuit could not readily consult their circuit Justice; in the Fourth Circuit, they consulted him whenever a troublesome case arose. Fuller seemed to suffer more distress (judging by his complaints to Mrs. Fuller) over difficult circuit cases than he did over Supreme Court cases. And he was compelled to go on circuit to South Carolina in June in very hot weather.

Three weeks after Fuller was sworn in as Chief Justice in October, 1888, President Cleveland was defeated for reelection. Fuller was desolate but, when he called at the White House the next morning, he found the Clevelands "very serene." Four days later he wrote to a Chicago friend: "The election returns depress me. The country parts *for four years* with one of its purest and ablest servants." Already he felt certain that Cleveland's defeat was only temporary and that he would be reelected in 1892. A few months later, in sending the former President a gift on his fifty-second birthday, Fuller wrote that he was looking forward with "profound confidence" to felicitating him on his fifty-sixth.

Cleveland, who had always felt like a prisoner in the White House, responded: "I did not receive your birthday gifts until my return from my Southern trip last Saturday. I am sure nothing I could write could convey the depth and warmth of my thankfulness to you for thus pleasantly remembering my fifty-second mile stone. Somehow I have found myself considering myself as a kind of cast off President—an old horse turned out to die. I know however that you will be pleased to learn that all during my recent trip I have been treated with such respect and consideration by the people whom I have encountered that I have been deeply touched. When I add to this such manifestations of friendship as your valuable gifts and kind letter afford I find much—very much—compensation for hard work and earnest endeavor.

"On one thing you and I cannot agree and that is the outcome of four years hence so far as I am concerned.

"I am expecting to see you about the 30th instant and hope that Mrs. Fuller may be with you.

"Give my love to the dear Lady and believe me with many thanks, Yours very Sincerely,

GROVER CLEVELAND"

The plans for the meeting in New York fell through; but in November, 1889, Mrs. Fuller invited the Clevelands to be house guests in the new Fuller home at the time of the Washington Centennial in December. Cleveland wrote an affectionate letter of regret that a speaking engagement in Boston would prevent their acceptance. He was distressed, he said, to miss the Chief Justice's oration.

All during 1890 they were in correspondence about the demands of the Iroquois Club in Chicago that Cleveland speak there on tariff reform, Fuller urging that the invitation be accepted and Cleveland only half-convinced that it should. "Of course, I had rather not go at all," he said, "but if there is a question of duty in the matter I must yield and do the best I can." But in September he declined. A month later Fuller wrote to him: "I do not see how you can do otherwise than in some form expressing your views & your hopes in a struggle directly upon issues with which your name is so indissolubly connected."

In February, 1891, Fuller was delighted with Cleveland's outspoken declaration against the free and unlimited coinage of silver. "If we won anything under your administration," he wrote in his letter of congratulation, "it was the reputation for honesty and safety, and the idea, after being rehabilitated, of being remanded into the quagmire of no principles is abhorrent to the vast majority of the party & to all the members of that great margin, whose votes enable us to carry elections. . . . I write in a hurry and being Ch. Justice, confidentially, & there's really no need of writing at all as you know me, but I can't help it."

In the meantime the invitation to speak at the Chicago Iroquois Club was renewed, and Cleveland again said that he would consider it. But in March he wrote to Fuller, asking his help in declining without wounding anyone. He wrote at length of the many importunities he received to make addresses:

"There are some things I cannot explain to all who press upon me these invitations, but I feel that perhaps I ought to impart them to you. At any rate it will be a relief to do so. . . . In my condition, every public effort involves careful and studious preparation. This brings with it much hard work. I cannot afford to do less than the very best I can. . . . Too frequent appearances before the people may tend to the weakening of my power for usefulness, and the loosening of my hold on the lines which guide public thought. Don't laugh at this, for I do not write it with a personal aspiration in my mind. No one knows better than you that in our party the greatest care is necessary on the part of somebody to be in condition to assist in dispelling errors and keeping the ranks steady. I am praying daily more and more fervently that the rest of my days may be unofficial, but there are things to be presented and things to be prevented. In these circumstances am I wrong in supposing that if there is any means of good in me it will best be displayed and exercised by waiting for the somewhat rare occasion when speech or action will *tell*? I am so clear that the Chicago trip had better be entirely abandoned that if you agree with me, I want you to help me to settle the matter in the negative with as much consideration for the good friends, who I believe will be really disappointed, as is possible."

Fuller responded that he had always been sympathetic with Cleveland's harried situation and was surprised that it was not better appreciated. "I think you are right," he said, "and I will of course help to alleviate the disappointment of our friends." But he took the opportunity to reciprocate Cleveland's candor. "You cannot escape," he warned, "from the consequences of your commanding position as a leader and leave the party staggering around in 1892 to be beaten on lines that would bring it into contempt and relegate it to the limbo of betrayal of principle and general imbecility. Years in a minority lost it the art of governing. You rehabilitated it and you cannot let it go back."

In 1890 Cleveland argued his first and only case before the Supreme Court. It was a very intricate suit against the City of New Orleans on drainage warrants. He wrote the Chief Justice apologetically, asking when the case was likely to be reached for argument. "I have often heard," he said, "that the most troublesome fellow in the legal profession is the Lawyer with but one case."

The case was argued in October, 1890. An incident occurred during the argument which has become part of the folk lore of the Court. The Court adjourns promptly on the minute set for adjournment—often to the consternation of counsel then arguing. As Cleveland was finishing his argument, he looked up at the clock above the Chief Justice and, seeing that it was only two minutes to closing time, observed that it was almost time for adjournment but that he would detain them for only a few minutes to complete his argument. The Chief Justice said courteously but firmly: "Mr. Cleveland, we will hear you tomorrow morning," and the Court adjourned.

The decision in the case was adverse to Cleveland, with Brewer writing the opinion and Harlan the dissent in which Lamar and Fuller joined. It was an extremely technical case in which the decision might well have been either way, but it tended to demonstrate that it is not wise for former Presidents who have appointed Justices to argue cases before the Court. Cleveland never did it again; and Taft, who as Solicitor General was doubtless aware of this case, emphatically refused to appear before the Court when he became an ex-President.

Cleveland wrote Fuller of his bitter disappointment but said that he was " 'well broken' to the harness of defeats." He was afraid, he confessed, that it was unjust to clients for him to present cases in the Supreme Court. Fuller performed with felicity the age-old task of the judge to bind up the wounds of defeated counsel. "No temporary visitation," he wrote to Cleveland, "should lead you into the mistake of supposing that the interests of any client could suffer anywhere by being confided to your charge." "Such an argument as you made entitles you to very high rank in the profession." That Cleveland cherished this letter is indicated by the fact that he wrote the word "rank" over Fuller's almost illegible scrawl for that word.

As the election year of 1892 approached, Fuller's friends began to suggest him as the nominee for President instead of Cleveland. In New York the former President was involved in a deadly quarrel with Tammany and Governor Hill which made it doubtful whether Cleveland could carry his own State.

It looked as though the candidate must be a Western man acceptable to Cleveland and also to Tammany and Hill. Fuller's friends were sure that he was that man.

In March, 1892, the Chief Justice's former partner Henry M. Shepard, in an interview in the Chicago *Journal,* suggested Fuller for President. A day or so later, Hugh Wallace, Fuller's son-in-law, told Shepard that the Chief Justice would be annoyed if he saw the report. Shepard then sent Fuller a copy of the newspaper, saying that Wallace had told him that Mrs. Fuller was "down on all of us who are tempting you." Shepard argued that loyalty to the party and to the country should forbid Fuller to decline if he were nominated. "Your boy and your girls," Shepard wrote, "certainly would be prouder if you had filled both of the great offices. . . . I find myself thinking only of my children . . . and I dare say it is so with you." Fuller responded that Shepard's friendship for him was "overleaping the bounds of discretion." He was "disgusted with me," Shepard wrote to Wallace. "I am a little afraid of the old man and don't dare to write to him . . . but you are not afraid of him—let me know what he says."

Shepard, Phelps, Doane, Morris, and other Chicago friends wrote Fuller at this time, urging that although Governor Hill's vendetta against Cleveland was failing to gain headway it would probably prevent his election if nominated, and that the convention, if convinced of this result, would not nominate him. Fuller was just then overwhelmed with Court work because of the illness of Justices Lamar and Gray. Mrs. Fuller wrote: "The C.J. is miserable in health but entirely subordinate to the ills of his associates—overworked abnormally as you know." And Fuller wrote to Morris: "You don't know how I am harassed and perplexed & the Court work is very onerous. . . . I don't know which way to turn. . . . If Cleveland can't be nominated I rather think old Palmer the next best man but I have not paid any attention to it." He wrote at length to Cleveland about Lamar's serious illness and never mentioned politics. But he found time to carry on a correspondence with

Judge Lambert Tree in Chicago in an effort to secure the support for Cleveland of the Chicago *Times,* then owned by Carter Harrison.

In May, 1892, the New York *World,* in a long dispatch from Washington, announced with many circumstantial details that Cleveland had been persuaded to withdraw and make Fuller his heir. The *World* said that this step had been decided upon when Governor Palmer captured the Illinois delegation to the Democratic National Convention. The story was too detailed not to have some elements of truth: the proposal had at least been presented to Cleveland. The Chief Justice immediately wrote him: "My messenger brought me yesterday the New York *World* containing a dispatch which first annoyed & then amused me. I have no doubt that Illinois is all right & Judge Tree, with whom I have been in communication in relation to a matter which he or Senator Vilas will explain, so assures me. You must not suppose that I talk or write politics—I don't—but I must say that my conviction that you are the only nominee absolutely certain of success remains unshaken & I entreat you not to be of any other opinion—Do not underrate your running qualities."

Five days later Fuller wrote to his wife with a marginal note of "strictly confidential": "Saw Lamar yesterday—he was rather languid but no worse. He had received a letter from Cleveland written before mine reached the latter. It showed that C. was considerably harassed about running. I always thought he would [be] a little indisposed to do it but I can't see how he can help it & have no doubt he should & that he will be elected."

In June, Fuller wrote his wife from Chicago: "This town is getting ready for the Democratic convention. . . . I am quite sure Cleveland is all right. . . . I am full of hope that he will be elected. . . . Though Harrison is a splendid fighter the general current is our way & that makes an immense difference." Cleveland was nominated on the first ballot. About 10:00 P.M. on November 8, 1892 (election day), Eugene

Brooks, the Chief Justice's colored messenger and houseman, began to receive a series of telegrams from Hugh Wallace in New York, the last of which read:

"*Eugene Brooks*
 1800 Mass. Ave.
  Washn. D.C.
"Everything looks brighter hourly. It looks like a land slide. Doane says that Illinois will go for Cleveland. My communications not for you. H. C. Wallace."

Cleveland did, in fact, carry Illinois, although no Democrat had seriously claimed that he would. His popular vote in the whole country was 5,556,000 to Harrison's 5,175,000.

Fuller was asked to pay for his part in persuading Cleveland to run. In the month after the election, while the Chief Justice was in New York, he was surprised to receive a letter from the President-elect requesting a "little talk." On their meeting, Cleveland asked him to resign from the Court and head the new Cabinet as Secretary of State.

Fuller took a few days to think it over and then wrote to Cleveland: "I have given the subject of our recent conversation the most serious consideration. I was bound to do this on account of its importance in every way, and the more in view of my sincere attachment to you personally, and my earnest desire for the success of your Administration for the sake of the party and your own. And the result is that I must ask you to allow me to decline the great place you were kind enough to wish me to accept. I am convinced that the effect of the resignation of the Chief Justice under such circumstances would be distinctly injurious to the court. The surrender of the highest judicial office in the world for a political position, even though so eminent, would tend to detract from the dignity and weight of the tribunal. We cannot afford this.

"Again, a change in the head of the court, situated as it is at this juncture, would inevitably involve delay to some extent in the transaction of its business, and invite criticism, which however transitory, it would be the part of wisdom to avoid.

"So far as I myself am concerned, I also think the effect would be unfortunate, though I admit that in the face of imperative duty, purely personal considerations should give way. I am fond of the work of the Chief Justiceship. It is arduous, but nothing is truer than that 'the labor we delight in physics pain.'

"I am deeply sensible of the confidence you repose in me, and it is difficult to decline doing as you would like, but I am clear that I am right on every ground in the conclusion to which I have come."

A month later, in writing to Fuller on another subject, Cleveland said: "I have hardly recovered from the knockdown you gave me in your last letter. I suppose I ought not to have cherished such a dream, but you know I thought I had a little sort of an encouragement for it, and my extreme desire to have you at my side in a very trying time, I suppose, led me on. I hope you do not think I did an improper thing in attempting to compass what I desired so much."

Fuller's old friend Judge Walter Q. Gresham was appointed Secretary of State.

CHAPTER XIII

°∽°

FULLER'S INCREASING INFLUENCE
ON THE COURT

1890–1892

Fuller's growing command of the Court, his firmness when
Field roared but his gentleness and forbearance with the errors
of a subordinate like the Reporter, are shown by certain cases
decided between 1890 and 1892. In the same period he began
to display a daring and resourcefulness in evolving novel legal
theories. And his increasing influence with his colleages frequently gave him majorities for these conceptions.

His first landmark decision was delivered in 1890 in the case
of *Leisy* v. *Hardin*.[1] It involved the power of a state to restrict
interstate commerce in intoxicating liquor. The central fact in
Fuller's life was the enormous growth of Chicago—a direct
result of interstate commerce. Restrictions on such commerce
were odious to him. When he came to the Court, it had recently
been decided that a state could not stop an interstate shipment
of liquor at the state boundary. But it had also been decided
several years before, that a state could forbid the sale of an
interstate shipment of liquor after it had arrived. In the *Leisy*
case, Fuller persuaded the Court to overrule this last decision
and adopt a rule called the "original-package doctrine."

The Leisys made beer in Peoria, Illinois, and shipped it in
kegs to a relative in Keokuk, Iowa, who sold it there. Under
an Iowa liquor-prohibition Act this beer was seized by the city
marshal in the original kegs in the hands of the Keokuk Leisy.
The Supreme Court, in an opinion by the Chief Justice, held

[1] 1890, 135 U.S. 100.

that the Iowa statute as thus applied was an unlawful interference with interstate commerce.

Fuller said that intoxicating liquor was a recognized article of commerce. Under the interstate commerce clause of the Constitution, a state could not prohibit its entry from another state. But the question remained: When does an interstate shipment cease to be such? At some point articles shipped into a state must become subject to its laws. Fuller then applied for the first time to interstate commerce a rule of thumb which had been suggested by Chief Justice Marshall to determine when a foreign importation ended so that a state could tax an imported article despite the constitutional provision against state taxes on imports. Importation does not end, Marshall had said, until the imported goods have become intermingled with the common mass of property in the state. It does not end, he held, while the goods are in the original package in the hands of the importer; and the right to import includes the right to sell. Under this test the city marshal of Keokuk had unlawfully interfered with interstate commerce when he seized these original kegs of beer.

An able dissent from Fuller's opinion in the *Leisy* case was delivered by Justice Gray, who was joined by Justices Harlan and Brewer. The dissenters argued that—Congress being silent on the subject—the states had a right to prevent importations which they thought harmful to the health of their citizens. Fuller responded that a state had no right under that guise to exclude entirely a recognized article of commerce. Otherwise a state could exclude any and all importations, and interstate commerce would exist only at the sufferance of the several states. The Constitution was adopted, he said, largely to avoid that condition, and "the magnificent growth and prosperity of the country attest the success which has attended the accomplishment of that object."

A great clamor arose over this decision from the anti-liquor people, who then had great political power. They forced through Congress an Act to the effect that intoxicating liquor when shipped into a state should become subject to its laws and should not be exempt therefrom because it was in the "original package." Fuller, in the *Leisy* opinion, had repeatedly said that such an Act of Congress would be proper. However, it was clear that Congress could not logically give to the states the power to determine the constitutional scope of interstate commerce. Fuller sustained the new Act by holding that Congress had not delegated such power to the states but had merely divested liquor shipments of their interstate character at an earlier date than that of the original-package rule. Several years later, the Court held that under this Act a state could not interfere with an interstate shipment of liquor prior to its arrival in the hands of the consignee. Only the consignee's right to sell was cut off by the law. The dispute over Fuller's original-package doctrine raged for several years, but he was eventually victorious and the rule became firmly embedded in the law.

The *Leisy* case shows Fuller's pluck in opposing a popular desire in favor of what he thought was a more fundamental need. The case also demonstrates his grit in overruling a prior decision. It indicates his resourcefulness in applying in a new way a doctrine having the sanction of Marshall's great name and transparent reasoning. It proves Fuller's influence on the Court in his ability to lead his colleagues in these strange paths. It shows his moderation through his invitation to Congress to legislate, and the subsequent cases show his adroitness in accepting the legislation in a restricted sense and without destruction of his original theory.

A sequel to the *Leisy* case—*O'Neil* v. *Vermont* [1] caused great trouble inside the Court. O'Neil was convicted of selling liquors in Vermont. He had sent the liquor by express in jugs and flasks from his store in New York to individual customers in Vermont. The shipments were made C.O.D., and the Supreme Court of Vermont held that the express company was therefore O'Neil's agent and that the sales were made by him in

[1] 1892, 144 U.S. 323.

Vermont through such agent. Title in the liquors did not pass to the buyer until they were paid for in Vermont. O'Neil was sentenced to pay a fine of some $6,500, and in default of payment he was to be imprisoned for more than fifty-four years.

The Supreme Court of the United States in an opinion by Justice Blatchford dismissed the case on the ground that no federal question had been decided by the Supreme Court of Vermont. The commerce clause had not been mentioned in the trial court. The Supreme Court of Vermont, under its rules, could not, therefore, consider that question.[1] The Vermont court never mentioned the commerce clause in its opinion as to O'Neil, though it did refer to that clause in deciding the cases brought against the express company for condemnation of the liquors.

Justice Field passionately dissented. He insisted that the commerce clause had been brought to the attention of the Supreme Court of Vermont. He pointed out that the arguments of counsel for O'Neil in that court as reported in the official report had expressly referred to that clause.

When he published these opinions, Bancroft Davis, the Reporter, set off this storm anew by the language which he used in the head note for the case. "No point on the commerce clause of the Constitution," he said, was "considered by the Supreme Court of Vermont *or called to its attention*." Blatchford's opinion had stated that the points made in the trial court were "too general to call the attention" of the Vermont Supreme Court to the commerce clause. Field immediately wrote the Reporter that the italicized words in the head note were not correct. Field's letter is not now available, but in view of his irascibility and his strong feeling in the case, its tone may be well imagined. Davis sent Field's letter to the Chief Justice, who wrote to Field:

---

[1] Blatchford said that perhaps a reason for the lack of argument on the commerce clause in the Vermont courts was that the case was argued there before the decision in the *Leisy* case and local liquor laws then took precedence over the commerce clause.

"My DEAR MR. JUSTICE FIELD:

"Mr. Davis has sent me a copy of your note to him of the 17th & you must allow me to say that it greatly surprises & pains me.

"The headnote numbered 5 expresses the facts as I understand & have always understood the record in O'Neil v. Vermont in this court. In your vigorous and eloquent dissent you arrive at a different conclusion upon the point but inasmuch as the headnote accords with the opinion of the majority in that regard, I do not see how it can be changed on the ground of being incorrect. It seems to me impossible for any misapprehension to arise on the part of any reader of both opinions and I deeply regret if you feel otherwise.

"Very sincerely & truly yours,
MELVILLE W. FULLER"

Fuller sent a copy of this correspondence to Justice Gray, who responded: "As to the Reporter's headnote in O'Neil v. Vermont, I unhesitatingly concur with you on both points: 1. It accords with the opinion of the court. 2. That is the whole office of a headnote."

In answer to Fuller's letter, Field wrote:

"DEAR MR. CHIEF JUSTICE FULLER:

"Your letter of yesterday's date, respecting the syllabus to the decision in O'Neil v. Vermont, is received. If my note to the Reporter surprises and pains you I regret it but cannot help it. The syllabus is incorrect and the statement that no point on the commerce clause of the constitution was called to the attention of the Supreme Court of Vermont is not correct and no repetition of it will make it so. The report of the case in the Vermont Reports contains a synopsis of the briefs of counsel before that court and shows that the point was expressly taken. . . . The decision in O'Neil v. Vermont and the opinion of the court are, in my judgment, destined to an unenviable notoriety, greater than has followed any previous decision of the Supreme Court. . . .

"If my associates, who concurred in that decision and opinion could read some of the letters I have received on the subject from distinguished judges, lawyers and legal writers, they would find that I am not alone in my views but that they are held by some of the ablest intellects of the country. I should have shown some of these letters to my associates had I not feared that they would consider that I intended to be rude to them; so I have refrained. I have selected one of the most moderate in expression of all of them from the distinguished writer on criminal law, Joel P. Bishop, Esq., and send a copy of it for your perusal.

"I am

> Very respectfully yours,
> STEPHEN J. FIELD"

Joel P. Bishop was a legal author of some renown in that period. But he had an "enormous vanity." His letter on this case was afterward published in an anonymous communication to a legal periodical. Bishop's letter did not mention the commerce clause but abused the Supreme Court for failing to hold the conviction void under the "due process" clause of the Constitution.

The Chief Justice responded to Field's letter:

"DEAR JUDGE FIELD:

"I received yours of the 19th yesterday but delayed acknowledgment until I could read Mr. Bishop's paper which I return as requested. I am obliged to you for giving me the opportunity but I do not think it adds anything to the force of your dissent and it is impertinent in its allusions to the court though that may be unintentional.

> "Very truly yours,
> MELVILLE W. FULLER"

A month later Field printed a long letter to the Chief Justice and sent copies to all of the Justices. "I have often wondered," he said, "how it happened that you, who I know wish in all cases to be correct, could concur in the erroneous statement. At last I think I have found out the cause of your error, and I do only as I would wish to be done by in calling your attention to what I suppose it to be."

Field said that it was very evident that Blatchford erroneously thought that only the lawyers for the express company, and not counsel for O'Neil, had relied on the commerce clause in the Vermont court. Field then quoted in full the Vermont brief for O'Neil on the commerce clause. It would appear, however, that Field was mistaken in his inferences from Blatchford's opinion. Blatchford knew that the commerce clause had been mentioned in the brief for O'Neil: he could hardly fail to know that fact, since it had been emphatically stated in the dissenting opinions. Blatchford's point was that the reference to the commerce clause in the brief was not sufficient to give the Supreme Court of Vermont jurisdiction to consider that clause because the subject had not been mentioned in the trial court. The *O'Neil* case shows how difficult Field could be, but it also shows Fuller's patience and firmness in handling him.

The first five to four decision in the Fuller regime did not occur until about three years after his appointment. The case— *Briggs* v. *Spaulding* [1]—involved the liability of directors of an insolvent bank for alleged neglect in permitting the president of the bank to have such control of its affairs that he was enabled, without their knowledge, in a few months' time to wreck the bank. No one knowing Fuller would doubt his answer to this question. He was generous in his judgments of men's conduct, and in order to condemn a director for mere inaction he would require strong evidence. The majority of the Court thought that there was no such evidence in the case, and Fuller wrote the opinion of the Court affirming the Circuit Court's exculpation of these directors. The minority thought that the misconduct of the president of the bank could have been discovered by reasonable diligence on the part of certain of the directors.

[1] 1891, 141 U.S. 132.

There is evidence that Fuller was originally a dissenter in this case and secured a majority for his dissenting opinion. Among the Chief Justice's papers is an undated note from Justice Brown:

"DEAR CHIEF JUSTICE:

"May I ask you to circulate your dissent as soon as you conveniently can. I happen to know that an effort will be made to postpone final adjournment to June 3. To give time to this would be as bad as a continuance to me as I am booked to sail for Europe June 1 and could not possibly be present without breaking up my summer.

"Very truly yours,
H. B. BROWN"

There are reasons to believe that this note refers to an original dissent by Fuller in *Briggs* v. *Spaulding*. He dated the note in his own hand "May 19/91" and carefully preserved it. No dissenting opinion was thereafter delivered by him in any case argued prior to this note. However, the five to four decision in *Briggs* v. *Spaulding* was rendered six days thereafter (May 25, 1891), when the Court adjourned for the term. The case had been argued on March 3, and Fuller perhaps knew when he dated Brown's note and put it away that his "dissent" would be the majority opinion. The dissenting Justices were Harlan, Gray, Brewer, and Brown. And it would seem that only a five to four decision could threaten postponement of Brown's trip to Europe. There was no other close division of the Court at that term or for some time thereafter. Moreover, the dissenting opinion in this case by Justice Harlan bears on its face some evidence that it was originally prepared as a majority opinion. It never refers to the majority opinion and lacks the usual tone of a dissenting opinion.

In this case there was more trouble about the headnote. Fuller corrected the proof sheets of the opinion and sent them to the Reporter in June, 1891. In September, in Chicago, he received a letter from Harlan, who had written the dissent in the case:

"DEAR CHIEF JUSTICE:

"I have read the head-notes in the Bank case. They are awful & are enough to make you & not me sick. There is time to correct them. Make the corrections & send to Banks Brothers & tell them they must be made. It will require some of the opinions of the next term to complete Vol. 141 & hence you have time to have the corrections made.

"Yrs.
"JNO. MARSHALL HARLAN"

This letter indicates the affection in which Fuller had come to be held by his colleagues. Here is a case about which Harlan had felt keenly enough to publish a long dissenting opinion—an appeal to posterity against the majority opinion. Yet when he discovered that the effect of Fuller's opinion had been ruined by the headnotes, he at once warned the Chief Justice and suggested the surest method of correction.

Harlan was right. The headnote was badly mangled and made Fuller's reasoning appear ridiculous. But the kindliness of Fuller's letter of correction to the Reporter was characteristic. It is reminiscent of Sir Isaac Newton's gentleness with the little dog that knocked over a candle and thereby burned up Newton's scientific paper on which he had labored for a year.

"CHICAGO
Oct. 8/91

"DEAR MR. DAVIS:

"The closing paragraphs of the head note to Briggs v. Spaulding, 141 U.S. 132 are so inaccurate as to require correction. I think it would be quite as well to omit the summing up entirely but if that can not readily be done, I would like to have the enclosed substituted for the defective matter. Mr. Justice Blatchford improved the notes as far as he went but I do not think he went far enough.

"My opinion in Rogers v. Durant, 140 U.S. 498 is attributed to Mr. Justice Field. If he does not object I do not know that I need to.

"I hope Mrs. Davis & yourself are very well. My eldest daughter, Mrs. Brown, has been lying dangerously ill for some weeks. Her condition was imminently critical last night—This morning, you will be glad to know there are grounds for hope of recovery.

"Very truly yours,
MELVILLE W. FULLER

Hon. J. C. Bancroft Davis"

No correction of the head note was ever made, apparently because Fuller's letter was received too late. If he had written directly to Banks Brothers, the publishers, as Harlan advised, the changes might have been made. Fuller doubtless did not adopt that course through fear of wounding the feelings of the Reporter.

The *Briggs* case illustrates Fuller's compassion for the defendants and his influence with his brethren on the Court. When the Court divided five to four, the majority was more likely to be on his side.[1] This case also indicates in a striking way Harlan's great affection for Fuller. And, more sharply, it shows the Chief Justice's restraint in dealing with the Reporter's errors.

Another case which discloses Fuller's compassion as well as his daring in evolving legal theories is *Boyd* v. *Nebraska*.[2] It also proves again his power in securing a majority for his ideas. And the subsequent correspondence shows once more the great regard in which his colleagues held him.

The case involved the right of James Boyd to be governor of Nebraska. He had been elected and inaugurated as governor, but the Supreme Court of Nebraska had decided by a two to

[1] Out of 64 such decisions in Fuller's 22 years on the Court, he was with the majority in 38 cases and in the minority in 26.
[2] 1892, 143 U.S. 135.

one vote that he was not a citizen of the United States and therefore not qualified for the office.

Boyd had been born in Ireland and brought to this country as a child by his father in 1844. His father had settled in Ohio and soon thereafter filed his declaration of intention to become a citizen of the United States. But it was alleged that he had not completed his naturalization before his son attained the age of twenty-one, although the father had voted and held political office in Ohio. In 1856 the son had gone to Nebraska, where he had since repeatedly voted and held many elective offices prior to his election as governor in 1890. The father was formally naturalized in Ohio in 1890, and this proceeding provoked the controversy in Nebraska over the son's citizenship. The son claimed that this 1890 naturalization had occurred only because his father was unable to find his citizenship papers issued many years before.

Fuller held that Boyd was a citizen of the United States, regardless of his father's citizenship, because he had been a resident in Nebraska when the Congressional enabling Act was passed and the State admitted into the Union. Those statutes declared that all residents of Nebraska who had filed their declarations of intention to become citizens were citizens of the United States. The son, Fuller said, had acquired an inchoate or potential citizenship by his father's declaration, which placed him in the same category which his father would have occupied had he moved to Nebraska. Furthermore, Fuller held that the son had duly alleged in his answer that his father had been fully naturalized during the son's minority. The Supreme Court of Nebraska had held the contrary.

The first basis on which Fuller put the case was rather bold, for statutes are not usually extended beyond their terms. But he was frankly moved by sympathy for a man who had been a pioneer in the State and had been a member of the legislature, a delegate to two constitutional conventions, mayor of Omaha, and had been fairly elected governor. Harlan, Gray, and Brown concurred in the opinion only on the second basis.

This ground was that Boyd had alleged on information and belief that his father had completed his naturalization in strict accordance with the Acts of Congress prior to the time when the son became twenty-one. The Supreme Court of Nebraska had held this allegation insufficient. Fuller pointed out that prior decisions of the Supreme Court of the United States had held that, where a naturalization certificate was lost, a jury might infer citizenship from voting and holding office for a long period of time. Since Boyd alleged these facts, Fuller held his allegation of his father's citizenship to be sufficient.

Fuller secured the concurrence in the decision of every Justice of the Court except Field. Field said that the federal courts had no power to determine a state election contest, that the states had the "absolute power to prescribe the qualifications of all their state officers," and that the decision was an unwarranted invasion of states' rights.

This point was the least vulnerable portion of Fuller's opinion. He had based the federal jurisdiction on the fact that Boyd had claimed to be a citizen of the United States under federal statutes, to which the Nebraska court had not given proper effect. But Fuller's opinion was labored and prolix, while Field's was sparkling and succinct. A week after the opinions were delivered, Justice Gray wrote to Fuller:

"DEAR CHIEF JUSTICE:

"I had in mind to say to you on your return from Richmond (but it escaped my mind yesterday) that Judge Field's dissent in *Boyd* v. *Thayer* is so insidious and plausible to the common mind that I hope you will enlarge upon the question of jurisdiction so as to meet it—which would not be difficult.

"Respectfully & truly yours,
HORACE GRAY"

It is typical of Gray's feeling for Fuller that in a case where Gray was only half-convinced that Fuller was right, Gray was still extremely anxious that the Chief Justice should not be disparaged by Field's dissent.

But whatever changes the Chief Justice made in the opinion in pursuance of this suggestion were quite inadequate. The *Harvard Law Review* in an editorial note condemned the decision for invading the rights of the states and commended the dissenting opinion of Justice Field. Perish the thought that the Harvard law professors were, in the terminology of Justice Gray, persons "of common mind!"

CHAPTER XIV

༄

MORE TRIUMPHS AND
SOME DEFEATS, CLEVELAND'S
SECOND TERM

1893–1897

On a stormy day in March, 1893, the Chief Justice gave the inaugural oath to Cleveland on the east portico of the Capitol. Fuller had administered another inaugural oath that day. In the morning at the Court he had given the oath of office to Howell E. Jackson, President Harrison's appointee to succeed the late Justice Lamar. Jackson was born in Tennessee in 1832 of an old Whig family. He had opposed secession but had held civil office under the Confederacy. His public life was a series of surprises. He practiced law very quietly in Jackson, Tennessee, until his election in 1880 to the Tennessee legislature. He was elected by a narrow margin as a Democrat. The first duty of this legislature was to choose a United States senator. They were deadlocked, and after several days a Republican member suddenly nominated Jackson, who was elected. He served in the Senate until 1886, when he resigned to become United States Circuit Judge on President Cleveland's appointment.

One of Jackson's colleagues on that court was Henry Billings Brown, of Detroit. Brown tells the rest of the story in his memoirs: "During his occasional visits to Detroit, he usually made his home at my house. . . . One day as we were returning from court, . . . he told me that he had been informed that Mr. Justice Matthews was fatally ill, and that in case of his death he proposed to go to Washington, see President Harrison, a former colleague of his in the Senate, and persuade him to appoint me to the vacancy. As my aspirations had never mounted to the Supreme Bench, and I had never dreamed of it as a possibility, I was naturally surprised. . . . He made his promise good, went to Washington in my behalf, and ultimately obtained my appointment. . . . It only remains to add that upon the occurrence of the next vacancy, by the death of Mr. Justice Lamar, I was instrumental in inducing President Harrison to appoint Mr. Justice Jackson in his place."

The newspapers said that Jackson looked like a miniature Uncle Sam; he was a tiny man with a goatee. Although he was an able lawyer and Judge, his service of less than two years on the Supreme Court prevented him from obtaining the eminence which is the natural result of long service there. But the brevity of his term did not debar him from establishing a cordial intimacy with the Chief Justice.

Even before he administered the oath to Cleveland, Fuller was deluged with requests for help in securing appointments. His old political partner Erskine M. Phelps wanted the third member of their triumvirate, John M. Doane, appointed Secretary of the Treasury. Shepard, Gregory, and other Chicago intimates sought Fuller's aid in having W. C. Goudy appointed Attorney General. But the appointment of Walter Q. Gresham of Indiana and Chicago as Secretary of State blocked another Cabinet appointment from Chicago, and Cleveland wrote Fuller asking his help in finding an Attorney General from the South. "Can you give me the name of a first rate lawyer in the South," Cleveland asked, "some one who has appeared in your Court and made a good impression? I am not sure but I shall need an Attorney General from that quarter—preferably from Alabama, Mississippi or that vicinity. . . . If such a man occurs to you and you can put me on the track of him, I shall be much obliged."

Judge Lambert Tree asked Fuller's help in securing his appointment as Ambassador to Great Britain, and Perry M. Smith wanted to be Minister to Denmark. General Joseph H.

Smith of Bangor desired a Canadian consulship. At Fuller's request Henry C. Morris, the son of his old Chicago office associate, John Morris, was appointed consul at Ghent. Robert T. Lincoln of Chicago and Francis Fessenden of Portland, Maine, wrote the Chief Justice about Army appointments. Henry M. Shepard was being strongly urged for Gresham's place on the Circuit Court of Appeals. Justice Harlan, who was in Europe on the Bering sea arbitration, wrote Fuller asking that Minister Coolidge be allowed to stay for a time in Paris and that James Harlan, the Justice's son, be appointed to the federal bench.

Harlan's letters from Paris at this time show that Fuller wrote a dissent that became the unanimous opinion of the Court. He was in a minority of three and he converted the entire Court to his position. The case was entitled *Metcalf* v. *Watertown*.[1] A statute of limitations in Wisconsin outlawed in ten years suits on judgments of the federal courts. The same law permitted suits to be brought on state court judgments for twenty years. This discrimination posed a sharp dilemma. It was inconsistent with the supremacy of the federal government to permit the judgments of its courts to be thus discriminated against. Yet the rule was well settled in the Supreme Court of the United States that state laws on this subject must be followed. In fact, the interpretation of such a law by the Supreme Court of a state was binding on the Supreme Court of the United States. And the Supreme Court of Wisconsin had held that the ten-year statute applied to suits on federal court judgments.

At first a majority of the Supreme Court of the United States concluded that they were bound by this state court decision. They accepted the discrimination as inevitable. Fuller, Blatchford, and Brown dissented. Harlan then wrote to Fuller: "If the matter has not gone too far I should like very much to prepare a dissenting opinion in Metcalf v. Watertown unless you or someone who was in the minority will do it."

[1] 1894, 153 U.S. 671.

Fuller, however, had already composed such a dissent. Three weeks later Harlan wrote him: "Your dissenting opinion in Metcalf v. Watertown hits the nail squarely on the head. I agree to every word of it & congratulate you upon the partial victory over against views that would 'without rhyme or reason' destroy rights plainly secured by the Federal Constitution. God has rewards for all this and I send greetings to you, Blatchford and Brown."

Harlan's reference to a "partial victory" meant that Fuller's dissent had resulted in the Court ordering a reargument. When the final decision was made a year later, it was a unanimous opinion written by Fuller. It subtly but boldly reinterpreted the Wisconsin statute so that the twenty-year period applied to both state and federal judgments.

A year later, in another case involving a conflict between the state and federal courts, Harlan wrote to Fuller: "Since reading your opinion in the *Moran*[1] case I am ready to take off my hat to you as the Wonder of Wonders. It is an unusually fine opinion." In this case Fuller sustained the admiralty jurisdiction of the federal courts as paramount to that of the state courts even in a case where the state courts had first acquired jurisdiction. Fuller's opinion distinguished the prior decisions which appeared to require a contrary result.

Another letter of Harlan's refers to a series of cases in which Fuller and Harlan were in the minority. A harsh law then prevailed that an injured workman could not recover damages from his employer if the injury had been due to the negligence of a fellow servant. In an effort to mitigate the rigor of that rule, a few courts had held that a train conductor was not a fellow servant of the other trainmen but was instead a vice principal in charge of a department of the railroad. Before Fuller's advent the Supreme Court had adopted this vice principal doctrine. It was in keeping with Fuller's predilections and sympathies that he should strive to ameliorate the fellow-servant rule. Almost at once he became an advocate of the

[1] *Moran* v. *Sturges*, 1894, 154 U.S. 256.

proposition that railroad conductors were vice principals.

In January, 1893, Harlan wrote Fuller at length about the opinion in *Lake Shore, etc. Ry. Co.* v. *Prentice.*[1] This was a suit against a railroad for the wrongful arrest of a passenger by a conductor. A judgment for the passenger was reversed. Harlan did not object to the decision so much as to some things said by Gray in the course of his opinion. "There is one paragraph in the opinion," Harlan wrote, "which will be interpreted as pretty nearly over-ruling our former decision holding the negligence of the conductor was the negligence of the corporation because he represented the personality of the corporation itself. . . . The first time a case comes up, where the question is whether a conductor and the brakeman are fellow-servants, that part of the opinion will be cited against the view for which you, Justice Field, Lamar and myself have contended."

Harlan was wrong in his prediction that the *Prentice* case would be cited to overthrow the doctrine that a railroad conductor was a vice principal. However, that rule was almost repudiated in a series of cases in which Fuller, Field, and Harlan dissented. But time was on Fuller's side in his opposition to the fellow-servant rule. It was eventually repealed by statute.

In this period the Chief Justice vigorously dissented from opinions of Justice Gray in two important cases. The first case was *Fong Yue Ting* v. *United States*[2] involving the deportation of resident Chinese. It was settled that the power to exclude aliens on arrival might be exercised by the Executive Department in a purely arbitrary way. And in time of war, it was clear that enemy aliens might be deported without constitutional restrictions. But the question was whether a friendly alien who had acquired a domicile here under a treaty was not entitled in peacetime to the protection of the Constitution. Gray delivered the majority opinion holding that deportation

[1] 1893, 147 U.S. 101.
[2] 1893, 149 U.S. 698; see 7 *Harvard Law Review*, 183.

of friendly aliens in peacetime was as much an attribute of sovereignty as exclusion of such aliens on arrival. He held that the constitutional guaranties of jury trial, of compulsory process for witnesses, against excessive punishments, and due process were therefore not applicable in such deportation proceedings.

Brewer, Field, and Fuller dissented in separate dissenting opinions. Their position was that these Chinese residents had acquired vested rights under treaties and that the Bill of Rights was applicable to noncitizens who were residing here. The Constitution provided that "no person" should be deprived of life, liberty, or property without due process of law. Exclusion on arrival, the dissenters conceded, might be arbitrary, but expulsion of those who had lawfully acquired a domicile was subject to constitutional limitations.

A week after the decision was announced, Field wrote to Fuller: "I send you my dissenting opinion in the Chinese deportation case. Please look it over carefully and make any suggestions which you may deem wise to adopt. I should like to have it returned at your earliest convenience as I wish to file it at once and let Justice Gray worry over it as much as he can." A few days later Fuller filed a short dissent in which he said: "No euphuism can disguise the character of the Act. . . . It . . . inflicts punishment without a judicial trial. It is, in effect a legislative sentence of banishment, and, as such, absolutely void. Moreover, it contains within it the germs of an assertion of an unlimited and arbitrary power in general incompatible with the immutable principles of justice, inconsistent with the nature of our government, and in conflict with the written Constitution by which that government was created and those principles secured." Field immediately wrote him: "I have just rec'd your dissenting opinion in the Chinese deportation cases. It is a gem, and its words ought to be printed in gold. It is brief but contains the pith of the whole case. It can never be met or answered. The last six lines announce the judgment of the country now and hereafter upon the strange and, to use the language of a distinguished lawyer and jurist of New York, hateful decision of the majority."

Justice Gray did "worry" over these dissents. He attempted to modify the sentence of his opinion which read: "Congress, under the power to exclude or expel aliens, might have directed any Chinese laborer, found in the United States without a certificate of residence, to be removed out of the country by executive officers, without judicial trial or examination, just as it might have authorized such officers absolutely to prevent his entrance into the country."

Field was furious at the modification. He wrote the Chief Justice: "I send you a copy of my opinion containing the note which I have affixed to page 9 of it stating that the words quoted by me were originally in the opinion of the court to which the dissent was directed and that in the revision of the opinion the phraseology is changed. This ought not to give offense to Mr. Justice Gray and the original language quoted shows that my comments were not uncalled for."

Gray was perturbed. On the same day as Field's letter, he wrote the Chief Justice: "I wish to see you about what we talked of Saturday afternoon. Shall I call on you at quarter past eleven this morning or would any other time or place suit you better?" And on the same day Gray wrote: "Dear C. J. As I understand it would be more convenient to you and will be equally so to me, I shall expect you here as you come back from the 1.15 train or after that when you please." Fuller apparently persuaded Gray to forego the proposed changes in his opinion, thus obviating Field's footnote.

Fuller had great influence with Field despite the latter's independence. Once when Field was ill and unable to attend a Saturday conference, he wrote to the Chief Justice: "You can cast my vote in all the cases with your own, with the exception of the case of the Northern Pacific. In all others I believe your opinion corresponds with my own. In that case I would affirm the judgment and you may not vote to that effect."

Fuller was also very fond of Gray, whose position as the scholar of the Court was undisputed after Justice Bradley's death. And Gray's desire to have the immense scholarship of his opinions appreciated by the Chief Justice was almost painful. Witness this letter from Gray to Fuller transmitting Gray's fifty-eight-page opinion in a famous case involving the title to tidelands in the Columbia River in Oregon:

"At last I hand you proof of Shively v. Bowlby which I should be very glad to have your criticism of before sending it round.

"I wish it were shorter. But the brief of the Ptf. in error was an able and ingenious and plausible attempt to warp and twist former decisions belittling Martin v. Waddell, Pollard v. Hagen, Knight v. U.S. Land Assn., exaggerating Dutton v. Strong, R. R. Co. v. Schurmeir, Yates v. Milwaukee, ignoring Barney v. Keokuk and like decisions of this court and misapplying state decisions depending on local law. Prosser v. Northern Pacific R.R. can now be quite short and after finishing that I shall devote myself to your opinion in Miller v. Caldwell (as I ought to have done before) before doing anything else of mine."

But Gray did not hesitate, when he felt it necessary, to correct the Chief Justice, although he preferred to do it privately rather than in a published dissent. A week after the foregoing letter he wrote Fuller: "Can you spare a few moments this afternoon to talk over Miller v. Caldwell? I believe it would result in modifications that would save my feelings and save time in conference. I dislike to write a concurring opinion. What hour shall I call on you? Or if you prefer within what limits may I expect you, so as to be sure to be at home?" It is a certainty that the Chief Justice modified the opinion in pursuance of Gray's suggestions.

Fuller's second notable dissent from an opinion by Gray

occurred in *Hilton* v. *Guyot*.[1] This case was a suit in the United States on a judgment obtained after a full trial in France. The majority, in an opinion by Justice Gray, held that since France did not recognize American judgments as conclusive, our courts should not so recognize French judgments: they were only *prima facie* evidence of the justice of the plaintiff's claim, and the defendant could retry the case.

Fuller's position was that the issues having been fully litigated, the judgment was like any other legal right acquired under foreign laws. Our courts had always recognized such rights unless contrary to some policy or prejudicial to the interests of the state.

The professional applause which followed the decision was all for Fuller. The *Harvard Law Review* said: "The dissenting opinion of Mr. Chief Justice Fuller seems entirely sound." Sir Julian Pauncefote, the British ambassador, wrote: "The reasons given for dissent are overwhelming." Justice Emery of the Maine Supreme Court wrote to Fuller: "The doctrine of retorsion [that is, basing our attitude toward French judgments on their attitude toward ours] is medieval and inconsistent with the higher modern sense of justice and morality. I am glad you had the firmness to oppose it."

But probably Fuller's most prized letter was from James Bradley Thayer of Harvard calling the Chief Justice's attention to the comments in the *Law Quarterly Review* of London. "No doubt it is Dicey who writes," Thayer said, referring to A. V. Dicey, the most distinguished authority on the subject. The comments in the *Law Quarterly Review* must have made Justice Gray wince. Dicey said, "This decision claims to be grounded in principle on English authorities which are set forth with extraordinary learning and elaboration by Mr. Justice Gray. . . ." Dicey then showed that the modern English authorities were wholly against the decision and that comity or politeness or good manners or reciprocal courtesy had nothing whatever to do with the question. "The dissenting opinion

[1] 1895, 159 U.S. 113.

of the Supreme Court admirably hits the true point" said Dicey. He then quoted Fuller's dissent that "it is difficult to see why rights acquired under foreign judgments do not belong in the category of private rights acquired under foreign laws."

Cleveland in his second term appointed two new Justices to the Court. In the summer of 1893 Justice Blatchford died, and in September the President nominated William B. Hornblower, a leading lawyer of New York and a nephew of Justice Bradley. Due to the quarrel between the President and Senator Hill of New York, Hornblower failed of confirmation, as did also Cleveland's next nominee, Wheeler H. Peckham,[1] another distinguished New York lawyer. On the rejection of his second nominee, the President surrendered to the Senate and appointed Edward Douglass White, a senator from Louisiana, who was immediately confirmed. White was a bachelor, forty-nine years old, already of generous proportions and serious mien. Of Irish descent, he had been educated in Jesuit schools and was a devout Roman Catholic. His father had been governor of Louisiana and a rich sugar planter there. White had spent practically all his life in public service. He had served in the Confederate Army and for one year on the Supreme Court of Louisiana.

He had a remarkable mind, distinguished principally by his prodigious memory and his tenacity of purpose in going to the root of any problem presented to him. His industry was monumental. He had learned well the lessons of humility taught by his Church and, probably from the same source, he had acquired a deep sense of majesty. But he was cordial, genial, and lovable.

The Chief Justice was as successful in winning White as he had been with the other brethren. Fuller gave his usual dinner for the new Justice; and after White's marriage, which occurred a few months after his appointment, Mrs. Fuller was gracious to his bride. But while Fuller and White's relations

[1] A brother of Rufus W. Peckham, who was thereafter appointed to the Court.

were always affectionate—they wrote each other long friendly letters during the summer vacations—the cases show that White very frequently differed from Fuller.

Upon one point, however, the Chief Justice and Justice White were together: neither of them valued very highly the right of the majority to enact Sunday blue laws when such laws came in conflict with the Constitution. Two decisions of Fuller in this period reflect his lack of sympathy for these laws. In this respect he occupied a position far in advance of most of his colleagues. He had come a long way since 1856, when he had written to the Augusta *Age* in horror that saloons and theaters in Chicago were open on the Sabbath.

The first case involved the Sunday opening of the World's Fair in Chicago. The United States filed a bill to enjoin such opening on the ground that the closing of the Fair on that day was an express condition of a certain federal appropriation. The Fair contended that the government had defaulted in that appropriation, thus relieving the Fair of its obligation. A three-judge United States Circuit Court issued the injunction. Fuller, speaking for the Circuit Court of Appeals, reversed it on the ground that there was no showing of irreparable injury or inadequate remedy at law which were prerequisites to an injunction.

The second case involved a Georgia statute forbidding the running of freight trains on any railroad in the State on Sunday. The Supreme Court held that this Act was not an unlawful interference with interstate commerce. Fuller in a dissent, in which only Justice White joined, said: "This statute in requiring the suspension of interstate commerce for one day in the week amounts to a regulation of that commerce. . . . As the freedom of interstate commerce is secured by the Constitution except as Congress may limit it, the act is void because in violation of that freedom."

Fuller was a deeply religious man; but when the religious prejudices of his day came in conflict with the Constitution, it was the Constitution that prevailed in his decision. Thus his dissent to the forfeiture of the property of the Mormon Church represented a conflict between the Bill of Rights and the powerful moral and religious prejudice against polygamy; his decision in *Leisy* v. *Hardin* represented a conflict between the constitutional freedom of interstate commerce and the great moral crusade for liquor prohibition led by American churches; his dissent in the Georgia Sunday law case, a conflict between a current religious value and the constitutional freedom of interstate commerce. In all of these cases time has vindicated his position.]

Cleveland's second appointee to the Court was Rufus W. Peckham, who was appointed in 1895 to succeed Justice Jackson. Peckham was born in Albany in 1838, the son of a New York lawyer. He never attended college but studied law in his father's office and was admitted to the bar in 1859, the same year in which his father was elected to the Supreme Court of New York. After twenty-four successful years at the Albany bar, the son also was elected to the Supreme Court and afterward to the New York Court of Appeals, where he had served for ten years when he was appointed to the Supreme Court of the United States. He had an intense fervor for the law, coupled with a fearless independence and an outspoken candor.

When he was appointed, the comment was made that he looked like the Chief Justice. They had the same bushy white hair, cameo face, and piercing eyes, but Peckham was a taller man. They had been friends for years in national Democratic circles, and on the Court they grew very much attached to each other.

In 1896 Fuller bought the old square red-brick house at 18th and F streets, where he lived for the rest of his life. This house had been built in 1801 by Tench Ringgold, the Marshal of the District of Columbia. Chief Justice John Marshall and all of the Justices of his Court had boarded there for two winters in 1831 and 1833. Fuller felt a great pride in holding Court conferences in the house where Marshall's Court had counseled.

The Court has always gloried in its traditions. In the same year that Fuller bought this house, the Court unanimously rejected a proposal by Congress that the Supreme Court move from its ancient, cramped quarters in the Capitol to the new and spacious Congressional Library Building.

CHAPTER XV

◦‿◦

THE INCOME TAX CASE

FULLER's most famous and most criticized decision is *Pollock v. Farmers' Loan & Trust Co.,*[1] in which the Supreme Court held the Income Tax Law of 1894 unconstitutional.

In August, 1894, Congress imposed a tax of 2 per cent on incomes above $4,000. Although an income tax had been levied during the Civil War, no such tax had been in effect since 1873. The agitation for the income tax of 1894 had come from the Populist party; but the vote in Congress was sharply sectional, and President Cleveland allowed the bill to become a law without his approval. With rare exceptions both Democrats and Republicans from the industrial states (where almost all of the tax would be collected) opposed it; but in Congress the South was solidly for it and secured enough scattering support from the agricultural states to pass it by a narrow margin. The South felt that the burden of the tariff had fallen largely on its people and, what was worse, the proceeds had been expended in great part for soldiers' pensions in the North. The ultimate division of the Justices on the Supreme Court was also sectional and the result produced more heat than any decision since the *Dred Scott* case.[2] As in that case, the subsequent discussion of this decision has been characterized by a marked absence of objectivity.

The issues in the case were simple. The Constitution provides: "Representatives and direct taxes shall be apportioned among the several states . . . according to their respective numbers." Another section reads: "No capitation or other di-

---

[1] 1895, 157 U.S. 429; 158 U.S. 601.
[2] *Dred Scott* v. *Sanford,* 1857, 19 How. 393.

rect tax shall be laid, unless in proportion to the census. . . ."
The questions were: (1) Were these clauses intended to prevent a majority of states from imposing direct taxes on a
minority except by apportionment among the states according
to population? (2) If so, what is a "direct" tax?

The procedure in the *Pollock* case was evolved by William
D. Guthrie, a young New York lawyer. Certain of his clients
wished to contest the constitutionality of the income tax. The
usual way to test the validity of a federal tax is to pay it and
then sue the collector to get it back. A federal law forbids an
injunction against the collection of a tax. Guthrie wished to
avoid the delay incident to paying the tax and then suing for
it. He therefore raised the issue of the validity of the tax by a
suit between private litigants. He had a stockholder of a trust
company demand that his company refuse to pay the tax and,
upon its declaration of intention to pay despite the demand,
sue for an injunction to prevent the corporation from paying
the alleged unlawful tax. Guthrie arranged for such a suit to
be brought against the Farmers' Loan & Trust Company by a
Boston stockholder named Pollock and for a similar suit to be
brought against the Continental Trust Company by a New
Jersey stockholder named Hyde. Guthrie agreed in advance
with the Solicitor General that they should seek a prompt decision in the lower court and take a speedy appeal. As usually
is done in such test cases, the trust companies retained a lawyer
who was instructed to do everything in his power to sustain the
law. The lawyer so engaged was James C. Carter, then one of
the ablest men practicing at the bar of the Supreme Court.
Guthrie secured Joseph H. Choate as his senior counsel.

In the Supreme Court (after denial of the injunction below)
the *Pollock* and *Hyde* cases were consolidated for argument
with a Pennsylvania injunction suit against a collector in
which former Senator George D. Edmunds was counsel. In
March, 1895, approximately six months after the enactment
of the law, these cases were argued for an entire week. The

THE COURT THAT DECIDED THE INCOME TAX CASES IN 1895

Top row: Justice Jackson, Justice Brown, Justice Shiras, Justice White
Bottom row: Justice Gray, Justice Field, Chief Justice Fuller, Justice Harlan, Justice Brewer

courtroom was crowded with Washington notables, and the daily press of the country carried full reports of the arguments. Even to those who had come from a distance to hear it, this debate by the country's eminent lawyers was no disappointment.

Attorney General Richard Olney, his assistant Edward B. Whitney, and James C. Carter made impressive and scholarly defenses of the law. Carter argued that taxes ought to be proportioned to the ability to bear the burden. He said that the poorer classes had been "prodigiously overburdened" by the tariff, and that the income tax would tend to right that wrong. "It is . . . said to be sectional legislation, and that . . . is true," he admitted, "but it is so only because wealth has become sectional."

No less powerful were the arguments against the law by William D. Guthrie, his partner Clarence A. Seward, Senator George D. Edmunds, and Joseph H. Choate. Choate pointed out that in 1873, with an exemption of $2,000 instead of $4,000, the four states of New York, Pennsylvania, Massachusetts, and New Jersey had paid four-fifths of the income tax. These states had less than one-quarter of the representation in the House of Representatives, where tax bills must originate. The income tax, he contended, was a direct tax which could not thus be imposed by a majority upon a small number of states.

Less than a month after the argument, the Chief Justice delivered the opinion of the Court holding the law invalid in part. The Court was unanimous in deciding that the law was unconstitutional in so far as it imposed a tax on any income received from state and municipal bonds. Prior decisions had held that the federal government could not impose any tax on the states or their municipalities. A tax on the income from such bonds would clearly be a burden on their borrowing power. With only two dissenting Justices—White and Harlan—the Court found the law unconstitutional to the extent that it imposed a tax on the income from land. The Court said that a tax on the income from real estate was a "direct" tax. The Court was evenly divided (four to four, Justice Jackson being ill) on the issues:

1. Whether the whole act was void because of the invalidity of the tax on the income from real estate.

2. Whether a tax on income from personal property was a direct tax.

It will be convenient to discuss this opinion of the Chief Justice in three sections, so that opposing views may be compared.

I

A preliminary issue was whether the direct-tax clauses were put into the Constitution to prevent a majority of states from voting taxes on a minority. The defenders of the income tax claimed that these provisions had been inserted in the Constitution only as a part of the compromise on slavery and, when slavery ended, these words had served their purpose.

This position is best stated by Professor Seligman in his book *The Income Tax,* published in 1911. But it must be remembered that Seligman was a partisan. He furnished the government lawyers with part of the material to defend the law and, since he was then writing a book on the income tax, he was doubtless disappointed when the law fell. At any rate, he abandoned his book for many years. His partisanship sometimes prevented him from stating accurately in his book the simplest facts regarding the case. For example, he said that the Court's decision in the first *Pollock* case was "close" and "several" judges dissented. Six to two is not very close and two Justices are not usually regarded as several.

Seligman's version of the adoption of the direct-tax clauses by the Convention of 1787 was as follows: After the adoption of the "Great Compromise" for equal representation of the states in the Senate and proportionate representation in the House of Representatives, a battle ensued over representation in the lower house. The North contended that, in apportioning representatives, no slaves should be counted and the South that all slaves should be counted. Both sides refused to accept Madison's old compromise whereby three-fifths of the slaves should be counted. In July, 1787, Morris made a motion that direct taxation ought to be proportioned to representation. He indicated afterward that he intended by this motion to bring the North and South together on the three-fifths compromise. If the South was to have representation for three-fifths of its slaves, it would have to pay taxes on the same basis. Morris was successful in effecting this compromise. After this purpose had been accomplished, Morris moved to strike out the words that he had inserted but the convention refused.

However, the direct-tax clause appears twice in the Constitution: once in this provision on representation, and again in the sentence which reads, "No capitation, or other direct tax, shall be laid except in proportion to the census. . . ." Here Seligman stated that a capitation tax was forbidden at the behest of the South to prevent a tax on slaves; and the words "or other direct tax" were inserted, as declared by their sponsor, to prevent the collection from the delinquent states of the unpaid requisitions of Congress against them under the Articles of Confederation.

The majority of the Court was not at all impressed by these arguments. The makers of the Constitution had just emerged, Fuller said, from the struggle for independence whose rallying cry had been that "taxation and representation go together." He showed that before Morris's motion was adopted, similar proposals had been made by several members of the convention. Morris's motion merely phrased a generally accepted principle. In the ratifying convention in Massachusetts, Rufus King, a delegate at the Philadelphia convention, declared: "It is a principle of this Constitution that representation and taxation should go hand in hand. . . . And it was adopted because it was the language of all America." And in the Virginia ratifying convention, Randolph had said: "Representation and taxes go hand in hand; according to one will the other be regulated." Fuller pointed to a wealth of similar expressions.

Furthermore, Fuller called attention to the fact that it was contemplated that the ordinary revenue of the federal government should be raised by "duties, imposts and excises" and that only in the event of war or "absolute necessity" should direct taxes be imposed. In the Massachusetts convention Adams, Dawes, Sumner, King, and Sedgwick all agreed that a direct tax would be the last source of revenue resorted to by Congress. The same thought was expressed in other state ratifying conventions. Massachusetts even proposed an amendment that Congress should not lay direct taxes unless the impost and excise were insufficient. South Carolina, New York, New Hampshire, and Rhode Island concurred in this amendment.

The Chief Justice concluded that these clauses for apportionment among the states by population of direct taxes were not mere incidents of the slavery compromise, but were important considerations in the formulation and ratification of the Constitution. "Nothing can be clearer," he said, "than that what the Constitution intended to guard against was the exercise by the general government of the power of directly taxing persons and property within any State through a majority made up from the other States." Seligman condemned this conclusion by Fuller and the Court as "an historical interpretation which is beyond all doubt erroneous." Corwin stated that no "respectable historical testimony" was adduced in support of it! But Seligman's argument that Gouverneur Morris had an ulterior motive in proposing one of the direct-tax clauses, even if true, is not as devastating as Seligman thought. While the private intention of the author of any constitutional phrase is perhaps pertinent in construing the clause, it is not necessarily of prime importance. More significant is the purpose and understanding of the convention in adopting it and the states in ratifying it. On this issue, Fuller's evidence was overwhelming. Seligman was not even able to convince counsel for the government that his theory was correct. Writing in the *Harvard Law Review* in criticism of the Court's decision ten years later,

Edward B. Whitney, the assistant attorney general who argued the case on this point, deplored the small amount of discussion of these clauses in the Constitutional Convention and said: "The evil feared was a combination of seven states, perhaps the seven smaller ones, to over-assess the property, . . . of the other six. The remedy was to prevent any apportionment of taxes otherwise than by the rule of population."

I I

The main issue in the case was: What is a direct tax? Fuller quoted Madison's notes of the Constitutional Convention: "Mr. King asked what was the precise meaning of direct taxation. No one answered."

Fuller said, however, that the framers of the Constitution were familiar with the use of the term "direct tax" in Adam Smith's *Wealth of Nations,* published in 1776. Smith's use of the words is best shown by the definition given in the *Oxford English Dictionary* on the authority of his usage: "Direct tax: one levied immediately upon the persons who are to bear the burden, as opposed to indirect taxes levied on commodities of which the price is thereby increased." [1] Fuller quoted Franklin in his famous examination in the House of Commons regarding the stamp tax. There Franklin had spoken of external taxes or duties on commodities where the duty is added to the price: "If the people do not like it at that price, they refuse it; they are not obliged to buy it. But an internal tax is forced from the people without their consent, if not laid by their own representatives." If Fuller had known it, he would doubtless have mentioned that Franklin (a member of the Convention of 1787) was a close friend of Adam Smith and that they had carefully discussed together chapters of *The Wealth of Nations* before it was published.

Fuller noted that John Marshall in the Virginia ratifying

[1] *O. E. D.,* 1897, *s.v.* Direct tax. Seligman's denial of Adam Smith's authority for this usage is not very convincing in the light of this definition attributed to Smith in an almost canonical English dictionary.

convention had said that "direct" taxation was well understood: direct taxes were the taxes that the states were then levy-
ing on land and personal property. Fuller showed that similar
direct taxes were imposed in all of the states before the Constitution. And in seven states a tax was levied on the profits of
professions, trades, and employments.

Fuller quoted from Albert Gallatin's *Sketch of the Finances
of the United States* published in 1796: "By direct taxes in the
Constitution, those are meant which are raised on the capital
or revenue of the people; by indirect such as are raised on their
expense." Gallatin indicated that this distinction came from
Adam Smith.

Fuller thus suggested four ideas that were involved in the
phrase "direct taxes." (1) A direct tax was levied directly on
the person who was to bear the burden. (2) It was used in
antithesis to "duties, imposts and excises" which were to be
the main source of revenue of the federal government. (3) It
was a tax, such as the states were then imposing, on real estate,
personal property, or incomes. (4) It was a tax on the capital
or revenue of the people rather than on their expense. He concluded that "the distinction between direct and indirect taxes
was well understood by the framers of the Constitution" in
these senses.

The criticism of this argument of the Chief Justice has been
shrill. His critics have said that he started by quoting Madison's notes of the convention indicating that the phrase "direct
taxes" had no "precise meaning" and ended by saying that the
words were then "well understood." But there is a vast difference between a well understood meaning and a precise meaning. Words with well understood meanings are many; words
with precise meanings are rare. The failure of any person in
a group to volunteer an answer to a request for a precise definition of a word does not give rise to any inference that the word
has no well understood meaning.

Fuller's critics claimed that the phrase "direct tax" was an
economist's term and that each economist used it in a different

sense. This criticism is certainly sound if the phrase is only an economist's term. Economists have discovered that the burden of a tax rarely rests entirely on him who pays it. The burden of a tax on rents could be shifted to the tenant, and yet under Fuller's conception it was a direct tax. But as Justice Holmes put it many years later: What is a direct tax is determined by traditional usage and not by scientific consideration of shifting the burden. "Upon this point," Holmes said, "a page of history is worth a volume of logic."

I I I

The government, the dissenting Judges, and the subsequent critics claimed that the Court had overruled five prior decisions in declaring the law unconstitutional.

All of these cases rested upon the early case of *Hylton* v. *United States* [1] involving a federal tax on carriages imposed in 1794. This case was important because the constitutionality of the carriage tax was debated by congressmen, argued by lawyers, and decided by Justices, many of whom had taken part in adopting the Constitution.

In the Congress of 1794 Fuller showed that Sedgwick of Connecticut had stated that "taxes on land and on property and income generally" were direct taxes. But Sedgwick did not think that a federal tax on a specific item of luxury such as a carriage was a direct tax. Others took the same view, but Madison thought the carriage tax was unconstitutional because it was a direct tax and not apportioned to the states by population. Fisher Ames in reply suggested that the tax was not a direct tax but a "duty" on the "use" of the carriage. The act provided for a tax on carriages "which shall be kept by or for any person for his or her own use, or to be let out to hire. . . ."

The case for the constitutionality of the carriage tax was successfully argued in the Supreme Court by Hamilton. Fuller showed that in his argument Hamilton had admitted that "general assessments, whether on the whole property of indi-

[1] 1796, 3 Dall. 171.

viduals, or on their whole real or personal estate," were "direct" taxes. Hamilton also argued that in England a duty on carriages was an excise and said: "It is fair to seek the meaning of terms in the statutory language of that country from which our jurisprudence is derived." Fuller then noted that in England income taxes had always been classified by law as direct taxes.

In the opinions of each of the three Justices in the carriage tax case, Fuller found support for his conclusions.

Thus Justice Chase said that he was inclined to think, but of this he did not "give a judicial opinion," that only capitation taxes and taxes on lands were direct taxes. He sustained the carriage tax as an indirect tax: (1) by the example of Great Britain and (2) as a tax on expense "because a carriage is a consumable commodity; and such annual tax on it, is on the expense of the owner."

Fuller showed that Justice Paterson had stated that a tax on land was a direct tax. He said that it was not necessary to determine whether a tax on the produce of land was a direct tax, but "Land, independently of its produce, is of no value." Fortified by extracts from Adam Smith, he had sustained the carriage tax as a tax on "expense or consumption."

Justice Iredell, Fuller showed, had indicated that it was not necessary for the Court to determine what was a direct or indirect tax in all cases. "Some difficulties may occur," Iredell said, "which we do not at present foresee." It was sufficient, he said, to find that this carriage tax was not a direct tax. Fuller concluded: "It will be perceived that each of the Justices, while expressing doubt whether anything but a capitation tax or a tax on land was a direct tax within the meaning of the Constitution, distinctly avoided expressing an opinion upon that question or laying down a comprehensive definition but confined his opinion to the case before the court."

In answer to this argument, Justice White in his dissent showed that not only Congress and the Treasury Department but Kent, Story, Cooley, Miller and a host of other writers—

in fact practically everyone who had written on the subject—had cited the *Hylton* case as holding that only capitation taxes and taxes on land were direct taxes. The "suggestion of the Justices" in the *Hylton* case, White said, had been adopted in subsequent decisions of the Supreme Court. "It is too late now to destroy the force of the opinions in that case by qualifying them as mere *dicta* when they have again and again been expressly approved by this court."

The only case that was difficult for Fuller to distinguish was the case of *Springer* v. *United States* [1] holding the Civil War income tax not to be a direct tax but an excise or duty. However, no income from real estate was involved in that case. And Fuller deftly suggested that the case would be of more value as a precedent if it had referred to the difference between a tax on professional earnings and a tax on the income from personal property. A tax on professional earnings, he said, might be an excise or duty, and a tax on the income from securities might be a direct tax. Furthermore, the *Springer* case involved a war tax, and Fuller strongly implied that a peacetime tax stood on a different basis. It was the expectation of those who framed the Constitution, he said, that the federal government should raise its funds by "duties, imposts and excises" except in extraordinary emergencies. This expectation had been realized, he asserted, until August 15, 1894, when the present Act was passed.

Fuller denied any intention to overrule a single case. He scrupulously examined each case cited and distinguished each of them. "It is conceded in all these cases," he said, "that taxes on land are direct taxes, and in none of them is it determined that taxes on rents or income derived from land are not taxes on land."

If the Constitution had in so many words forbidden a tax on real estate without apportionment, he asked, could Congress impose an annual tax on the income from land? He quoted from *Coke upon Littleton* that a grant of the entire

[1] 1880, 102 U.S. 586.

profits of land conveyed the land: "For what is the land but the profits thereof." He concluded that a tax on the income from land was different only in form, not in substance, from a tax on land.

Let us turn now to the critics on this point. Corwin asserted that the words from Coke, "What is the land but the profits thereof?" had "about as much bearing on the matter at issue as a text from *Al Koran*." Justice White, with more pertinence, pointed out in his dissent that this quotation from Coke had been pressed on the Supreme Court without effect in *Pacific Insurance Co.* v. *Soule*,[1] one of the five cases that Fuller had distinguished as not decisive of the question at issue here. Justice White also suggested that the income tax, instead of being a "direct" tax on land, was doubly indirect: a tax on rent was only an indirect tax on land and a tax on income was only an indirect tax on rent.

But White was here using the term "indirect" in a loose, popular sense. Fuller had analyzed its traditional usage much more acutely. Fuller's opinion in this case was undoubtedly his greatest. Justice Gray immediately wrote him.

"Apr. 5/95

"DEAR CHIEF JUSTICE

"I have just read through your opinion, with the greatest pleasure and admiration. You must permit me to say that it deals with the subject in a manner worthy of the importance of the case, and of the Chief Justice of the United States.

"I cannot imagine a fitter or more felicitous form of laying the matter before the Judges tomorrow, and, whatever may be done then, I am sure the head and hand that framed it will find little to change, whether it stands as it is, or goes a little further. As to matters of detail, those can be considered hereafter.

"Very truly yours,

HORACE GRAY

The Chief Justice"

[1] 1868. 7 Wall. 433.

Brewer a few years later delivered an address on the income tax cases to the graduating class of the law department of the State University of Iowa. He predicted that this opinion of the Chief Justice would "in days to come . . . be classed among the great historic opinions of the court." Some of the graduates before him, Brewer suggested, would perhaps one day sit on the Supreme Court. "I can ask no higher glory for you," he said, "than that you write into the records of that court opinions equally majestic and immortal."

But the decision holding the income tax void only as to taxes on rents and on the income from state and municipal bonds was received with disappointment on all sides. It was not a clean-cut decision either way and created too much uncertainty. Southern newspapers in general applauded the dissenters (Harlan and White, both from the South) ; and northern newspapers, Republican and Democratic, commended the Justices of the majority.

An incident occurred in connection with this decision which had a peculiar effect on the writing of American history. Two days before the opinion was delivered, the Chicago *Tribune*, in a seven-column article, purported to tell the most intimate details of the arguments in the conference room and gave precisely what proved to be the ultimate result. The *Tribune* story had been so detailed that the Associated Press immediately sent out a summary of it from Chicago.

The *Tribune* stated that the Court had made great efforts to preserve the secrecy of its decision. "All the officials of the court were kept at arm's length, and pages and private secretaries were rigidly excluded from the consultation room, so that it was manifestly impossible for any of them to secure any information . . . except in the improbable contingency that some one of the Judges should talk in his sleep or leave papers lying around where stragglers might pick them up. . . . Contrary to the usual custom the decision was not at once sent to the Government Printing Office, although it finally reached that institution, where extraordinary precautions were at once taken to prevent its getting out."

The newspapers of the country cried out against this leak, and the Associated Press formally complained to the President about it. The story had been secured by Raymond Patterson, head of the *Tribune's* Washington bureau, who went to his grave without disclosing its source. There was evidence in the *Tribune* article itself, however, that the leak came from someone close to Justice Harlan. The *Tribune* story gave an entirely disproportionate amount of space to his individual view on a feature of the law which was barely mentioned in the opinions. But of course it would be easy for a reporter to throw blame on any Justice in that way and thus conceal the true source.

When the accuracy of the main portion of the *Tribune's* report was proved by the delivery of the opinions, most newspapers accepted the *Tribune's* story of the part played by individual Justices in the decision. In fact, the *Tribune* reported that many Washington correspondents merely sent out a telegram reading: "Chicago *Tribune* story all straight." The *Tribune* had said, "Justices Harlan, Brown, Shiras and White voted to sustain the law as a whole."

This statement was copied into many American newspapers and was the basis of the subsequent newspaper charge that Justice Shiras had switched his vote in the next hearing of the case. Almost every American historian has accepted this widely prevalent newspaper report. After denials that Shiras changed his vote, some historians have speculated at length on what other Justice shifted his position and selected one Justice or another as the "vacillating judge." As will appear in the next chapter, these speculations rest on no safe basis.

CHAPTER XVI

○‿○

THE INCOME TAX CASE
ON REHEARING

ONE week after the decision in the income tax case, the opponents of the tax filed a petition for rehearing of the questions on which the Court was evenly divided. To this petition the Attorney General responded that if a rehearing were granted it should cover all the questions involved. The rehearing was allowed, and on May 6 the case was reargued before a full bench.

There has been some speculation on the circumstances of Justice Jackson's return to the Court to hear this case. Since October, 1894, he had been absent from Washington and was known to be seriously ill—he died a few months after the final decision. The letters from Justice Jackson to the Chief Justice show how desperately ill Jackson was. They also show the pressure that was put on him to participate in this rehearing. The two dissenting Justices in the first *Pollock* decision (Harlan and White) were the only Justices from the South then sitting. Justice Jackson's residence was in Nashville, Tennessee. That city was also the home of Congressman Benton McMillin, who had introduced the Income Tax Law of 1894, had charge of the bill during its passage, and made the principal speech in support of it. No Southern senator had failed to vote for the tax. Local pressure was immediately put on Justice Jackson to resign so that a pro tax Justice could be appointed in his place. His attendance on the rehearing under these circumstances was almost the only alternative to his resignation.

Two months before the first decision, the Chief Justice had received the following letter from Justice Jackson's brother:

"BELLE MEADE
NASHVILLE, TENN.
Jany 28/95

"*Chief Justice Fuller*
"MY DEAR SIR

"I have just returned from a visit to my brother, Justice Jackson, at Thomasville, Ga. and regret to say that I found his condition much changed and for the worse. His lung affection [tuberculosis] has greatly improved and his diabetes trouble has almost disappeared but another and more serious disease has developed itself in the form of *Dropsy*. For several weeks past his liver has been affected—enlarging with inflammation—and is secreting water which is collecting in the lower bowels, legs and feet with considerable swelling of the parts. His local physician pronounces his present trouble *dropsy* and says he will probably have to be tapped both in the bowels and legs. He is further of the opinion that the disease will progress and that Justice Jackson will never be able to resume his official duties on the bench. Under these distressing circumstances and conditions it has occurred to me that Justice Jackson should be retired if it can be done. He feels it to be his duty to retire from the bench, but this ought not to be done, in my opinion, without giving him his salary. Since he has served the government faithfully on the Circuit & Supreme benches for nearly eight years,[1] I think, and his health has been shattered we have a precedent in the case of Justice Hunt whose health gave way while he was on the Supreme bench and he was retired on full salary.

"Justice Jackson has no income outside of his salary. His wife has valuable real estate near Nashville but it yields little or no income. It is a constant source of worry to him that he

---

[1] After ten years' service, on attaining the age of seventy a Justice could retire on full salary.

is unable to resume his duties on the bench. For him to retire without his salary annuity would hardly be just I think. I write to you on the subject of his retirement because of his admiration and friendship for yourself. Will you think the matter over and if you deem it proper confer with the President and Attorney General and give me your suggestions in the matter.

"You are at liberty to make such use of this letter as you may deem proper.

"With high respect & my kind regards,

Yours Very Truly,

W. H. Jackson"

On receipt of this letter Fuller conferred with his associates. All of the Justices agreed that nothing should be done, because, as Fuller wrote the Attorney General, other letters seemed to show that the "end" was very near. However, a bill was introduced in the Senate for Justice Jackson's retirement on full salary.

Three weeks later Justice Jackson wrote to the Chief Justice:

"NASHVILLE, TENN.
Feby 21/95

"DEAR CHIEF JUSTICE

"My dropsical condition has improved considerably during the past few days and my Physicians encourage me to hope that it can and will be ultimately relieved without further resort to tapping. I am gaining strength gradually and am able to walk about the house a little. Altogether the outlook is not so discouraging as when I wrote you last and I have for the present abandoned the idea of retiring from the bench and will await developments as you and the Brethren have so kindly suggested. I have accordingly requested that no further action should be taken on the bill for my retirement which my brother caused to be introduced in the Senate when he considered my condition hopeless. (Such was the opinion of Several Eminent Physicians.) While I am trying to cultivate a spirit of resignation to the Will of Him who knows all things and does all things well even though that Will should be that my judicial career and life should close, still I shall hope and pray that my health & strength may be so far restored as to enable me at no distant day to resume my judicial labors and have my share of the Bench's work.

"I have recently received from the Commissioner of Internal Revenue or one of his deputies a circular calling for report as to my *income* for 1894 under the Income Tax Act.

"Does that Act include our salary as members of the Supreme Court? Under the Constitutional provision that the salary shall not be reduced during the term of office can the salary or any portion thereof be taxed? It seems to me that it cannot. That Congress cannot do indirectly what it is prohibited from doing directly. What is your view and that of the members of the Court on this subject?

With kindest regards & best wishes, I remain

Yours truly,

HOWELL E. JACKSON"

On the day that the first decision in the Income tax case was rendered (but before he knew of it), Jackson wrote the Chief Justice:

"NASHVILLE, TENN.
April 8/95

"DEAR CHIEF JUSTICE

"Your kind note of recent date came duly to hand and as I am feeling pretty fresh today I answer it in person. I feel very hopeful of being able to resume the duties of the Bench by next fall. While I am still weak and very much reduced in flesh my Physicians express great confidence in my restoration to health. They were out to see and examine me yesterday and professed to see steady and satisfactory improvement in my condition. I regret missing the Income Tax Argument and the conference on the questions involved. In thinking over the subject I have reached the conclusion that the law would be partially sustained and partially declared unconstitutional by the Court.[1] And I am consequently awaiting the announcement of the decision with much interest. . . .

"With best regards and best wishes,

Sincerely yours,

HOWELL E. JACKSON"

The day after this letter was written, the Nashville newspapers contained long reports of the first decision in the *Pollock* case. The Nashville *American* concluded seven columns of these reports with the statement: "It is universally regretted that there was not a full bench to hear the case and should Justice Jackson resign there is good reason to believe his successor would almost certainly be favorable to the law." The *Morning News* of Savannah, Georgia, said that the situation would probably hasten the resignation of Justice Jackson. The editorial said: "Congress at the last session ought to have passed the bill that was proposed for his retirement. It doubtless would have acted in the matter if there had been the remotest expectation of a divided court on the income tax law."

Such statements as these almost compelled Jackson either to resign or participate in the rehearing. A few days later, he wrote the Chief Justice:

"AT HOME

April 15/95

"DEAR CHIEF JUSTICE

"I see from the newspapers that a rehearing has or will be asked for in the Income Tax Cases. If such an application is made and granted as to the questions undisposed of by the recent decision and it is the wish of the court to have the matter disposed of at the present term I will make the effort to come to Washington & participate in the rehearing which could be

[1] The completeness of Jackson's about-face from the point of view indicated in this correspondence is shown by the fact that he was said to have been the only Justice on the reargument who did not agree that the tax was void as to income from state and municipal bonds. See Whitney, "The Income Tax and the Constitution," 20 *Harvard Law Review,* pp. 280, 286–287, note 3.

set for some day early in May. I think I could stand the trip without any serious backset and after getting there could with safety sit in the rehearing and take part in the conference. It seems highly important that the whole matter should be finally and speedily settled. Its settlement now will prevent much embarrassment and prevent a multitude of suits. I feel that I should make the effort to secure a speedy disposition of a matter of such importance. I am still improving slowly in strength and regaining my flesh gradually.

"With kindest regards, I remain

Sincerely yours,

HOWELL E. JACKSON"

On April 20, Jackson again wrote the Chief Justice: ". . . I will at once act upon your suggestion & consult my Physician as to whether I can come on without any serious risk. Will see him tomorrow (Sunday) morning & telegraph you. Either the 6th or 13th of May will suit my convenience. . . . Send me your opinion whenever it is ready."

On the following day Jackson telegraphed: "My Doctor says I can go on without risk. I prefer to hear the oral arguments."

On April 26, 1895, Justice Jackson wrote to Fuller: "Your letter extending an invitation to stop with you while in Washington is received and highly appreciated. We will however have to decline your invitation as we will be accompanied by our Niece and her husband and Mrs. Jackson thinks we should not separate from them. I expect to reach Washington on the Morning of the 5th (Sunday). I rec'd copy of your opinion yesterday & read it with great interest and pleasure."

Commencing on May 6, the case was again strenuously argued for three days. During the argument the Chief Justice called counsel's attention to a side-light upon the *Hylton* case which had not previously been mentioned. His letter to the Reporter a week later gave this comment in detail.

Fuller had found in Tucker's Blackstone a statement by Judge Tucker that John Marshall had argued the constitutionality of the carriage tax against Hamilton. "Each of these gentlemen," Tucker said, "was supposed to have defended his own private opinion" in the case. "Judge Tucker," Fuller said, "was undoubtedly acquainted with the opinion of Chief Justice Marshall upon the particular subject." If John Marshall thought that even the carriage tax was a direct tax, then it was clear that he would also have thought that an income tax was such.

Two weeks after the argument the Chief Justice again delivered the opinion of the Court holding the law unconstitutional not only as to taxes on income derived from state and municipal bonds and real estate but also as to taxes on income derived from personal property. Furthermore, the Court held that since the Act was invalid in its greater part, Congress would not have passed the law in its mutilated form and declared the whole law void.

The opinion of the Chief Justice followed his first opinion, but his points were somewhat sharpened. He said that if changes in the wealth of the states had made the rule of apportionment operate unequally, it was an inequality demanded and agreed to as a condition of the formation of the Union. In the same way the equal representation of the states, however small, in the Senate was demanded and agreed to. "The Constitution ordains affirmatively," Fuller said, "that each State shall have two members of that body, and negatively that no State shall by amendment be deprived of its equal suffrage in the Senate without its consent. The Constitution ordains affirmatively that representatives and direct taxes shall be apportioned among the several States according to numbers, and negatively that no direct tax shall be laid unless in proportion to the enumeration."

But he pointed out that these latter clauses were open to amendment, and that if the federal government ought to have the power to impose income taxes the only just procedure would be to propose a constitutional amendment which would give time for "the sober second thought of every part of the country to be asserted." Eighteen years later this suggested amendment to the Constitution was adopted.

He answered the contention that the income tax was not a tax upon property at all, but a tax upon spending power as shown by a taxpayer's revenue for the year preceding—in other words a tax on money-in-pocket from whatever source derived. He pointed out that the Court had unanimously held the present tax void as to income from state and municipal bonds, but that the money-in-pocket theory would apply equally to such income. However, Justice White, when he agreed that the tax on income derived from such bonds was unconstitutional, had anticipated this argument. White had said: "In the one case [income from land], there is full power in the Federal government to tax, the only controversy being whether the tax imposed is direct or indirect; while in the other [tax on state bonds] there is no power whatever in the Federal government, and, therefore, the levy, whether direct or indirect is beyond the taxing power."

On the division of the Court after the rehearing, Justices Jackson and Brown joined with Justices Harlan and White (the original dissenters) so that the decision was five to four. The line of cleavage on the Court was in strict accord with the wealth per capita of the states in which the Justices resided as shown by the census of 1890:

AGAINST CONSTITUTIONALITY OF THE TAX		
Justice	State	Wealth Per Capita by census 1890
Fuller	Illinois	$1,324
Field	California	2,097
Gray	Massachusetts	1,252
Brewer	Kansas	1,261
Shiras	Pennsylvania	1,177
FOR CONSTITUTIONALITY OF THE TAX		
Harlan	Kentucky	$ 631
Brown	Michigan	1,001
Jackson	Tennessee	502
White	Louisiana	443

In view of the exemption of $4,000, it is clear that almost no part of this tax would have been collected in the home state of any of the dissenting Justices. The vote on the Court was thus on the same lines as the vote in Congress.

All of the dissenting Justices were from the South except Justice Brown, who came from Michigan, then an agricultural state. Brown voted against the constitutionality of the tax in the first decision and in favor of its validity in the second decision. By his own statement Justice Brown owed his seat on the Court entirely to Justice Jackson.[1] The importunities of Jackson, who was near death and was being shamefully treated by the demands for his resignation, would have been hard for any friend to resist. In Brown's dissent in the second case he quoted the foregoing figures of the wealth per capita in certain states (but not in Michigan) in an effort to show the unfairness of any apportionment of direct taxes by population to the states. Suppose, he said, the United States wished to raise the equivalent of $1 from each inhabitant. Suppose the assessment had to be apportioned to the states according to population. Massachusetts has a per capita wealth of $1,252; South Carolina, a per capita wealth of $348. "Assuming that the same amount of property in each State represents a corresponding amount of income, each inhabitant of South Carolina would pay in proportion to his means three and one-half times as much as each inhabitant of Massachusetts." These figures had apparently been pressed upon Brown to induce him to change his mind. The relatively low per capita wealth of Michigan could hardly have been omitted in the arguments made to him.

In America no argument inspires more heat than a sectional controversy. Justice Harlan delivered an extemporaneous dissent in which he banged his fist on his desk and glared at the Chief Justice. The *Nation* said: "Remembering . . . that it was to the Southern members mainly that we owed the insertion of the income tax in the tariff-reform bill, it is not sur-

[1] See Chapter XIV, p. 180–181.

prising that of the four judges who stood by the tax three should be Southerners. Nor is it surprising, remembering Justice Harlan's antecedents, that he should have made himself their mouthpiece in the most violent political tirade ever heard in a court of last resort." All of the dissents were heated. Some of Justice Brown's language ill comported with his concurrence with the majority only a month before. He hoped, he said, that the decision might not be the first step in submerging the "liberties of the people in a sordid despotism of wealth."

But not all of the heat was on the side of the dissenters, although no trace of warmth was perceptible in either of the Chief Justice's opinions. In the first decision, Justice Field delivered a concurring opinion in which he said that, while he agreed with the majority, he would go further and hold the entire law unconstitutional because of the many breaches of uniformity in the imposition of the tax. In conclusion Field said: "The present assault upon capital is but the beginning. It will be but the stepping stone to others, larger and more sweeping, till our political contests will become a war of the poor against the rich; a war constantly growing in intensity and bitterness." He predicted that our national decadence would inevitably follow from such a war.

The intensity of Field's feeling in the case is displayed in a letter which he wrote to the Chief Justice three days before the final opinions were delivered:

"May 17, 1895

"My dear Chief Justice:

"I had an experience last evening which nearly brought me to the close of my career, and I mention it to you simply to make a suggestion that it might be well, considering my condition, that the decision of the Income Tax case be announced as soon as practicable.

"I had been advised by some friends to try an injection of carbolic acid into my knee joint, upon the idea that it would remove the possible cause of the continued severity of the internal pain. I yielded to the suggestion and received an injection of carbolic acid but the result was anything but pleasant. There followed from it a pain that was perfectly uncontrollable, and lasted for some hours. Indeed, the paroxysms of pain were so great, that I thought for some time that I should not be able to survive them; and what gave me additional pain was the thought that if I did not survive, our action in reference to the Income Tax cases would be entirely defeated. I however am this morning relieved from the pain to a very considerable extent; and I trust that I shall not be weak enough to yield to any more experiments with my knee joint. But the experience of last night has taught me, that I have no fair assurance of continued life, and the consequences that might follow from my yielding to one of these paroxysms of pain, to which I may be subjected, has led me to venture the suggestion that, as soon as possible, the decision be announced by the court. This, I suppose, of course cannot be before Monday, but I suggest that it be announced on that day, even if further time be taken to complete the opinion which you may wish to write. My hold upon life is too slight for me to trust, with any reasonable assurance, to the certain continuance of it beyond a day.

"I am

Very sincerely yours,

Stephen J. Field

To the Chief Justice
of the United States"

It will be noted that the strength of feeling of the Justices in this case was roughly in proportion to the wealth per capita of their states. Thus Field, from California, the state with the highest wealth per capita, felt the strongest against the tax; and White, from Louisiana, the state with the lowest wealth per capita, felt the strongest for it. The range of fervor among the other Justices fairly approximates the position of each

Justice's state in the scale with Brown, whose state was in the middle area, fluctuating from one side to the other.

As soon as the final decision was announced, the pro-tax newspapers charged that one of the Justices, who had been originally pro-tax, had switched to the other side. From the viewpoint of these partisans such a man was a turncoat, an apostate, and a renegade. On the basis of the Chicago *Tribune* scoop, described in Chapter XV,[1] Justice Shiras was selected by rumor as the guilty Justice and great obloquy was heaped upon him. Thus Myers in his *History of the Supreme Court* wrote:

> When the final vote was taken, it turned out that one Justice had changed his mind, "over night" and arrayed himself against the income tax. This Justice was said to be Shiras who, as we have seen, came from the same State as Senator Quay, and who had been counsel at Pittsburg for the Baltimore and Ohio Railroad system. The pro-income tax newspapers freely stated that the vacillating Justice was Shiras, and denounced him. This tergiversation caused a very consequential sensation, and was bitterly commented upon in the speeches and declarations of supporters of the income tax.

Myers was a frank Marxist and his history is a confessed effort to tear down the Court as the alleged bulwark of "capitalism," in the "conflict of classes." His book is full of errors of fact which no one has ever dignified by refuting. But other critics of this decision have followed Myers in his analysis and even sometimes in his language.

Thus Professor E. S. Corwin, under the caption "The Mystery of the Vacillating Jurist," stated that for many years it was supposed that the "backslider" was Justice Shiras, but that denials from three sources that Shiras changed his vote in the case have raised a doubt. Professor Sidney Ratner, under the headline "The Mystery of the Vacillating Judge," stated that a rigorous analysis of the evidence proved that Shiras was not the Justice who shifted.

---

[1] The *Tribune* had said, "Justices Harlan, Brown, Shiras and White, voted to sustain the law as a whole." This statement only meant that these Justices were not in favor of declaring the whole law invalid because of the unconstitutional tax on the income from land.

However, Corwin argued at length that Ratner was wrong in selecting Brewer as the vacillating Judge. Brewer, Corwin said, was fanatical against Communism and therefore must have been against the income tax. "Even as early as 1883," Corwin wrote, "we find Brewer sounding the alarm against Communism in an address called 'The Scholar in Politics'; and ten years later he is in full cry against . . . 'the fiend, fool or fanatic' who would support these 'assassins of liberty.' "

Gray was chosen by Corwin as the true vacillating Justice because he was a "very learned man . . . whose final presence among the Justices opposed to the act is certainly something which requires to be explained on its own account." Gray, Corwin said, was a "great precedent judge, whereas the Pollock Case played 'ducks and drakes' with the precedents." "Finally," Corwin concluded, "it is the tradition of the Court that Gray was the Justice who changed his mind, *a fact which I have from first hand sources*."

This last statement was too much for Ratner. He abandoned his espousal of Brewer as the "vacillating Judge" and said, "Professor Edward S. Corwin has been able to demonstrate that Justice Gray was the man." Gray, Ratner said, was a radical free-soiler when he was a young man and became a strong nationalist on the Court. "These facts and his great respect for precedent undoubtedly influenced him to uphold the constitutionality of the 1894 income tax law on most points at the first hearing."

However, Gray's letter to Fuller on reading the Chief Justice's opinion in the first case makes such a suggestion impossible.[1] Justice Gray certainly was not in favor of upholding the constitutionality of the law at the first hearing, as stated by Ratner and Corwin. Even "the tradition of the Court," if received at first hand, could not prevail against Gray's letter to the contrary.

---

[1] *Supra*, Chap. XV, p. 204, Gray's letter was written on Friday, April 5. The Chicago *Tribune* of Saturday, April 6, reported that Fuller's opinion was delivered to the other Justices on the evening of Friday, April 5. The opinion was adopted by the Court on Saturday, April 6, and delivered on Monday, April 8, 1895.

Furthermore, it seems very doubtful whether there was any vacillating Justice except Justice Brown in the sense in which these critics use the term. The supposition that there was such a Judge is based on the Chicago *Tribune* story, from an undercover source, that Justice Shiras was in favor of sustaining the law as a whole at the time of the first decision. If correct, this statement meant that he did not think that the Court's conclusion (in which he concurred) that the law was invalid as to income from land made the remainder of the law void. Apparently his position then was that to hold the entire law void, the tax on the income from personal property should first be annulled. Such was eventually his recorded judgment. If the Chicago *Tribune* scoop was correct, Shiras, instead of vacillating, forced the Court to come to his position. Gray indicated in his letter to the Chief Justice that he was not averse to having Fuller's first opinion "go a little further." Apparently, therefore, he was then in favor of holding the entire law void on the basis of the invalidity of the tax on income from land. Perhaps Gray was not then in favor of invalidating the tax on income from personal property but preferred to reach the same result by another path. His change, if any, was only a change of route to a result which he had strenuously advocated from the first.

It has been the practice of the Supreme Court from the beginning not to make known the alignment of the Justices on an equally divided court. Such cases are frequently reargued before a full Court, and the divulgence of the prior vote would prejudice the reargument. After a decision on reargument the disclosure of the individual Justices on the prior equal division would weaken the force of the final decision, and such revelation has therefore never been made. Nevertheless, Corwin and Ratner decried the court for not designating by name the supposed "vacillating Justice." Corwin said: "It is the secretiveness, not to say furtiveness of the manoeuvre, which has added another heavy count against the court's disposal of this case."

It seems clear that the subsequent criticism of the decision is not entirely disinterested. There are legitimate arguments against the Court's decision, ably expressed by Justice White in his dissent in the first *Pollock* case. But the subsequent disparagement of the Chief Justice and the Court is not justifiable. The decision cannot be used, as these critics attempt to use it, to picture the Court as the partisan of the rich. On the Court, as in Congress, the income tax was a sectional controversy. The case merely emphasizes the value of the American tradition that a fair geographical distribution should be preserved among the Justices of the Supreme Court.

Fuller's opinions in the income tax case again display his daring. A timid man would have followed the trend of the Court's prior decisions and the comments of the text writers. Fuller's opinions in this case also evidence his influence on the Court in securing a majority for so revolutionary a decision. They reveal his courage and independence, as Attorney General Olney said on Fuller's death, in deciding so important a case against the Cleveland administration. They demonstrate his capacity for scholarly research. They manifest also his New England conservatism in his insistence on a "sober second thought," through a constitutional amendment, as to whether the whole country really wanted such a tax. On this issue of policy he expressed not the slightest intimation of his views.

CHAPTER XVII

SENILITY ON THE COURT

1897–1902

SENILITY strikes hardest at men of strong personality. Age intensifies a man's principal characteristics; and, when such expansion is accompanied by a failure of mental powers, the situation is difficult for those who must collaborate with a man so stricken. Fuller's gentle and kindly but firm and effective handling of this problem on the Court is a model for future Chief Justices.

In the early nineties Justice Field's mind began to fail, but his independence and irascibility did not abate as his mental powers waned. As early as 1892, Justice Gray in returning certain opinions of the Chief Justice with, as Gray said, only a "little criticism," added: "I wish I could say the same of Brother Field's who seems this term to be behaving more like a wild bull than before."

Field soon had difficulty, even in simple cases, in writing opinions that would receive the approval of his brethren, and he had to revise them again and again. The last case in which he wrote the opinion of the Court was *Telfener* v. *Russ*,[1] involving a Texas land contract. He sent the opinion to the Chief Justice after many such revisions, stating that he had now included every material fact and every provision of the statute involved in the case. "I hope," he concluded, "it will prove satisfactory to you and wind up the case." Although the opinion was still in deplorable shape, he was allowed to read it

[1] 1896, 162 U.S. 170; on rehearing 163 U.S. 100. Doubtless this case was assigned to Field because he had rendered an opinion several years before in the same case, *Telfener* v. *Russ*, 1892, 145 U.S. 522.

from the bench a few days later. But petitions for rehearing were filed, and the Court reluctantly concluded that they must be granted. Field then wrote to Fuller that he was leaving for California. "There is nothing to detain me," he said, "as the only case in which I was deeply interested (the *Telfener* case) has been held up. . . . It seems to me that there are members of the Court who will not allow that case to be considered if possible ever again." However, Field was permitted to read another weak opinion correcting his prior opinion and denying the rehearing.

The *Telfener* case was probably the subject of an incident which Walter Wellman reported in the Chicago *Times-Herald* after Field's retirement. Wellman's story was that in this period Fuller sent two of the Justices to Field's home to discuss a certain case with him. They found him in an unusually lethargic condition. "He sat in a big armchair, his head bowed down upon his breast and his eyes closed. It was with difficulty that he recognized the callers and exchanged a few words with them. Then his eyes closed again.

"Finally one of the visitors took from his pocket some memoranda he had prepared on the case. . . . He asked permission to read this to Justice Field and taking silence as consent proceeded to read aloud." For a time Field's head lay still upon his breast. Finally he opened his eyes, and it seemed as though the legal phrases had "at last roused his sleeping brain to activity."

"Read that again," he commanded.

When it had again been read, he said:

"That is not right. That is not good law. You err when you say so and so."

"And then Mr. Field, now thoroughly roused, delivered an argument which for depth, clearness and force astonished both his listeners. This done he relapsed into his former comatose condition." Such flashes of lucidity are, of course, a common experience with senility.

The Chief Justice assigned no more cases to Field for opinions. The assignments to him had been declining for years. When he was in his full powers, he had written twenty-five to thirty opinions a year; but in the 1893 term he delivered only 9; in the 1894 term, only 6; and in the 1895 term, only 4, including the two opinions in the *Telfener* case.

After each Saturday conference the Chief Justice sent out a printed slip designating the cases assigned to each Justice for opinions. In 1896, on receipt of such a weekly slip, assigning one case to each of six Justices with blanks after the names of Field and two others, Field wrote to Fuller: "I return to you the enclosed memorandum of the cases assigned to the different Justices made yesterday. I do not care to retain any memorandum of assignment of cases where none are assigned to myself. I do not know and shall not ask the reason that no cases have been assigned to me within the past six months."

After discussion, the Justices deputized Justice Harlan to suggest to Justice Field that he should resign. He had a right to retire under the law and continue to draw his full salary. Harlan approached him in the robing room, where he was sitting on a settee with his head bowed, apparently oblivious of his surroundings. Harlan had difficulty in rousing him and finally asked Field if he remembered the occasion when Field had been a member of a committee to suggest to Justice Grier that he ought to resign. At this Field sat up, his eyes blazing, "Yes, and a dirtier day's work I never did in my life," he cried out. Harlan retired without effecting his purpose.

Finally, in the spring of 1897, Justice Field's brother, the Reverend Henry Field, a distinguished clergyman, came to Washington and persuaded the Justice to resign. Apparently Henry Field acted at the instigation of the Chief Justice and Justice Brewer, Field's nephew; at any rate, Henry Field delivered the resignation to Fuller and Brewer for presentation to the President. Justice Field was anxious that his resignation should not take effect until after August 16, 1897, several months later, because on that date he would equal the length of service of Chief Justice Marshall and would thereby surpass in the length of his service any other Justice in the history of the Court.

On May 3, 1897, Field wrote to Fuller:

"MY DEAR CHIEF JUSTICE:

"My brother Henry called upon you yesterday, as he informed me, and handed you my resignation differing in some few exceptions from the one previously handed you; and he remarked to me, as I understood him, that you stated to him that you and Justice Brewer would look the matter over and arrange it satisfactorily. My brother left this morning for New York.

"On last evening I told him that I would be glad if he would drop you & Judge Brewer a line stating that whatever you and Judge Brewer agreed upon as to form, terms and manner of the resignation would be entirely satisfactory to me. He left this morning without writing to you to this effect as he intended. I therefore wish to convey to you the sentiment which I told him he might express to you. I shall be entirely content to abide by whatever you and Judge Brewer may decide to do in the premises and will give you my thanks in advance.

"I am

with profound respect,
very sincerely yours,
STEPHEN J. FIELD" [1]

Fuller and Brewer lost no time in presenting the resignation to the President before Field could change his mind. The day after the foregoing letter, Fuller responded:

"DEAR MR. JUSTICE FIELD:

"I received your communication yesterday and today Justice Brewer & myself concluded, after carefully considering the matter, that your letter of resignation in which you fixed De-

---

[1] Genet papers. Only the signature is in Field's handwriting.

cember 1 as the date of its taking effect was much to be preferred to the other, both with respect to expression and as to the date in view of the assembling of Congress.

"Accordingly we have just delivered it to the President with whom we had a very pleasant and agreeable interview. Neither the President nor ourselves will give publicity to the fact.

"With kind regards and sincere hope that you may be spared for many years to come, I am dear Mr. Justice

Very sincerely yours,

MELVILLE W. FULLER"

But Field would not stay resigned. In August, Brewer wrote the Chief Justice: "I have . . . received a letter from Uncle Henry in which he says he has just returned from a visit to Uncle Stephen & that the latter is so much better physically that he talks of another year's work on the bench, intimated that you wish it, & expects me to insist upon it as a personal matter. Uncle Henry wishes me to write to the Judge, but I do not propose to do so. I can do more by talking to him when the time demands it. You may hear from the Judge on the matter—I did think of writing to the President & stating the situation & suggesting that he write to the Judge accepting the resignation, complimenting him on his long service & expressing a desire to consult with him about his successor. A little flattery like this might prevent any attempt to withdraw his resignation or any feeling of bitterness at retiring. Perhaps however the less said or done the better. It may only call his attention to the matter & suggest the doing of that which ought not to be done."

As soon as Fuller returned to Washington, he wrote to Mrs. Fuller: "Judge Field bothers me a good deal. I am going to see him this afternoon. He is physically better and that is all that can be said."

In October, however, on the opening of the 1897 term, Field's resignation was announced by an exchange of letters between him and the remaining Justices. On December 1, 1897, when his resignation took effect, he had served thirty-four years and seven months—a term, as he pointed out, longer than that of any of his predecessors. He had been appointed by President Lincoln; and one of his early associates on the bench had been Justice Wayne, who had sat with Chief Justice Marshall, who was appointed in 1801—thus, Field said, "binding into unity nearly an entire century of the life of this court." Field's farewell letter gives no indication of any mental difficulty, but the reason is apparent from Fuller's papers.

On October 4, Harlan had written to Fuller: "I called last week to see Justice Field and in the course of the conversation he said that he talked with you & that he was preparing a letter to the court. He expressed a wish that I should see it when prepared & make suggestions.

"I supposed that would be the last of the matter. But this morning he sent for me & read what he had prepared, most of it in print. He finally pressed for suggestions when I said to him that in my judgment it was too long & had too many references to his own opinions. As it is it will not do at all. Having said that he had consulted yourself and Brewer about his letter to the President, I advised him to consult you two & take your judgment. If he brings to you the letter he read to me it will be seen at once that it will not do. I spoke frankly to him in order to make your work the easier. He does not know that you and I talked." It is clear that Fuller followed Harlan's suggestion, because his papers contain several sheets, with many interlineations, of a draft in Fuller's handwriting of Field's published letter of farewell.

The newspapers that announced Field's resignation also stated that his successor would be Joseph McKenna, who was then Attorney General. McKenna was born in Philadelphia of Irish parents in 1843. When he was eleven, his family moved to California. Educated in Catholic schools there, he was admitted to the bar in 1865, and immediately turned to politics. After service as county attorney and in the state legislature, he was elected to Congress, where he became a member of the

Ways and Means Committee of the House of Representatives and formed a fast friendship with its chairman, William McKinley. President Harrison had appointed McKenna to the United States Circuit Court in California, where he had served for five years when he resigned to become Attorney General in President McKinley's Cabinet. His appointment to the Cabinet was made, according to rumor, to scotch the story that McKinley was friendly to the American Protective Association, the anti-Catholic society of that period. McKenna had objected to giving up his life position on the federal bench for a Cabinet post because of his lack of financial means to maintain his family in Washington. He had been promised, according to the newspapers, the first vacancy that occurred on the Supreme Court.

A month before the official announcement of Field's impending retirement, the Chief Justice received a letter from Charles B. Bellinger, the United States District Judge in Oregon, protesting against the appointment of McKenna. "I know the estimate," Judge Bellinger wrote, "in which the Attorney General is held by the Judges who were associated with him in the Circuit Court of Appeals in this circuit and what is said of his qualifications among lawyers who practiced before him. He had no standing at the Bar at the time he was appointed Circuit Judge. He had never been connected with an important case nor appeared in any Federal Court, nor, as I am informed, in the Supreme Court of the State. He was without legal training, or knowledge or acquaintance with the literature of the law. Nor did he develop any of the qualities required by his office of Judge during the time he held it. His associates in the Circuit Court of Appeals were under the necessity of revising his opinions and correcting his syntax and mistakes of grammar. I believe that such portions of his opinions as did not require correction will be found to have been taken mainly from the briefs of counsel. His capacity for work is shown in his record as Judge. When he retired from the bench he left more than thirty cases undecided that had been taken under advisement by him, and these reached back over a period of some two and a half years.

". . . It is extremely unpleasant for me to say these things of Judge McKenna. My limited personal acquaintance with him is a pleasant one. He is an agreeable and, I believe kindly disposed man. I would rather do him a service than otherwise. I only regret that he lacks the qualifications to be a Justice on the Supreme Bench. It is beyond my comprehension how such a man can wish for such a place."

The Chief Justice immediately made an investigation which appeared to confirm the statements made in Judge Bellinger's letter and resulted in a similar letter to the Chief Justice from C. H. Hanford of Seattle, the United States District Judge in Washington. Judge Hanford, who was a Republican, wrote: "My relations with Judge McKenna have always been pleasant and I bear no animosity toward him, but his unfitness for a judicial office is glaring and well known to the judges and lawyers of the ninth circuit."

It was clearly the duty of the Chief Justice to bring these letters to the attention of President McKinley, and there is evidence that he did so. On the day that McKinley nominated McKenna to the Supreme Court, the President's Secretary wrote the Chief Justice: "Will you please call here at your convenience to talk with the President about a matter which he wishes to explain to you personally?" Probably the President told the Chief Justice that he had promised the Attorney General the position and could not recant. McKenna was confirmed a month later after violent opposition, during which these letters were aired. Naturally he never became a very strong Judge: his associates always felt in him some judicial inadequacy. But he had the good sense to attach himself to his coreligionist White. McKenna usually voted with White when the Court divided. And McKenna was honest and courageous, and the great valley of his lack of education and experience was gradually filled up to some extent. Fuller took care to assign to him the simpler cases, and their relations were satisfactory, though they were never very close.

The Chief Justice had hardly solved the embarrassments arising from Justice Field's condition when he was confronted with another situation of the same sort. The subject was John Chandler Bancroft Davis, the Reporter of the Court.

Davis had been born in Massachusetts in 1822. His mother was a sister of George Bancroft, the great historian, and he was thus a remote relative of the Chief Justice. After attending Harvard, Davis had practiced law in New York and then served for several years as Assistant Secretary of State. He had achieved distinction as the American agent in the arbitration of the *Alabama* claims between the United States and Great Britain. Following his success in that effort, he became Minister to Germany, succeeding his uncle, George Bancroft. He was serving as a Judge of the United States Court of Claims when in 1883 he was appointed Reporter of the Supreme Court under Chief Justice Waite.

Doubtless because he had previously held such eminent positions, Davis always assumed a rather condescending attitude toward his work as Reporter and toward the Justices of the Court. The Bancroft-Davis papers in the Library of Congress are replete with letters of correction from various Justices to the Reporter. Frequently he failed to make the suggested corrections and grew heated toward those who requested them. In such cases the Chief Justice in his early years assumed a mollifying attitude. Thus in 1891, apparently in response to an angry telegram from Davis, Fuller wrote: "My dear Kinsman: I shall feel deeply grieved if my returning the proofs this morning worried you in the least degree as your telegram made me suppose. I know what is due to people who are ill." Later, however, Fuller spoke quite firmly to Davis. In 1896, in sending a correction to him, Fuller wrote, "I have called your attention to this before." However, they remained fast friends.

They were both active in St. John's Episcopal Church in Washington, and much of their correspondence related to this subject.

As Davis approached eighty years of age in the late nineties, the loftiness of his condescension increased as his mental capacity to do his work diminished. Once he wrote to the Chief Justice: "There is too much dissent on the Court. It weakens its authority." This revelation from a subordinate on a subject which had been the Chief Justice's main concern for many years would have irritated a less tolerant man than Fuller. In another case Davis wrote in a headnote: "The Reporter feels himself unable to prepare a headnote which would convey an adequate and just account of the opinion and decision of the Court." Many a Reporter must have felt a similar frustration, but to surrender to it in print was hardly respectful to the Court.

Again, in a tariff case, the issue was whether certain glass beads were taxable at 60 per cent as articles of thin blown glass or at 10 per cent as imitations of precious stones. The Court held them dutiable at 60 per cent under the statutory provision that an article should be taxed at the higher rate when it fell within two categories under the tariff law. Davis, however, copied into his headnote a confusing paragraph from McKenna's opinion. McKenna had a habit of asking rhetorical questions in his opinions, and the paragraph which the Reporter reproduced as a headnote contained five of these questions. It read as follows:

It was impossible to have in contemplation glass beads, loose, unthreaded and unstrung (445), and not have the exact opposite in contemplation—beads not loose, beads threaded and strung and made provision for them. What provision? Were they to be dutiable at the same or at a higher rate than beads unthreaded or unstrung? If at the same rate—if all beads were to be dutiable at the same rate, why have qualified any of them? Were some to be dutiable at one rate and some at another rate? If made of plain glass, were they to be dutiable at sixty per centum under paragraph 108; if tinted or made to the color of some precious stones, were they to be dutiable at ten per centum under paragraph 454?

It is difficult to resist the conclusion that the Reporter was making sport of the opinion.

Many of Davis's headnotes were so vague that they gave no impression of the decision of the Court and sometimes they were quite misleading. The *Harvard Law Review* sharply criticized one of his headnotes on this score.

In 1900 Davis was seventy-eight, but Fuller wrote that he looked and behaved like a much older man. "He no longer," Fuller wrote, "comes in duty to the Court as he formerly did and in some ways—perhaps particularly in his headnotes, which is the chief point—exhibits failing powers. . . . Signs of restiveness on the part of some of the brethren are plainly evident."

The situation finally grew intolerable to the Justices, and they pressed the Chief Justice to secure Davis's resignation. Fuller's letter, in doing so, displays not only his sensitivity and delicacy but his firmness and effectiveness. Never was a demand for a resignation more tactfully phrased. He wrote the Reporter:

"As the vacation draws to its close, I feel constrained as a matter of duty, and of friendship to communicate with you in respect to the subject of our interview June 3d, the day after the adjournment of the Court. You then expressed the wish to retain the Reportership for another term so that your occupancy of the position might exceed that of Mr. Howard.

"Now some year and a half ago the members of the Court were given to understand that you would retire after October Term, 1901, and the subject is certain to come up as soon as the Court reconvenes.

"I have seen only two of my colleagues since Court rose, and have not sought to consult the others by correspondence. When we get together the views of all will be ascertained.

"But I thought you would like in the meantime to be informed of the situation."

Davis sent his resignation by return mail and was obviously grateful to the Chief Justice for writing as he had.

CHAPTER XVIII

❦

THE McKINLEY ADMINISTRATION

1897–1901

FULLER ceased to be a Democrat in 1896, when the party repudiated Cleveland, declared for the free coinage of silver, denounced the income tax decision, and nominated Bryan.

All his life Fuller had fought those who would depreciate the currency. In February, 1896, he wrote to Morris: "Times are dreadful. I have not seen the like since 1873 & the way Congress behaves seems to postpone relief & give those who wish a depreciated currency a strong hold on the people." In the same letter he voiced a faint fear of what eventually happened. "The silver men are pretty rampant," he said, "& may put somebody of theirs on the Democratic ticket."

In April, he wrote: "If we have a sound money platform & above all a sound money candidate we shall win." But in May, doubt began to creep over him. "I hope Illinois will send a sound money delegation," he said. "That is the point—let them vote for whom they please."

In June, before the convention met, his fears began to grow into horror. "The Convention looks squally," he wrote. "Still I can't believe that they can carry 16 to 1 as applied to existing contracts." A great part of the lands in the West were mortgaged to insurance companies and banks in the Eastern states. Fuller thought it was dishonest to depreciate the currency by the free coinage of silver on the ratio of sixteen ounces of silver to one ounce of gold and require these mortgage holders to accept the new currency in payment of their loans. "If that is what they are up to," he wrote, "it'll be for New York, Pa., Ct.,

N. J., etc., to say whether they will submit or withdraw. . . . That involves the destruction of property."

When in July the convention refused to endorse the Cleveland administration and was stampeded into nominating Bryan on a free-silver platform, Fuller wrote to Morris: "Politics! Good Lord Deliver Us."

Just before the election in November, Morris wrote him that to protect himself against Bryan's possible election Fuller should withdraw his Chicago bank account. " 'If the election goes wrong' you say," Fuller responded, "but I believe it is going right." Nevertheless, he did withdraw his balance and bought a New York draft. Apparently he thought the New York banks would be more likely to pay in gold. He administered the inaugural oath to McKinley with relief.

On the Court the era of the McKinley administration (1897–1901) was marked by the growing influence of the Chief Justice, the eminence among the Associate Justices of Gray, and the rising power of White. It is odd that, with each battle between them, these three men were drawn closer into each other's affections.

Fuller and Gray's greatest contest (except for the original-package cases) was on the question of whether Chinese children who were born in this country were citizens. " 'Wong Kim Ark,' " the Chief Justice wrote to his wife in 1898, "has finally been put on file. I am glad." He meant that he was relieved to have the case ended, for it was perhaps his worst defeat on the Court. But his letter then continues: "Another—and a very serious case has come out my way. I was the only one on that side a year or two ago. But you must not speak of this & I'll tell you about it when you come home."

Wong Kim Ark [1] involved the meaning of that clause of the Fourteenth Amendment which reads, "All persons born or naturalized in the United States and subject to the jurisdiction thereof are citizens of the United States." Was a child born in the United States of Chinese parents—who were by treaty and

[1] *United States* v. *Wong Kim Ark*, 1898, 169 U.S. 649.

by law not subject to naturalization—a citizen? The answer turned on whether such a child was "subject to the jurisdiction" of the United States.

Justice Miller had said, both in his lectures on constitutional law and in a remark in a famous case, that children born here of foreign subjects were not within the scope of the amendment. On the other hand, Justice Field had decided in a California case that children born in this country of Chinese parents were citizens.

After debating the case for more than two years, the Supreme Court in a strong opinion by Justice Gray held that all Chinese who were born here were citizens. Gray pointed out that there were two rules for fixing citizenship: it could be determined by the place of birth, as in England, or by the nationality of the parents, as on the Continent. The English rule that citizenship was fixed by the place of birth had been the law of the Colonies, Gray said, before our separation and had become the law of the United States prior to the Fourteenth Amendment, which had merely declared the preexisting law. Furthermore, the citizenship of Chinese born in this country had been discussed in the Congressional debates on the Fourteenth Amendment, and it had been said that such children would be citizens under the amendment.

To this argument Fuller responded that the English rule was based on a theory of allegiance to the feudal lord or sovereign which was incompatible with our conception of citizenship. Under the English law such allegiance to the sovereign could not be thrown off, whereas we had always recognized the right of a man to change his citizenship. Fuller denied that the English rule had been adopted in this country after the Revolution. He said that the adoption of such a rule would produce many inconveniences. Under it, children born to our citizens while abroad would not be citizens of the United States. Children of foreign subjects born here might claim, when taken home, the protection of our armed forces. If war came, we could not expel persons who had acquired citizenship by such a rule. If

Fuller's view had been adopted, we would not have been confronted with the very difficult constitutional problem of the relocation of the American-born Japanese in the recent war. The Constitution, Fuller noted, provided that only a "natural-born citizen" could be President. Did the framers of the Constitution, he asked, intend to provide that a child born while his alien parents were passing through our country might become our President but that a child born to American citizens while abroad was not eligible to that office?

Fuller proposed a logical method of meeting the statements in the Congressional debates on the Fourteenth Amendment. The question was whether, in the language of the amendment, a Chinese child born here was "subject to the jurisdiction" of the United States. Fuller said that the amendment was passed two months after the Civil Rights Act and for the purpose of giving constitutional validity to that law. The Civil Rights Act provided that all persons born in the United States and not "subject to any foreign power" should be citizens. Senator Lyman Trumbull had declared in the debates on the Fourteenth Amendment that the words "subject to the jurisdiction thereof" in the amendment meant the same thing as the words "not subject to the jurisdiction of any foreign power" in the Act.

The parents of a Chinese child born in this country owed allegiance to the Emperor of China, whose laws provided decapitation for a person renouncing his allegiance, strangling for those who concealed the crime, enslavement for the criminal's wives and children, and banishment for his parents, grandparents, brothers, and grandchildren. Since Chinese in this country could not throw off this allegiance by naturalization under our laws, they clearly owed allegiance to a foreign power.

But Gray's opinion was too powerful for the Court to resist: only Harlan joined in Fuller's dissent. And this time the professional applause was for Gray, though Mr. Dooley asked his friend Hennessy, "If cats were born in an oven wud they be biscuits?" Senator George F. Edmunds wrote to Gray that Gray had interpreted the Fourteenth Amendment as the members of the Senate understood it when they passed it. Edmunds commended the Court's opinion but said that he also had a "sincere admiration" for the "great ability" displayed in the dissenting opinion.

The case of *Wong Kim Ark* illustrates the diverging attitudes of Justice Gray and the Chief Justice toward the precedents. Gray was a legal historian—perhaps the greatest that the Court has ever had. His investigation of the ancient precedents was tireless and completely objective; once he had reached a conclusion from his research, he applied it relentlessly to the problem before him.

Fuller's experience on the other hand was only as a practicing lawyer. He had immense industry in research and shrewd acuteness in distinguishing any precedents that obstructed his client's interests. On the Court he regarded posterity as his client. He usually studied the precedents to distinguish them rather than to apply them; to unshackle the future from the past.

But what was the case that compensated Fuller for the loss of *Wong Kim Ark*—the case that "came out" his way, according to his letter to Mrs. Fuller—the case of which he wrote, "I was the only one on that side a year or two ago"? It was undoubtedly one of the original-package cases which were decided at this time.

When Fuller first laid down the rule in the Iowa liquor case of *Leisy* v. *Hardin* [1] that a state could not interfere with an interstate shipment in the original package, Justice Gray had dissented. But Gray had his day a few years later in *Plumley* v. *Massachusetts,* [2] when the Court held valid a Massachusetts statute in effect forbidding the importation of oleomargarine which was colored to look like butter. The Court said that the freedom of interstate commerce did not include freedom to cheat the people of a state, that "*Leisy* v. *Hardin* must be re-

---

[1] 1890, 135 U.S. 100, *supra,* Chap. XIII.   [2] 1894, 155 U.S. 461.

strained in its application to the case actually presented." This statement was practically a polite overruling of *Leisy* v. *Hardin*. Four new Justices had come on the Court since that case, and all of them had apparently been converted to Gray's views in the *Leisy* case.

Fuller, Field, and Brewer dissented in the *Plumley* case. Fuller said that colored oleomargarine was a recognized article of commerce which a state could not exclude. It was characteristic of him not to suggest that the claim of cheating in coloring the oleomargarine was a sham in the interests of the butter industry. But his critics had no such kindness or reticence; the *Plumley* decision was thereafter used to disparage the Chief Justice. When feeling ran high over his income tax decision, a hostile critic suggested that that decision should be overruled just as *Leisy* v. *Hardin* had been in effect overruled by *Plumley* v. *Massachusetts*. It was natural, therefore, that Fuller should have had some feeling on this subject.

The week before he wrote Mrs. Fuller about *Wong Kim Ark*, two cases had been argued—and probably had been decided in conference—in which the Court held void the antioleomargarine laws of Pennsylvania and New Hampshire under the original-package doctrine of *Leisy* v. *Hardin*. The Pennsylvania statute absolutely prohibited the sale of oleomargarine, and the New Hampshire statute prohibited it unless the oleomargarine was colored pink. In each case Gray and Harlan dissented on the basis of the *Plumley* case. But the Court distinguished that case on the ground that the statute there did not forbid the sale of oleomargarine except when it was colored in imitation of butter.

Another decision which might fit Fuller's description of a case that "came out" his way was *Rhodes* v. *Iowa*,[1] also argued a week before his letter to Mrs. Fuller. This case applied the original-package doctrine to a shipment of liquor into the State of Iowa. It held that the Wilson Act when it provided that the state laws should be applicable to liquor "upon arrival" in the

[1] 1898, 170 U.S. 412.

state, "regardless of its being introduced therein in the original package," did not refer to arrival at the state line but to arrival in the hands of the consignee. Only the consignee's power to sell the liquor was cut off by the statute. Thus the federal law passed by the prohibition forces to overrule *Leisy* v. *Hardin* was restricted in its effect. The opinion of the Court was by White. Gray again dissented and was joined by Harlan and Brown.

It was typical of Fuller that he did not write any of these original-package opinions himself. To do so might have given him satisfaction, but it would also have emphasized the conflict between him and Gray and the consequent rift on the Court. Fuller assigned the oleomargarine cases to Peckham and the liquor case to White. But the influence of the Chief Justice may be seen from these cases. On some aspect of the original-package doctrine he had originally stood alone; but he had finally, after years of debate against the ablest adversary on the Court, converted more than a majority of the Court to his position.

A rather humorous case involving the original-package doctrine arose a year later. Tennessee passed a statute forbidding the importation of cigarettes. The tobacco companies thereafter shipped cigarettes into that state in packages of ten cigarettes each, claiming that these were original packages.

The Supreme Court of Tennesee said that cigarettes were not legitimate articles of commerce because they were "wholly noxious and deleterious to health." "Their use is always harmful, never beneficial. They possess no virtue, but are inherently bad and bad only. . . . Beyond question, their every tendency is toward the impairment of physical health and mental vigor." The Supreme Court of Tennessee said that these facts required no scientific proof but that the court could take judicial notice of them.

The Supreme Court of the United States unanimously held that cigarettes were a legitimate article of commerce: they had been so recognized by Congress in the revenue laws. But for a year the Court was divided four to four, with Justice White in the middle, on whether packages of ten cigarettes shipped loose in baskets were original packages. Naturally Gray, Harlan, and Brown, who were opposed to the original-package doctrine, were sure that these were not original packages. They were joined by McKenna, while the Chief Justice and Justices Brewer, Shiras, and Peckham were on the other side. In the summer of 1900 Brewer wrote the Chief Justice: "I have been thinking of some additions to my cigarette opinion which I can but think would convince White if he took pains to think them over carefully. At any rate it will strengthen the dissent if it must be a dissent."

White finally wrote a concurring opinion in which he said that if the opinion of the Court weakened the force of *Leisy* v. *Hardin* [1] or *Rhodes* v. *Iowa*,[2] he would be unable to concur in it. But he thought that the small size of the packages, their trifling value, the absence of an address on each package, and the fact that they were thrown together in an open basket, to be segregated on arrival, indicated that they were not original packages. The position of Brewer for the dissenters was that the size of the package or intention to evade the state law had nothing to do with the question: the law was void because the state had no power to interfere with interstate commerce. He failed to find in the Constitution, he said, any limitation of the size of the package over which Congress was given exclusive power in interstate commerce.

Fuller's relations with White became closer during this period. In 1897 the Whites spent their summer in Camden, near Sorrento, Maine, where Fuller had his summer home. From Camden, White wrote to the Chief Justice:

"MY DEAR CHIEF:

"We are fixed in our new home which is small but engaging and very comfortable. Small as it is, there is a LITTLE room which we have mentally designated as yours should you alone

[1] 1890, 135 U.S. 100.   [2] 1898, 170 U.S. 412.

or Mrs. Fuller and yourself tire of the *heat* of Sorrento and long for the cool breeze of the Camden mountains. . . . I have very diligently studied the covers of the books which I brought with me and have walked and driven hereabouts to my heart's content. We look out upon the summit of . . . Mount Desert and know that under its shadow you and yours are sheltered. It seems and is so near that I am sure some fine day you will sail down this wonderful bay and give us the pleasure of seeing you. . . .

"Yours faithfully,

E. D. WHITE

Mr. Chief Justice Fuller"

Several letters like this are preserved among Fuller's papers. They are notable for their style, which has an almost Gaelic lightness of touch, such as one might expect from White's Irish blood. Never was there a greater disparity between a man's letters and his judicial opinions. White's decisions are not sprightly, to say the least.[1]

White and Gray sometimes clashed. In the summer of 1898 a controversy developed between them which eventually resulted in a five to four decision of the Court. In the beginning each of them sought the favor of the Chief Justice for his cause. White first wrote him: "I wrote Judge Gray shortly after coming here [Cooperstown, N.Y.] but have heard nothing from him. I hope it is not because he is unwell. Maybe he is mortally exercised over the fire boat case: If by any chance you have the opinion with you I would be very glad if you would go over it again. It is in its present shape much too long and is encumbered with too many authorities. The more I think of it the stronger is my conviction that the lines of decision in New York and Mass. are wrong. Gray & Peckham will, as a matter of course, stand by them."

[1] See Holmes-Pollock *Letters,* Vol. II, pp. 67–68, Holmes: "I have never greatly admired the Chief's [White's] mode of writing"; Vol. I, p. 130, "His mode of exposition rarely strikes me as felicitous or as at all doing justice to his great ability."

Before the summer was over, Fuller had a letter from Gray complaining that White had written the opinion in this fireboat case contrary to the decision at the last conference. Gray said that he was not able to write the opinion in a certain case assigned to him in accordance with the vote of the Court. But in view of the Chief Justice's instructions in such a case, Gray said that he would not write the opinion the other way until he had reported to a conference of the Court. "I wish," Gray wrote, "Justice White had done the like in *New York* v. *Workman* [1] [the "fireboat" case]. His lucubration seems to me quite unconvincing and mostly wide of the mark. But I am in no hurry to write a counterblast as that will be impossible except in a huge library and will take as much time and space as our Chinese *enfant terrible*.[2] Considering how decidedly the Court came to the other opinion presently after the argument and the length of time that has since elapsed, I do hope that his suggestion of ordering a re-argument may be adopted as tending to put us on a more even keel."

The "fireboat" case involved the question whether the City of New York was liable in admiralty for the negligent operation of a fireboat resulting in a collision. A reargument was ordered, and the case was not decided until two years later. The general rule was that a city was not liable for a negligent injury by its fire department. White and the majority of the Court doubted this rule and held it not applicable in any event in admiralty. They sustained a decree against the city. Gray, speaking for himself, and Brewer, Shiras, and Peckham, dissented.

There is also evidence that Fuller's relations with Brown— somewhat shattered by the income tax case—improved at this time. In May, 1901, Brown wrote to Fuller: "I dislike to trouble you when you are so busy, but as you are an expert on jurisdictional questions and always have an opinion on the subject I want to state to you the difficulty I have in case No.

[1] 1899, 179 U.S. 552, 14 *Harvard Law Review*, 450.
[2] Doubtless a reference to *United States* v. *Wong Kim Ark*, 1898, 169 U.S. 649.

151, Hale v. Lewis." [1] Brown then presented a complicated problem, too lengthy to be set out here, and concluded: "I should like to know what you think about it as I am in grave doubt." Three days later Brown wrote the Chief Justice. "Thank you for the attention you have given to the question of jurisdiction. I fully concur in your conclusion and am adopting your suggestions in an opinion I am preparing in the case." Brown states in his Memoirs that Fuller was the Court's recognized authority on questions of practice and procedure.

In December, 1901, Fuller received a note from Brown which, in contrast to his usual formality and dignity, was warm and jocular. He wrote: "Dear Chief, Oh! certainly I will write No. 303 with a 'grin' and polish it off with a 'shine.' As I presume our good friend the Czar is anxious to meet up with this particular grin as soon as possible I will give the case precedence and try to have the opinion ready for the opening of court."

This note related to a five to four decision on the extradition of a Russian sailor who had deserted from a group of seamen sent here to man a warship being built in Philadelphia for the Russian government. The Court allowed the extradition. Since the case included questions of both admiralty and extradition law, which were Brown's specialties, it is easy to see why it was assigned to him. It is harder to understand why the Chief Justice made the assignment, since he, together with Gray, Harlan, and White, dissented. When the Chief Justice is in the minority, the assignment of the opinion is made by the senior Justice of the majority—in this case, Brewer, the fourth Justice in seniority. But of course the Chief Justice could make the assignment and afterward change his mind and join the minority.

Gray's dissent was devastating. The situation almost raises the suspicion that the Court decided, perhaps at the suggestion of the State Department, to let the Russian sailor be extradited to preserve friendly relations with the Czar but to put on

[1] 1901, 181 U.S. 473.

record so vigorous a dissent by the senior Justices that the case could never be cited as a precedent.

Justice Harlan's relations with the Chief Justice are portrayed by a letter which Harlan wrote him in 1898:

"DEAR CHIEF:

"Let me celebrate the 21st anniversary of my judicial life by a slight growl.

"Two Saturdays in succession you have not assigned to me any case but have assigned cases and important ones to Justice Gray. I was in the majority in each case assigned to him.

"I fear that you have the impression that my health is failing while that of Justice Gray is vigorous. I hope his is on the mend.[1] I know I am in good health and wish to do my full share of the work. The cases on my hands to be written are not as many in number as in the case of some others.

"Now tear this up & think no more of the growl.

"Yrs.

JOHN M. HARLAN"

There were other indications of jealousy of Gray on the Court in this period. The Chief Justice spoke to the Reporter on the impropriety of starting successive volumes of the official reports by opinions of Justice Gray. This complaint was doubtless made by some of the Associate Justices. Fuller assigned to Gray more than his share of important opinions and selected Justice Gray's nephew, Roland Gray, as his Secretary in the Venezuelan boundary arbitration. With the advent of a new Reporter in 1902, the practice, which still prevails, of printing the decisions in strict order of seniority of the Justices was adopted.

The most important occurrence in the McKinley adminis-

---

[1] On the same date (Dec. 18, 1898) Fuller received a letter from Gray: "I have a bad cold again not so serious as last time but enough to have Dr. Johnston think it very unwise for me to go out of the house today" (Genet papers). Gray's health was not very good during this period. On May 25, 1898, Brewer had written Fuller: "I shall call on Mrs. Gray tomorrow and insist on her taking the Judge away where he will cease to worry" (Genet papers).

tration was the war with Spain, which was declared in April, 1898. On March 30 the Chief Justice had written to his wife: "I had not supposed we should have war but it looks like it today. . . . Peckham insists that we shall be bombarded at Sorrento if we go there. I have just had a letter from Shepard in reference to Stuart [Shepard's son] going to the war." In an effort to secure a commission in the Navy for Stuart Shepard, Fuller saw his old friends Admiral Crowninshield and Secretary of the Navy Long. From them he learned that the war, if it came, would be short because of the inferiority of the Spanish Navy. These predictions were confirmed at Manila Bay and Santiago.

In August the Chief Justice received at Sorrento the following telegram: "It would give me special pleasure if you would permit me to consider you for membership on the Peace Commission. Wire answer. William McKinley." He at once responded: "I fully appreciate the honor you pay me and cannot refuse to assent to the consideration of my name but sincerely hope you can get along satisfactorily without designating me." But after a restless night he again wired the President: "I answered too hastily. I really could not accept if offered. Will write."

His letter was as follows:

"MY DEAR MR. PRESIDENT:

"Your telegram of yesterday came during my absence and I did not receive it until later in the afternoon. This led to haste in my reply and I answered as I did partly from a feeling that perhaps it might be a duty to accept if you thought fit to tender the appointment and partly out of my personal regard for you if perchance you were embarrassed as to a choice. But on reflection I became absolutely convinced that the path of duty laid distinctly the other way and accordingly telegraphed you this morning. I would have done so last night but the office was closed.

"I am as you are aware one of the arbitrators under the Anglo-Venezuelan treaty and although the hearing will doubtless not be had until next summer, either Mr. Justice Brewer or myself or both of us may be compelled to go over to Paris in February to attend the organization of the tribunal. At the time I assented to the wish that I should accept the position it seemed best that I should do so but I have become satisfied since that I was mistaken in the view that I then entertained.

"My duty to the country lies in the discharge of my duty to the Court over which I preside and the labors of the Court are, as you know arduous and many matters of detail necessarily devolve upon the Chief Justice. Nothing but some imperative exigency ought to be allowed to interfere in any way with the conduct of the business that we are appointed to perform and I am quite sure that the Chief Justice should not take on any additional burden.

"I think moreover that considering the nature of the office it is far wiser that the Chief Justice should not participate in public affairs. The circumstances of today are not those which existed in the day of Jay and Ellsworth nor of Marshall who was Secretary of State as well as Chief Justice for a few weeks.

"I have endeavored not to allow my personal inclinations to affect me. The position is attractive as well as most honorable and my friendship for you personally is sincere, but I should not feel justified in taking the place.

"I fully appreciate the confidence you show me in wishing to consider my name in this connection and heartily congratulate you on your success in dealing with the problems that confront us."

Thereafter the President offered a position on the Peace Commission to Justice White, who also declined. In September, Fuller wrote to Shepard: "I am glad Judge White did not consent to act as a Peace Commissioner." It was fortunate that neither Fuller nor White were on the commission, because the Treaty of Peace afterward came before the Court in the insular cases. A Justice of the Court who had served on the peace commission would probably have disqualified himself in those cases, and the result would perhaps have been different.

There were also a number of admiralty prize cases coming

before the Court at this time which involved the seizure of Spanish merchant ships as prizes of war. Since the Court was divided in some of these cases, it would have been embarrassing to have had the Chief Justice or any Justice serving on the peace commission. In four of these prize cases Fuller wrote the opinion of the Court. In one, however—*The Paquette Habana* [1] —he wrote a dissent from Gray's opinion. In this case Spanish fishing ships of twenty-five to thirty-five tons were seized in the Caribbean by the United States Navy. In an opinion by Justice Gray these seizures were set aside. Gray traced the history of the treatment in war of coastal fishing boats from the early 1400's and showed that in most wars such ships, either by treaty or by executive order, were not seized. He concluded that this practice had become a settled rule of international law except where fishing ships were used for war purposes or where fishing was a large commercial operation.

Fuller, with Harlan and McKenna, dissented. He said that no such settled rule existed and that the Executive power should be left free to decide the question as the circumstances of war demanded. Furthermore, he suggested that these ships were not ordinary coastal fishing boats but were engaged in commercial ventures. Later he regretted that he had not given more emphasis to this aspect of the case. He wrote to Shepard: "In the Paquette—the fishing smacks—the fact is the supposed rule did not apply & I ought to have written so."

This remark illustrates the attitude of the Chief Justice toward dissents. He thought they should be short but restrained and respectful toward the majority. In his judgment, a dissent was no place for heat. In another letter to Shepard at this time, he wrote: "Did you notice the decision of the Court in the last Legal News on a question of jurisdiction? I dissented but with not half the vigor I felt."

[1] 1900, 175 U.S. 677.

CHAPTER XIX

o‿o

VENEZUELAN BOUNDARY ARBITRATION

In 1897 Fuller, with Justice Brewer as his colleague, accepted appointment as an arbitrator in the boundary dispute between Venezuela and British Guiana.

These countries lie side by side on the north coast of South America, with Venezuela to the west and British Guiana to the east. The disputed territory was between the Orinoco River in Venezuela and the Essequibo River in British Guiana, a distance on the coast line of nearly two hundred miles. Venezuela at one time claimed as far east as the Essequibo, and the British had extended their demands as far west as the mouth of the Orinoco, so that the coastal claims overlapped for a distance of about two hundred miles. In the interior the British claims had been pressed still further to the west. For more than fifty years the dispute had raged intermittently, with Great Britain expanding her claims from time to time and refusing Venezuela's pleas for arbitration.

Venezuela had early appealed to the United States for aid, and the State Department had tried since 1876—first gently and later with increasing insistence—to induce Great Britain to settle or to arbitrate the dispute. These efforts came to a crisis in 1895, when Great Britain definitely refused to arbitrate concerning any part of the territory lying within its so-called Schomburgk line. This line had originally been drawn in 1841 by an enthusiastic explorer named Robert Schomburgk. His line went far beyond any area occupied by the British and included control of the mouth of the Orinoco. When the line was marked, Venezuela had protested and had been told by Lord Aberdeen, the British Prime Minister, that it had been drawn only for the purposes of discussion and, after further protest, the posts marking the line at the coast were cut down by Lord Aberdeen's orders. Thereafter he had offered to settle on a line short of the Schomburgk line, but this proposal had been rejected by Venezuela.

In 1896 President Cleveland and his Secretary of State, Richard Olney, scored a diplomatic triumph by compelling arbitration. They drafted a message to Lord Salisbury, the British Prime Minister, in which they stated that under the Monroe Doctrine the honor and interests of the United States were involved in the dispute and requested a "definite decision" as to whether Great Britain would "consent or would decline" to submit the whole matter to impartial arbitration.

After some delay Salisbury replied, explaining in a patient, didactic tone that the Monroe Doctrine might enjoy great popularity in the United States but that it had no application to a boundary dispute such as this. He refused to arbitrate except as to territory beyond the Schomburgk line. Cleveland laid Salisbury's reply before Congress and asked for a commission to find the true line. "When such report is made and accepted," he said, "it will, in my opinion, be the duty of the United States to resist by every means in its power . . . the appropriation by Great Britain of any lands . . . which after investigation we have determined of right belong to Venezuela." Congress immediately appropriated the requisite funds, and the President appointed a commission of five distinguished citizens, with Justice Brewer as chairman, to determine the true boundary.[1]

All through 1896 two lines of effort went feverishly forward. Justice Brewer's commission engaged a group of cartographers and historians who ransacked the archives in London and Holland for material bearing on the historic boundary. It soon

---

[1] The other commissioners were: Chief Justice Alvey of the Court of Appeals of the District of Columbia, Frederic R. Coudert, of New York, Daniel C. Gilman, president of Johns Hopkins University, and Andrew D. White, president of Cornell University.

became apparent that the report of the commission would probably be adverse to most, if not all, of the British claims. As this outcome became clearer, Salisbury and Olney negotiated strenuously to draft an arbitration treaty which would obviate a report by the commission. Salisbury finally was glad to accept a treaty which not only applied to all the disputed territory but provided in effect that possession of any part of it for less than fifty years should not make good title. (Few persons then realized that Great Britain was being drawn inexorably into the orbit of the United States.) Although the arbitration treaty was not signed until February 2, 1897, Olney wrote Brewer in strict confidence on November 10, 1896, that it had been agreed upon. Olney indicated that it was of great importance that he should be able to assure the parties that the commission would immediately suspend its "deliberations." He therefore had secured the President's authority to ask the commission to make no findings.

As soon as the boundary commission was appointed, on January 1, 1896, the British prepared a Parliamentary Blue Book to present their side of the controversy. The eminence of the author of this anonymous work and the speed with which it was prepared are shown by a letter dated February 1, 1896, from Sir Frederick Pollock to Oliver Wendell Holmes, Jr., then a Justice of the Supreme Court of Massachusetts. "For the last 3 weeks," Pollock wrote, "I have been hard at work drafting a statement of our case in the Venezuelan affair. . . . It is to be laid before Parliament as soon as possible. . . . The thing had to be done against time—I should have liked to have [had] 2 or 3 months instead of 3 weeks." Pollock apparently started to prepare this book within a week after the American commission was appointed. Two months after Pollock's letter to Holmes, Sir Julian Pauncefote, the British ambassador, sent a complimentary copy of the Blue Book to the Chief Justice, whose interest in the subject was then only academic.

Under the terms of the treaty one arbitrator was to be designated by the President of Venezuela and one by the Justices of the Supreme Court of the United States, while two British arbitrators were to be nominated by the Judicial Committee of the Privy Council. The four so selected were to name the fifth arbitrator, who was to be president of the tribunal.

In January, 1897, overtures were made to Fuller to act as an arbitrator. He thought it his duty to accept but hesitated because embarrassing questions of precedence might arise if the Privy Council should appoint his opposite number, the Lord Chancellor. But on January 10, 1897, Olney wrote to Fuller that former Lord Chancellor Herschell was likely to be the principal arbitrator for Great Britain. "If I do not hear from you," Olney wrote, "I shall understand that Ex-s do not count—that your judgment as to being on the Commission yourself is not changed." Fuller was modest as a mouse until the dignity of his office was involved, and he tried to avoid situations where the deference due his position might be slighted.

In February the President of Venezuela appointed Fuller and the Justices of the Supreme Court selected Brewer as arbitrators under the treaty. As soon as the arbitrators were appointed, the British suggested that the governments agree on the fifth arbitrator and save the arbitrators the burden of his selection. Fuller and Brewer acceded. "Judge Brewer thought that there was no objection," Fuller wrote to Olney, "to the representatives of Great Britain & Venezuela agreeing on the fifth arbitrator & so signified to Sir Julian.[1] . . . In respect to the choice I am perfectly clear that it is a jurist & *Not* a diplomatist that is needed."

But when no selection had been made by the end of July, with the ninety days for the appointment almost half gone, the Venezuelan minister suggested to Fuller that he and Brewer write their British colleagues on the subject. Justice Brewer concurred. He said: "I should put the matter as a query, saying we had been advised that the two nations would agree on the fifth Arbitrator or at least suggest names [and] that hear-

[1] Sir Julian Pauncefote, the British ambassador.

ing nothing we ask if the following names would be satisfactory, suggesting Calvo, Bar, Martens. I have no objections to President Díaz, but is he a jurist? [1] . . . Would it be better to ask them [the British arbitrators] to suggest names in the first instance, leaving to us to pick from the names they suggest?" Fuller adopted this last course because he could not get a reply to his letters to the Venezuelan authorities requesting approval of any names. "If you had had as much experience as I have had," Brewer wrote, "with those gentlemen at Caracas you would not be so much astonished. . . . I think however the testimony has been so fully collected that they can not blunder much." The documents submitted to Brewer's commission were being published in four volumes, and its report (without any findings), in three volumes. Brewer's overconfidence in this great mass of material was to prove a weakness before the arbitration had ended.

But weeks passed and no reply came from either London or Caracas. "I do not wonder at your irritation," Brewer wrote. "I never would put anything in which I had any interest in the hands of those gentlemen of South America. They seem to have no idea of promptness." But Brewer thought that no further letters on the subject should be written to the British arbitrators. He wrote to Fuller: "As to writing again to our British friends, I doubt the wisdom of it. Do we want to appear anxious about the matter? Are we any more responsible than they? Does the duty rest upon us alone? Are they to pose as the indifferent ones and we to revolve around or ask favors of them? It seems to me that, in the dignified suggestion we made we have done our duty. If their response leads to nothing we can justly say that we moved in the matter & they did not."

But just before the time for the appointment expired, Venezuela notified the Chief Justice that Great Britain had sub-

[1] Carlos Calvo (1824–1906), Argentine jurist; Karl Ludwig von Bar (1836–1913), German jurist; Frédéric Frommhold de Martens (1845–1909), Russian jurist, who was subsequently accepted as the fifth arbitrator; José de la Cruz Porfirio Díaz (1830–1915), President of Mexico.

mitted a list of names from which Venezuela had chosen Frédéric de Martens, a Russian jurist, as the fifth arbitrator. "Monsieur de Martens," the Venezuelan minister wrote, "was formerly the President of the Institute, Professor of the University and of the Law School at St. Petersburg, and for a long time member of the Council of Foreign Affairs of Russia. He stands it appears very high as a writer and as a man. He is considered a person of independent mind and his writings show judgment and practical good sense." Martens had acted as an arbitrator in the Newfoundland controversy in 1891 and the Bering Sea arbitration in 1893. He had received honorary degrees from Oxford and Cambridge and—because he had presided at so many international arbitrations—was sometimes referred to as the "Lord Chancellor of Europe."

Under the treaty each side was to file its printed case with its evidence within eight months; its countercase within four months thereafter, and its printed argument three months after that. Extensions were granted on request, and the last arguments were not filed until December, 1898. These documents embraced 23 printed volumes and make, with the 7 volumes of the American Boundary Commission, 30 volumes. It is not surprising that, as this flood of material poured in upon him, the Chief Justice began to doubt whether he should have accepted a place on the tribunal. "At the time I assented to . . . accept the position," he wrote to President McKinley, "it seemed best that I should do so but I have become satisfied since that I was mistaken." Every day that passed in the next year made Fuller more certain of this error.

The treaty provided that the arbitrators should meet in Paris within sixty days after the filing of the printed arguments. It was early apparent that this date would fall in the midst of the court term of 1898 and 1899. As soon as this situation was discovered, Fuller wrote to Lord Herschell: "It is well nigh impossible for two Justices of the Supreme Court to be absent next winter and absolutely so as to the Chief Justice. It is true that I might withdraw, and, except that I should regret being deprived of the pleasure of making your acquaintance and that of our colleague [Lord Collins], I am personally entirely willing to do so, but I cannot help thinking that it would be awkward and inadvisable.

"I should be gratified if the hearing could be postponed to the middle of May or the first of June, 1899. As such an adjournment would require the tribunal to meet, either Justice Brewer or myself, perhaps both, could come over to participate in that action, which, necessarily should be assented to beforehand."

Fuller wrote to the same effect to Martens, who immediately responded, reluctantly consenting to the extension of time for the hearings. In January, 1899, Brewer went to Paris, and a brief meeting of the Tribunal was held, continuing the hearings to May 25. They were afterward continued to June 15.

Lord Herschell died suddenly at the British Embassy in Washington on March 1, 1899. He had been in this country for several months as a member of the Joint High Commission to consider several subjects of controversy between the United States and Canada, including the Alaskan boundary. It appears from the letters of John Hay, the Secretary of State, that Herschell was trying to pay off the United States for the defeat the British had suffered in being compelled to arbitrate the Venezuelan boundary. He demanded an arbitration treaty on the Alaskan boundary which would submit to arbitration large tracts of what had always been regarded as territory of the United States. It was characteristic of Fuller, under the circumstances, to exert all of his charm upon Herschell. Fuller gave a dinner party for him and had called on him at the Embassy just before his death. The day after his death the Supreme Court adjourned to honor him; it was the first time that such a compliment had been paid to a foreign dignitary. Lord Russell of Killowen, the Lord Chief Justice, succeeded Herschell on the Venezuelan boundary tribunal.

By the time the arbitration tribunal met in Paris in the summer of 1899, the lines of argument were well marked out.

It must be remembered in considering these arguments that, in the greater part of the disputed territory, neither side had any settlement that had existed for more than fifty years.

Venezuela's position was that Spain had discovered Guiana from the Amazon to the Orinoco and had perfected her title by exploration and occupation. Spain's explorers had circumnavigated the so-called "island" of Guiana by ascending the Amazon and the Río Negro rivers and coming down the Orinoco. Spain had taken ceremonial possession of the whole province and island and had founded settlements at Santo Thome and other places. Spain's grant to Holland of the territory which subsequently became British Guiana was limited to the area occupied by the then existing Dutch settlements which did not include any substantial part of the disputed territory. Venezuela had succeeded to all the rights of Spain in Guiana.

The arbitration treaty provided that the tribunal should ascertain the extent of the territory which might be lawfully claimed by Holland and by Spain in 1814, when Great Britain acquired British Guiana from Holland. It also provided that "adverse holding" for fifty years should make good title. Venezuela claimed that under the treaty the fifty-year period must be measured back from 1814. The British protested against this interpretation and produced the diplomatic correspondence between Salisbury and Olney indicating that the fifty-year period was to be figured from the date of the treaty. Sir Richard Webster, the Attorney General, made it clear at the outset that if the Venezuelan position on this point were accepted by the tribunal, the British counsel would leave the room and end the arbitration.

Britain's position was that the claim of Spanish possession of the disputed territory was not well founded; that the territory was essentially no man's land and that the Indian tribes living in it had alliances with the Dutch rather than the Spanish. The Dutch, they argued, had thus acquired a sphere of influence in the territory which was continued and fostered by the English so that the Indians in effect became British subjects.

For fifty-five days the arbitrators listened to the arguments. Great Britain was represented by her Attorney General, Sir Richard Webster, afterward Lord Chief Justice as Lord Alverstone. He was assisted by the Attorney General of the prior administration, Sir Robert Reid, afterward Lord Chancellor as Lord Loreburn. They were supported by George Askwith, later Sir George Askwith, and Mr. Rowlatt, later Mr. Justice Rowlatt. The senior counsel for Venezuela was former President Harrison, though Mr. S. Mallet-Prevost, General Benjamin F. Tracy, and James Russell Soley all took a prominent part.

In the course of the arguments a question of the production of a document arose. The British had printed as part of their case the correspondence between Lord Aberdeen and the governor of British Guiana at the time the Schomburgk line was drawn. One such letter was omitted, although it was known to exist because a subsequent letter referred to it. It seemed probable that this missing letter gave the reasons which induced Lord Aberdeen to repudiate the Schomburgk line and offer a line nearer the Essequibo. In the course of the argument Fuller called Sir Robert Reid's attention to the absence of this letter. Reid answered that it could not be produced because it related to high governmental policy. Two days later the president of the tribunal stated that some of the arbitrators desired to see the dispatch in question, but the Attorney General absolutely refused to produce it. The president then stated that all the members of the tribunal agreed that it was sufficient to have the statement in the record that the document could not be produced. The letter must have been damaging indeed to the British case to cause the Attorney General deliberately to submit to the inferences which would flow from his refusal to produce it.

But the British made the better presentation of the arguments, both printed and oral. Their Attorney General was ex-

perienced in international arbitrations. The British love of con-
ciseness and organization was invaluable in a case involving
such an immense mass of material. The Venezuelans had no
counsel comparable to Sir Frederick Pollock to prepare the
original outline of the argument. Although President Harrison
was probably the ablest lawyer ever to be President,[1] the mistake was made of letting him speak last, at the end of weeks
of argument, when all ears were wearied of the subject. Similarly in the printed cases, countercases, and arguments, the
British developed their full theory in their case, the first document submitted; the Venezuelans withheld theirs for the final
printed argument. The British printed argument was a short
outline of their case; the Venezuelan filled two thick volumes.
On oral argument Venezuelan counsel could only repeat what
they had just said in print, while the British had a fresh story
to tell. Furthermore, Lord Alverstone thought, after experience
in three international arbitrations between English and American advocates, that the British division between barristers and
solicitors showed to advantage in such a proceeding. The
American presentation, he said, was adversely affected by the
lengthy labor of securing the evidence. The lawyer who pre-
pares the case is inclined to emphasize the points that he has
dug out, but the barrister, with all the evidence laid before
him, is more likely to choose his emphasis to impress his
tribunal.

The heat was oppressive in Paris in the summer of 1899,
and the Chief Justice found the arguments tedious. His family,
however, enjoyed in France, during the arbitration, their first
automobile ride. But Fuller was caught up in a social whirl:
every member of the tribunal gave a dinner party—a thing

[1] Roland Gray, of Boston, who was the Chief Justice's Secretary in Paris,
commented on reading this statement: "I think he [Harrison] was more than
that. I never heard him argue in Washington and he did not appear very well in
Paris. But my uncle [Justice Horace Gray] once said to me that in his opinion
the four ablest counsels who argued before him in Washington were Mr. James
Carter, Mr. Joseph Choate, Mr. John Johnson of Philadelphia and President
Harrison." Gray to the author, Nov. 2, 1948.

that he had always found distressing. The Dreyfus case was then being retried at Rennes; and it, rather than the arbitration, was the principal topic of conversation.

With relief the arbitrators heard the end of the arguments and went into their final conference. That their ultimate unanimity was not spontaneous is apparent from the fact that this conference lasted six days. The British theory that the Dutch had acquired sovereignty over the territory by alliance with the Indians roaming in it was preposterous to American lawyers. No sovereignty had ever been acquired by giving presents to the Indians and making alliances with them. The American Indians were never considered as having any sovereignty. Chief Justice Marshall had declared that the governments of Europe in settling America, and especially England, had agreed to the rule that discovery gave to the nation making it the sole right of acquiring the soil from the natives. "The absolute ultimate title," Marshall said, "has been considered as acquired by discovery, subject only to the Indian title of occupancy, which title the discoverers possessed the exclusive right of acquiring." Spain was the admitted discoverer of Guiana.

But Martens fervidly desired a unanimous decision, and this attitude on his part gave the British an advantage. The fact that they had been dragooned into the arbitration made them desperate in their threats to ignore the award if it did not suit them. Counsel for Venezuela were not of a temper to threaten to withdraw from the arbitration or refuse to produce an obviously pertinent document as the British did. And similarly, the American arbitrators were not able in the conference to assume the fire-breathing attitude of their British colleagues. The Americans doubtless threatened to dissent, but without the heat with which the British threatened. Furthermore, Britain had an equity in its favor which was cut off by the arbitration treaty. For some years (though not fifty) British subjects had been operating gold mines in the disputed territory. One cannot help sympathizing with a man whose possession has existed for a long time but is a few years short of the period prescribed by a statute of limitations. Martens wavered and finally leaned toward the British view. Perhaps Marshall's pronouncement did not seem as conclusive to a Russian jurist as it did to the Americans.

In the main the Schomburgk line was adopted as the boundary, but the American arbitrators forced two great gaps in it. On the coast the line was pushed back several miles from the mouth of the Orinoco, giving Venezuela undisputed control of that river. In the interior the line of the Wenamu River was adopted instead of the Cuyuni, allowing Venezuela another substantial area east of the Schomburgk line. Thus Venezuela was awarded substantial parts of the territory which Britain had originally refused to submit to arbitration, as well as all the territory claimed by Britain beyond the Schomburgk line.

But the British were jubilant over the result and the Venezuelans disappointed. Great Britain received all the gold mines and the far greater part of the disputed territory. Sir Richard Webster was made a baronet and Sir Robert Reid received the Grand Cross of St. Michael and St. George for their services as advocates in the case and the British arbitrators on their return were feted by the Royal Societies Club.

However, the suggestions of a British publicist that Venezuela received practically nothing of value under the award is far from true. Barima Point at the mouth of the Orinoco may be swampy and worthless land, but the possessor of it could levy duties on Venezuelan commerce, for it controls the mouth of a river which is the great inland waterway of Venezuela. And for Venezuela to have the boundary settled after more than fifty years of strife and constant encroachment by a powerful neighbor was in itself a victory.

Fuller's rare good will—his capacity for cultivating those who irritated him—is illustrated again by this arbitration. Though he privately expressed some bitterness toward the British, he carried on for the remainder of his life a cordial correspondence with his English colleagues. The following year Lord Russell of Killowen invited Fuller to visit him in England and, upon Russell's death a few months later, Fuller was an active member of the memorial committee. The next year Martens received an honorary degree from Yale, and the Chief Justice gave a dinner for him in Washington. Fuller exchanged many letters with Lord Alverstone and Lord Collins, visited Lord Collins in England in 1905, and in 1907 gave Justice Holmes a letter of introduction to Lord Loreburn, the Lord Chancellor, eliciting an enthusiastic response.

Fuller's capacity for suppressing his resentment and his unusual facilities for friendship were thus a factor in creating the present relations between Great Britain and the United States. "You will be just as likely to be chosen President," Grandma Weston had written to her hot-headed grandson when he was twenty-three, "if you don't knock everybody down who presumes to differ from you." [1] For more than forty years, under the spur of that advice, he had cultivated a capacity for controlling his temper. Anglo-American relations are perhaps indebted to Paulina Weston. It was prophetic that among the Chief Justice's book purchases in London in 1899 was a book called *The River War,* dedicated to Lord Salisbury by a young English writer named Winston Churchill.

[1] See Chap. III, *supra.*

CHAPTER XX

THE INSULAR CASES

Whether the "Constitution follows the flag"—whether Congress was limited by the Constitution in governing Puerto Rico and the Philippines—this is usually said to be the question decided in the insular cases. Actually, these cases involved a much narrower question: whether Congress could impose a tariff on the commerce between these islands and the states. The reports of these cases are the debris of the battle fought by the tobacco and sugar producers to preserve their tariff protection against the products of these territories.

Puerto Rico and the Philippines were ceded to the United States in the peace treaty with Spain. In 1900, after a military occupation, an Act for the government of Puerto Rico, called the Foraker Act, was passed. The President had recommended free trade with Puerto Rico, but the protective-tariff forces secured a temporary, token tariff of 15 per cent of the rates imposed by existing law. Their purpose was to save the principle of protection and to test in the courts whether such a tariff could constitutionally be imposed. By testing the question for Puerto Rico, they could settle it for the Philippines.

It was agreed that the United States could acquire territory under the war and treaty powers of the Constitution. It was settled that such territory could be governed by Congress without the consent of its inhabitants. But in such control Congress was restricted to some extent by the Bill of Rights. And it was immediately pointed out that a tariff between these islands and the states was invalid under the constitutional provision that "all duties, imposts and excises shall be uniform throughout the United States." Chief Justice Marshall in emphatic language had construed this clause to extend to the territories. "The District of Columbia, or the territory west of the Missouri," he said, "is not less within the United States, than Maryland or Pennsylvania."

In January, 1899, two articles by distinguished authors simultaneously appeared, arguing that Marshall was wrong in this conclusion. One such argument was by Christopher C. Langdell, long-time Dean of Harvard Law School, and the other was by Harry Pratt Judson, who a few years later became president of the University of Chicago. They said that the term "United States" was used in the Constitution either as the collective name of the states that were united thereby or as the title of the entity or sovereignty created by the Constitution. These words were not used, they argued, in the "map" sense to designate a geographical area. That usage was conventional but not legal or constitutional.

Langdell attempted to dispose of Marshall's opinion to the contrary by calling it a dictum or a remark not necessary to the decision. Both he and Judson indicated that Marshall might have rested his decision on better and surer grounds. As opposed to this dictum of Marshall, Langdell proposed a dictum of Webster where, in arguing a case, Webster had said that the Territory of Florida was "no part of the United States."

But one cannot brush aside a portion of an opinion of John Marshall as a dictum: American constitutional law rests largely on his dicta. It is an aphorism of constitutional law that a dictum of Marshall is better authority than a decision of any other judge. Furthermore, Marshall's statement that the United States included the territories was made as a step in the reasoning by which he reached his conclusion in the case before him and was in no proper sense a dictum. And heated arguments of lawyers in prior cases—even those of Webster— are not compelling authority for any purpose, much less to overcome an alleged dictum of Marshall.

If the protectionists were to prevail, it was necessary for them to find a theory which did not involve a direct collision with John Marshall. A young Boston lawyer, Abbott Lawrence Lowell, climbed the first step toward his subsequent eminence as president of Harvard University by evolving such a theory. In an article in the *Harvard Law Review* he suggested that all prior treaties or laws for acquisition of territory had "incorporated" the inhabitants into the Union. The treaty with Spain, he said, on the contrary, provided: "The civil rights and political status of the native inhabitants . . . shall be determined by Congress." Lowell then reviewed the authorities and concluded that while they were "certainly meagre," the weight of them was to the effect that, unless "incorporated" by treaty or legislation, acquired territory did not "become a part of the United States."

In the meantime a group of Puerto Rican tariff cases was coming up for argument in the Supreme Court. The Attorney General in his briefs and oral argument presented the Langdell-Judson theory rather than the Lowell theory. He argued that the uniformity clause on duties was limited to the states. The sugar and tobacco interests rested their arguments on the same basis.

The validity of the tariff on Puerto Rican products coming into the states was sustained in the insular case of *Downes* v. *Bidwell.*[1] The so-called "opinion of the Court" in this case was by Justice Brown, and it was based on the Langdell-Judson theory that "uniform throughout the United States" means uniform only in the states. Brown said that Marshall's famous opinion included certain "observations" which had occasioned some "embarrassment" and which "were not called for by the exigencies of the case."

All eight of his associates disagreed with Brown on this basis. But they did not agree with each other. White, who with Shiras and McKenna concurred in the result, rested his opinion on the Lowell theory that Puerto Rico had not yet been "incorporated" by the treaty or any statute into the United States. He

[1] 1901, 182 U.S. 244.

held that territory could not be "incorporated" by a treaty: incorporation of territory into the United States required an Act of Congress.[1] He said that the uniformity clause in the Constitution was fully applicable to any territory once it had been "incorporated" into the Union. White said that it was "entirely inadmissible" to question "as mere *dicta*" the "rulings" on this point of Chief Justice Marshall as Brown had done. Justice Gray also concurred in the result. He agreed in substance with White but indicated that he would limit the necessity for "incorporation" to territory acquired by war. Fuller, Harlan, Brewer, and Peckham dissented. Since Brown disagreed with White's theory, a majority of the Court repudiated each of the two theories on which the case was decided.

Fuller's dissent was calm and restrained. He observed that the majority "widely differed" on the reasoning by which the conclusion was reached. Brown had spoken of the "embarrassment" arising from Marshall's "observations." "Manifestly this is so in this case," Fuller said, "for it is necessary to overrule that decision to reach the result herein announced." He then reviewed Marshall's opinion and repeated White's conclusion that the pertinent language could not be rejected as a dictum. He called attention to other clauses in the Constitution where the words "United States" embraced the territories.

In answer to White, Fuller noted that White, unlike Brown, conceded that Congress in making laws for the organized territories was completely limited by the Constitution. White's position was that Puerto Rico had not been "incorporated" into the United States. Fuller said that the clause in the treaty that the "civil rights and political status" of the inhabitants should "be determined by Congress" merely stated that Congress need not give the inhabitants the full status of citizens. Full citizenship had never been given the inhabitants of the

[1] Lowell's article was not mentioned in White's opinion, but a recent biography of Lowell (Yeomans's *Abbott Lawrence Lowell,* 1948, p. 47) states: "White . . . generously gave Lowell much credit."

territories. But this clause in the treaty with Spain, Fuller said, could not enlarge the constitutional powers of Congress. No grant from Spain could increase those powers.

If "incorporation" were necessary, Fuller showed that the territory had already been incorporated. Congress had passed an Act to carry out the obligations of the treaty, thus accepting the cession. It had created a civil government for Puerto Rico with a governor, secretary, attorney general, and other officers appointed by the President and confirmed by the Senate. It had provided for a court with a district judge, attorney, and marshal also appointed by the President. This court was called the District Court of the United States for Puerto Rico. By the terms of the Act, it had the same jurisdiction as the District and Circuit Courts of the United States. From this court appeals were allowed to the Supreme Court of the United States. All officers of Puerto Rico were required to take an oath to support the Constitution of the United States.

Fuller said that Puerto Rico had thus clearly been made an "organized territory" of the United States. If it were not "incorporated," that word must have some "occult" meaning. If a discriminatory tariff could be passed against it, it was "because the power of Congress over commerce between the states and any of the territories was not restricted by the Constitution." "This," Fuller said, "was the position taken by the Attorney General with a candor and ability that did him great credit."

Other cases of less significance were decided at the same time as the *Downes* case. In one case it was unanimously decided that Puerto Rican tariffs imposed under the war powers by the military authorities prior to the ratification of the treaty were valid. In another case, that of *DeLima* v. *Bidwell*,[1] it was held that after the ratification of the treaty and before the passage of the Foraker Act, Puerto Rico was not a "foreign country" within the terms of the existing tariff laws imposing taxes on goods "imported from foreign countries." Brown de-

[1] 1901, 182 U.S. 1.

livered the Court's opinion in this case and was joined by Fuller, Harlan, Brewer, and Peckham, the dissenters in the *Downes* case. McKenna, Shiras, White, and Gray vigorously dissented. It is difficult to see why they should dissent so strenuously on this simple question of statutory construction until it is noted that Brown's opinion (given on behalf of the Court) disparaged, if it did not overrule, one of the "meagre" authorities which Lowell said were all he could find to sustain his theory of the necessity for "incorporation" of a territory.

Brown's view was that Puerto Rico after the cession was not a foreign country under the tariff act but that no territory was a part of the United States within the Constitution. He suggested that Congress might extend certain provisions of the Constitution to the territories and that, once extended, such provisions could not be withdrawn. Puerto Rico was governed, he asserted, under the plenary power of Congress over the territories. This power, he declared, was "without limitation" in the Constitution except for certain "fundamental" restrictions and those provisions of the Bill of Rights which cut off all power of Congress to do certain things such as to pass a law abridging freedom of speech. White's position was that the power of Congress over the territories was subject to all applicable constitutional limitations but that until a territory had been "incorporated" into the Union by Congress the constitutional provision for uniformity of tariff laws was not applicable.

The published reaction of the legal profession to the *Downes* case was adverse to Brown and White and favorable to Fuller. Probably the public reaction was the other way. The public understood the decision to be in accord with the spirit of nationalism that was then sweeping the country. We had colonies: we had become a nation. The protectionists were fortunate enough to get astride of this national sentiment and ride it toward their goal. Apparently the public understood that it was the citizenship of the inhabitants that was involved in the insular cases instead of how their commerce should be taxed.

Our war with Spain had been started with a formal declaration that we sought no sovereignty over Cuba. At the end of hostilities, however, we were in military possession of the island of Puerto Rico and the city of Manila in the Philippine Islands. Reluctantly President McKinley accepted a cession of these islands, paying Spain $20,000,000 for the Philippines. He had difficulty in securing ratification of the treaty in the Senate, and it was only approved when William Jennings Bryan advised his followers to vote for it. In the campaign of 1900, however, Bryan made an issue of alleged "imperialism" against the administration and demanded that the Philippines be freed as soon as a stable government should be established. Aguinaldo, a Filipino leader, had revolted against our military rule, and we were then engaged in suppressing this insurrection. Bryan was badly beaten in the election, and the result was claimed to be a popular mandate for expansion or nationalism.

The country was as pleased with its new nationalism as a man with a new house. Two letters received by Fuller from eminent lawyers exhibit this attitude on the insular cases. His old friend Judge Lambert Tree wrote him: "In my judgment no more important question has ever come before the Court, for it involves shaping the future policy and destiny of the *Nation*—I begin to like this last word in speaking of this country and people." John N. Jewitt, an eminent lawyer of Chicago and Fuller's intimate friend since Bowdoin days, wrote him: "The United States of America is a *Nation,* made such by . . . the acknowledgment of all the Nations of the world. In its outward relations it is an independent power. The implied powers, accompanying that independent position, are or may be as important as the express powers."

This argument from the necessities of our new nationalism found a place (though a slight one) in the opinions in the *Downes* case. Brown said, "A false step at this time might be fatal to the development of what Chief Justice Marshall called the American Empire." Fuller noted that it had been argued by the government that "absolute power is essential" to the acquisition of "distant territories" and that the Court should "regard the situation as it is today rather than as it was a century ago." His answer was that this argument was "merely political": the question was whether the Act of Congress was within the Constitution.

Bryan, in his campaign against imperialism, had coined the catch phrase, "The Constitution follows the flag." Finley Peter Dunne played on this phrase in his syndicated column "Says Mr. Dooley":

"I see," said Mr. Dooley, "th' Supreme Court has decided th' Constitution don't follow th' flag."

"Who said it did?" asked Mr. Hennessy.

"Some wan," said Mr. Dooley. "It happened a long time ago, an' I don't raymimber clearly how it come up, but some fellow said that ivrywhere the Constitution wint, th' flag was sure to go. 'I don't believe wan wurrud iv it,' says th' other fellow. 'Ye can't make me believe th' Constitution is goin' thrapezin' around ivrywhere a young liftinant in the ar-rmy takes it into his head to stick a flag pole.' "

Then followed a colloquy on the utter confusion of the judges in the decision and the impossibility of understanding the result. It concluded:

"Some say it laves th' flag up in the air, an some say that's where it laves th' Constitution. Annyhow, something's in th' air. But there's wan thing I'm sure about."

"What's that?" asked Mr. Hennessy.

"That is," said Mr. Dooley, "no matter whither th' Constitution follows th' flag or not, th' Supreme Coort follows th' illiction returns."

American historians have sometimes quoted this last sentence from Mr. Dooley as though it were a flash of revealing light on the insular cases. It gives a false emphasis. While the Act sustained had been passed in Congress by a strict party vote, the division of the Court was not at all on political lines. One Democrat (White) voted with the majority, and two Republicans (Brewer and Harlan) were with the minority. Much

more important than a sense of national destiny to explain the
decision was a particular judge's sympathy or lack of sympathy
with the policy of a protective tariff. White had been all his life
a sincere advocate of a protective tariff for American sugar producers. When he was appointed, he had incurred sharp criticism by refusing to take his seat on the Court until he had
finished the battle in the Senate for what he regarded as necessary protection for sugar in the Wilson-Gormley tariff. His
explanation was that "the people of Louisiana were in the
throes of almost a struggle for existence" and he felt that he
was "acting in line of duty." He was the owner of a large sugar
plantation there. Fuller thought that a protective tariff was
wrong. And eight of the nine judges agreed (according to contemporary, professional comment) that the "Constitution follows the flag"; that Congress could not in general legislate for
the territories except under the limitations of the Constitution.

But it was natural for those who were outraged by the
breach that the protectionists had made in the constitutional
limitations on congressional power over the territories to say
that the Court had held that the Constitution did not apply
to the territories. Thus Harlan wrote the Chief Justice a few
weeks after the decision: "The more I think of these questions
the more alarmed I am at the effect upon our institutions of
the doctrine that this country may acquire territory inhabited
by human beings anywhere upon the earth and govern it at the
will of Congress and without regard to the restraints imposed
by the Constitution upon governmental authority. There is
danger that commercialism will sweep away the safeguards of
real freedom and give us parliamentary in place of constitutional government." The next year, when Holmes was appointed to the Court, Harlan wrote: "The indications in the
papers are that he is sufficiently 'expansive' in his views to
suit those who think that it is the destiny of the United States
to acquire & hold outlying possessions 'outside of the Constitution.' " And three years later Brewer wrote to Fuller: "Take
good care of yourself. You must stay on the court till we over-

throw this unconstitutional idea of colonial supreme control."

The *Downes* case and the subsidiary insular cases were decided just before the Court adjourned for the summer in May, 1901. At the request of Justice Brown two cases were held over until fall and were not decided until the following December.

The first such case was entitled *Fourteen Diamond Rings*,[1] and involved the seizure of these rings by the customs authorities from a soldier who had brought them from the Philippines after the cession of those islands and before the enactment of any Philippine tariff act. The case was governed by the *DeLima* case holding that Puerto Rico was not a "foreign country" under existing tariff laws unless the situation of the Philippines was different.

Two differences were suggested:

1. It could be argued that the Philippines *were* a foreign country because, due to Aguinaldo's insurrection, we had not taken possession of them pursuant to the cession from Spain.

2. After the ratification of the treaty the Senate had passed the McEnery Resolution to the effect that it was not intended to incorporate the inhabitants of the Philippines into citizenship in the United States.[2]

During the summer Harlan wrote to Fuller: "I think it would be well for you to prepare something on the Fourteen Rings case to be used as a concurring or dissenting opinion as the situation may require. I do not feel sure that we will hold the judgment in that case. In the DeLima case something was said about the treaty not taking effect . . . until there was delivery of possession by the ceding power. It will be said that we had not obtained such possession in the Philippines. . . . I have some apprehension that Brown may accept this view. If so whatever you write will become or can be turned into a dissenting opinion."

[1] 1901, 183 U.S. 176.
[2] Resolution of Feb. 14, 1899, proposed by Senator Samuel Douglas McEnery of Louisiana.

Fuller prepared such an opinion, which was skillfully drawn to secure Brown's acceptance. On every page it cited Brown's decision in the *DeLima* case. The Chief Justice disposed of the contention that possession had not been taken by saying, "We must decline to assume that the government wishes to disparage its title [under the treaty] or to place itself in the position of waging a war of conquest." On the effect of the resolution, he noted that it was in form a joint resolution of both Houses, but was passed only by the Senate and there only by a bare majority, whereas the treaty had been ratified by the constitutional two-thirds. "The meaning of the treaty," he said, "can not be controlled by the subsequent explanation of some of those who may have voted for it."

Fuller sent his draft of this opinion to Harlan, who responded: "I have received & read (& return herewith) your concurring opinion in the Diamond Rings case. It covers the ground fully. . . . If Brown indicates to you when court meets that he intends to adhere to his vote it will not be necessary, I take it, for us to have a concurring opinion. In that event you could let him have your opinion as embodying your views & thus make it certain that he will say all that ought to be said. My fear that Brown might change his vote in the Diamond case arose from what he said, & his manner of saying it when he asked that the Diamond case go over to the next term."

It was not necessary, of course, for Harlan to coach Fuller in diplomacy. The Chief Justice immediately sent the draft opinion to Brown, who responded: "Have just received yr letter with copy of opinion in the Rings case. I withheld my opinion last term as I had no time to answer the dissent. Of course I had intended to state my views of the McEnery resolution in a revised opinion but you have covered the ground so completely I think yours shd stand as the opinion of the Court. There is every reason in the world why the opinion in this case shd be delivered by the Chief Justice. I may write a short concurrence and call attention to one or two cases I had in mind but it will contain nothing inconsistent with yours. I have also some figures wh I wish to call up in conference as an answer to Brother White's pessimistic views of the consequences."

Brown's suggestion was followed. The Chief Justice delivered the majority decision and Brown concurred in a short opinion. The dissenters merely noted their dissent, without comment.

When Fuller sent to Harlan the letter from Brown stating that he would concur in Fuller's opinion in the *Diamond Rings* case, Harlan suggested that Fuller ought now to prepare an opinion in the one case remaining and try to secure the same result in it. This procedure was followed but without success; Fuller's opinion became a dissent with the same division of the Court as in the *Downes* case. Brown delivered the decision of the Court, White a concurring opinion, and Fuller a dissenting opinion for himself, Harlan, Brewer, and Peckham.

This case involved a duty under the Foraker Act on goods shipped from New York to Puerto Rico. It was claimed to be void under the constitutional clause that "no tax or duty shall be laid on articles exported from any State."

Brown held that "exported" in this clause meant "exported to a foreign country," and Puerto Rico had been held, after its cession, not to be a "foreign country." Furthermore, since the tax was collected in Puerto Rico and the proceeds were segregated for the sole benefit of Puerto Rico, he held that it was a tax on an import in Puerto Rico rather than on an export from New York.

Fuller said that there was no warrant for qualifying the absolute prohibition on Congress to tax "exports from any state" by inserting after the word "exports" the words "to any foreign country." "The right to carry legitimate articles of commerce from one state to another state without interference by national or state authority was . . . secured," Fuller asserted, "by the Constitution." The prohibition on Congress to tax exports therefore applied to exports from one state to another, and applied to Puerto Rico whether it was "a foreign territory, a domestic territory or a territory subject to be dealt with at the will of Congress regardless of constitutional limitations."

On Brown's second point that this was a tax on an import into Puerto Rico rather than an export from New York, Fuller quoted a statement of Marshall's that the prohibition on Congress to tax exports could not be evaded by stationing revenue cutters off the coast of New York and collecting the tax.

Fuller thought that this was the most significant of the insular cases. He wrote to Morris: "The *important* opinion is my dissent in No. 207 as you will see when you read it. The papers have not 'caught on.' " He meant that the establishment of the principle that Congress could tax exports from one state to another was a hazard to commerce between the states. Congress might crucify any state or section of the country by laying a prohibitive tax upon its exports to other states. Brown answered that it was not intended by his opinion to authorize such a tax. He suggested that it would be difficult, if not impossible, to impose such a tax without violating the uniformity clause in the Constitution.

Two years later a case from Hawaii arose which was similar in some aspects to the insular cases. Hawaii had been "annexed" in 1898 by a joint resolution of Congress which provided that the local laws not "contrary to the Constitution of the United States" should remain in force until Congress should otherwise determine. Before Congress acted, a man was convicted of manslaughter, in conformity with the local laws, on an information filed by the Attorney General of Hawaii instead of on an indictment and by a verdict of nine out of twelve jurors. These practices violated two clauses of the Constitution, although some of the states had adopted both of these procedures and they had been held valid under the state constitutions and the due-process clause of the Fourteenth Amendment.

A majority of the Court in an opinion by Brown held that the annexation resolution, while it literally required the full application of the Constitution, should not be interpreted to

bring about the absurd consequence of freeing all persons convicted of infamous crimes before Congress could set up laws to
govern Hawaii. This construction, Brown said, was particularly
applicable because the constitutional principles violated were
not fundamental. Brown reached this result by interpretation
of the annexation resolution and not by any reference to the
insular cases. White, joined only by McKenna, wrote a concurring opinion in which he said that Hawaii had not been
"incorporated" into the United States under his doctrine in
the *Downes* case. Fuller, for himself, Harlan, Brewer, and
Peckham, dissented. He saw no necessity for straining—and
Brown admitted that he was straining—to avoid the full application of the Constitution. Harlan wrote a long dissent pointing out in detail that the treaty with Hawaii (in pursuance of
which the annexation resolution was passed) expressly provided
for "incorporation." He voiced again the fear manifested in his
letter to Fuller that commercialism was subverting the constitutional guaranties for its own purposes.

The issues of the insular cases again flared up in the following
year in the case of *Dorr* v. *United States*,[1] in which the majority
of the Court, in an opinion by Justice Day, held that the constitutional guaranty of jury trial was not applicable to the
Philippine Islands. Day said that the Philippines had "not
been made a part of the United States by Congressional action." While Harlan dissented, Peckham, Fuller, and Brewer
reluctantly concurred on the ground that the Hawaii case, previously discussed, was adequate authority for the present decision. They warned, however, that the *Downes* case was not in
point and that neither of the theories proposed in that case had
been accepted by the majority of the Court.

An amusing recurrence of the controversy arose in the following year. In holding an Act of Congress providing for a jury
of six in Alaska void as a denial of constitutional jury trial,
Justice White devoted a large part of his opinion to showing
that Alaska *had* been "incorporated." This exposition was too

[1] 1904, 195 U.S. 138.

much for Justice Brown. In a specially concurring opinion he said that in the *Downes* case the "incorporation" argument was "simply the individual opinion of three members of the court." "The point was not pressed on our attention in the briefs or arguments of counsel in that case," he said. "It has never since that time received the endorsement of this court and in my opinion it is wholly unnecessary to the disposition of this case."

Charles Henry Butler, the Reporter, told how as soon as White delivered his opinion in this case the Justice sent for the Reporter to meet him behind the screen in the rear of the bench. "As he came toward me," Butler said, "the breeze from the open window blowing out his gown, he was flourishing the proof sheets of his opinion in one hand and shaking the fist of the other at me it seemed. Then he exclaimed in a voice that was probably heard by all who were on the other side of the screen: 'Butler, now *Downes* vs. *Bidwell* is the opinion of the Court and I want you to make it so appear in your report of this case.' "

But it was only after the deaths of Fuller, Brown, Brewer, Peckham, and Harlan that White could state his doctrine of "non-incorporation of territory" without outraged protests. However, in 1921 Chief Justice Taft declared: "The Insular cases revealed much diversity of opinion in this court as to the constitutional status of the territory acquired by the treaty of Paris . . . but the *Dorr* case shows that the opinion of Mr. Justice White of the majority in *Downes* v. *Bidwell* has become the settled law of the court." But Taft was not quite an unprejudiced commentator in this field, as Holmes perhaps indicated by concurring only in the result of the case containing this last remark. Taft as governor of the Philippines had imposed the Philippine tariffs and had himself drawn the Acts of Congress which ratified them. The first such Act had been found ineffective under the *Fourteen Diamond Rings* case in an opinion by Holmes. On rehearing, White and McKenna had dissented. A new Act to ratify these tariffs was then drawn by Taft and was held effective in an opinion by White. It was Taft's custom to say that this last opinion first drew his attention to White's supreme judicial capacities, resulting in his appointment as Chief Justice by Taft as President. Taft spoke on this subject with his usual jovial candor and would probably have readily agreed that he was not entirely objective on the subject of White and the insular cases.

CHAPTER XXI

‿‿

FULLER AND HOLMES
THE APPOINTMENT OF HOLMES

1902

Eᴀʀʟʏ in 1902 Justice Gray fell ill. "He will be seventy-five on Monday," Fuller wrote, "& at that age recuperation is slow." But in June, Fuller reported that Gray had been absent for most of the term—"three weeks at the opening and all the time after February 17." The loss of such a stalwart threw a heavy burden on the Court. The Chief Justice said that it was the hardest year since he had been on the bench.

Rumors soon spread of Gray's impending resignation; and as early as May 20, Senator Henry Cabot Lodge of Massachusetts wrote his close friend President Theodore Roosevelt about it. Senator Lodge was also a lifelong intimate of Chief Justice Oliver Wendell Holmes of the Supreme Judicial Court of Massachusetts. Their youthful association is shown by an excerpt from a speech made by Holmes in Chicago in 1902. "Only twice before in my life," Holmes said, "have I had a glimpse of your wonderful city. Once in 1867, with Mr. Cabot Lodge, not then a Senator of the United States, on our way to shoot prairie chickens. We had met a perfidious friend who hoped we had thick boots on account of the rattlesnakes. So we rose early before even Chicago was awake in the hope of buying some and jumped a yard on the prairie every time a cricket stirred in the grass." It was understood in 1902 that Lodge would suggest Holmes for the vacancy if Gray resigned.

Holmes, after almost thirty years on the Supreme Court of

the United States, has since become such a towering figure—rivaling, if not surpassing, Marshall—that it is difficult to view him as he was in 1902, before he had attained that stature. Eight years younger than Fuller, he was born in Boston in 1841, the son of Dr. Oliver Wendell Holmes, the famous professor of anatomy and author of the Autocrat papers. Immediately upon graduation from Harvard, he marched away to the Civil War, where he suffered three grievous wounds and emerged a brevet colonel. After the war he went to Harvard Law School, from which he graduated in 1866. A trip to England that summer began his lifelong fascination with the English intellectuals. Admitted to the Massachusetts bar in 1867, he practiced law in Boston for fifteen years. At the same time he edited, for three years, the *American Law Review;* prepared the twelfth edition of Kent's *Commentaries on American Law;* and in 1881 published his great legal classic, *The Common Law.* He had served only a few months as a Professor of Law at Harvard Law School when, in 1882, he was appointed to the Supreme Court of Massachusetts. He had been on that court for twenty years—three as Chief Justice—when he was appointed to the Supreme Court of the United States. His legal scholarship was then recognized to be broad and deep and his English style pungent. But, had he died then, at the age of sixty-one, his fame, apart from legal academic circles, would have been small.

When President Roosevelt received Gray's resignation in July, 1902, he wrote to Senator Lodge on Holmes's qualifications for the position. The President recited the many reasons why he wished to appoint Holmes: eminent father, high character, a gallant soldier, highest professional standing, and especially his freedom from class prejudice as demonstrated by certain labor cases in which Holmes had taken the position that picketing "disassociated with violence" was not unlawful. But the President asked to be reassured as to Holmes's political philosophy. Was he a "party man" like John Marshall? Holmes's recent speech on Marshall, Roosevelt said, seemed to show "a total incapacity to grasp what Marshall did" for his party and his country.

"The majority of the present Court," the President wrote, "who have, although without satisfactory unanimity, upheld the policies of President McKinley and the Republican party in Congress, have rendered a great service to mankind and to this nation. The minority—a minority so large as to lack but one vote of being a majority—have stood for such reactionary folly as would have hampered well-nigh hopelessly this people in doing efficient and honorable work for the national welfare, and for the welfare of the islands themselves, in Porto Rico and the Philippines." The President then demanded to know how Holmes would stand on the insular cases.

Probably Lodge did not show this letter, as the President suggested, to Holmes, who, judging by what we now know of him, would have resented it deeply. Lodge had once suggested to him that he run for governor of Massachusetts, and when Holmes asked "Why?" Lodge had answered, "Because from there you could go directly to the United States Senate." "But I wouldn't give a damn to be a Senator," Holmes responded.

In 1886, in a speech at Harvard, he had spoken of the "secret isolated joy of the thinker, who knows that, a hundred years after he is dead and forgotten, men who never heard of him will be moving to the measure of his thought." Holmes toiled for the ages. The United States Senate seemed to him contemporary and trivial. He did not even read the daily newspapers. "I don't understand ambition for an office," he wrote to Pollock apropos of Taft's statement that he had always had an ambition to be Chief Justice. Who could bargain with such a man on the terms of his appointment? Senator Lodge probably assured the President that Holmes was "regular." Two weeks later, in a personal interview, Roosevelt offered Holmes the position. That the President did not dare to mention any conditions of the offer is apparent from Holmes's subsequent votes on the Court, which roused Roosevelt's wrath, and from a letter to Lady Pollock in which Holmes spoke of his "joy of the way" in which the President tendered the appointment. As editor of the *American Law Review,* Holmes had condemned President Grant for appointing Justices Bradley and Strong with an apparent pledge to reverse the legal-tender decision.

After the President announced the appointment, Lodge said that he had never known a "nomination received in the press with such a chorus of praise." But Holmes was "sick" with disappointment: it was such flabby, undiscriminating approval of his life work. The New York *Post* had even written that he was " 'brilliant' rather than sound." He had hoped that they would mention his contributions to the law in the last twenty years and not "bully" him, as he said, with "Shaw, Marshall and the rest."

But what plagued him most in the newspaper notices of his appointment was the inevitable statement that he was the son of the celebrated author. The mainspring of the judge's life had been his will to rise above his station as his father's son— to achieve a place of his own.

Fuller had always been a great admirer of the Autocrat papers. He liked to quote them to his friends. "Everybody says how well you look," he had written to Morris, "but that only means, according to Oliver Wendell Holmes, 'I'm growing old.' " Fortunately, Fuller did not mention his new colleague's father in his letter of congratulations. "Allow me," Fuller wrote, "to express my gratification at your appointment—It seems to me in natural succession to Mr. Justice Story, Mr. Justice Curtis and Mr. Justice Gray, and I am happy in the thought that you will follow them with equal steps—I can assure you of the warmest welcome from us all."

Fuller then regarded Holmes only as "equal" to the great Massachusetts judges on the Supreme Court—Story, Curtis, and Gray. The Chief Justice was to revise this estimate in the next few years. But no one was more delighted with the appointment than Fuller. He had first met the Massachusetts judge in 1888, in Chicago, immediately after his own nomination as Chief Justice. In the interval he had heard Holmes make one of his captivating speeches and had followed his career with pleasure.

In October, after his appointment, Holmes went to Chicago, at the invitation of Dean Wigmore, to attend the dedication of the new Northwestern University Law School and the installation of Edmund J. James as president of the university. With gusto he reported on the trip to Lady Pollock: "I was in alternate crowds of College Presidents . . . and of Judges and leaders of the bar, so I was a howling swell for a time and they seemed to like it and I did. . . . I made two speeches which was two more than I felt up to but they also seemed to please. Indeed as I soaped the Dean, I was sure of having one hearer in my favor. But I said no more than I meant." The deference paid to Holmes in Chicago was not diminished by an item which had appeared two days before in the Chicago *Legal News*. It was headed "A Compliment to Chief Justice Holmes" and reported a recent decision of the English Court of Appeal, in which Fuller's old friend Collins, of the Venezuelan arbitration, had decided a case on the basis of a quotation from Holmes's *Common Law,* which Collins had referred to as an "admirable" work.

The source of this item has been found among the Morris papers in a confidential letter from the Chief Justice:

"Oct. 16, '02

"Private

"DEAR JOHN:

"Judge Holmes will be in Chicago as I understand it the latter part of next week on the occasion of the dedication or opening of the Law School and the installation of Pres't. James. It occurred to me that Bradwell would like to print in the Legal News the matter I enclose. It might be headed 'compliment to Judge Holmes.' But I do not wish Bradwell to know that *I* had anything to do with it and I fear that if I send it to him he would get me in his paper somehow.

"So I send it to you. Can't you write on top of page 1—'Compliment to Judge Holmes' & give it to Bradwell, or get Harry to do so. If *B*. publishes it, send me an extra copy.

"All this is in confidence. I do not wish our honorable friend to know that it comes from me. Harry can look at the advance sheets of English Reports for himself.

"I hope to hear from you about Shepard.

"Yrs. affectly.
M. W. FULLER

"Of course keep this letter to yourself."

When this letter was received, John Morris had suffered a stroke, and so his son, Harry Morris, carried the enclosure to Bradwell of the Chicago *Legal News*. Judge Shepard, who is mentioned in the letter, was seriously ill in a sanatorium. Morris and Shepard were Fuller's closest friends. Morris died a few months later and Shepard never recovered from his illness. Holmes took their place in the Chief Justice's affections.

As soon as Holmes was appointed, a peculiar situation arose on the Massachusetts Supreme Court. His senior associate, Judge Marcus Perrin Knowlton, was promised by the governor the appointment to succeed Holmes as Chief Justice. But if Holmes were not confirmed, and consequently did not resign until after January, 1903, a new governor would make the appointment and another person might receive it.

A "Dear Theodore" letter from Senator Lodge to the President tells the story of the anxiety:

"I had a note from Holmes telling me what he had written you. The very first rate man who is to succeed him as Chief Justice has put the idea in his head that if he remains C. Justice [of the Supreme Court of Massachusetts] it will be interpreted that he does not want the Supreme Bench. I wrote him that he would be confirmed unanimously, that unless you desired to appoint him in the recess, which was not usual in appointments to the Supreme Court, the proper and dignified and natural thing for him to do was to remain Chief Justice until his name had gone into the Senate and was confirmed. . . . I trust sire that this advice founded on truth and wisdom will meet your approbation."

The difficulty was that Senator George F. Hoar of Massachusetts, who was chairman of the Judiciary Committee of the Senate, had supported another candidate for the position on the Supreme Court; while he had promised the President not to oppose the confirmation of Holmes, he might very well delay it for a few weeks, which would perhaps mean a great disappointment to Justice Knowlton of the Supreme Court of Massachusetts. But the Supreme Court of the United States desperately needed Holmes; and Fuller told Senator Hoar of this need, received the necessary assurances from him, and wrote Holmes to prepare to take the oath on December 8. Holmes responded:

"My dear Chief Justice:

"Of course I will do as you desire, and hold myself ready to take the oath and my seat on December 8, if the Senate should have confirmed me before that date. I had supposed from my talk with the late Judge Gray that it was not likely that I should be wanted before January but it will make no difference to me and it will make my senior associate happy if it turns out as you predict.

"With great respect,
Sincerely yours,
O. W. Holmes"

Senator Hoar, however, could not resist telling the Chief Justice what he thought about Holmes. He wrote Fuller on November 5, 1902:

"I have no reason to suppose there will be any delay in acting upon Judge Holmes' nomination. The nomination has been received with very great favor throughout the country, and I have not seen in any newspaper or heard in any political quarter, any suggestion of an objection.

"Judge Holmes is a gentleman, a man of integrity. He will bring to the decisions of all judicial questions an honest purpose to do his duty. He will not be prejudiced or warped by his relations to any party, or desire to affect the political course of the government one way or the other. He is a man of learning and has an excellent style. He is a man of great industry and of courteous manner. He has been a very faithful student of the origins of the English law. So I think he will be a delightful associate to you and the other members of the Court, and will have the good will of the Bar.

"The best lawyers of Massachusetts, almost without exception, think that while he has these excellent qualities, he is lacking in intellectual strength, and that his opinions carry with them no authority merely because they are his. We have contributed from New England some very tough oak timbers to the Bench, State and National. Our lawyers in general, especially those in the country, do not think that carved ivory is likely to be as strong or enduring, although it may seem more ornamental.

"I trust you will not think me guilty of indelicacy in telling you, in strict confidence, exactly what is on my mind. It will not have any effect, and it ought not to have any effect, upon my action in the Senate.

"I am, with high regard, faithfully yours,

GEO. F. HOAR"

Fuller, however, was so confident of Holmes's prompt confirmation that he issued invitations for a dinner party for him at Fuller's home on December 9. Holmes responded:

"DEAR MR. CHIEF JUSTICE

"I accept your kind invitation for Tuesday, December 9, 8 P.M. with much pleasure subject to this implied proviso—Senator Lodge said that he would suggest to you that a hint to Senator Hoar of the need of prompt action might be advisable. Speaking between ourselves, I suppose that the Senator wanted his nephew to be appointed and I am afraid that he does not like me but I suppose that he will offer no opposition, and if so I should suppose that he would do whatever the convenience of the Court required.

"Yours Resptly

O. W. HOLMES"

President Roosevelt, however, feared to accept an invitation to a dinner for a nominee not confirmed. He wrote the Chief Justice:

"MY DEAR MR. CHIEF JUSTICE

"Three cheers for you. . . . Now my dear Mr. Chief Justice I know you will understand my feeling that under the circumstances it will be better for me not to go. I hate to say no, for it is depriving me of a very real pleasure, but I think it will be wiser taking into view all the facts.

"With hearty regards

Sincerely yours,

THEODORE ROOSEVELT"

Senator Lodge was more practical. He wrote the Chief Justice on December 2:

"It will give me great pleasure to dine with you on Monday next.

"Judge Holmes' name came in today and ought to be reported and confirmed tomorrow. I think if you could send a line to Senator Hoar (1605 Connecticut Avenue) asking him to have the report and confirmation at once it would be of great assistance. We will probably adjourn over on Thursday to Monday.

"Hence it is very important to dispose of this nomination tomorrow if possible. A line from you to Mr. Hoar tonight would, I am sure, bring this about."

Doubtless Fuller wrote Senator Hoar, as Lodge requested, because Holmes was confirmed on December 4. Charles Henry Butler, the new Reporter of the Court, tells in his reminiscences how, just as Holmes went on the Bench to take the oath, he handed Butler a telegram, to be sent to the governor of Massachusetts, containing his resignation as Chief Justice of the Supreme Court of Massachusetts. It was like Holmes to take no chances and to turn his corners squarely. And so Judge Knowlton was appointed Chief Justice of the Supreme Judicial Court of Massachusetts.

The bar at Boston gave a farewell dinner for Holmes. Among the young lawyers present was Dixon Weston, the son of Fuller's favorite cousin, Paulina. She had been reared in the same household with the Chief Justice and was like a sister to him. Dixon Weston and his friends thought that Holmes talked too much about the Civil War. Even though he *had* been seriously wounded three times,—he went on talking about the war after everyone else had stopped. Amused glances were exchanged when in his farewell address, after saying that it was a wrench to leave, Holmes remarked: "But . . . to have one's chance to do one's share in shaping the laws of the whole country spreads over one the hush that one used to feel when awaiting the beginning of battle. We will not falter. . . . We will reach the earthworks if we live. . . . All is ready. Bugler, sound the charge."

After the dinner Dixon Weston wrote his mother's cousin, the Chief Justice of the United States. "There is about to be a charge upon your Court," he said. He then described the speech and to clinch his point referred to the Chief Justice's favorite, Dickens. "The readiness of Holmes for battle," he suggested, "was reminiscent of Mr. Winkle's famous readiness for battle on a certain occasion." An ominous silence on the part of the Chief Justice followed: he never answered that letter, and Dixon Weston knew that he had been rebuked. But a few months later, in writing to Dixon's mother, the Chief Justice remarked: "Tell Dixon that it was Snodgrass,—not Winkle." Twice rebuked!

Holmes's colleagues on the Court gloried—perhaps more than he—in his Civil War valor. They did, however, criticize him from time to time for rapturous passages in his opinions. "State the reason for your conclusion directly," they said. A small volume of Holmes's speeches had been published in 1900, and in 1904 Holmes presented a copy to the Chief Justice with a letter:

"DEAR CHIEF

"In view of your repeated taunts as to the pure reason I think I must convince you that I can drool on occasion and therefore send you this little volume with my affectionate regards.

"Sincerely yours,
O. W. HOLMES"

The Chief Justice responded:

"MY DEAR COLLEAGUE

"I am delighted with your note and the volume of charming 'Speeches' which accompanies it—

"Enthusiasm is not eliminated from these nor even a touch of rapture, but I shall endeavor to take the lesson to heart that what is elevating and appropriate in the one case may be 'drooling' in the other, though it is a sacrilege to use such a word as applied to these thoughts under any circumstances—I heard you in June, 1895, & the allusion at the close to the line of spearheads put me in mind of something in Hallam's Middle Ages about the first gleam of the lances of France in the depths of the Alps."

In this speech, Holmes, speaking of the long development of the common law, had concluded: "And so the eternal procession moves on, we in the front for the moment; and, stretching away against the unattainable sky, the black spearheads of the Army that has been passing in unbroken line already for near a thousand years."

CHAPTER XXII

○◡○

FULLER AND HOLMES ON THE COURT

1902–1905

HOLMES was enthralled with the work of the Court. Soon after he arrived, he wrote to Pollock: "Yes—here I am—and more absorbed, interested and impressed than ever I dreamed I might be." Exuberantly he reported that he had already written opinions in cases from such faraway places as California, Arkansas, and Wisconsin. On the same date he wrote to Fuller:

"DEAR CHIEF JUSTICE

"Or ought I to have said Mr. Chief Justice? I enclose another opinion and have my third nearly ready. I have not heard from Harlan, Brewer, Shiras or Peckham J J as to 41 Otis v. Parker.[1] I suppose I am to do nothing until the next conference? Mr. J. Harlan to be sure said on the day that he received it that he had read it and I understood him to agree— I also want to consult you as to what we are to do on New Year's day as to the President. But perhaps I shall hear from him on Tuesday as I believe we are to dine and go to the play

---

[1] 1903, 187 U.S. 606—Holmes's first case. The opinion held valid a provision of the California constitution forbidding sales of stock on margin. Brewer and Peckham dissented. The opinion contains an oft-quoted dictum: "It by no means is true that every law is void which may seem to the judges who pass upon it excessive, unsuited to its ostensible end or based on conceptions of morality with which they disagree."

with him on that day.[1] I cannot tell you how much I am impressed by and enjoy the work here.

"With much respect

Sincerely yours,

O. W. HOLMES"

Holmes's doubt of Harlan's approval of this first opinion suggests that Harlan stood somewhat aloof from Holmes. Harlan had judged from newspaper reports that Holmes had committed himself to the President on the wrong side (to Harlan) of the insular cases. Years later Holmes told how the Chief Justice had averted a clash between him and Harlan in the conference room. Harlan was expounding his theory of a case when Holmes, violating the rule against interruptions, cut in and said, "But that just won't wash." Harlan was outraged; his fists clenched and his eyes bulged. But the Chief saw instantly what was happening, flashed his radiant smile, started a quick washboard motion with his hands, and said, "But I just keep scrubbing away, scrubbing away." The Justices laughed and the incident was passed off. Holmes told the tale to illustrate Fuller's skill and dexterity as a moderator. "As a presiding officer," Holmes said, "Fuller was the greatest Chief Justice I have ever known." Holmes made this comment after he had served under Chief Justices Fuller, White, Taft, and Hughes. Mr. Justice Miller, who served under Chief Justices Taney, Chase, Waite, and Fuller, had made almost an identical statement about Fuller to Senator Cullom many years before.

As Holmes struck his stride on the Court and his intimacy with the Chief Justice increased, it became his custom to ask for additional cases instead of waiting for assignments. The following letters, written in February, 1903, in the rush that precedes the February recess, are typical of many such letters:

---

[1] It was customary for all Justices of the Court to call on the President on New Year's Day. Holmes was in his "honeymoon" period with President Roosevelt. The next year a coolness developed.

Feb. 5, 1903

"DEAR CHIEF JUSTICE

"I am on my last case barring the one you told me not to write until further notice and the getting in of McKenna.

"If you will give me some of yours I shall be grateful.

"Sincerely yours,

O. W. HOLMES

"P.S. I shall finish the last tomorrow."

Feb. 6, 1903

"DEAR CHIEF JUSTICE

". . . If there are 2 more weeks—I can write almost any old thing that anyone will give me. A case doesn't generally take more than two days if it does that.

"Yours sincerely

O. W. HOLMES"

Holmes's zeal and speed, while it pleased the Chief Justice, did not add to his popularity with the other Justices. A few days after the last letter, Fuller wrote to Peckham: "Are you willing to part with No. 121 to Holmes, J? I shall be glad to put it in his hopper." Peckham returned the letter with an endorsement: "I will part with it in spite of —— —— as Brother Harlan would say! P." Peckham's blanks may not refer to Holmes, but Harlan's vituperation usually had a subject.

Fuller's delight with his new colleague's zest for work is indicated by a letter to Mrs. Fuller written just before the February recess: "We shall dispose of more than fifty cases at our next meeting—more than ever before I believe—The Nimble Holmes has got out his last—I delayed his progress for about a week but he deserved the obstacle & is free and clear & I suppose eager for more work."

One of the cases decided at this time was the famous *Lottery* case, holding valid a federal statute excluding lottery tickets from interstate commerce. The case had been argued three times; and the division of the Court was five to four, with Harlan writing the majority opinion and Fuller the dissent for himself, Brewer, Peckham, and Shiras. Fuller's position was that lottery tickets (like insurance policies) were not articles of commerce and, if they were, the federal power to "regulate" interstate commerce did not include power to exclude articles therefrom. This opinion shows again Fuller's strong desire to preserve interstate commerce from all unnecessary restriction, state or federal, as previously indicated in the original-package cases and the insular cases.

Holmes was on the other side—the majority—in this case. Before the decision was announced, Fuller's fellow dissenter, Shiras, wrote to him: "I have read with care your dissenting opinion in No. 2 [the Lottery case]. It is just the thing—clear and convincing. I wonder if White and Holmes may not yet come over. I will talk with the former." Apparently White and Holmes had not been very firm in their attachment to the majority. But Shiras's aversion to arguing with Holmes is apparent. Shiras suggests by innuendo that the Chief Justice is the proper person to win Holmes for the dissenters. But if Fuller talked to Holmes on this case, he was not successful. Holmes seldom changed his mind once he had decided a question, and he was very reluctant to hold any law, state or federal, to be unconstitutional.

Another case in Holmes's first term in which Fuller apparently tried without success to persuade Holmes to join the dissenters was *Snyder* v. *Bettman*.[1] It was held in this case that a federal estate tax could constitutionally be imposed upon a legacy to a city despite the settled law that the federal government could not tax the property of the states or their municipalities and the states could not tax the property of the federal government. The federal estate tax was said not to be on the property but on the right to succeed to it. The dissenters were Fuller, White, and Peckham, the only Democratic Justices on the Court.

[1] 1903, 190 U.S. 249.

It had previously been held that the states could impose a similar tax on bequests to the federal government. Brown, for the majority, argued that Congress should have the same power to tax legacies to states as the states had to tax legacies to the United States. White in his dissent pointed out that the states could repeal the privilege of inheritance entirely, which the federal government could not do. The validity of the federal tax on legacies to states could not be based, therefore, on the validity of the state tax on federal legacies. Holmes wrote to Fuller that he agreed with White's distinction and thought Brown was wrong in basing the decision on the state cases. But Holmes thought that since the tax was upon the entire estate, the portion of the tax falling on the city was only incidental, and should be upheld.[1]

The most important case of Holmes's second year was the famous merger case of the Northern Securities Company.[2] Morgan and Hill attempted to merge the competing Great Northern and Northern Pacific railroads through the acquisition of a majority of the stock of both railroads by the Northern Securities Company, a New Jersey corporation. With great fanfare President Theodore Roosevelt ordered Attorney General Knox to secure an injunction against the merger under the Sherman Act.

[1] Holmes to Fuller, May 13, 1903: "230 [*Snyder* v. *Bettman*] lies in my mind thus. I agree with White that the State and U.S. taxes stand on different grounds. The U.S. taxes the faculty of testation (to use a bad word) and must be judged purely on grounds of taxation. This is not brought out as it should be. Brown and his conclusion that the U.S. should not have less power than the States is misleading. But taking the tax as I have stated it, it is good in general and I should be prepared to say that as the indirect effect on property coming to a city was only incidental and accidental the tax should be upheld even as against the city. We recognize in other cases the difference of degree—not every tax that in some slight degree falls on interstate commerce, for instance, is bad. There is this difficulty in the other view. We say generally that when the law does not distinguish we cannot—and it must be good in all cases or it is bad altogether. I fear we shall meet that in this case—and have to hold that if this tax is bad as to legacies to cities, the law is wholly void, as it makes no distinction. I am writing without looking at the papers—trusting to memory" [Genet papers].

[2] *Northern Securities Company* v. *United States*, 1904, 193 U.S. 197.

As soon as the injunction was issued by the United States Circuit Court in Minnesota, the legal periodicals teemed with discussion of it. This case raised the issue of whether the purchase of a controlling interest in competing corporations violated the Act. The Act condemned contracts or combinations in restraint of trade or commerce among the states. It prohibited attempts to monopolize any part of such trade or commerce. It had been previously applied to contracts not to compete or to fix rates or prices, but it had never been applied to a consolidation, merger, or fusion. If it were so applied, then the creation of a partnership between two small merchants operating across a state line was apparently criminal. The railroads in the United States had developed through consolidation or merger, and the question was whether this traditional procedure was a violation of the law.

The Court divided four to four, with Harlan, Brown, McKenna, and Day for affirming the injunction and Fuller, White, Peckham, and Holmes against it. Brewer was in the middle but leaned toward sustaining the injunction. A month before the decision was announced, Fuller wrote to Holmes: "I had an interesting interview with Brewer yesterday & he is inclined to write out his own views—Yours will hit him between wind and water."

Harlan delivered the opinion of the Court affirming the injunction, and Brewer a specially concurring opinion disavowing portions of Harlan's opinion. Harlan held that in any event this colossal merger was within the Act. It would be time enough, he said, to consider the case of individual or corporate purchases of controlling interests in small competing corporations when that case arose. Brewer in his specially concurring opinion said that the prior cases had been wrong in not limiting the scope of the Act to "unreasonable restraints of trade." Furthermore, he held that under the Constitution, Hill, as an individual, had the right to buy the stock of the two railroads and that no law could prevent him. But the Northern Securities Company was only an instrumentality, he concluded, to permit several individuals to pool their stock in a manner which constituted an unreasonable restraint of trade. White, joined by Fuller, Peckham, and Holmes, dissented on the ground that Congress had no power under the commerce clause to control the acquisition and ownership of stock in railroads. Such control was purely a matter of state law.

Holmes read a dynamic dissent. "Great cases," he suggested, "like hard cases, make bad law. For great cases are called great, not by reason of their real importance in shaping the law of the future, but because of some accident of immediate overwhelming interest which appeals to the feelings and distorts the judgment."

"The statute of which we have to find the meaning," he noted, "is a criminal statute. The two sections on which the Government relies both make certain acts crimes. . . . The words cannot be read in one way in a suit which is to end in fine and imprisonment and another way in one which seeks an injunction. . . . Before a statute is to be taken to punish that which always has been lawful it must express its intent in clear words."

This Act should be interpreted, he suggested, so as not to raise grave doubts of its constitutionality. Congress was in a dubious field, he argued, when it attempted to regulate "contracts the bearing of which upon commerce would be only indirect." "Commerce depends upon population, but Congress could not, on that ground, undertake to regulate marriage and divorce."

The Act first forbade contracts or combinations in restraint of trade. Holmes said that these terms were defined by the common law, and they did not include restraint of trade arising inevitably from partnerships, mergers, or fusions.

The Act then forbade "every person" from "attempting to monopolize" "any part" of the trade or commerce among the several states. The word "monopolize" might be used here in the popular sense of the campaign orator or it might be used in the legal, technical sense of the law of "restraint of trade."

Combinations in restraint of trade at common law were not objectionable unless they amounted to a monopoly. "The notion of monopoly [in contracts in restraint of trade] did not come in unless the contract covered the whole of England."

The word "monopolize," Holmes said, clearly could not have been used in the popular sense. "There is a natural inclination to assume that it was directed against certain great combinations. It does not say so. On the contrary, it says 'every' and 'any part.' "

"Every railroad monopolizes, in a popular sense, the trade of some area. Yet I suppose no one would say that the statute forbids a combination of men into a corporation to build and run such a railroad between the States." In any sense, he declared, in which the proposed merger in this case creates a monopoly, the original charter of each of the constituents created monopolies. If the word "monopolize" is used in the popular sense, it clearly applies to the individual who purchases competing companies; and yet a majority of the Court, he said, held that it had no such application.

"There is a natural feeling," he ended, "that somehow or other the statute meant to strike at combinations great enough to cause just anxiety on the part of those who love their country more than they love money, while it viewed such little ones as I have supposed with just indifference." But "the very words of the act," Holmes said, "make such a distinction impossible."

This was Holmes's first great dissent. The scene as he delivered it was described by the Chief Justice in a letter to Mrs. Fuller. "When his voice, refined and clear, rose in the Court Room you could have heard a pin drop & his sentences were as incisive as the edge of a knife." It was many years before the world discovered the immense power of Holmes's opinions, but Fuller early came to know it. One of his secretaries tells how, whenever a new opinion by Holmes was brought to the Chief Justice, he would stop whatever he was doing and read it aloud with exclamations of pleasure and admiration. "Isn't that marvelous? Doesn't he write superbly?" he would say. Fuller's style was rather stodgy, but so was every other judge's in comparison with Holmes's.

To Holmes's surprise President Roosevelt resented his dissent in the Northern Securities case; Holmes was frequently oblivious of how barbed his words were. Years later, after Roosevelt's death, Holmes wrote to Pollock, quoting a senator, "What the boys like about Roosevelt is that he doesn't care a damn for the law." Holmes then said: "It [that is, this attitude] broke up our incipient friendship however, as he looked on my dissent in the *Northern Securities case* as a political departure (or, I suspect, more truly, couldn't forgive anyone who stood in his way.) We talked freely later but it was never the same after that, and if he had not been restrained by friends, I am told he would have made a fool of himself and would have excluded me from the White House—and as in his case about the law, so in mine about that, I never cared a damn whether I went there or not. He was very likeable, a big figure, a rather ordinary intellect, with extraordinary gifts, a shrewd and I think pretty unscrupulous politician. He played all his cards—if not more. *R.i.p.*" Holmes's sentiments about Roosevelt were fully shared by the Chief Justice.

Holmes's next great dissent, given the following year in *Lochner* v. *New York*,[1] is one of his most famous. The majority (Fuller, Brewer, Brown, Peckham, and McKenna) held unconstitutional, as a denial of "liberty" under the Fourteenth Amendment, the New York ten-hour law for bakers. This law made more than ten hours' work in one day a crime by both employer and employee. There was no exception for emergencies. The majority opinion was by Peckham, and dissents were delivered by both Harlan and Holmes. The case was first decided the opposite way, and Harlan's dissent was originally prepared as the opinion of the Court. One of the attorneys who brought the case to the Supreme Court was a young baker who had studied law and had become impressed with the idea that the ten-hour law was an unconstitutional infringement of the

[1] 1905, 198 U.S. 45.

liberty of bakers. He was admitted specially in the Supreme Court to argue this case. The Court had previously held valid a Utah eight-hour law for miners on the ground that the health of the workers was involved. It was agreed that a state had the right to protect the health of its people even at the expense of their liberty. But the majority in the *Lochner* case held that an Act limiting the hours of bakers could not be sustained as a law to protect their health. Nearly every housewife baked!

Holmes dissented in language now almost as well known as Lincoln's Gettysburg Address:

"This case is decided upon an economic theory which a large part of the country does not entertain. If it were a question whether I agreed with that theory, I should desire to study it further and long before making up my mind. But . . . I strongly believe that my agreement or disagreement has nothing to do with the right of a majority to embody their opinions in law. . . . The Fourteenth Amendment did not enact Mr. Herbert Spencer's Social Statics. . . . I think that the word liberty in the Fourteenth Amendment is perverted when it is held to prevent the natural outcome of a dominant opinion, unless it can be said that a rational and fair man necessarily would admit that the statute proposed would infringe fundamental principles as they have been understood by the traditions of our people and our law."

This case came into great notoriety because it was a main basis of Theodore Roosevelt's presidential campaign plank in 1912 for the recall of judicial decisions. The *Lochner* case is sometimes cited to condemn Fuller and his colleagues of the majority as reactionaries without social consciousness or ordinary humanity. This condemnation is unfair. Holmes often disclaimed the title of "humanitarian." "I loathe," he declared, "the thick-fingered clowns we call the people." Fuller, on the other hand, was deeply sympathetic with the laboring man, as many of his decisions show. But the ten-hour law for bakers seemed to him to be "featherbedding," paternalistic, and depriving both the worker and employer of fundamental liberties. He was not as farseeing as Holmes. But few were.

However, Fuller's restraint in applying the Fourteenth Amendment to strike down state laws was greater even than Holmes's. During the nine years of their joint service, the Court in 21 cases declared state action invalid under the Fourteenth Amendment; out of these, Fuller dissented in 8 cases and Holmes in 6. They dissented together in 5 of these cases (Fuller and Holmes were together in every such dissent by Holmes except the *Lochner* case), and in addition Fuller dissented in 3 cases where Holmes did not.

The Chief Justice and Holmes were drawn closer together by Mrs. Fuller's death in the summer of 1904. She died suddenly of a heart attack while picking flowers for a guest at their summer home at Sorrento, Maine. She was twelve years younger than Fuller, and her death was a great shock. Holmes immediately wrote to him:

"MY DEAR CHIEF

"We were deeply grieved by your telegram. It is the fall of a great town and we shall feel that a large space has been left empty. Of your loss I do not venture to speak but . . . both of us so appreciated her high and noble qualities and were so single in our admiration of them that to us also the loss will be very great. I know your courage and that you will rise to your duties in the same heroic way you always have and if it is any pleasure to you to hear that I think of you always with the same affection and faith I like to tell it to you and hope that you know it beyond a doubt. We shall await some further information as to the arrangements for the funeral.

"Affectionately yours,

O. W. HOLMES"

Fuller responded:

"MY DEAR COLLEAGUE

"Your letter of 18th was & is comforting to me—It shows that you & Mrs. Holmes appreciated the nobility of character of my beloved wife—She crossed the continent—she crossed the sea—she went to & fro covering her brood beneath her wings—and her children arise up & call her blessed—of course her husband does & 'Praiseth her'—Six of our daughters and her only sister, to whom she has been mother as well as sister, were with us at the grave—One daughter & one son were too ill to be present—

"The day was beautiful & she was laid at rest by the side of our first born son & near her father to whom she was devotedly attached & leaving room for me—we had services here Thursday & went on to Chicago, where the final service was had on Saturday—I was so stunned that I did not telegraph again as I ought to have done—Her birthday was Friday, the 19th—

"Dear colleague, this was a love match and it continued for more than thirty eight years—The heart has reasons that Reason knows not of, according to Pascal and the fact. I was introduced to her on Saturday, with her the next Saturday & engaged to her the Wednesday after—And amidst trials and tribulations we lived happy ever afterwards—and she died in my arms—

"I should be unworthy of her if I did not struggle to perform my duty—The separation to her cannot be more than a moment—in fact not measurable by time, & to me not very long—

"I gave Brewer last fall on our return from Europe a copy of an epitaph *we* read in Gray Friars Church Yard, Edinburgh—

" 'She was

What words are wanting to express,—
Think what a wife should be,
And she was that.—'

"Affectionately yrs

MELVILLE W. FULLER"

Thereafter in Washington Holmes called on Fuller nearly every Sunday. Holmes told the Chief to send for him whenever he was needed. The next year Fuller could not stay in Sorrento and returned to Washington in September. From there he wrote to Holmes:

"My very dear colleague

"I arrived here on Saturday night—The truth is that Sorrento grew so sad that I could not remain . . . though I carried in my heart that if I summoned you you would come I did not feel that I ought to do it as the melancholy days had come. . . . I hope you & Mrs. Holmes are very well—give my love to her—and accept mine."

CHAPTER XXIII

◦‿◦

"I AM NOT TO BE 'PARAGRAPHED' OUT OF MY PLACE."

1902–1910

WHEN Justice Shiras in October, 1902, told President Roosevelt that he wished to retire from the Court, the President's choice for a successor was William Howard Taft. Roosevelt sincerely admired Taft and was indebted to him for his own political advancement, for Taft had taken considerable part in securing Roosevelt's appointment as Assistant Secretary of the Navy in 1897. Before McKinley's death, when Roosevelt did not regard himself as eligible for the Presidency in 1904, he had declared that he felt "in honor bound" to make Taft either President or Chief Justice. (All his life Taft had said that he would rather be Chief Justice than be President.) After Roosevelt became President—and as a result a candidate for the nomination in 1904—there was an additional reason for him to put Taft on the Supreme Court. To do so would eliminate a rival (though an unwilling one) for the Republican nomination for President. Roosevelt's enemies—and he made many—mentioned Taft as a possible opponent.

This situation explains Roosevelt's frantic efforts to get Taft to accept the Shiras vacancy and, when Taft refused, to induce Fuller to resign so that Taft might be appointed Chief Justice. The President first cabled, offering Taft, then governor of the Philippines, the position as Associate Justice. Taft declined by cable the following day. He was engrossed in his task in the Philippines and sincerely felt that he must finish it. A month later Roosevelt wrote him: "I am awfully sorry, old man, but

. . . I shall have to bring you home and put you on the Supreme Court. . . . After all, old fellow, if you will permit me to say so, I am President, and see the whole field." Taft cabled: "Recognize soldier's duty to obey orders. . . . However, I presume on our personal friendship even in the face of your letter to make one more appeal." This plea, strongly reinforced by cables from the other Philippine commissioners and leading Filipinos, proved too powerful for the President.

But Roosevelt had another shot in his locker. He was the inventor of a presidential device called the "trial balloon," under which the President gave a fanciful story to the newspapers and forbade them to print it as coming from him. Then the President watched the public reaction. A few days after Taft's cable pleading that he be allowed to finish his task in the Philippines, a "White House" story appeared in the press to the effect that Taft would not accept the offer of the Shiras vacancy and that the appointee would probably be Judge William R. Day of Ohio. The item stated that the President would appoint Taft to the Supreme bench when he had concluded his work in the Philippines. It then continued:

> The suggestion is made that Chief Justice Fuller may soon wish to retire and that Governor Taft would be a suitable man for the vacancy.

This sentence produced a flood of speculation in the newspapers. The Chief Justice read the original item with consternation. He was seventy years of age, but he had not thought of resigning. However, over the next six years, he was to become accustomed to the President's trial balloons on the resignation of the Chief Justice. "I am not," he once commented to Justice Holmes, "to be 'paragraphed' out of my place." Shortly after his original suggestion of Fuller's retirement, the President sent Wayne MacVeagh to inquire of the Chief Justice whether there was any basis for the rumor. Fuller assured him there was none.

On January 29, 1903, Roosevelt dramatically announced the

appointment of Judge Day by addressing him before a large audience as "Mr. Justice Day." Day's and Fuller's relations had been cordial during Day's term as Secretary of State. Fuller immediately wrote congratulating him and the next month gave his usual dinner for the new Justice. A significant bit of repartee at this party is preserved in the reminiscences of Charles Henry Butler, the Reporter:

"While coffee was being served in the drawing room, a young officer called to say good-by to the Chief Justice and Mrs. Fuller. He had been suddenly ordered to the Philippines. . . . Mrs. Fuller . . . called from the floor above to the young officer, and said that, though she could not come downstairs, she would talk to him over the bannisters. After the exchange of farewells, and just as the young officer was going out the front door, Mrs. Fuller called to him . . . 'And when you get to the Philippines you tell Willie Taft not to be in too much of a hurry to get into my husband's shoes.' "

Apparently the Fullers blamed Taft for the suggestion of the Chief Justice's resignation. They were almost certainly mistaken in the light of letters which have since been published. Although Taft never concealed his yearnings to be Chief Justice rather than President, his conviction at that time was supreme that he must complete his work in the Philippines. Roosevelt's trial balloon was probably directed quite as much at Taft as at Fuller.

However, the news stories of Fuller's impending retirement were disturbing to his friends. Grover Cleveland wrote to Judge Putnam: "I wonder if there is anything in the talk of Chief Justice Fuller's retirement. . . . I don't know what the Court will come to unless a little more strength is vouchsafed in new appointments." Putnam wrote to Fuller referring to an article in *Harper's Weekly* to the effect that Fuller's retirement would be a misfortune. "Mr. Cleveland wrote me about the rumors," Putnam said, "and he was evidently somewhat disturbed by them. I was gratified to reply to him that your health never seemed better than when I met you at Boston last Autumn, and that I was assured that it was still most excellent and further that I did not credit that there was any reason to fear the occurrence of the rumored catastrophe."

Fuller then wrote to Cleveland that he was reminded of a remark made by Chief Justice Weston of Maine, Fuller's grandfather, about Federal Judge Ware. A group of politicians in Maine, Fuller said, were discussing the possibility of Judge Ware resigning. It was suggested that he was growing old and was tiring of his judicial duties and besides, his wife was very wealthy and had just built a large block of buildings. Soon they had practically selected his successor. But Judge Weston cut in gruffly to say, "In my opinion Judge Ware will resign when it pleases God." Fuller often told this story when he was plagued by the trial balloons.

Cleveland responded: "Of all men in the world I ought to be the last to believe what I read in the newspapers; but somehow I connected what I read there about your retiring with something I heard about your having rheumatism and thought it not amiss to refer to the rumor when writing to Judge Putnam feeling assured he would know if there was anything in it. When I heard from him I put the report where it belongs— among newspaper canards—Since that time I have recovered for good, my place among those who believe you should only 'resign when it pleases God.'"

The next year, when Taft returned to Washington to be Secretary of War, Fuller, as president of the Harvard Law School Association, introduced him with gentle raillery as Orator of the Day at the annual banquet at Cambridge. Fuller said:

"When the late Governor of the Philippines arrived at Washington, as soon as I penetrated the dense thicket of laurels that embowered him, he propounded this question: 'How's the Docket?' I recognized at once the demonstration of his fitness for the highest judicial station. It is very true that I knew my friend had been a professor and Dean of a law school, had been a judge of a state court, had been Solicitor General of the United States and Judge of the Circuit Court of the United

States, and Governor as aforesaid and had discharged the duties of all these positions to great acceptance, but I had not realized before that he felt that interest in the docket which is considered a principal qualification of Chief Justices.

"Of course I make that remark with some reservation. I make it as the love letters of a young man by the name of Guppy were written,—without prejudice. But letting the future take care of itself, we now find Mr. Secretary Taft occupying a different position from any heretofore filled by him and I think I can assure him that we all have no doubt that the duties of that rather novel place will be discharged with the same success as those which have preceded it.

"His present position brings him into close connection with the Chief Magistrate, and on that account I venture to ask him to allow me in giving the health of the Orator of the Day to couple with it the health of a Harvard boy of 1880—the President of the United States."

These remarks are typically Fuller. They indicate how absurd was any suggestion that he was senile. Though he had a grievance against Roosevelt and, as he thought, against Taft, he made light of it. He did not snarl at them, but neither did he truckle to them. His personal complaints did not prevent him from recognizing their merits. In other words, he kept his head.

William Rufus Day, who became the junior Justice of the Court on March 2, 1903, was the son of a Chief Justice of the Supreme Court of Ohio and the grandson of another Justice of that court. A great-grandfather had been Chief Justice of Connecticut. Born in 1849, Day graduated at the University of Michigan and studied law in a lawyer's office with one year at the University Law School. He was admitted to the Ohio bar at the age of twenty-three and established himself at Canton, Ohio. As a trial lawyer he built a fine reputation at the local bar and became the fast friend of another Canton lawyer, William McKinley. Reluctantly, Day went to Washington in 1897 at McKinley's request to serve as First Assistant Secretary of

State when John Sherman, the Secretary, began to show signs of mental weakness. Day was thereafter Secretary of State and president of the Spanish-American Peace Commission. In 1899 President McKinley appointed him to the Circuit Court of Appeals in the Sixth Circuit, where he had served for three years when he came to the Supreme Court. He was small in stature and was noted for his tact and reticence. Day's relations with Fuller were always happy. A few years later, Fuller chose as his secretary one of Day's sons.

The next vacancy on the Court arose in 1906, with the resignation of Justice Brown. Again Roosevelt tendered the place to Taft, but this time the President did not demand acceptance: Taft had become Roosevelt's choice for his successor in 1908. This prospect was a nightmare to Taft, who reiterated his desire to be Chief Justice rather than President. But Mrs. Taft took a firm hand for the Presidency and against a judicial career, especially one that did not start with the Chief Justiceship. Taft's interest in Fuller's health became acute. "If the Chief Justice would retire, how simple everything would become," Taft wrote to his wife. Again there was a storm of published rumors that Fuller would resign. Again his friends were concerned. Holmes spoke to him directly on the subject, and the next day Fuller wrote him: "Dear Holmes, thank you very much for your expressions yesterday of the hope that I would not yield to newspaper paragraphs & retire—Of course I won't —But I am glad to be assured that my brethren see no particular reason why I should."

A few months later, S. S. Gregory, of Chicago, wrote to Fuller that he had had a long talk with William H. Moody, the Attorney General. "He referred," Gregory said, "to the newspaper talk about the likelihood that you might retire and then said with emphasis that there was no reason why you should— that none of the members of the Court asked you to, that you discharged the duties of your office in a most admirable manner."

The next year, when the "paragraphs" continued, Cleveland

wrote: "Remembering how a few years ago you quieted my ap-
prehensions . . . by relating the Maine story of a man who
would only retire . . . 'when God willed,' I am fervently praying every day that God's will may be long postponed and that
you will continue to await it. I am not sure that you feel as
deeply as some of your countrymen the importance to our
country of your resignation to divine disposition in this
matter."

In 1908 Justice Shiras, now retired, whose resignation had
raised the discussions of Fuller's retirement, wrote him: "It is
to be hoped that there will be no occasion for any change in the
personnel of the Supreme Court. On this delicate subject I need
say no more." But in the same year Elihu Root, the third member of the so-called "Three Musketeers" of Roosevelt, Taft,
and Root, wrote that he had concluded that Fuller would "stay
indefinitely." "They will have to shoot him on the day of
judgment," Root said.

William Henry Moody of Massachusetts, the Attorney General, was appointed to succeed Justice Brown in December,
1906. Moody was born in 1853 on a Massachusetts farm, educated at Phillips Andover and Harvard University and attended Harvard Law School for a few months, completing his
legal education in the office of Richard H. Dana, Jr., and being
admitted to the bar in 1878. He early laid down the rule for
himself: "The power of clear statement is the greatest power
at the bar." He attracted favorable comment from both Gray
and Holmes when he argued cases before them in the Supreme
Judicial Court of Massachusetts. As prosecutor in the Lizzie
Borden murder case, he acquired wide public recognition. In
1902, after several years in Congress, he was appointed Secretary of the Navy by President Roosevelt and in 1904 Attorney
General. In that office he personally argued many more cases
than his predecessors and made a brilliant record. In one important case when he apologized for the length of his argument,
the Chief Justice interrupted. "Your argument is very interesting," he said. "You need offer no apology." When Moody was

THE COURT AS IT STOOD FROM 1906 TO 1909

Top row: *Justice Day, Justice McKenna, Justice Holmes, Justice Moody*
Bottom row: *Justice White, Justice Harlan, Chief Justice Fuller, Justice Brewer, Justice Peckham*

appointed to the Court, Fuller wrote to Gregory: "I have always liked his way of stating things"; and Holmes wrote to Pollock: "We have a new Judge, another Mass. man whom I think well of." Unfortunately, Moody served only three years, being compelled to retire by extreme ill health in 1910.

In view of the pressure that had been put upon Fuller to resign, it is not surprising that he stayed on the bench slightly longer than he should. Perhaps the worst year in the history of the Court was the term commencing in October, 1909, and ending in May, 1910, just prior to Fuller's sudden death in July of that year. Justice Moody was entirely incapacitated; Justice Peckham died in October and Justice Brewer the following March. These casualties would have disrupted the Court under a young and vigorous Chief Justice. Fuller was seventy-eight and beginning to be feeble. One day his cousin Paulina, who was visiting him in Washington, rode to the Capitol with him in his carriage; and as he got out, he was unsteady on his feet. "Paulina," he remarked, "I totter." But Holmes wrote after Fuller's death, "I never thought that the time had come when it would be wise for him to resign until this last term."

However, Taft, who was then President, was quick to discern the signs that he had been expecting so eagerly for so long. When Fuller administered the oath to him in March, 1909, Taft said that the Chief Justice made him swear to "execute" the Constitution instead of supporting and defending it. Taft wrote to Circuit Judge Lurton in May, 1909, "Really the Chief Justice is almost senile."

It is possible that Taft asked Justice White to feel out Fuller and perhaps suggest his resignation. In October, 1909, White had sent word to the President through Wickersham, the Attorney General, "not to bring any important cases before the Court" as it was then constituted. This advice, however, was apparently based on the illnesses of Peckham, Brewer, and Moody. However, in 1910 the President asked White to make certain investigations of persons suggested for the bench, and White reported thereon to the President. Among the Fuller papers is an undated letter from White to Fuller reading as follows:

"Wednesday
"MY DEAR CHIEF

"Thanks so much for the photograph. It has a value not only for the present ties of affectionate regard which it constantly will serve to vivify but also for the future which with God's Holy Help may it foreshadow. I put then the image of both the Chief who is and the one who is to be on the wall of my study.

"Yours

E. D. WHITE"

Much speculation can be hazarded on this letter. Did White and Fuller agree on Fuller's successor and White put up two pictures? It seems improbable. And no one close to White at that time recalls two such pictures in his study. It seems more probable that Fuller sent White one of his photographs, perhaps the one taken on December 2, 1909 (opposite page 330); that White had previously discussed with Fuller his possible resignation and the Chief Justice had indicated that he had no intention to resign. White's letter might refer to such a conversation. But this hypothesis remains a speculation.

After Fuller's death in July, 1910, Holmes wrote to his friend Baroness Moncheur: "The Chief died at just the right moment, for during the last term he had begun to show his age in his administrative work, I thought, and I was doubting whether I ought to speak to his family, as they relied on me."

It is noteworthy that Holmes refers to deficiencies of age in Fuller's "administrative" work rather than in his opinions. Fuller wrote several opinions at this last term, and they seem no different than his prior opinions. The experience of American industry is that persons in responsible executive positions must be retired earlier than others. Perhaps a Chief Justice should retire sooner than an Associate Justice. If Holmes had been Chief Justice, he might not have been able to serve until he was ninety-one.

One magnificent performance by Fuller in the year preceding his death indicates that neither his acumen nor his literary capacities were then impaired. The occasion was his speech at the Cleveland Memorial in New York on March 16, 1909. President Taft was the principal speaker and spoke with his usual candor and sincerity, "hailing the late President," as a New York newspaper reported, "as a great American and claiming his fame for the whole country." "But," said the paper, "even more than by Mr. Taft, the analysis definitive was given by Chief Justice Fuller."

In this address Fuller quoted Cleveland's memorial on Grant that he "trod unswervingly the path of duty, undeterred by doubts, single minded and straightforward." "In these words," Fuller said, "Mr. Cleveland indicated the qualities he thought most commendable in a public servant and in eulogizing another unconsciously portrayed himself, for he was single-minded and straightforward and unswerving and nothing doubting in his adherence to duty." "He was indeed a great man," Fuller said, "and it was character that made him great." The Chief Justice concluded: "It is very right that this tribute be paid to him, and that the President of the United States and the Governor of New York,[1] the successor of Mr. Cleveland have joined in it. I find in the President that adherence to duty and those plain and practical utterances that were Mr. Cleveland's, and I mark with delight the salutary influence on the Governor of the fearlessness of his illustrious predecessor.

"At the simple rites with which he was committed to the grave, Wordsworth's poem of The Happy Warrior was read, and applicable as it was, I still could not help thinking of Valiant-for-truth's last words: 'My sword I give to him that shall succeed me in my pilgrimage and my courage and skill

[1] Charles Evans Hughes.

to him that can get it. My marks and scars I carry with me to be a witness for me that I have fought His battles who will now be my rewarder.' "

There was no evidence of senility in this speech. And it was too characteristic of Fuller not to be his own composition. Five days before the meeting he had written to Gregory, "I hope you will come on to the Memorial Exercises at Carnegie Hall, Mr. 16th at 3 P.M. I am booked for some remarks, which I have not yet prepared & am trying to get together."

CHAPTER XXIV

◦◡◦

FULLER AND HOLMES

1904–1910

THE friendship of Fuller and Holmes is one of the most notable in the history of the Court. It was unusual because they were so different. Holmes was a Republican; Fuller a Democrat. Fuller was a devout churchman; Holmes a skeptic. Holmes had fought valiantly in the Civil War; Fuller had been lukewarm about it. Fuller had an immense sympathy for the common man; Holmes was an aristocrat and repudiated the title of humanitarian. Fuller suffered fools gladly; Holmes abhorred them. But they were together in their devotion to the Bill of Rights, as well as in their reluctance to strike down state laws under the Fourteenth Amendment. Both were descendants of a long line of New England intellectuals, and their schooling had been similar. They had the same cultural heritage, but Holmes's long years of reading and pondering philosophy sharply distinguished his mental equipment from Fuller's.

The correspondence between them shows Fuller's delight in Holmes's learning and acuteness but without any surrender of his own independence of thought. With all his great deference to Holmes, Fuller quietly insisted on the recognition of his own headship of the Court. And Holmes cultivated the Chief Justice—as an Associate Justice must—without the slightest suggestion of subservience.

A case which illustrates their divergent approach to certain legal problems is *Slater* v. *Mexican National R.R. Co.*[1] An

[1] 1903, 194 U.S. 121.

American company operated a railroad in Mexico. By its negligence it fatally injured in Mexico one of its employees. The injured man was an American citizen and died at his home in Texas; his wife and children brought suit there for his death. The question was whether the Mexican law gave a right to sue for wrongful death which could be enforced in the United States. Mexico allowed such a suit but gave alimony and pensions to the wife and children until remarriage or during necessity, instead of a lump sum as was usual in the United States. Holmes, speaking for the majority of the Court, denied all recovery. The law of Mexico, he said, was the sole source of the claim. That law must equally determine its extent. Justice to the defendant therefore would not permit the substitution of a lump sum in Texas for the periodical payments under the Mexican law.

Fuller, joined by Harlan and Peckham, dissented. He pointed out that the English law permitted a recovery under similar circumstances and attempted to distinguish the American cases to the contrary. Again, Dicey, the eminent English authority on this subject, agreed with Fuller. Fuller would strain to allow a recovery in such a case; Holmes would not.

Among Fuller's papers is a letter from Holmes that reveals the relations between them. The Chief Justice was always vigilant to prevent dissents from growing acrimonious. Once he cautioned Holmes on this score. Holmes responded:

"DEAR CHIEF

"I will omit 'anomalous.' I half forgot it. I meant to speak to you also about any expression that seems to chafe the majority. Nothing was further from my mind. I shall have a chance to talk with you before anything is done I hope.

"Yours ever

O. W. HOLMES"

In a few years Holmes became very influential on the Court. His weight with his colleagues is shown by an admiralty case in 1905 where he converted a dissenting opinion into the opinion of the Court. The question was whether a ship which had been abandoned on the high seas was entitled to collect freight charges when the cargo had been restored to the owner by salvors.

The *Eliza Lines,* a Norwegian bark, was bound from Pensacola, Florida, to Montevideo, Uruguay, with a cargo of lumber. Because of dangers of the seas, the ship was abandoned by her officers and crew. It was undeniable that they were justified in such abandonment, but the vessel was picked up by salvors and brought into Boston. The master there claimed the right to resume his voyage and earn the freight, but the cargo owners demanded that the cargo be sold. This request was granted, but the Circuit Court on appeal deducted the freight from the cargo owners' proceeds of the sale.

The minority opinion was by Justice Brown, who was an authority on the law of admiralty. Brown admitted that, under the English Admiralty decisions, an abandonment of the vessel, even though justifiable, put an end to the obligation to pay freight or at least gave the cargo owners the option to do so. But this rule, he said, had been criticized and was unjust when the cargo was recovered, particularly where the freight had almost been earned. An involuntary abandonment, Brown said, was not an act showing an intention to repudiate the contract to carry the cargo to its destination.

It is clear from a letter from Holmes to Fuller that Brown's opinion was originally the opinion of the Court. In the summer of 1905 Holmes wrote to the Chief Justice: "I have not written an opinion contra Brown in the Admiralty case but I wrote letters to White and Harlan developing the further point that it could not be said that the vessel was not abandoned out and out when the only ground for salvage was that it had been— and that salvage was due was decided as *vs*. all parties."

Apparently Holmes won White by his arguments. Soon after the Court assembled in October, Holmes delivered the opinion of the Court adopting the English rule. The vote was five to four. Holmes said that the American law of admiralty should not be different from the British law unless strong reasons compelled the difference. The master and the crew in this case, he suggested, were not torn from the ship by the force of the storm. "A continuous intent . . . to go on with the voyage," he held, "is an essential condition to the obligation to pay freight." Any cessation of performance excuses the other party just as in ordinary contracts a repudiation of the contract excuses the other party.

After 1906 Fuller and Holmes had a protégée on the Court in the person of Justice Moody. He was a dangerous man in winning members of an opposite group on the Court, as witness this note from Holmes to Fuller: "Dear Chief, In the telegraph case, which Harlan handed down to me this morning, No. 65,[1] Peckham tells me that he has gone over to Moody, as White had done already. Thereupon I suggested to Moody that he go ahead and write an opinion to which he properly replied, not until you told him to, and I said I would write to you and report, which I hereby do."

The note is tantalizing because the opinion in the case was ultimately delivered by Holmes and was unanimous. Did Holmes reconvert Moody and his cohorts or write the opinion as Moody thought it should be? Since Holmes's opinion dismissed the case for lack of federal jurisdiction, it is possible that Holmes discovered that method of avoiding a closely divided Court on the merits.

Another record of Moody's prowess is contained in a letter from Fuller to Harlan: "I have not returned Moody's opinion in 412.[2] I do not agree with it and I hope you have or will look at it. On the vote Peckham, Brewer, Harlan and the Chief Justice were the other way." When Moody's opinion in this case was delivered, however, only the Chief Justice dissented, and he did so without a dissenting opinion.

---

[1] *Western Union Telegraph Company* v. *Wilson,* 1909, 213 U.S. 52, a suit for delay in transmitting a telegram.

[2] *Honolulu Rapid Transit Co.* v. *Hawaii,* 1908, 211 U.S. 282, suit to prevent streetcar company from reducing service.

It is clear that Moody, despite his short term of service (three years), was one of the ablest Justices of his period. Longevity has usually been the first prerequisite to eminence on the Court. But Moody had been admired by Holmes in their Massachusetts days and had won the esteem of Fuller and the other Justices by his brilliant work as Attorney General.

Holmes's sponsorship of Moody before he came on the Court may be seen from these notes written in 1905: "Dear Chief, I heard Moody expressing a doubt or uneasiness as to whether you had received an invitation to dine from him so without saying anything to him I thought it proper to tell you—especially as he expressed a very nice feeling about sending the invitation."

And the same day: "Dear Chief, I have written to Moody that I mentioned to you what I heard him say—that you replied as you did and that I should write to you that I had said to him that you would take the will for the deed if the invitation was not rec'd through any mistake and thus save you the bother of further writing."

It was generous for Holmes to intercede for the Attorney General in a misunderstanding with Fuller about a dinner invitation. Inviting the Chief Justice to dinner was a delicate matter. From the first he had found that Washington dinner parties made him ill. One of his excuses to avoid attending dinners was that the dignity of his office might be impaired. If the dinner party was for a foreign guest, "he ought to call first upon the Chief Justice." If members of the diplomatic corps were to be present, it was their contention that, as the personal representatives of their sovereigns, they were entitled to precede the Chief Justice.

At the annual President's Judiciary Reception the Chief Justice and the Justices always headed the line, but in 1907 someone in the State Department had made the error of suggesting to the Dean of the Diplomatic Corps that the Corps appear at all receptions in full regalia. To the horror of the

Secretary of State they came to the Judiciary Reception that year in official attire and made it clear that they expected to lead the line. Just as the Chief Justice and his daughter were about to start the procession, an aide came to him and said, "Mr. Chief Justice, the Secretary of State asks me to tell you that the Diplomatic Corps will precede you tonight." Some of the Justices and their wives wanted to go home at once. Harlan afterward insisted that "the little whippersnapper" of an aide "actually and violently assaulted the Chief Justice of the United States." The aide touched Fuller's lapel as he spoke to him, which is a technical assault. But the Diplomatic Corps went first. Thereafter the precedence of the Justices at the reception was reestablished by making the invitations read "in honor of the Chief Justice" instead of "to meet the Chief Justice," as previously.

Holmes's delicacy in inviting Fuller to a dinner may be seen from the following letter: "Dear Chief, I am making a little dinner for my old pupil and friend, Baron Kentaro Kanako, now a great man in Japan—on Wednesday, April 6 at 8 o'clock. If you would honor us with your presence he would come to meet you rather than you to meet him, on the general principles of gravitation. You would add greatly to our pleasure, and I don't think that the dignity of your office would be impaired."

Holmes's scholarship and industry are displayed by a note from him to the Chief Justice regarding an opinion by Holmes to the effect that the territory of Hawaii could not be sued without its permission. The rule is usually stated that a sovereign, without his consent, is exempt from suit. But Hawaii was a territory with a legislature whose laws could be repealed by Congress. It had little or no sovereignty. This situation compelled historical investigation to find out the true basis for the exemption of governments from suit without their consent. Holmes found that the exemption did not rest on the conception of sovereignty but on the "practical ground that there can be no legal right as against the authority that makes the law on which the right depends." Twelve days after the opinion was delivered, Holmes wrote to Fuller: "I suppose there is no objection to my adding to my French quotation from Bodin in Kawananakoa v. Polyblank[1] the following from Baldus which takes it back to the 14th Cent. greatly to my delight. I found it like a needle in a bundle of hay in a search through abbreviated black letter folios: Nemo suo statuto ligatur necessitative. Unless you forbid I shall send it to the reporter."

Holmes frequently quoted Latin in his notes to the Chief Justice. Thus: "Will you let me know as soon as convenient the cases you assign to me. I worry until I know. Nil factum reputans dum quid superesset agendum." But in the next note he could be very earthy, as: "Why dont you send me a real stinker that will be of some real relief to you."

One of the foundations of Holmes's fame was his cultivation of his own skepticism. He read sociological works, he once said, to "multiply" his "scepticisms." His open-mindedness up to the last minute before a decision is shown by a letter to the Chief Justice in a case where Holmes wrote two decisions—one each way. The question involved was whether a city could construct its own waterworks system after it had granted an exclusive franchise to a private water company. Holmes wrote the Chief Justice: "I have sent a memo in favor of the former opinion and an opinion reversing it to the printer—to be submitted to the boys. If the former opinion is sustained, I hope some one else will do it. I am about on the fence as to the merits and therefore inclined to sustain." Day subsequently wrote the opinion in this case denying the city's right to erect its own water system, and Holmes concurred.

Holmes's objectivity even after a decision had been made is shown by a case where a defeated lawyer published an article in a legal periodical attacking one of Holmes's decisions. The case involved the title to the land under the waters of a lake. Fuller wrote to Holmes: "I have a letter from Mr. Dent of Chicago, an old fellow practitioner of mine, in respect of an

[1] 1907, 205 U.S. 349.

article he contributed to the Central Law Journal—He expressed, or intimated, the desire, that it might reach you—I replied that I had read it with interest, & that I would call your attention to it—So I enclose the number." One might expect Holmes to express a mighty wrath at Dent's article. Public criticism of a court by defeated counsel comes with ill grace. But Holmes responded, referring to his criticized opinion, "I think myself it was doubtful or wrong but I think the Court had decided it per Bradley, et als." In other words he felt that he was bound by a former decision.

At Fuller's request Holmes sometimes made suggestions on the Chief's opinions. Such criticisms were gratefully received and adopted unless Fuller had strong reasons against them. For example, in the boundary dispute between Louisiana and Mississippi, the opinion, as in most state boundary cases, was by the Chief Justice. But it is clear that Holmes contributed to it, as shown by the following letter from Fuller to Holmes:

"My dear colleague, I am deeply obliged to you for your suggestions in No. 11 Original [1] & rather ashamed that I put you to so much trouble—I have improved the opinion by adopting most of them though I could not all because I thought it would require a recasting [to] which I did not feel equal, though I saw how much better the opinion would be. I do not wish to refer to Mr. Justice Clifford in this connection. His style was something awful and Mr. Justice Gray was never tired of quoting the old gentleman's exclamation, 'My style is my own.' . . . Robert Smith once called my attention to a sentence by Judge Clifford of a man convicted of murder on the high seas—Bob said that Clifford was so charmed with it that he made the Clerk print it, (at his own [Clifford's] expense),— it contained a paragraph to this effect: 'If you had obeyed the sixth commandment, and *kept the provisions of your shipping articles,* you would not now be' &C. I believe the epitaph on

---

[1] *Louisiana* v. *Mississippi,* 1906, 202 U.S. 1.

Boyle's tomb was: 'He was a celebrated chemist & brother of the Earl of Cork.' . . .

"Yrs Affectionately
MELVILLE W. FULLER"

[PS.] "I received a letter from Shiras yesterday—He writes in re Missouri v. Illinois: [1] 'I quite agree with your favorable estimate of Justice Holmes' opinion—No other conclusion, I think could have been reached—Still the opinion is entitled to praise for a clear and cautious treatment of a novel and difficult subject.' "

The extent to which Fuller went in excusing his failure to follow Holmes's suggestion in *Louisiana* v. *Mississippi* is typical of Fuller's diplomacy. And the sugar plum for Holmes at the end in Shiras's compliment about Holmes's opinion is also characteristic.

Fuller had more experience than any of his colleagues in the practice and procedure of the federal courts. His associates usually deferred to him when a question of that sort arose. It is not surprising that in this field he was not moved by strong pressure from Holmes.

Thus, Section 724 of the United States Revised Statutes provided that the courts might order the "parties" to a suit to produce documents in their possession. A suit was started against the Pennsylvania Railroad by a coal company for discrimination in rates. On motion of the plaintiff, the president of the railroad was ordered, after hearing, to produce certain books. The president contended that he was not a "party" within the statute and took an appeal. The view of the Chief Justice was that the order was not a final order so as to be appealable.

But Holmes wrote him: "I think the power given by §724 is confined to requiring the 'parties' to produce as it says. I

---

[1] *Missouri* v. *Illinois and the Sanitary District of Chicago,* 1906, 200 U.S. 496.

think the remedy [judgment against the 'party' refusing to produce] leaves it entirely unnecessary to issue an order to anyone else . . . and therefore *I think the Circuit Court had no power to make the order it did.* I think the cases of parties or subpoenaed witnesses, both, are different from this. And I think that persons against whom an order is issued without warrant or jurisdiction ought to be allowed to have it set right at once without waiting to be sent to prison. I shall bow to whatever you decide to do but thems my sentiments. Your afft and humble but stubborn colleague

O. W. Holmes"

Fuller wrote a short opinion holding that the order was not appealable and Holmes did not dissent.[1]

Another case that illustrates the intimate relations prevailing between Fuller and Holmes, as well as the difference in their approach to certain legal problems, is *Selliger* v. *Kentucky.*[2] In 1909 Holmes delivered an opinion in this case holding that the State of Kentucky could not tax warehouse receipts held in that State for whisky in a warehouse in Germany. It was settled that a state could not tax property outside of the state, but it was contended that these warehouse receipts were property *within* the state. The owner, a Kentuckian, had pledged them there for a bank loan.

When Holmes presented his opinion, Fuller indicated that he would dissent and Holmes wrote him: "I am sorry that my moderation in 115 did not soften your inexorable heart. But I stand like St. Sebastian ready for your arrows." Holmes then said that he did not see how Fuller could possibly answer his opinion in this case. But three days later Holmes wrote, "You knocked me rather silly yesterday by your attack on my opinion." The basis of Fuller's attack is a matter of surmise, but it is fairly clear that he argued that the warehouse receipts were property in Kentucky just as bonds issued in a foreign

[1] Holmes to Fuller, Nov. 9, 1907, Genet papers. The case is *Webster Coal Co.* v. *Cassatt,* 1907, 207 U.S. 181.
[2] 1909, 213 U.S. 200.

country would be taxable property when held in Kentucky. The warehouse receipts could be *used* as collateral and be sold and transferred in Kentucky just as the bonds could.

However, Holmes's letter to Fuller then continues: "But I am stronger on my second line [of defense] than on my skirmishers. The tax is *not* a tax on the *use* of the receipts. It is a tax on the receipts as *property in the hands of the owner of the whiskey*. A tax on the use, e.g. transfers, would raise different questions. But the owner is taxed as owner of the documents, just as he might be taxed as owner of the whiskey where the whiskey is—So the question is the one I have discussed. The tax would be the same if he had covenanted never to use the papers, and I guess—if they were simple receipts not running to order." Holmes made a revision of the opinion to meet Fuller's position. As published, the opinion states that the warehouse receipts are not in the record and that for all the Court knows they may be simple receipts not transferrable without the consent of the warehouseman. Fuller did not dissent to this revised opinion. Holmes's pistol had missed fire, but he knocked the dissenters down with the butt of it.

The last great collaboration between Fuller and Holmes occurred in the case of *United States* v. *Shipp*.[1] In January, 1906, a white woman in Chattanooga, Tennessee, was raped by a Negro. Ed Johnson was charged with the crime and, for fear of mob violence, was removed to a jail in Nashville. Thereafter a mob stormed the Chattanooga jail and only dispersed when they found that the prisoner was not there. A few days later the State militia was called out to protect the jail from another expected mob. Shortly thereafter Johnson was convicted and sentenced to be hanged. Immediately after his trial, he was taken to a jail in Knoxville. Six reputable lawyers, assigned by the local court to defend him, agreed that no appeal should be taken to the State Supreme Court because of the risk that the prisoner would be lynched if any delay in his execution occurred. Johnson, while protesting his innocence, agreed to

[1] 1906, 203 U.S. 563; 1909, 214 U.S. 386; 215 U.S. 580.

waive the appeal to save himself from death by lynching.

A colored attorney, however, filed a petition for *habeas corpus* in the United States Circuit Court on the ground that all Negroes had been excluded from the grand and petit juries and that the attorneys had been intimidated by fear of mob violence from making a proper defense or taking an appeal. This petition was denied by the federal court, but the prisoner was ordered to be held for ten days so that he could take an appeal from such denial to the Supreme Court of the United States. The day after this order was made, the prisoner was brought back from the jail at Knoxville, where he had been kept since his trial, and lodged in the Chattanooga jail. The Supreme Court of the United States allowed the appeal, and the Clerk of the Court notified the sheriff by telegram. This action made Johnson a federal prisoner. Previously he had been guarded by several deputies; but that night the customary guards were withdrawn, leaving only the night jailer, and Johnson was taken from the jail and killed by a mob. Neither the sheriff nor the jailer made any effort to protect him.

The sheriff, Shipp by name, gave an interview to a newspaper in which he said: "The Supreme Court of the United States was responsible for this lynching. . . . The people . . . were willing to let the law take its course until it became known that the case would probably not be disposed of for four or five years by the Supreme Court of the United States. The people would not submit to this and I do not wonder at it." The sheriff was running for reelection.

The day after the lynching the Chief Justice sent a note to each of his colleagues: "I write the brethren to come to my house tomorrow, Wednesday, at 11 o'clock—The Times of this city announces that the man whose appeal we granted yesterday has been hanged by lynch law." The speed of Fuller's action when the dignity of the Supreme Court was impugned is noteworthy.

At the request of the Court, Attorney General Moody made an investigation at Chattanooga and two months later filed in the Supreme Court an information for contempt against Shipp and some of his deputies as well as several alleged members of the mob. Shipp and the night jailer were charged with failing to protect the prisoner and with "pretending to do their duty" but "really sympathizing" and "conspiring" with the members of the mob.

The defendants answered, denying the charges under oath and moving to dismiss. They claimed that neither the Circuit nor Supreme Court had jurisdiction of the original case. They urged that the defendants should go free on their disavowal under oath of any intentional contempt. In December, 1906, these motions were unanimously denied by the Court in an opinion by Holmes. His conclusion must have sent a shiver through the defendants. "It may be found," he said, "that what created the mob and led to the crime was the unwillingness of its members to submit to the delay required for the trial of the appeal. From that to the intent to prevent that delay and the hearing of the appeal is a short step. If that step is taken the contempt is proved."

Through the years 1907 and 1908 testimony was taken before a commissioner appointed by the Court, and the case was argued in March, 1909. Apparently it was first assigned to Justice Holmes, but before he had done much on it, the Chief Justice took it over. Perhaps it was thought that he could secure a larger majority on the Court than Holmes. Perhaps the novelty and importance of the case suggested that the Chief Justice should deliver the opinion. At any rate, among Fuller's papers is a letter from Holmes: "Dear Chief, I send you some notes in 5 original [*U.S.* v. *Shipp*] the first pages (2) as I had begun to write the case—the rest indications of the points and pages of record prominent in my mind."

In a masterly opinion, the Chief Justice analyzed the evidence. He reviewed the overwhelming proof of Shipp's knowledge of the danger as shown by his secrecy in taking the prisoner away from Chattanooga, his awareness of the first mob, his calling out of the militia, his employing extra guards, and purchasing guns to protect the jail. There was evidence that the sheriff had said that Johnson would be lynched if his execution were stayed. A few hours before the mob came, the night jailer told a white woman prisoner who was at large in the jail to get back in her room because a mob was coming.

The opinion then detailed the sheriff's derelictions: "failure to make the slightest preparation to resist the mob; the absence of all deputies, except Gibson from the jail"; Shipp's "failure to make any reasonable effort to save Johnson or identify the members of the mob." "When the mob left the jail with Johnson, Shipp did not follow or make any effort to rescue Johnson or get others to help rescue him." "There was in the crowd around the jail a substantial number of law abiding men of good character yet he asked no one for help." "He could have gone about three blocks to a police station and got the police." "The militia was drilling," on the night in question, "three blocks from the jail." "It was not called upon to assist in suppressing the mob, although it had been called out twice before by the governor and was bound to respond to another call by him. The governor had given assurances that any help asked for would be given."

Fuller quoted Shipp's statement that "the people" were willing to let the law take its course until the Supreme Court allowed the appeal and that the "people" would not submit to this delay. "His reference to the 'people,'" Fuller said, "was significant, for he was a candidate for re-election and had been told that his saving the prisoner from the first attempt to mob him would cost him his place, and he had answered that he wished the mob had got him [Johnson] before he did."

"Only one conclusion," Fuller ended, "can be drawn from these facts, . . . Shipp not only made the work of the mob easy, but in effect aided and abetted it."

After this opinion was prepared but before it was announced, Holmes wrote to the Chief Justice that he must prepare for a dissent by White. "He dilates with horror," Holmes said, "and says that he shall write a dissent. I confess that I don't see how he can do more than suggest unreal doubts but then I don't see how you are going to answer 115!" [1] The dissent in the *Shipp* case, however, was delivered by Peckham, with White and McKenna concurring. Holmes's prediction of its lack of substance was correct. It dwelt repeatedly on Shipp's high reputation in the community, his advanced age, and the absence of direct evidence of his participation in the conspiracy of the mob.

Fuller's opinion did not fix the punishments. Holmes had written him: "I am sore distraught as to our duty re Shipp. But if he ought to be convicted I don't see how we can treat it as less than a grave offense—I am inclined to say one year's imprisonment." When the Chief Justice announced the sentence, however, Shipp was given, for his contempt, ninety days in the jail of the District of Columbia. Most people would agree with Holmes that one year's imprisonment would have been more appropriate. But Fuller was no person to lead the Court in imposing a harsh penalty. Although he was profoundly attached to the Bill of Rights, outraged by the lynching of the prisoner in this case, and resolved to maintain the dignity of the Court in all events, he was wholly devoid of vindictiveness toward the defendants.

[1] Holmes to Fuller, March 26, 1909, Genet papers. No. 115 is *Selliger* v. *Kentucky*, 1909, 213, U.S. 200; supra, pp. 322–323.

CHAPTER XXV

°᠊ᨅ᠊°

DEATH AND ESTIMATE

M̲RS. FULLER once told a neighbor at their summer home in Sorrento, Maine, that both she and the Chief Justice hoped they would die there. It was an idyllic place. The house was in the woods near Frenchman's Bay. About a hundred yards to the rear the Chief Justice had built a cabin, where he smoked and read and fed the wild squirrels which ran in and out. The next owner of the house had to shoot the squirrels to make the premises habitable.

Fuller's childhood interest in pets had lasted all his life. In Washington he had cats, canaries, and a brilliant-plumed parrot named Bonito, a gift of the Mexican minister. Sometimes the Chief Justice fed the parrot in the walled garden beside the house; he had the brim of a straw hat cut away on one side so that Bonito could ride more easily on his shoulder. Once when the Court was holding its Saturday conference at the Fuller home, a "cat walked in and jumped on Judge Brown's lap," as the Chief Justice reported by letter to his wife.

But troubles crowded in upon him after Mrs. Fuller's death. The arrears in disposal of cases on the Court were ever on his mind; his health was never sturdy; some one or more of his children was always distressingly ill. However, no man took greater joy than he in his grandchildren: the Beecher girls from Tarrytown, the Aubrey children and Cony Moore from Chicago, the Wallace children from Tacoma, Washington, and the Mason children from Washington, D.C. They were with him frequently, both in Washington and Sorrento.

He died at Sorrento of a heart attack in the early hours of

Monday, July 4, 1910. He had been to church as usual the day before and had only time to call his daughter Jane and to say, "I am very ill"—when he was gone. Like Jefferson, John Adams, and Monroe, he died on the birthday of the country with which his life had been so intimately entwined.

Funeral services were held in the little church at Sorrento and later in Chicago, where he was buried in Graceland Cemetery, beside his wife. There was no eulogy. The Reverend James E. Freeman, the young rector at Sorrento, a close friend, and later Bishop of Washington, read the liturgy of the Protestant Episcopal Church. Justice Holmes wrote to Judge Putnam: "The services at Sorrento moved me through and through. It was a beautiful day and there was a touch of the loveable and no false note. The coffin spread with a coverlet of flowers was put on a buckboard to go from the house to the church. The birds were singing, the clergyman, a fine fellow, whom I daresay you know, read extremely well, a little choir of four young men sang touchingly. The church built by Richardson was the right thing for the place. It is rare indeed for me to find everything so conspire with the natural feelings of the moment."

On Fuller's death, the press concurred that not even the greatest of his predecessors had more enjoyed the respect and confidence of the country. He was called by some "the most beloved of all the Chief Justices." Even the *Outlook*, reflecting the frank hostility toward Fuller of one of its editors, Theodore Roosevelt, agreed that Fuller was "perhaps the most popular," though "not the strongest or most famous Chief Justice."

There were reasons for Fuller's place in men's affections. His appearance had endeared him to many. His small stature, his silver hair and mustache, his bright, sensitive, and poetic face gave him a rugged and patriarchal aspect and made him, it was said, the most striking man in Washington. Americans were proud of him as they were proud of Admiral Dewey: his appearance was commensurate with the dignity of his exalted office. "Mr. Fuller was small in size," the *Outlook* noted, "and yet—by reason of . . . his striking figure, the fineness of his hair, the agility of his step, the alertness of his movement, the clearness and combined vigor and gentleness of his eye, the moderation of his manner, and his evenly modulated, musical, low and clear voice—was a forceful, if not commanding, presence."

When he presided over the Court, he seemed the very embodiment of the dignity of the highest judicial tribunal on earth. Aloof, yet attentive and alert, his demeanor was almost majestic; yet he was gracious and courteous, even deferential, to his colleagues and the bar. Quickly he put at their ease the young lawyers who were awed by the Court. Off the bench he was approachable and affable and—on the bench or off it—his dignity commanded respect without making familiarity possible. A Philadelphia newspaper said that it was no disparagement of the Marshalls and the Taneys, the Jays and the Rutledges who had preceded him, to suggest that none of them was superior to him in dignity.

One of his best loved qualities was his wealth of quiet, gentle humor. A quaint turn of phrase or a salty old New England word always fascinated him. Thus writing to Morris in Chicago about the selection of an arbitrator to appraise a property belonging to the Peck family and on which Fuller had a lease, he asserted: "The Pecks have horse-shed everybody" in Chicago. In New England, to "horse-shed" a man was to talk with him secretly in the place best adapted for such communication: the horse-shed back of the church. Again, writing about a spinster in the family who had married at the age of fifty, he quoted what his grandmother's ancient dressmaker in Augusta had said about Eliza Dillingham who was married late in life: "If I had been Eliza," she remarked, "I'd have *toughed it out*."

Fuller's courage and independence inspired great respect. President Taft testified: "He was noted for his independence of thought and his courage of action." And the *Outlook* conceded that Fuller "was dominated by strong convictions and gentle but inflexible courage in maintaining them." His deci-

CHIEF JUSTICE MELVILLE W. FULLER

Taken December 2, 1909

sions against the prohibition forces, against Sunday blue laws, and his dissent to the forfeiture of the property of the Mormon Church are all examples of high courage in the face of popular demands. His dissent in the *Neagle* case, despite the strong sympathy of himself and his colleagues for Justice Field (who was defending the man who had saved his life), is another instance. Fuller's opinion declaring the Income Tax Law unconstitutional, against strong popular clamor and against the interests of the Cleveland administration, is perhaps the prime example. As the Detroit *Free Press* put it: "He was absolutely fearless of President or mob."

The country had complete confidence in his impartiality and nonpartisanship. None of his great predecessors had surpassed him in this respect. "No man," the Philadelphia *Public Ledger* asserted, "has ever more completely realized the impartial, impersonal integrity and dignity of the Court in its splendid aloofness from prejudice and passion." It was recalled on his death that his confirmation had been delayed because of his appointment by a Democratic President and particularly in view of his own record of strict adherence to his party. But all conceded that these fears had proved groundless. Furthermore, as the Boston *Globe* noted: "He was not against the rich because of their wealth, nor with the poor because of their poverty. He was neither for nor against any class or section. He stood for justice under the Constitution."

The wide range of his scholarship astonished his colleagues. His years of trying all sorts of cases for other lawyers; a lifetime of insatiable reading, both in law and literature; his retentive memory and his earnest zeal for research on the Court: all these were brought to a focus in his opinions. Today, recognition of his scholarship is somewhat obscured by the fact that his colleagues Gray and Holmes surpassed him in pure legal erudition. But he in turn surpassed them in the breadth of his practical experience. And Gray's acclaim of Fuller's opinions on many occasions, as well as Holmes's outspoken admiration, show their estimate of him.

While Fuller's opinions were held in high esteem, their style was not as impressive as that of Marshall or Holmes. Fuller's judicial opinions are labored and cannot compare in sparkle with his rare after-dinner speeches. His opinions contain no lofty phrases, no grandiloquent passages, no personal conceits to betray a hungry ego in their author. The largest number of Fuller's opinions related to questions of jurisdiction or practice in the federal courts. Most of these were models of pithy brevity. But some of his opinions are not as tightly knit or as well organized as an ideal opinion of the Court should be. In his eternal battle to keep up with the docket, he tried to write too many opinions himself. Many of his cases concerned intricate commercial transactions. His statements of the facts in these cases were written with great pains. Sometimes these factual statements were longer than was necessary to present the point for decision. But their length was not due to any prolixity on his part but rather to his overzealous care not to omit a minor fact which counsel thought to be pertinent.

Fuller's gentleness, kindliness, and human sympathy were also factors in the country's affections. These traits were demonstrated in his opinion exempting from the demands of creditors life insurance taken out by an insolvent man in favor of his family. They were shown by his struggle to mold the law in favor of an injured workman and to cut down the harsh doctrine that a workman could not recover damages if his injury had been caused by the negligence of a fellow servant. They were indicated again in his split with Holmes on whether suit could be brought in the United States for the death of a railroad worker killed by defective cars in Mexico. When Fuller died, the newspapers spoke of his thoughtfulness for others and his broad compassion.

Perhaps most of all, the country loved the modesty of the man. Never has there been so unobtrusive a Chief Justice. This quality is strikingly shown in his assignment of cases. When he first came on the bench, Justice Lamar advised him not to "give away" an important case but to write the opinion himself. He did not follow this advice but assigned the case to Justice Miller. And so it was in his entire career on the Court; almost always he assigned to others the cases which attracted national attention.

Thus it was Fuller who assigned to Justice White *Knowlton* v. *Moore*,[1] the famous case upholding the validity of the federal estate tax. It was Fuller who assigned to Justice Brown *Holden* v. *Hardy*,[2] in which Brown delivered the most brilliant opinion of his career, sustaining the Utah eight-hour law for miners. Similarly, Fuller assigned to Justice Brewer the leading case of *Muller* v. *Oregon*[3] holding valid the Oregon eight-hour law for women. It was Fuller who assigned to Justice Moody the much-cited case of *Twining* v. *New Jersey*[4] to the effect that the Fourteenth Amendment did not compel a state to grant a witness exemption from answering questions that might incriminate him. Many similar cases could be cited where the Chief Justice spurned an opportunity to put himself in the limelight.

On his death a Philadelphia newspaper noted that he had left behind fewer opinions in great cases than some of the Associate Justices. "He was a modest man," the paper said, "and as he had the assignment of the opinions . . . he selected other Justices . . . to . . . give the argument for the decision reached." A Massachusetts paper observed: "No one on the bench in his time was less disposed to put himself forward or to deny opportunity to his colleagues in favor of himself." And a Peoria, Illinois, newspaper commented: "During his 22 years of service he received less publicity than the ordinary congressman of the louder variety."

But Fuller's most remarkable abilities were largely unknown to the country. They lay in his great skill as an executive in managing the business of the Court. When he became Chief Justice, the Court was clogged with cases; it was more than four years behind with its work. In a few years, by securing

[1] 1900, 178 U.S. 41. [2] 1897, 169 U.S. 366. [3] 1908, 208 U.S. 412.
[4] 1908, 211 U.S. 78.

the passage of the Circuit Court of Appeals Act, he brought the calendar almost up to date. And by painful struggle he kept it so for the remainder of his life. In this effort he wrote far more than his share of the opinions.[1] "Justice Fuller's greatest ability," the Pittsburgh *Sun* said, "was made more manifest to the members of the court than to outsiders. . . . In keeping up with the work of the court, none of his predecessors ever equalled him." The Pittsburgh *Sun* probably secured this information from Justice Shiras, who was then living in Pittsburgh.

The same newspaper also referred to another of Fuller's talents which was not generally known: "In making his assignments of judges he displayed rare discretion." Twenty years after Fuller's death, Holmes mentioned Fuller's conscientiousness and wisdom in selecting judges to write particular opinions. "In the assignment of decisions to the different judges," Holmes said, "his grounds were not always obvious, but I know how serious and solid they were and how remote was any partiality from his choice." Apparently Fuller sometimes discussed with Holmes his reasons for assigning a case to one Justice or another.

The Pittsburgh *Sun* mentioned still another of Fuller's accomplishments which was known only inside the Court: "In maintaining the harmony of the bench, his efforts were little short of remarkable." The stories of his great adroitness in this respect, as told by both Gray and Holmes, have previously been detailed.

Holmes said of Fuller's executive abilities: "Of course the function of the Chief Justice differs from that of the other judges only on the administrative side, but on that I think he was extraordinary. He had the business of the Court at his fingers ends, he was perfectly courageous, prompt, decided. He turned off the matters that daily called for action easily, swiftly, with the least possible friction, with inestimable good humor and with a humor that relieved any tension with a laugh."

[1] See Appendix I.

But was Fuller a great Chief Justice? Was he worthy to be compared with Marshall or Taney, the greatest of his seven predecessors? At his death there was some difference of opinion on these questions. Many newspapers, while praising Fuller highly, thought that he did not rank with Marshall or Taney. Others thought that he occupied a place beside them, and still others said, "It is too soon to know."

In the forty years since Fuller's death, the opinions on this subject of two of his nineteen colleagues have come to light. They were the two Justices who, because of their length of service, had the best basis for comparison. Samuel Freeman Miller, who sat under Taney, Chase, Waite, and Fuller, stated to Senator Cullom that "Fuller was the best presiding judge" in Miller's time. Oliver Wendell Holmes, who had served under Fuller, White, Taft, and Hughes, told Justice Frankfurter that Fuller was the best presiding officer that Holmes had ever known. When Fuller died, Justice Holmes wrote to Judge Putnam: "The Chief had outlived most of his contemporaries and I think the public will not realize what a great man it has lost."

But Fuller cannot be ranked with Marshall any more than our Presidents, except Lincoln, can be compared with Washington. Marshall marked out the main trails in which the Court has since walked. He was a man of immense force and acumen and dominated the Court as no Chief Justice after him has done. He could do this because his associates did not change rapidly; and they were not, except for Story, judges of such force or ability as Miller, Field, Bradley, Gray, White, or Holmes. Marshall established the foundations of American constitutional law and built for himself an imperishable fame; Fuller skillfully guided the Court through a period of great difficulty and enhanced the respect in which it was held. "The Supreme Court," a Philadelphia newspaper said, "has steadily strengthened its influence and grown in importance since he presided over its deliberations."

The comparison of Fuller with Marshall was most aptly

made by a Chicago newspaper. It told how, on his appointment, Senator William P. Frye of Maine, who was a senior at Bowdoin when Fuller was a freshman, had remarked, "There is a wide gulf between John Marshall and Mel Fuller." Later Frye confessed that he had underestimated Fuller. "Few will agree," the Chicago *Post* said, "that the gulf ever was bridged but Fuller looked across it from an eminence of his own."

What was the source and secret of his success? It lay in his character rather than in his intellect. His mental attainments inspired respect—even admiration—but not awe. Nevertheless, he was an extraordinary Chief Justice in his relations with his colleagues. They fought for his good will. The bases for this relation were his deep humility, his sense of humor and humanity, his strict impartiality, his rare capacity for friendship, and his complete freedom from rancor. He had a strong habit of command, but the poison of power never affected him.

But other qualities are necessary in a successful Chief Justice. He must have serene confidence in his own mental processes and yet respect for the opinions of others. He must be as disinterested as the stars in making his decisions and yet as hot as the sun in supporting them. He must have his eye ever on remote posterity and yet be conscious of the needs of his day. For posterity will find him wanting if he courts popularity and yields to the fleeting demands of the moment. These great qualities Melville Fuller had.

White and Holmes, McKenna and Day, and two recently appointed Justices, Lurton and Hughes, brought Fuller's body back to Chicago. The guns on the lake front sounded their seventeen salutes to him for the last time. None of the two million people in the city could compare this pomp with his humble entrance into Chicago in 1856. But he had realized the American dream. The manifest destiny, personal and national, of his New England boyhood had come to pass. When he was born, Andrew Jackson was President and there were only 13,000,000 people in the country. Now William Howard Taft presided over 91,000,000. And of all that mighty horde there was no intelligent American to say that Melville Fuller had not borne his part nobly in the nation's history.

OPINIONS OF THE COURT

TERM	1888	1889	1890	1891	1892	1893	1894	1895	1896	1897	1898	1899	1900	1901	1902	1903	1904	1905	1906	1907	1908	1909	Total
Fuller	45	56	58	55	48	65	69	60	42	32	25	38	30	34	34	35	27	16	23	16	14	18	840
Miller	24	27																					51
Field	25	18	21	19	10	9	6	4															112
Bradley	20	18	19	0																			57
Harlan	32	34	37	37	4	28	23	34	25	25	19	24	19	12	20	13	15	14	18	11	9	18	471
Gray	22	30	29	26	25	32	18	27	20	13	13	14	14	4									287
Blatchford	39	50	34	36	34																		193
Lamar	26	24	26	14																			90
Brewer		23	38	35	36	42	40	16	32	27	14	25	16	24	29	26	22	23	24	14	18	12	536
Brown			31	36	37	43	37	43	28	15	21	31	33	23	24	12	18	15					452
Shiras					28	31	31	32	25	17	14	17	24	20	8								247
Jackson					16	30																	46
White						10	21	31	26	23	24	20	18	18	22	24	21	15	23	22	27	25	370
Peckham								21	29	22	22	23	21	25	24	24	21	18	22	20	17	0	309
McKenna										8	22	22	22	23	20	25	23	21	25	21	17	24	273
Holmes															29	28	28	29	33	30	31	34	242
Day																26	23	18	24	25	21	27	164
Moody																			15	21	28	0	64
Lurton																						19	19

TERM	1888	1889	1890	1891	1892	1893	1894	1895	1896	1897	1898	1899	1900	1901	1902	1903	1904	1905	1906	1907	1908	1909	Total
Fuller	0	2	1	3	4	2	1	2	1	1	0	2	3	0	3	3	0	0	0	1	1	0	30
Miller	2	4																					6
Field	0	0	2	2	5	1	0	6															16
Bradley	1	1	1	1																			4
Harlan	3	2	0	4	1	4	6	6	2	2	2	7	9	2	3	6	3	1	4	4	6	1	79
Gray	0	1	0	0	0	1	1	0	1	2	1	0	2	1	0								10
Blatchford	0	0	0	0	0	0																	0
Lamar	0	1	1	1	0	0																	3
Brewer			4	2	5	4	4	0	1	1	2	1	2	0	3	2	2	2	2	1	1	0	42
Brown			4	2	3	3	5	3	1	3	2	1	1	3	1	2	2	3	0				39
Shiras					3	1	1	2	0	2	1	2	1	1	0	0							14
Jackson						3	1	0															4
White							1	1	2	1	4	2	4	1	5	2	3	6	1	1	0	3	37
Peckham								2	0	0	1	0	1	0	1	0	1	0	0	0	1	0	7
McKenna											0	0	1	1	0	1	0	1	2	1	1	1	9
Holmes															0	2	3	0	2	3	4	3	17
Day																0	1	0	1	0	1	1	4
Moody																			1	3	1	0	5
Lurton																							

DISSENTS WITHOUT OPINIONS

TERM	1888	1889	1890	1891	1892	1893	1894	1895	1896	1897	1898	1899	1900	1901	1902	1903	1904	1905	1906	1907	1908	1909	Total
Fuller	1	5	2	1	2	5	6	4	6	4	7	5	4	7	3	14	9	5	9	3	2	8	112
Miller	4	5																					9
Field	4	5	5	12	1	8	5	9	5	0													54
Bradley	2	3	2	0																			7
Harlan	1	6	5	10	1	9	8	6	19	15	13	7	10	8	10	13	17	13	12	12	6	7	208
Gray	0	7	9	1	3	2	1	4	4	3	4	2	3	2									45
Blatchford	0	0	0	0	0	0																	0
Lamar	0	4	1	3	0	0																	8
Brewer		8	4	8	4	12	9	4	6	11	6	5	11	13	14	12	11	13	12	5	3	6	177
Brown			7	6	4	7	3	4	13	4	5	4	7	2	8	11	4	7					96
Shiras					0	3	4	3	4	4	4	7	12	3	5	0							49
Jackson					1	6	2																9
White						2	1	9	7	9	8	16	18	8	12	10	6	9	1	3	5	3	127
Peckham								1	8	9	11	10	14	13	13	13	14	13	13	3	4	0	139
McKenna										5	12	9	16	5	10	11	5	14	4	7	6	11	115
Holmes															1	2	1	4	1	2	1	7	19
Day															0	2	7	5	7	2	3	2	28
Moody																			3	3	5	0	11
Lurton																						1	1

JUDGES AGREEING AND DISAGREEING WITH FULLER ON DIVIDED COURTS

Name of Judge	Number of Cases Agreeing	Number of Cases Disagreeing
Miller	17	21
Field	178	85
Bradley	54	21
Harlan	426	321
Gray	328	113
Blatchford	98	18
Lamar	93	14
Brewer	468	264
Brown	376	203
Shiras	271	108
Jackson	54	21
White	374	250
Peckham	351	182
McKenna	301	181
Holmes	232	72
Day	202	80
Moody	62	29
Lurton	14	6
	3,899	1,989

It will be noted that Field, Bradley, Gray, Blatchford, Lamar, Shiras, Jackson, Holmes, Day, and Moody most frequently agreed with Fuller. Fuller's ratio of disagreements to agreements is higher with Harlan, Brewer, Brown, White, Peckham, and McKenna. Miller's relatively large number of disagreements with Fuller is accounted for by the fact that Miller frequently was a sole dissenter without opinion. Blatchford's small number of disagreements is due to the fact that he rarely dissented in any case.

BIBLIOGRAPHY

Adams, Henry, *Education of Henry Adams*. Boston, 1918.

Alverstone, Viscount (Richard Everard Webster), *Recollections of Bench and Bar*. London, 1915.

Andreas, A. T., *History of Chicago*. Chicago, 1885.

Anthony, Elliott, *Constitutional History of Illinois*. Chicago, 1891.

Bailey, John C. W., *Chicago City Directory*. Chicago, 1864–1865.

Beard, Charles and Mary, *The Rise of American Civilization*. New York, 1927.

Beveridge, Albert J., *The Life of John Marshall*. New York, 1916.

——, *Abraham Lincoln*. New York, 1928.

Blatchford, Eliphalet Wickes, *Blatchford Memorial II*. Chicago, 1912.

Bowdoin College, Class of 1853. Boston, 1873.

Bowdoin College catalogues, 1849–1853. Brunswick, Me., 1849–1852.

Bowen, Catherine Drinker, *Yankee from Olympus*. Boston, 1944.

Bradley, Charles, *Miscellaneous Writings of Joseph P. Bradley*. Newark, 1902.

Brooks, Van Wyck, *The Flowering of New England*. New York, 1936.

Brown, George Rothwell, *Washington, a not too serious history*. Baltimore, 1930.

Browning, Orville H., *The Diary of Orville Hickman Browning, 1850–1881*, ed. Theodore Pease and J. G. Randall. Springfield, Ill., 1925, 1933.

Butler, Charles Henry, *A Century at the Bar of the Supreme Court of the United States*. New York, 1942.

Carson, Hampton Lawrence, *The History of the Supreme Court of the United States*. Philadelphia, 1910.

Cate, Wirt Armistead, *Lucius Q. C. Lamar: Secession and Reunion*. Chapel Hill, N. C., 1935.

Chicago Directory. D. B. Cooke and Company, 1858.

Clark, Floyd Barzilia, *The Constitutional Doctrines of Justice Harlan*. Baltimore, Md., 1915.

Cleveland, Grover, *The Venezuelan Boundary Controversy*. Princeton, 1913.

Cole, Arthur Charles, *Centennial History of Illinois*, Vol. III, *The Era of the Civil War*. Springfield, 1919.

Commager, Henry Steele, *Theodore Parker*. Boston, 1936.

Corwin, Edward Samuel, *Court over Constitution*. Princeton, N. J., 1938.

Cullom, Shelby M., *Fifty Years of Public Service*. Chicago, 1911.

Currey, Josiah Seymour, *Chicago: Its History and Its Builders*. Chicago, 1912.

Democratic National Convention, Official Proceedings of the. Chicago, 1864.

Democratic National Convention, Official Proceedings of the. Baltimore, July 9, 1872.

Democratic National Convention, Official Proceedings of the. St. Louis, 1876.

Dickerson, Oliver Morton, *The Illinois Constitutional Convention of 1862.* Urbana, 1905.

Directory of Chicago. Case & Company, 1858.

Dow, Neal, *The Reminiscences of Neal Dow.* Portland, Me., 1898.

Edwards, Richard, *Annual Directory for Chicago,* 1866, 1871, 1872, 1873.

Fairman, Charles, *Justice Miller and the Supreme Court.* Cambridge, Mass., 1939.

Fessenden, Francis, *Life and Public Services of William Pitt Fessenden.* Boston, 1907.

Fish, Carl Russell, *The Rise of the Common Man, 1830–1850.* New York, 1927.

Foraker, Joseph Benson, *Notes of a Busy Life.* Cincinnati, 1916.

Frankfurter, Felix, *Mr. Justice Holmes and the Supreme Court.* Cambridge, Mass., 1938.

——, and Landis, James M., *The Business of the Supreme Court.* New York, 1928.

Gabriel, Ralph Henry, *The Course of American Democratic Thought.* New York, 1940.

Gager, John, *Gager's Directory of Chicago,* 1857.

Goodrich, Samuel Griswold, *Recollections of a Lifetime.* New York, 1856.

Gookin, Frederick William, *The Chicago Literary Club.* Chicago, 1926.

Gray, Wood, The Peace Movement in the Old Northwest. Unpublished doctoral thesis, University of Chicago, 1933.

Greeley, Adolphus Washington, *Reminiscences of Travel and Adventure.* New York, 1927.

Gregory, Charles N., *Samuel Freeman Miller.* Iowa City, Iowa, 1907.

Gresham, Matilda, *The Life of Walter Q. Gresham.* Chicago, 1919.

Halpin, T. M., *Halpin & Bailey's Chicago City Directory,* 1861–1863.

Hamlin, Charles Eugene, *The Life and Times of Hannibal Hamlin.* Cambridge, Mass., 1899.

Harrison, Carter H., *Growing up with Chicago.* Chicago, 1944.

Harvard Law School, catalogues of, 1853–1855.

Harvard Law School Association, Report of the Eighteenth Annual Meeting of. Cambridge, Mass., 1904.

Hatch, Louis Clinton, *The History of Bowdoin College.* Portland, Me., 1927.

——, *Maine, a history.* New York, 1919.

Hawthorne, Nathaniel, *Fanshawe.* Boston, 1828.

——, *American Notebooks*. Boston, 1868.

Hoar, George F., *Autobiography of Seventy Years*. New York, 1903.

Holmes, Oliver Wendell, *Speeches*. Boston, 1900.

Howard, Oliver Otis, *Autobiography of Oliver Otis Howard*. Burlington, Vt., 1909.

Howe, Mark De Wolfe, ed. *Holmes-Pollock Letters*. Cambridge, Mass., 1941.

——, *Touched with Fire: Civil War Letters and Diary of Oliver Wendell Holmes, Jr.* Cambridge, Mass., 1946.

Hubbard Brothers, *Living Leaders of the World*. Chicago, 1889.

Hughes, Charles Evans, *The Supreme Court of the United States*. New York, 1927.

Hutchinson, William Thomas, *Cyrus Hall McCormick*. New York, 1935.

Illinois Constitutional Convention, Journal of the. Springfield, 1862.

Illinois House of Representatives, Journal of the. Springfield, 1863.

James, Cyril F., *The Growth of Chicago Banks*. New York, 1938.

James, Henry, *Richard Olney and His Public Service*. Boston, 1923.

Johnson, Allen, *Stephen A. Douglas: A Study in American Politics*. New York, 1908.

Judd, Sylvester, *Margaret*. Boston, 1845.

——, *Richard Edney and the Governor's Family*. Boston, 1850.

Keim, De Benneville Randolph, *Handbook of Official and Social Etiquette and Public Ceremonials at Washington*. Washington, 1889.

Kent, Charles A., *Memoir of Henry Billings Brown*. New York, 1915.

Kinsley, Philip, *The Chicago Tribune: Its First Hundred Years*. New York, 1943–1946.

Klinkhamer, Sister Marie Carolyn, *Edward Douglas White*. Washington, 1943.

Koerner, Gustave, *Memoirs of Gustave Koerner, II, 1809–1896*. Cedar Rapids, Iowa, 1909.

Lardner, Lynford A., The Constitutional Doctrines of David Josiah Brewer. Unpublished doctoral thesis, Princeton University, 1938.

Latane, John Holladay, *America as a World Power*. New York, 1907.

Long, Peirce, *From the Journal of Zadoc Long*. Caldwell, Idaho, 1943.

Lusk, D. W., *Eighty Years of Illinois Politics and Politicians*. Springfield, Ill., 1889.

McDevitt, Brother Mathew, *Joseph McKenna*. Washington, 1946.

McElroy, Robert, *Grover Cleveland, The Man and the Statesman*. New York, 1923.

McLaughlin, Andrew Cunningham, *A Constitutional History of the United States*. New York, 1935.

McLean, Joseph E., *William Rufus Day*. Baltimore, 1946.

Martineau, Harriet, *Retrospect of Western Travel*. London, 1838.

Mayes, Edward, *Lucius Q. C. Lamar: His Life, Times and Speeches*. Nashville, Tenn., 1896.

Milton, George Fort, *The Eve of Conflict*. Boston, 1934.

Moses, John, *Illinois, Historical and Statistical*. Chicago, 1895.

Myers, Gustavus, *History of the Supreme Court of the United States*. Chicago, 1925.

Nevins, Allan, *The Emergence of Modern America*. New York, 1927.

———, *Grover Cleveland: A Study in Courage*. New York, 1932.

———, *Letters of Grover Cleveland*. New York, 1933.

North, James W., *The History of Augusta*. Augusta, 1870.

Norton, David, *Sketches of the Town of Old Town*. Bangor, 1881.

Nye, Russell B., *George Bancroft: Brahmin Rebel*. New York, 1944.

Oberholtzer, Ellis Paxson, *A History of the United States Since the Civil War*. New York, 1917–1937.

Palmer, John McAuley, *The Bench and Bar of Illinois*. Chicago, 1899.

Parker, George F., *Recollections of Grover Cleveland*. New York, 1909.

Parrington, Vernon L., *Main Currents in American Thought*. New York, 1927.

Pierce, Bessie Louise, *A History of Chicago*. New York, 1937.

Power, John Carroll, *Abraham Lincoln, his life, public services, death and great funeral cortege*. Springfield, 1875.

Pringle, Henry Fowles, *The Life and Times of William Howard Taft*. New York, 1939.

Ratner, Sidney, *American Taxation*. New York, 1942.

Rhodes, James Ford, *History of the United States from the Compromise of 1850*. New York, 1920.

Roosevelt, Theodore, and Henry Cabot Lodge, *Correspondence, 1884–1918*. New York, 1925.

Rusk, Ralph L., *The Letters of Ralph Waldo Emerson*. New York, 1939.

Schurz, Carl, *The Reminiscences of Carl Schurz*. New York, 1909.

Seligman, Edwin Robert, *The Income Tax*. New York, 1911.

Slifer, H. Seger, and Hiram L. Kennicott, Centennial history and biographical directory of the Chi Psi fraternity. Ann Arbor, Mich., 1941.

Smith, Joseph E., *Oakridge*. Chicago, 1871.

Spiller, Robert E., and others. *Literary History of the United States*. New York, 1948.

Stanwood, Edward, *James Gillespie Blaine*. Boston, 1905.

Stowe, Harriet Beecher, *Oldtown Folks*. Boston, 1869.

———, *Poganuc People*, New York, 1878.

Strachey, (Giles) Lytton, *Eminent Victorians*. London, 1918.

Sullivan, Mark, *Our Times*. New York, 1926.

Swain, Robert T., *The Cravath Firm*. New York, 1946.

Swisher, Carl Brent, *Stephen J. Field: craftsman of the law*. Washington, 1930.

Taft, William Howard, *Our Chief Magistrate and His Powers*. New York, 1916.

Thayer, William Roscoe, *John Hay*. Boston, 1908.

Thompson, Lawrance Roger, *Young Longfellow*. New York, 1938.

Trimble, Bruce R., *Chief Justice Waite, Defender of the Public Interest*. Princeton, 1938.

Turner, Frederick Jackson, *Frontier in American History*. New York, 1920.

——, *The United States, 1830–1850*. New York, 1935.

Warren, Charles, *The Supreme Court in United States History*. Boston, 1922.

Webster, Fletcher, *The Private Correspondence of Daniel Webster*. Boston, 1857.

Weston, Daniel C., *Scenes in a Vestry*. Augusta, Me., 1841.

Wiener, Frederick Bernays, The Life and Judicial Career of William Henry Moody. Unpublished thesis, Harvard Law School, 1930.

Willis, William, *A History of the Law, the Courts, and the Lawyers of Maine*. Portland, 1863.

Williston, Samuel, *Life and Law*. Boston, 1941.

Wilson, Forrest, *Crusader in Crinoline: the Life of Harriet Beecher Stowe*. Philadelphia, 1941.

NOTES

Bold face figures refer to pages of the text.

[2] Interviews R. D. Weston of Boston and Nathan Weston of Augusta; North: History of Augusta, 502, 954; Willis: Law, Courts and Lawyers of Me., 510; 33 Maine Reports, 593; IV Chicago Legal News, 300. [3] Nathan Weston to Henry W. Fuller, November 9, 1849, Dorothy Fuller papers; Mrs. Nathan Weston to Melville Fuller, November 9, 1851; Nathan Weston to M. W. Fuller, August 16, 1856; Melville M. Weston to M. W. Fuller, May 1, 1888, Genet papers. [5] North: History of Augusta, 170; VI Appleton's Cyclopaedia of Am. Biog., 675; Samuel Cony and Joseph H. Williams, grandsons of Daniel Cony, were Governors of Maine; Rusk: Letters of RWE, III, 58. [6] Interviews and correspondence with Dr. B. A. G. Fuller; North: History of Augusta, 516, 869; Willis: Law, Courts and Lawyers of Me., 700; Webster to Fuller, Dec. 21, 1802, July 2, 1803, Dr. B. A. G. Fuller papers. [7] DAB on Hannah Flagg Gould and Benjamin Apthorp Goulds, Sr. and Jr.; Fuller: Augusta Centennial Oration, June 9, 1897. [9] Fuller: Bowdoin Centennial Address, June 28, 1894. [10] Original Court files on divorce, Clerk of Sup. Ct. Kennebec County, Augusta; Last Will of Frederick A. Fuller on file in Probate Ct., Augusta, leaves a legacy of $200 to his son "G. Melville Fuller" indicating that Frederick by 1841 (date of will) did not even know his son's correct name. [11] Letters Mrs. Nathan Weston to Mrs. William

Dewey, June 2, 1836, September 25, 1836, February 11, 1839 on Catharine's music pupils, Genet papers; several letters from Oliver Ditson to Catharine Fuller are in the Genet papers; he was the founder of Oliver Ditson & Co. music publishers. See his biography in DAB. [12–13] Weston: Scenes in a Vestry; Drown: There Was War in Heaven, N.E. Quarterly Vol. IV No. 1, p. 30, 1930; Stowe: Poganuc People, pp. 34, 68. [14] Mrs. C. M. Wadleigh, Old Town to Mrs. Nathan Weston, Augusta, Feb. 18, 1845; same from "Milwaukie" Wisconsin to same, Augusta, Me., Sept. 6, 1845, Genet papers. [15] Melville Fuller, Duanesburg, N. Y., to Mrs. Nathan Weston, Augusta, Me., "Satteday," May 1846, June 10, 1846, Genet papers. [16] Fuller: Augusta Centennial Oration, June 9, 1897; For Polk's speech see Hamlin: Life & Times of Hannibal Hamlin, pp. 175–176. [17] Catalogues of Dialectic Club in Bowdoin College Library; many programs of the club in Genet papers. [18–20] Mrs. C. M. Wadleigh to Fuller, Aug. 18, 1850; Mrs. Nathan Weston to Fuller, Mar. 7, 15, Feb. 20, July 30, Aug. 8, 1850, June 10, 1851; Mrs. C. M. Wadleigh to Fuller, Feb. 7, Mar. 29, July 13, 1850, June 22, Oct. 18, 1851, Genet papers; See DAB for Upham, Cleaveland and Woods. [21] Catalogues of Bowdoin College, 1849–1853; Hawthorne, Fanshaw, 76; Class of 1853, Bowdoin College, published by the Class in 1873; Minutes of Chi Psi fraternity at Bowdoin. **[22]** Records of Library and minutes of Athenaean Society; theme dated July 5, 1852, Genet papers. **[23]** Minutes of Athenaean Society, July, 1853, manuscript of address in Genet papers. **[24]** Poems in Bowdoin College Library; Undated College theme, Genet papers. **[25]** Fuller: Webster Centennial Address, Dartmouth, 1901. Boston Post, Sept. 27, 1852. **[26]** Interview Nathan Weston, Augusta, Me. in August, 1945; Mr. Weston had the story from Chief Justice Fuller; theme dated July, 1853, Bowdoin College manuscripts. **[27]** Genet papers. **[28]** Manuscript poem in Maine State Library, Augusta, Maine. **[29]** Catalogues of Harvard Law School 1854–1855; Oration in archives of Chi Psi fraternity, Ann Arbor, Michigan. **[30]** Fuller to Prof. George T. Little, Aug. 9, 1888, Bowdoin College Library. **[31]** Augusta Age and Kennebec Journal, 1856; Stanwood: James G. Blaine, p. 43. **[32]** Mrs. C. M. Wadleigh to Fuller, July 16, Oct. 16, 1852; Mrs. Nathan Weston to Fuller, Oct. 15, 1852, Genet papers. **[33]** Manuscript poem dated 1854 in Maine State Library, Augusta, Me. **[34]** R. D. Rice, Augusta, Me. to J. Y. Scammon, Chicago, undated but obviously written in 1856; Benjamin E. Smith to Fuller, July 14, 1856, Genet papers. **[35–36]** These letters are anonymous but they are indubitably Fuller's. They appear in the Age on June 5 and 12, July 3, August 7, 1856, January 29 and March 5, 1857. **[37]** Mrs. Nathan Weston to Fuller, May 29, 1856; Nathan Weston to Fuller, August 16, 1856, Genet papers. **[38]** Census figures show that in 1860, 50.77% of Chicago's population was male and 49.23% female; Pierce: As Others See Chi-

cage, II, 186. **[39–40]** Mrs. Nathan Weston to Fuller, September, 1856, Genet papers; *Pearson* v. *Chapman,* 1859, 21 Ill. 650; Chicago Tribune, June 26, 1861, contains report of Pearson's death; *First M. E. Church* v. *City of Chicago,* 1861, 26 Ill. 482. **[41]** Address of the Young Men's Democratic Union Club of the City of Chicago, October 9, 1856. A printed copy in the Genet papers bears the inscription in his handwriting "Written by M. W. Fuller." It is a lengthy address of considerable merit. **[42]** Augusta Age, June 12, 1856; Mrs. Nathan Weston to Fuller, August 12, September —, 1856, Genet papers. **[43]** Mrs. Nathan Weston to Fuller, May 29, September —, June 11, 1856, Genet papers. These bound volumes of the New York Herald were found by me in the summer of 1945 in the Fuller home in Sorrento, Maine. Through the kindness of Mrs. Thomas Stone, the present owner of the house, I have had the opportunity to examine them with care through the ensuing years. I have made exhaustive but unsuccessful efforts to secure direct evidence of Fuller's authorship of these articles. However, I am convinced, for the reasons mentioned in the text, that he wrote some of them. The first letter from the Herald's Special Correspondent is dated at Leavenworth, December 21, 1857 and was published on January 4, 1858. Its phraseology is characteristic of Fuller. It refers to "Quilp" in Dickens' Old Curiosity Shop. In 1846 Fuller had named the pet turtle on the farm at Duanesburg, New York, "Quilp." To me some of these articles are recognizable as Fuller's just as the face of a friend is recognizable from a host of details no one of which would be sufficient standing alone. The following articles in the Herald of 1858 I would thus tentatively identify as Fuller's:

Date of Article	Date of Publication in Herald
December 21, 1857	January 4, 1858
December 30, 1857	January 12, 1858
January 3, 1858	January 15, 1858
January 7, 1858	January 16, 1858
January 8, 1858	January 16, 1858
January 15, 1858	January 25, 1858
January 30, 1858	February 13, 1858
February 10, 1858	February 20, 1858
February 12, 1858	February 22, 1858
February 9, 1858	February 23, 1858

[44] New York Herald, Jan. 15, Feb. 22, 1858. [45–46] Fuller's speeches for Douglas reported in Chicago Daily Times, Oct. 19, 20, 22, 23, 24, 25, 27, 28, 29, 30, 1858. Chicago Herald article quoted from reprint in Chicago Daily Press and Tribune, July 29, 1858. [47] Dispatch from Chicago dated June 13, 1860 and published in New York Herald June 26, 1860; Chicago Times & Herald, October 5, 1860; Anonymous article on Fuller, identified by intrinsic evidence as by S. S. Cox in Living Leaders of the World, Hubbard Brothers, Chicago, 1889. [48] Chicago Tribune, February 23, 1861; Thomas Dent's Diary, February 22, 1861, Chicago Historical Society. Fuller to Nathan Weston, June 19, 1861, Genet papers. Chicago Tribune, October 31, November 7, 1861; Fuller to Nathan Weston, November 19, 1861, Genet papers. [49] Chicago Tribune, November 7, 1861. Daily Illinois State Register, January 20, 1862. See Anthony's enthusiastic description of this address in his Constitutional History of Illinois, p. 114. [50] Journal of Illinois Constitutional Convention of 1862, pp. 30–35, 138, 450; Daily Illinois State Register, February 19, 25,

March 3, January 23, 1862. Daily Illinois State Register, February 8, 1862. [51] Daily Illinois State Register, March 13, 1862; Journal of Illinois Constitutional Convention of 1862, p. 695. [52] Daily Illinois State Register, March 11, 1862, Dickerson: The Illinois Constitutional Convention of 1862; Daily Illinois State Register, March 10, 11, 13 and 20, 1862; Dickerson: The Illinois Constitutional Convention of 1862, pp. 20–6, 53–4. [53] Fuller to Nathan Weston, July 14, 1862, Genet papers; Chicago Morning Post, April 4, 1862; Chicago Times, August 12, 1862; Fuller to Nathan Weston, August 18, 1862, Genet papers. [54] Fuller to Nathan Weston, November 10, 1862, Genet papers; *People, ex rel Fuller* v. *Hilyard,* 1862, 29 Ill. 413; Schurz: The Reminiscences of Carl Schurz, II, pp. 310–314; Browning: Diary I, p. 586. [55] Chicago Tribune, January 6, 8, 9, 1863; The Pacification Resolution, speeches of Hon. Albert G. Burr and Melville W. Fuller, February 11, 1863, The Chicago Times Book and Job Printing Establishment, Chicago, 1863, Illinois State Historical Library; Journal of Illinois House of Representatives, 1863, pp. 728–732. [56] *People* v. *Hatch,* 1863, 33 Ill. 9; Gray: The Peace Movement in the Old Northwest. [57] Chicago Tribune, January 22, February 3, 12, June 11, 1863; Chicago Times, January 15, 1863. Journal of Illinois House of Representatives, 1863, pp. 462, 360, 663–65; Chicago Times, January 26, February 11, 1863; Chicago Tribune, February 18, 1863; Pierce: History of Chicago, II, p. 416. [58] *People* v. *Hatch,* 1863, 33 Ill. 9; *Wabash Railway Co.* v. *Hughes,* 1865, 38 Ill. 174; *People ex rel Harless* v. *Yates,* 1863, 40 Ill. 126; Journal of Illinois House of Representatives, 1863, pp. 707–711; Chicago Tribune, June 9, 10, 12, 1863; M. W. Fuller to Nathan Weston, November 23, 1863, Genet papers. But see Pierce: History of Chicago, II, pp. 327–8; Andreas: History of Chicago, II, p. 120. Fuller to Sidney Breese, December 2, 1863, Illinois State Historical Society. **[59]** Fuller to George S. Kimberly, First Vice President Democratic Invincible Club, April 7, 1864, published in Chicago Times, April, 1864. Official Proceedings of the Democratic National Convention held in Chicago in 1864. On Fuller's self-criticism see Memorial Address on Fuller by Judge Edward Osgood Brown quoted in Currey: Chicago, Its History and Its Builders, III, p. 313. **[60]** Fuller to Joseph E. Smith, September 14, 1864, published in Chicago Times, October 15, 1864. Power: Abraham Lincoln, His Life, Public Service, Death and Great Funeral Cortege, p. 191. **[61]** In addition to the articles on Kansas in the New York Herald mentioned in Chapter III, pp. 43–44 and the articles on the campaign of 1860 referred to in Chapter IV, p. 47, Fuller apparently wrote a series of articles for that paper on the famous Burch divorce case in 1860. In 1863 he mentioned in a letter to Judge Breese that he was writing for the New York World (Fuller to Breese, October 30, 1863, Illinois State Historical Society). Fuller's trips to Memphis and Minnesota in 1864 were apparently made for that newspaper. Fuller to Nathan Weston, May 20, 1860, February 4, May 17, 1861, September 20, 1862. **[62]** Fuller to Nathan Weston, May 17, June 19, July 1, 1861, November 20, 1862, Genet papers. His eight cases before the Supreme Court of Illinois in 1861 are all reported in

volume 26 of the Illinois reports. All but one of these cases came up on Fuller's appeal. He lost 5 and won 3. On Lectures see Daily Chicago Post, February 1, 1861 (report of Lecture on Self Help before the Young Men's Association); Chicago Tribune, February 23, 1861 (Toast to the Ladies at Washington's Birthday celebration); Chicago Tribune, March 25, 1861 (lengthy report of Library Committee of Young Men's Association). Fuller to Nathan Weston, January 14, May 23, 1862, March 2, 1863, Genet papers. Halpin & Bailey's Chicago Directories for 1861–2 and 1862–3. Cases won were *Stone* v. *Atwood,* 1862, 28 Ill. 30; *Young* v. *Graff,* 1862, 28 Ill. 20; *Chicago Fire & Marine Ins. Co.* v. *Keiron,* 1862, 27 Ill. 501; *Tinkham & Co.* v. *Heyworth,* 1863, 31 Ill. 519; *White* v. *Walker,* 1863, 31 Ill. 422; *Connor* v. *Nichols,* 1863, 31 Ill. 148; *Pratt* v. *Grimes,* 1864, 35 Ill. 164; *Jupitz* v. *People,* 1864, 34 Ill. 516; *Dunbar* v. *Hallowell,* 1864, 34 Ill. 168. **[63]** *Jupitz* v. *People,* 1864, 34 Ill. 516; Fuller to Sidney Breese, March 11, 1864, Illinois State Historical Society. Fuller to Nathan Weston, March 24, May 25, July 14, 1864, Genet papers. Petition for probate of Calista Ophelia Reynolds Fuller's will filed December 1, 1864, Abstract of Title to Fuller premises in possession of Kirkland, Fleming, Green, Martin & Ellis, Chicago. **[64]** John C. W. Bailey's Chicago Directory for 1864–5; Andreas: History of Chicago, III, p. 237; Chicago Journal, March 12, 1892; Fuller to Nathan Weston, May 25, 1864, Genet papers. Fuller to Nathan Weston, March 3, 1865, Genet papers. Abstract of title to Fuller premises; Fuller to Nathan Weston, May 25, 1864, March 3, 1865,

Genet papers. Edwards Chicago Directory for 1866; Chicago Record-Herald, July 5, 1910; William F. Coolbaugh to Stephen A. Douglas, February 7, April 10, 1860, Douglas papers, University of Chicago; James: The Growth of Chicago Banks, pp. 418, 506–8. **[65–67]** H. M. Shepard to Fuller, December 21, 1890, Genet papers. Fuller, Diary, 1866. Entries quoted are under dates of June 27, 29, July 2, August 2, 6, 1866, Genet papers. **[67–68]** *Schwartz* v. *Gilmore,* 1867, 45 Ill. 455; *Schwartz* v. *Saunders,* 1867, 46 Ill. 18; *Schwartz* v. *Daegling,* 1870, 55 Ill. 342; *Daegling* v. *Schwartz,* 1875, 80 Ill. 320. **[69]** Chicago Tribune, May 2, 1867, June 10, 1868. Pierce: A History of Chicago, II, pp. 35–117; Atlantic Monthly, XIX, 325, March, 1867; Andreas: History of Chicago, III, p. 237; Chicago Journal, March 12, 1892. Interviews Henry C. Morris; correspondence with Maud Smith Briggs, Mrs. Aimee Lane and Joseph E. Smith, Jr., daughters and son of Joseph E. Smith; many references to Smith and some letters from him in the Genet papers; obituary of Joseph E. Smith in Chicago Tribune, June 17, 1881. **[70]** Andreas: History of Chicago, II, pp. 412–15; *Gorham* v. *Bishop of Exeter,* 1849, 2 Rob. Ecc. 1; Strachey: Eminent Victorians, Cardinal Manning, pp. 53–58. *Chase* v. *Cheney,* 1871, 58 Ill. 509; Brief and Argument for Defendant in Error by Melville W. Fuller, pp. i–xx, 1–127. **[71]** *Calkins* v. *Cheney,* 1879, 92 Ill. 463. Fuller to Mrs. Fuller, March 10, 11, 20, 21, 23, August 10, 14, 1874, Genet papers. **[72]** Palmer: Bench & Bar of Illinois, pp. 646–47. Minutes of Chicago Law Institute, November 2, 1874; Chicago Legal News, IV, p. 85, December 30, 1871;

V, p. 41, October 19, 1872. *Dows* v. *Chicago,* 1871, 78 U.S. 108; official records of Supreme Court show his admission on February 29, 1872 on motion of Thomas Hoyne, Esq.; that he immediately thereafter secured the dismissal of the appeal in the case of *Baldwin,* assignee, v. *Ludington* (unreported) and a few days later argued the case of *Traders Bank* v. *Campbell,* 1872, 81 U.S. 87. Fuller to Mrs. Fuller, March 1, 1872, Genet papers. **[73]** *Tappan* v. *Merchants National Bank,* 1874, 86 U.S. 490; Lusk: Politics and Politicians of Illinois, p. 461; Carson: The Supreme Court of the United States, II, p. 536. Gift of house reported in letter, Fuller to Nathan Weston, June 2, 1869, Genet papers; dates of births from memorandum in Fuller's handwriting in Class of 1853 volume in Fuller Library at Bowdoin College; death of Melville from interviews Henry C. Morris and Chicago Times, January 17, 1874. Fuller to Mrs. Fuller, March 11, 1874, March 29, 1876, Genet papers. **[74]** Musham: Monograph on Chicago Fire, Papers in Illinois History, Illinois Historical Society, 1940, p. 69. Class of 1853, Bowdoin College, printed by order of the Class in 1873, p. 53; Chicago Tribune, October 14, 1871; Fire edition Edwards Chicago Directory, December 12, 1871; 543 Wabash Avenue in 1871 is now 1120 and 1122 South Wabash Avenue; Edwards Annual Directory of Chicago for 1872 and 1873; Abstract of title of Fuller property. **[75]** Class of 1853, Bowdoin College, printed by order of the Class in 1873. Chicago Tribune, October 13, 1871. **[76]** James: The Growth of Chicago Banks, I, pp. 417–58. **[77]** Chicago Morning Post, January 8, 1863; Chicago Tribune, January 6, 1863. Chicago Times, October 27, 29, 1867, report of proceedings and speech by Fuller on October 26, 1867. Chicago Times, May 15, 1868; Cole: Centennial History of Illinois, III, p. 410. **[78]** Speech of Hon. M. W. Fuller, Chicago Young Men's Democratic Association, Chicago Times, August 19, 1868; Speech at Fort Wayne, Indiana, September 21, 1868, Fort Wayne Democrat, September 22, 1868. Songs in Chicago Times, July 30, August 21, 22, 1868. Fuller to Mrs. Fuller, December 12, 1869, Genet papers; Debates Constitutional Convention, 1870, p. 50. **[79]** Moses: Illinois Historical and Statistical, on Democratic State Convention of 1870, pp. 797–98; Fuller wrote a laudatory poem on Grant's death several years later. Genet papers. **[80]** Randall: Diary of Orville Hickman Browning, II, under dates June 30, July 27, 1871; Fuller to Browning, July 26, 1871; Browning papers, Illinois Historical Society. Fuller to Mrs. Fuller, February 26, 27, 1872, Genet papers. **[81]** Memoirs of Gustave Koerner, II, pp. 560–61; Official Proceedings of National Democratic Convention, 1872; Speech of M. W. Fuller reported in Chicago Tribune, September 1, 1872. Fuller to John M. Palmer, August 15, 1872, McCormick Historical Society papers; see Hutchinson: Cyrus Hall McCormick, II, pp. 316–24. **[82]** Fuller to McCormick, September 7, October 20, 30, 1880, McCormick Historical Society papers. Fuller to Mrs. Fuller, March 12, April 1, 9, 1876, Genet papers. Official Proceedings of the National Democratic Convention of 1876, pp. 123–24; reprinted in Chicago Times, May 1, 1888. **[83]** T. A. Hendricks to Fuller, July 2, 1876,

Genet papers. **[84]** Fuller to Mrs. Fuller, March 31, 1877; Fuller to Coolbaugh, August 10, 1877, Genet papers. Chicago Times, October 29, 1878. Fuller to Mrs. Fuller, June 21, 1880, Genet papers. **[85]** Chicago Tribune, October 15, 1880. **[86]** Chicago Tribune, November 15, 16, 17, 18, 1877; Chicago Times, November 15, 16, 17, 1877; Chicago Evening Journal, November 14, 15, 1877; Chicago Inter Ocean, November 15, 1877; Probate Court files in Cook County, Illinois, on estate of William F. Coolbaugh. **[87]** Gookin: History of the Chicago Literary Club; the records of the Club show Fuller's nomination on December 3, 1877 and his election on February 28, 1878. **[88]** Randall: Diary of Orville Hickman Browning, II, p. 501, January 10, 1879. **[89]** *Bunn* v. *People*, 1867, 45 Ill. 397, pp. 408–9. In citing an opinion by Chief Justice Weston, Breese said that he was "eminent for all the attributes that distinguish the jurist." Fuller to Breese, October 30, 1863, December 2, 1863, March 11, 1864, Breese papers, Illinois State Historical Society; Breese to Fuller, May 5, 1868, published in Chicago Daily Times, May 15, 1868; two books in Fuller's library at Bowdoin College bear Breese's signature. Proceedings of Chicago Bar at Chicago Law Institute on June 29, 1878 in memory of Sidney Breese. Proceedings of Illinois State Bar Association, 1879. **[90]** Whittier to Browne, August 19, 1892, Browne papers, Newberry Library, Chicago; Lloyd Lewis: Francis Fisher Browne, Newberry Library Bulletin, No. 2, pp. 23–36. The Dial, October, 1880, pp. 101, 103; see editorial on this review in Chicago Tribune, October 25, 1880; Beveridge: Life of John Marshall, I, p. 147.

[91] The Dial, January, 1881, pp. 188–89; April, 1882, pp. 282–84; May, 1883, pp. 4–6. [92] The Dial, May, 1885, pp. 10–13, May, 1887, pp. 13–15. [93] Fuller to Mrs. Fuller, March 20, 1878, Genet papers. Clara Louise Kellogg and Annie Louise Cary were noted singers of the day. Books read are from letters to Mrs. Fuller and inscriptions on books in Fuller Library, Bowdoin College. On extent of his practice see Chicago Times, March 25, 1888, Chicago Tribune, May 1, 1888; Loesch: The Chicago Bar in the Seventies and Eighties, 21 Chicago Bar Record, 360, 400; Obituary of Joseph E. Smith, Chicago Tribune, June 17, 1881; Chicago Directories, 1882–8. [94] Samuel Weston to Robert T. Lincoln, February 20, 1915, Henry C. Morris papers; interviews Henry C. Morris; Chicago Record Herald, July 10, 1910, part IV, p. 3. Manuscript office diary of Fuller, 1882, Bowdoin College Library; Loesch: Chicago Bar in the Seventies and Eighties, 21, Chicago Bar Record, pp. 358, 359, 361, 400; James S. Harlan in Who Was Who. *Field* v. *Leiter*, 1885, 18 Ill. App. 155; 1886, 118 Ill. 17; Fuller to John Morris, January 5, 1891, Morris papers. [95] *People* v. *Illinois Central Railroad Company*, 1888, 33 Fed. 739; 1892, 146 U.S. 387. [96] Loesch: The Leslie Carter Divorce Case, typescript reminiscences in Chicago Bar Association Library. Harper's Weekly, XXXII No. 1638, May 12, 1888, p. 340. MANDAMUS: *People ex rel Caton* v. *Needles*, 1880, 96 Ill. 575; *Timm* v. *Harrison*, 1884, 109 Ill. 593. QUO WARRANTO: *People ex rel Evans* v. *Callaghan*, 1876, 83 Ill. 128; *People ex rel Badger* v. *Loewenthal*, 1879, 93 Ill. 191; *Attorney General* v. *Chicago & E. R.R. Co.*, 1884, 112 Ill.

520. PERSONAL INJURY: *Chicago B. & Q. R.R. Co.* v. *Warner*, 1884, 108 Ill. 538; 123 Ill. 38; *Illinois Central R.R. Co.* v. *Zang*, 1882, 10 Ill. App. 594. TRADE-MARK: *Frazer* v. *Frazer Lubricator Co.*, 1887, 121 Ill. 147; 18 Ill. App. 450. TAX: *Coolbaugh* v. *Huck*, 1877, 86 Ill. 600; *People ex rel Johnson* v. *Springer*, 1883, 106 Ill. 542; *South Park Com'rs* v. *Chicago B. & Q. R.R. Co.*, 1883, 107 Ill. 105. Proceedings of Illinois State Bar Association, 1886, pp. 76–83. [97] Proceedings of Illinois State Bar Association, 1887, pp. 59–68. Frankfurter & Landis: The Business of the Supreme Court, p. 83 n. 126. [98] Interviews Henry C. Morris, George Packard, Judge Dennis Normoyle; correspondence with descendants of W. C. Goudy; Nevins: Grover Cleveland, pp. 445–47. [99] Harrison: Growing Up With Chicago, pp. 265–6; Parker: Recollections of Grover Cleveland, pp. 365–8. Peoria Daily Transcript, July 3, 1884. [100] Fuller to Cleveland, February 28, 1885, Cleveland papers. Fuller to Lamont, September 24, 1885; January 22, 24, May 24, 28, June 11, August 11, December 10, 1886; January 18, February 12, April 9, 16, May 9, November 9, 26, 1887; Fuller to Cleveland, March 4, April 16, 1887; March 29, 1888, Cleveland papers. [101] Telegram and letters Fuller to Cleveland, October 29, 1885, January 4, 1887, Cleveland papers. Cleveland to Fuller, July 19, 1886, Wallace papers. Fuller to Cleveland, July 22, 1886; to Lamont, August 11, 1886, Cleveland papers. [102] Fuller to Lamont, February 12, March 31, April 5, 9, 1887; to Cleveland April 3, 1887, "Easter," 1887, Cleveland papers. [103] Fuller to Lamont, March 31, April 5, 9, 1887; to Cleveland April 16, 1887, Cleve-

land papers. The Chicago Law Times, I, p. 227, July, 1887; Fuller to Lamont, March 15, May 12, 1887, Cleveland papers; Gookin: History of the Chicago Literary Club, p. 253. Fuller to Lamont, May 4, 1887; to Cleveland July 25, 1887, Cleveland papers. Fuller to Lamont, August 7, September 23, 26, 1887, Cleveland papers. [104] Fuller to Lamont, October 7, 1887; February 6, 16, 25, 1888, Cleveland papers. New York Herald, April 5, 9, 1888; Chicago Times, March 26, 28, April 1, 1888. [105] Fuller to Hamlin, October 29, 1877, National Archives. Chicago Tribune, April 11, 1888, editorial. Greeley: Reminiscences, pp. 254–55. Stetson to Cleveland, April 7, 1888, Cleveland papers. [106] Cleveland to John G. Carlisle, April 10, 1900 in Nevins: Letters of Grover Cleveland, p. 528. New York Herald, April 17, 1888. "He [Cleveland] is reported to have been considerably annoyed about it [the petition for Gray signed by 27 Senators] and to have made no secret of the fact; Nevins: Grover Cleveland, p. 446. Swisher: Stephen J. Field, p. 319; Fairman: Mr. Justice Miller and the Supreme Court, pp. 250–79, 373–74; Warren: The Supreme Court in United States History, III, pp. 275, 414; And see former Justice Owen J. Roberts in 35 American Bar Association Journal, pp. 1–4, advocating a Constitutional Amendment to preclude appointment of Associate Justices as Chief Justice. [107] Interview with E. C. Craig, Chicago, whose father was consulted by Scholfield. And see New York Herald of April 14, 1888 where Scholfield's refusal is put on the ground that his wife had never traveled and was averse to doing so. "She is quite content with

her chickens . . . and would not consent under any circumstances to going to Washington." Chicago Times, April 1, 4, 6, 8, 15, 1888; Chicago Tribune, April 4, 1888. Chicago Times, March 24, 31, 1888. See Loesch: The Chicago Bar in the Seventies and Eighties (21 Chicago Bar Record, p. 399) on Goudy's bitterness as expressed to Loesch over Cleveland's rejection of him on account of his age; Goudy to Fuller, April 27, 1888, Genet papers; for Goudy's war record see p. 55; for his piqued behaviour at farewell dinner for Fuller see pp. 122–23. Phelps to Cleveland, April 2, 1888, Cleveland papers; Farwell to Fuller, April 3, 1888, Genet papers. [108] Stetson to Cleveland, April 7, 1888, Cleveland papers. Fuller to Mrs. Fuller, April 14, 1888, Genet papers. Shepard to Fuller, April 16, 1888, Lincoln to Shepard, April 12, 1888, Genet papers; Chicago Tribune, April 11, 1888; Gresham to Fuller, April 13, 1888, Genet papers; Chicago Times, April 12, 1888, Fuller to Mrs. Fuller, April 16, 1888, Genet papers. Fuller to Gresham, April 17, 1888, Gresham papers, Library of Congress. [109] Gresham to Fuller, April 17, 1888, Genet papers. April 18, 1888, Cleveland papers. [110] Fuller to Putnam, April 19, 1888, published in the Purple & Gold, Official Magazine of the Chi Psi fraternity, April, 1915. Fuller to Mrs. Fuller, April 19, 1888. Springer to Fuller, April 21, 1888, Genet papers. [111] Harlan to Fuller, April 23, 1888, Genet papers; Fuller to Mrs. Fuller, April 23, 25, 1888, Genet papers. Garland to Cleveland, April 14, 1888, Cleveland papers. [112] Harlan to Fuller, May 10, 1888, Genet papers. Cullom: Fifty Years of Public Service, pp. 237–38. Telegrams Lamont and Cleveland to Fuller are in the Genet papers. **[113]** Cleveland papers. **[114]** Newspaper comments are collected in Public Opinion, V, No. 4, May 5, 1888; New York Herald, May 1, 1888. **[115]** Draft of letter (undated) in hand of Davis in J. C. Bancroft Davis papers, Library of Congress. Case in which Fuller and Edmunds were counsel was *Lees* v. *Fowler*, 1887, 122 U.S. 646—Fuller mentioned the heat of his argument with Edmunds in a letter to Lamont of March 31, 1887, Cleveland papers. For Edmunds' attitude on Phelps' appointment see Cullom: Fifty Years of Public Service, p. 238; Nevins: Letters of Grover Cleveland, p. 528. **[116]** Printed pamphlet in Genet papers. The charges contained in the pamphlet were widely copied in the newspapers. See New York Tribune, May 8, 1888, St. Louis Globe-Democrat, May 7, 9, 1888, New York Herald, May 8, 1888, Bloomington, Illinois, Pantagraph, May 26, 1888. Leonard Swett to Cleveland, April 23, 1888, Genet papers. Chicago Tribune, May 9, 1888. Medill had been quoted in the New York Herald of May 1, 1888, the day after the appointment, that Fuller was "no Copperhead." **[117]** Lyman Trumbull to Edmunds, June 22, 1888, National Archives. St. Louis Globe-Democrat, May 8, 1888; Memoranda in National Archives from Illinois State Journal of June 9, 10, 11, 12, 17, 19, 24, 1863 and from Governor Yates' veto message of the Horse Railroad bill as well as of proceedings of House of Representatives on June 8, 1863, the date of its passage; Letters from Henry M. Shepard to W. M. Springer, May 29, 1888, W. C. Goudy to W. M. Springer, May 28, 29, 1888 in National Archives; Chicago Tribune, June 12, 1888; see p. **58**. Chicago Tribune, June 12, 1888. **[118]** Edmunds to Fuller, June 11, 1888, Genet papers. Fuller to Edmunds, June 13, 1888, National Archives. Edmunds to Fuller, June 14, 1888, National Archives. Fuller to Edmunds, June 15, 1888, National Archives; Fuller to Cleveland, June 14, 15, 1888, Cleveland papers. The correspondence was widely published. **[119]** On *Lay* case: R. S. Thompson to Edmunds, June 26, 1888; A. Tracy Lay to Edmunds, June 20, 1888; E. J. Harkness to Edmunds, June 22, 1888; George W. Smith to Edmunds, June 20, 1888, National Archives. On *Kerr* case: William H. Bradley to Edmunds, June 1, 2, 8, 1888; A. W. Green to Edmunds, June 18, 1888, National Archives. On *Doolittle* case: William H. King to Edmunds, June 14, 21, 1888, National Archives; Ex U.S. Senator J. R. Doolittle to Senator James F. Wilson, May 7, 1888, Doolittle papers, Wisconsin State Historical Society. On *Dunlevy's character:* F. H. Kerfoot to Farwell, May 31, 1888; Goudy to Springer, May 29, 1888; S. J. Dolan to Senator J. J. Ingalls, June 15, 1888, National Archives; Chicago Tribune, May 29, June 3, 5, 12, 17, 1888. *On Cullom's attitude:* Chicago Tribune, July 4, 1888; New York Herald, July 4, 1888. *Public comment:* Albert Crane to Edmunds, June 14, 1888; J. C. Robinson to Edmunds, June 16, 1888, National Archives; Boston Journal, June 20, July 3, 1888; Boston Daily Globe, July 5, 1888; New York Herald, July 16, 1888. **[120–121]** Fuller to Cleveland, July 5, 1888, Cleveland papers. Cullom: Fifty Years of Public Service, pp. 238–40; Chicago Record

Herald, July 5, 10, 1910; Journal of the Executive Proceedings of the Senate, 50th Cong., 1st Sess. pp. 252, 254, 287, 313. The Republican Senators who voted in favor of confirmation were Cameron of Pennsylvania, Farwell and Cullom of Illinois, Davis of Minnesota, Frye of Maine, Jones of Nevada, Mitchell of Oregon, Plumb of Kansas, Quay of Pennsylvania, and Riddleburger of Virginia; Many friendly messages from Senator Edmunds are in the Genet papers. On "Judge" story see Chicago Record Herald, July 10, 1910. **[122]** Complete story of Farewell Banquet in Chicago Legal News, September 29, 1888, Vol. 21, pp. 25–28. On Goudy's disappointment, see p. 107. **[123–124]** Fuller to Cleveland, August 6, 1888. Genet papers. W. P. Drew in the Purple and Gold, Official Magazine of the Chi Psi fraternity, Vol. XV, No. 4, pp. 270–6. **[125]** Interviews R. D. Weston, Roland Gray. Gray quotation is from Samuel Williston, Justice Gray's secretary in 1888–9, in interview, August 3, 1945. **[126]** Chase quotation is from Strong: Samuel Freeman Miller, Annals of Iowa, January, 1894, p. 247. To same effect see letter Miller to Ballinger, July 27, 1892: "I doubt if my effective influence on the court would be increased by being made its chief" quoted in Fairman: Mr. Justice Miller and the Supreme Court, p. 256. Address by Miller in 20 Albany Law Journal, July 12, 1879, p. 29. Professor Williston says that bus-driver story was told him at the time, probably by Justice Gray, as being told by Fuller. The story is part of the American folk-lore though it is usually not attributed to Fuller. It may have been true—it is certainly typical Maine bus-driver—or it may

have been adapted by Fuller to the occasion. Address in Commemoration of the Inauguration of George Washington delivered December 11, 1889, 132 U.S. 706, see favorable description of this speech in Cullom: Fifty Years of Public Service, p. 240. **[127]** Fuller to Bancroft Davis, January 18, 1890; Bancroft Davis papers, Library of Congress. Cullom: Fifty Years of Public Service, p. 241. **[128]** Swisher: Stephen J. Field, Craftsman of the Law. **[129]** Centennial Celebration addresses in 134 U.S. 711, 728–9; Fuller to Field, February 14, 1890, Field papers, University of California. Fuller *to* Mrs. Fuller, January 13, 1891, Genet papers. Bradley: Miscellaneous Writings of Joseph P. Bradley. **[130]** Bradley to Fuller, December 5, 1889, Genet papers. Fairman: Mr. Justice Bradley's appointment to the Supreme Court and the Legal Tender Cases, 54 Harvard Law Review, 977, 1128. Mr. Justice Frankfurter has written me: "I rejoice over the view you have formed of Bradley. For myself I place him at the top of the heap for breadth and penetration and the qualities that endure. 'Objectivity' was indeed his quality to a very rare degree for here was the corporation lawyer *'par excellance'* and yet he did things like his dissent in the Minnesota Rate Case in 134 U.S. which if it had been in the Court's opinion would have saved the country much friction and folly and the Court a sad chapter in its history —all the 'reproduction' story and the rest." **[131]** Holmes-Pollock Letters, II, pp. 7–8. **[132]** Fairman: Mr. Justice Miller and the Supreme Court, p. 370 quoting letter of December 25, 1880; on Harlan's political activities; see also Butler: A Century at the Bar of the Supreme Court, pp. 71,

172; Williston: Life and Law, An Autobiography, pp. 96–7; Official record of appointment of James Harlan, as Fuller's secretary dated October 8, 1888; Chicago Legal News, XXI, p. 41. Letter quoted from Harlan to Mrs. Fuller, December 11, 1889, Genet papers. There are more than a hundred letters from Harlan to Fuller in the Genet papers and three letters from Fuller to Harlan in the Harlan papers at the University of Louisville. See Appendix II on Harlan's disagreement with Fuller. **[133]** Hoar: Memorial in Proceedings Massachusetts Historical Society, 2d Series, Vol. XVIII, pp. 155–87; Adams: Same publication, Vol. XVI, pp. 251–68. Interviews Samuel Williston and Horace Gray. Williston: Life and Law, An Autobiography, pp. 91–97. **[134]** On morning handshake see Bert Andrews in New York Times, June 16, 1946. Mr. Andrews had the story of Fuller's inauguration of this practice from Mr. Justice Frankfurter and Charles Elmore Cropley, the present clerk of the Court. Swaine: The Cravath Firm, I, pp. 31–32. See Appendix I. And see tabulation in Mayes: Lucius Q. C. Lamar, p. 547 and Blatchford's compilation in Fairman: Mr. Justice Miller and the Supreme Court, p. 387. **[135]** On Fuller's reporting for the New York Herald, see page 43 and note. Some of the articles in the Herald covering Seward's campaign trip to Illinois, Wisconsin, Minnesota, Kansas and returning to Springfield, Illinois, seem to be in Fuller's style. Fuller's library at Bowdoin contains a shelf of books by and about Seward, —a peculiar interest in Fuller unless based on personal experience, in view of his early strong anti-Republican bias. I have tried for many years to secure direct evidence of Fuller's

authorship of these Seward articles in the Herald but without success. The circumstantial evidence however is strong. He wrote some articles for the Herald at that time. He bound and saved the newspapers containing these articles. He bought many books about Seward. Furthermore the Springfield article of October 16, 1860 published in the Herald on October 20, 1860 states that Seward would not have stopped at Springfield except that his failure to do so would be misconstrued. Fuller wrote Lamont in 1887 a peculiar letter to the effect that Cleveland's failure to stop at Springfield and visit Lincoln's tomb would be misconstrued. Fuller to Lamont, September 23, 1887, Cleveland papers. Blatchford to Fuller, June 22, 1891, Genet papers. Many dinner acceptances from Blatchford are in the Genet papers. (On Blatchford's superior dinners, see Williston: Life and Law, An Autobiography, pp. 97–98.) Blatchford to Fuller, June 24, 1891, May 17, 1893, Genet papers. Cate: Lucius Q. C. Lamar; Mayes: Lucius Q. C. Lamar. **[136]** Quotation from Fuller is from Mayes: Lucius Q. C. Lamar, p. 546. Lamar to Fuller, October 13, 1888, Genet papers. The case is *U.S.* v. *Bell Telephone Co.,* 1888, 128 U.S. 315; and see Williston: Life and Law, An Autobiography, p. 98. Cleveland to Fuller, December 15, 22, 1889, Wallace papers. **[137]** Mrs. Lucy M. Clarkson, May 12, 1947, to the author. **[138]** *Washington Central Bank* v. *Hume,* 1888, 128 U.S. 195. Williston: Life and Law, An Autobiography, pp. 91–3; 256–8; 25 American Law Review, 185. **[139]** Howe: Holmes-Pollock Letters, II, p. 136, Holmes was speaking of Chief Justice Taft; on 5 to 4 decisions see Judgments of the Supreme Court

Rendered by a Majority of One, 24 Georgetown Law Journal, p. 984; for Fuller's insistence that dissents be respectful see infra, Chapter XXIV. *In re Neagle,* 1890, 135 U.S. 1; Swisher: Stephen J. Field, Craftsman of the Law, Chapter XIII; Green: *In re Neagle,* 14 Rocky Mountain Law Review, 29; for contemporary story of the case with picture of Mrs. Terry see Frank Leslie's Illustrated Newspaper, August 31, 1889, Vol. LXIX, p. 64. [140] *Ex Parte Terry,* 1888, 128 U.S. 289. *Terry* v. *Sharon,* 1889, 131 U.S. 40. [141] Fuller to Morris, April 21, 1890, John Morris papers, Chicago Historical Society. Cleveland to Fuller, April 16, 1890, Wallace papers. [142] *Whitten* v. *Tomlinson,* 1895, 160 U.S. 231, 247; *Baker* v. *Grice,* 1898, 169 U.S. 284; Act of August 23, 1916, c. 399, 39 Stat. 532. Fuller to Bancroft Davis, January 7, 1889; similar letters are dated February 17, March 30, April 5, May 23, 25, 30, 1889, March 1, July 3, 6, December 31, 1890, Bancroft Davis papers, Library of Congress. Fuller to Bancroft Davis, April 7, 1889 (correction requested is in *City Bank* v. *Hunter,* 1889, 129 U.S. 577); April 17, 1889 enclosing head note for *Gibbs* v. *Baltimore Gas Co.,* 1889, 130 U.S. 396; May 24, 1889 enclosing head note for *Veach* v. *Rice,* 1889, 131 U.S. 293 and *Hawkins* v. *Glenn,* 1889, 131 U.S. 319; November 5, 1890 enclosing head note for *Texas, Etc. R'y Co.* v. *Southern Pacific Co.,* 1890, 137 U.S. 48; November 19, 1890 enclosing head note for *Fitzgerald Const. Co.* v. *Fitzgerald,* 1890, 137 U.S. 98. [143] *U.S.* v. *American Bell Tel. Co.,* 1888, 128 U.S. 315, see p. **136;** *The Chinese Exclusion Case,* 1889, 130 U.S. 581, holding that if subsequent treaty conflicted with a statute,

the treaty must yield to the statute. Two complicated cases in Fuller's first year where he wrote the opinions are *City Bank* v. *Hunter,* 1889, 129 U.S. 557 and *Reynes* v. *Dumont,* 1889, 130 U.S. 354. *In re Baiz,* 1890, 135 U.S. 403; Fuller to Bancroft Davis, May 5, 9, 11, 1890, Bancroft Davis papers, Library of Congress. Putnam to Fuller, September 14, 1902, Genet papers. Adee to Fuller, May 14, 1890, Genet papers. [144] Blaine to Fuller, April 15, 1890, Genet papers. [145] Bradley to Fuller, February 2, 1890, Genet papers. *McGahey* v. *Virginia,* 1890, 135 U.S. 662. [146] *Cole* v. *Cunningham,* 1890, 133 U.S. 107; for criticisms of the decision see Williston: 5 Harvard Law Review, 210–221; Corwin: 81 University of Pennsylvania Law Review, 371, 384, note 54; Langmaid: 24 Illinois Law Review, 383, 408–411. [147] Bradley to Fuller, undated letter, Genet papers. *Mormon Church* v. *United States,* 1890, 136 U.S. 1. Joint resolution of October 25, 1893, see *United States* v. *Mormon Church,* 1893, 150 U.S. 145. [148] Reports of Attorney General of the United States, 1889, 1890, 1891; see Frankfurter & Landis: The Business of the Supreme Court, pp. 93–102. Miller to Ballinger, January 18, 1885, printed in Fairman: Mr. Justice Miller and the Supreme Court, p. 391. [149] For number of opinions written by each Justice see Appendix I; Fuller to John Morris, February 4, March 7, 1889, Morris papers; Fuller to Bancroft Davis, May 5, 1890, Bancroft Davis papers. See for example of appeals dismissed on technical grounds *Estis* v. *Trabue,* 1888, 128 U.S. 225 (Writ of error dismissed because judgment rendered against "the claimants" and their sureties in a bond and sureties did not join in writ of error); *Chapman* v. *Barney,* 1889, 129 U.S. 677 (Allegation that joint stock company, plaintiff, is citizen of State different from that of defendant not sufficient); *Stevens* v. *Nichols,* 1889, 130 U.S. 230 (Diversity not alleged with sufficient strictness); *Spalding* v. *Manasse,* 1889, 131 U.S. 65. (Seven cases affirmed because no showing that stipulation for trial before court without jury was in writing.) Out of 233 cases in which opinions were written in Fuller's first term (1888) 31 were patent, copyright or trademark cases; Crotch case is *Patent Clothing Co.* v. *Glover,* 1891, 141 U.S. 560; interview R. D. Weston, August, 1945. 99 out of 233 cases in which opinions were written at the 1888 term were cases based on diversity of citizenship. See substantially same proportion of these cases at 1889 term reported in 21 Cong. Record, p. 10221. **[150]** See Frankfurter & Landis: Business of the Supreme Court, pp. 86–102; J. H. Raymond: Relief of the Federal Court's Docket, Proceedings of Illinois State Bar Association, 1889, pp. 65–82; 21 Cong. Record, pp. 10217–10232; 10278–10288; 10302–10318; 10363–10365; Walter B. Hill: 12 Reports of American Bar Association, pp. 289–326. Acceptances and regrets for Brewer dinner on January 8, 1890, Genet papers. And see Stealey: Twenty Years in the Press Gallery, p. 62 "strongest [Judiciary] Committee . . . ever named"; Barry: Forty Years in Washington, pp. 214–15, repeating anecdote of Senators Pugh and Vest at this dinner showing their great appreciation of the honor. George P. Bradford, Clerk of the Judiciary Committee to the Chief Justice, February 18, 1890; Gray to Fuller with printed report and sug-

gested letter of transmission, March 6, 1890, Genet papers; Answer of Justices of the Supreme Court, March 12, 1890, Records of the United States Senate, 51st Congress, The National Archives. Two omissions are significant: They did not recommend abolition of their circuit duties. However onerous these duties were, the Justices had a sentimental attachment to them. They did not recommend allowing appeals from the new Circuit Court of Appeals by certiorari in the Supreme Court but suggested leaving such appeals entirely to certification of "novelty, difficulty or importance" by two judges of the Circuit Court of Appeals. **[151]** Act of March 3, 1891, 26 Stat. 826; 138 U.S. 709. Reports of Attorney General of the United States, 1892, 1893. **[152]** Great Men & Good Manners, Wide Awake, July, 1889; Fuller to Morris, February 5, 1889, Morris papers. **[153]** Interview Professor Samuel Williston, August, 1945. Mrs. Cleveland to Mrs. Fuller, January 2, 1889; Fuller to Mrs. Fuller, January 12, 1891, Genet papers; Keim: Handbook of Official and Social Etiquette and Public Ceremonials at Washington, 1889. Brewer to Fuller, August 21, 1904; Taft to Fuller, August 20, 1904, Genet papers. **[154]** Wellman: "Mell" Fuller at Work, Chicago Tribune, December 2, 1888; Dr. B. A. G. Fuller to the author, February 13, 1948; Fuller to Mrs. Fuller, January 13, 16, 19, 1891, January 18, 1892, Genet papers. **[155]** Interview Roland Gray, Esq., August, 1947; *Budd* v. *New York,* 1892, 143 U.S. 517, 551; Acceptances and regrets for Brewer dinner on January 8, 1890 in Genet papers. Fuller to Mrs. Fuller, January 13, 1891, Genet papers; Lardner: The Constitutional Doctrines of

David Josiah Brewer, unpublished Doctoral thesis, Princeton University. [156] Kent: Memoir of Henry Billings Brown; Fuller to Mrs. Fuller, January 13, 1891, Genet papers; interviews R. D. Weston, Esq. and Roland Gray, Esq., Boston, Henry C. Morris, Esq., Chicago. [157] XXXI Annual Reports of Pennsylvania Bar Association, 1925, pp. 106–8; 12 Green Bag, 553; many letters, Shiras to Fuller, Genet papers; Butler: A Century at the Bar of the Supreme Court, p. 89; Fuller Library, Bowdoin College; "Anecdotes of Justice Shiras" by George Shiras, 3d, The Daily Mining Journal, Marquette, Michigan, August 1, 1934. Fuller to his cousin, Mary Fuller, May 25, 1888, Henry M. Fuller papers. [158] Harlan to Fuller, May 3, 1888, Genet papers. Fuller to Cleveland, August 6, 1888, Cleveland papers, Library of Congress. Circuit assignments in 128 U.S. 701; Fuller to Mrs. Fuller, January 19, 30, February 2, 1891, Genet papers; Fuller to Bancroft Davis, June 7, 1891, Bancroft Davis papers; Fuller to Mrs. Fuller, November 7, 1888, Genet papers; Fuller to W. C. D. Grannis, November 11, 1888, Grannis papers (italics supplied). [159] Fuller to Cleveland, March 15, 1889, Cleveland papers. Cleveland to Fuller, April 8, 1889, Wallace papers. Cleveland to Fuller, November 24, 1889, Wallace papers. [160] Cleveland to Fuller, February 28, March 19, September 13, 1890, Wallace papers; Fuller to Cleveland, October 6, 1890, Widener Library, Harvard College. Nevins: Grover Cleveland, A Study in Courage, pp. 467–68; Fuller to Cleveland, February 17, 1891, Cleveland papers. Cleveland to Fuller, March 10, 1891, Wallace papers. [161] Fuller to Cleveland, March 12, 1891, Cleveland papers. Cleveland to Fuller, February 28, March 19, 1890, Wallace papers. [162] Butler: A Century at the Bar of the Supreme Court of the United States, p. 123. *Peake* v. *New Orleans,* 1890, 139 U.S. 342. Since Justice Brown did not sit, the decision was 5 to 3. Cleveland to Fuller, March 10, 1891, Wallace papers; Fuller to Cleveland, March 12, 1891, Cleveland papers. [163] Henry W. Scott to Fuller, June 30, 1891, Genet papers. Chicago Evening Journal, March 12, 1892; Shepard to Fuller, March 17, 1892; Shepard to Wallace, April 19, 1892, Genet papers. Shepard to Fuller, April 17, 1892; Morris to Fuller, April 30, May 16, 1892; Phelps to Fuller, February 16, 1892; Doane to Wallace, March 23, 1892; Doane to Fuller, April 12, 1892, Genet papers; Mrs. Fuller to Morris, March 31, 1892; Fuller to Morris, February 20, 1892, Morris papers; Fuller to Cleveland, March 30, 1892, Cleveland papers; Tree to Fuller, April 13, 24, 29, 1892, Genet papers. [164] New York World, May 3, 1892; Fuller to Cleveland, May 4, 1892, Cleveland papers, Library of Congress. Fuller to Mrs. Fuller, May 9, June 12, 1892, Genet papers. [165] Wallace telegram, Genet papers. Nevins: Grover Cleveland, A Study in Courage, pp. 507–8. Cleveland to Fuller, December 27, 1892, Genet papers. Fuller to Cleveland, January 2, 1893; Nevins in The American Scholar, III, p. 248. [166] Cleveland to Fuller, February 1, 1893, Wallace papers. [167] Recent case was *Bowman* v. *Chicago & N.W. Ry. Co.,* 1888, 125 U.S. 465. Overruled case: *Peirce* v. *New Hampshire,* 1847, 5 How. 504. [168] Marshall's case was: *Brown* v. *Maryland,* 1827, 12 Wheat. 419. Quotation from *In re Rahrer,* 1891, 140 U.S. 545,

561. [169] Act of August 8, 1891, 26 Stat. 313 c 728 commonly called the Wilson law. Case sustaining Act is *In re Rahrer*, 1891, 140 U.S. 545. See Bikle: The Silence of Congress, 41 Harvard Law Review, 200; Trickett: The Original Package Ineptitude, 6 Columbia Law Review, 161. The later case was *Rhodes* v. *Iowa*, 1898, 170 U.S. 412, discussed in Chapter XVIII. [171] Fuller to Field, May 18, 1892, Genet papers. Gray to Fuller, May 19, 1892, Genet papers. Field to Fuller, May 19, 1892, Genet papers. [172–173] On Bishop see 27 American Law Review, 938 and DAB on Joel P. Bishop. His letter was published in 40 American Law Register & Review, 619–23. Fuller to Field, May 21, 1892, Genet papers. Field to Fuller, June 28, 1892, Genet papers. [174] Brown to Fuller, May 19, 1891, Genet papers. [175–176] Harlan to Fuller, September 11, 1891, Genet papers. Bancroft Davis papers, Library of Congress. [178] Gray to Fuller, February 8, 1891, Genet papers. [179] 6 Harvard Law Review, 43–4. [180] Chicago Herald, March 5, 1893. Kent: Memoir of Henry Billings Brown, pp. 27–29; Thompson: Mr. Justice Jackson, Tennessee State Bar Association Reports, 1897, pp. 168–9; Dictionary of American Biography, IX, p. 544; James: Richard Olney, pp. 21–22; In Memoriam Howell Edmunds Jackson, 159 U.S. 701; see correspondence between Jackson and Fuller, Chapter XVI. [181] Phelps to Fuller, November 9, 1892; Gregory to Fuller, November 16, 1892, January 29, 1893, February 3, 1893; Shepard to Fuller, January 18, 29, February 11, 1893, Genet papers; Cleveland to Fuller, February 1, 1893, Wallace papers. Tree to Fuller, March 25, 30, April 1, 22, 1893; William M. Booth

to Fuller, February 7, 1893. [182] Smith to Fuller, November 5, 1893, Genet papers. Fuller's first wife was a sister of Smith's first wife; John Morris to Fuller, February 20, October 28, November 2, 1893, Genet papers; Fuller to Morris, April 20, 28, May 9, 14, 20, 27, October 27, 28, 30, November 2, 1893, John Morris papers; Shepard to Fuller, February 19, 25, 1893; Lincoln to Fuller, November 11, 1893; Fessenden to Fuller, October 15, 1893, Genet papers; Harlan to Fuller, February 28, March 25, 1893, and see Booth to Fuller, September 27, 1892, Gregory to Fuller, November 1, 1892, Genet papers, on appointment of James Harlan to Federal Bench. On *Metcalf* case: Harlan to Fuller, January 6, 1893, Genet papers. [183] Harlan to Fuller, January 23, 1893, Genet papers. Files of Supreme Court show order for re-argument in *Metcalf* case entered January 9, 1893. Harlan to Fuller, May 21, 1894, Genet papers. Vice principal case was *Chicago Mil. etc. Ry. Co.* v. *Ross*, 1884, 112 U.S. 377. [184] Harlan to Fuller, January 17, 1893, Genet papers. Vice principal rule dissipated in *Baltimore & Ohio R.R. Co.* v. *Baugh*, 1893, 149 U.S. 368, see 8 Harvard Law Review, pp. 57–8; *Northern Pac. R.R. Co.* v. *Hambly*, 1894, 154 U.S. 349; *Cen. R.R. Co.* v. *Keegan*, 1895, 160 U.S. 259; *Northern Pac. Ry. Co.* v. *Peterson*, 1896, 162 U.S. 346; see 10 Harvard Law Review, p. 185; and *Northern Pacific R.R. Co.* v. *Dixon*, 1904, 194 U.S. 338. [185] Field to Fuller, May 22, 30, 1893, Genet papers. [186] Field to Fuller, May 29, 1893, Genet papers; Field to Gray, May 27, 1893, Gray papers, Supreme Court Library. Gray to Fuller, May 29, 1893, Genet papers. The footnote is

not in Field's dissenting opinion as
published but it appears in the original dissenting opinion of Field on
file in the Supreme Court. (Vol. 2,
Opinions for 1892 Term, p. 1532.)
It occurs after the following sentence:
"I utterly dissent from and reject the
doctrine expressed in the opinion of
the majority that 'Congress under the
power to exclude or expel aliens,
might have directed any Chinese
laborer found in the United States
without a certificate of residence to
be removed out of the country by
executive officers, without a judicial
trial or examination just as it might
have authorized such officers absolutely to prevent his entrance into
the country.' " This sentence appears
without the footnote in Field's published dissent (149 U.S. at p. 755)
and is a correct quotation from Gray's
opinion as published (149 U.S. at p.
728). Field to Fuller, December 16,
1893, Genet papers. **[187]** Gray to
Fuller, February 24, 1894, Genet
papers. Cases referred to are: *Shively
v. Bowlby,* 1894, 152 U.S. 1; *Martin
v. Waddell,* 1842, 16 Pet. 367; *Pollard
v. Hagen,* 1845, 3 How. 212; *Knight* v.
U.S. Land Assn., 1891, 142 U.S. 161;
Dutton v. *Strong,* 1861, 1 Black 23;
R.R. Co. v. *Schurmeir,* 7 Wall. 272;
Yates v. *Milwaukee,* 1870, 10 Wall.
497; *Barney* v. *Keokuk,* 1876, 94 U.S.
324; *Prosser* v. *Northern Pac. R.R.,*
1894, 152 U.S. 59; *Miller* v. *Caldwell—
Hutchinson Investment Co.* v. *Caldwell,* 1894, 152 U.S. 65. *Hutchinson
Investment Co.* v. *Caldwell,* 1894, 152
U.S. 65; Gray to Fuller, March 3,
1894, Genet papers. For a similar
incident between Gray and Miller see
Fairman: Mr. Justice Miller and the
Supreme Court, pp. 320–21. **[188]** 9
Harvard Law Review, p. 430; Pauncefote to Fuller, December 22, 1895;

Emery to Fuller, February 4, 1896;
Thayer to Fuller, October 16, 1896,
Genet papers; 12 Law Quarterly Review, pp. 302–3. **[189]** Klinkhamer:
Edward Douglas White. **[190]** On
frequent differences between White
and Fuller see Appendix II and
Klinkhamer: Edward Douglas White,
Appendix C, p. 295; many letters
from White to Fuller are in the Genet
papers. *World's Columbian Exposition* v. *United States,* 1893, 56 Fed.
654. *Hennington* v. *Georgia,* 1896, 163
U.S. 299; see 10 Harvard Law Re-
view, pp. 378–79. **[191]** *Mormon
Church* v. *United States,* 1890, 136
U.S. 1, supra, pp. 167–69; *Leisy* v.
Hardin, 1890, 135 U.S. 100, supra, pp.
147–48; *Hennington* v. *Georgia,* 1896,
163 U.S. 299, supra, p. **190.** On Peckham see 1910 Reports of N.Y. State
Bar Association, pp. 629–712; 30 American Law Review, 100; Memorial, 215
U.S. v–xiii; many letters from Peck-
ham to Fuller are in the Genet papers.
On house at 1801 F St.: Fuller to
John Morris, March 31, April 11,
September 11, 1896, John Morris
papers; Warren: The Story-Marshall
Correspondence, William and Mary
Law Quarterly, Second Series, Vol.
21, No. 1, January, 1941, reprint pp.
24–25; Interview with Mrs. Robert
Low Bacon, the present owner of the
house. **[192]** J. G. Cannon, Chairman, Appropriations Committee of
House of Representatives, to Fuller,
December 16, 1896; Fuller to Cannon,
December 21, 1896, Genet papers.
[193] The vote in the Senate was 39
to 34; 26 Congressional Record, p.
7136; Seligman: The Income Tax, p.
505. **[194]** Swaine: The Cravath
Firm, I, pp. 518–22. **[196]** See Carter's argument, 157 U.S. pp. 523–24;
White's dissent, 157 U.S. pp. 617,
641–42. Seligman: The Income Tax,

p. 564, n. 2, pp. 576–78, n. 1 last paragraph, p. 579. **[197]** Seligman: The Income Tax, pp. 548–59. One of Fuller's references was to the Pinckney draft of the proposed constitution and Fuller was criticized by Worthington C. Ford in The Nation, Vol. 60, p. 398 for giving authority to that draft which was inaccurate. Since then, however, the researches of Messrs. Jameson and McLaughlin have enabled Farrand to reconstruct the authentic Pinckney draft. If it had been available then it would have served Fuller's purpose substantially as well as the draft from which he quoted. See Farrand: The Records of the Federal Convention, III, p. 607. **[198]** Seligman: The Income Tax, p. 558; Corwin: Court Over Constitution, p. 181: "Although he [Choate] was unable to adduce any respectable historical testimony in support of this theory . . . it was swallowed hook, line and sinker by the court." **[199]** Whitney: The Income Tax and The Constitution, 20 Harvard Law Review, pp. 280, 295. On Franklin and Adam Smith see Dictionary of National Biography, XVIII, p. 415. **[200]** Seligman: The Income Tax, pp. 568–69; Corwin: Court Over Constitution, p. 182. Seligman: The Income Tax, pp. 535–40. **[201]** *New York Trust Co.* v. *Eisner,* 1921, 256 U.S. 345, 349. **[204]** Corwin: Court Over Constitution, p. 189. White's dissent, 157 U.S. at pp. 647–48. The *Pac. Ins. Co.* case involved a tax on the business of an insurance company measured by its premiums, dividends and net gains. Fuller had said, p. 576: "The arguments for the insurance company . . . took a wide range, but the decision rested on narrow grounds, and turned on the distinction between an

excise duty and a tax strictly so termed." He said that the tax there was a tax on the privilege of doing business which was increased or diminished by the amount of business done. Gray to Fuller, April 5, 1895, Genet papers. **[205]** Brewer: The Income Tax Cases, Address Delivered before the Graduating Class of the Law Department of the State University of Iowa at the Annual Commencement, June 8, 1898, Published by the University, Iowa City. On newspaper comments see Literary Digest, Vol. X, No. 25, p. 1, April 20, 1895; The Daily Picayune, New Orleans, April 9, 1895; Birmingham Age Herald, Birmingham, Alabama, April 9, 1895; Morning News, Savannah, Georgia, April 9, 1895; The Nashville American, Nashville, Tennessee, April 9, 1895. **[206]** Chicago Tribune, April 6, 7, 9, 1895; Kinsley: The Chicago Tribune, III, p. 264; interview Leon Stolz, Chief Editorial Writer, Chicago Tribune, July, 1949. **[208]** Genet papers. William Hicks Jackson had been a General in the Confederate Army and was a large landowner at Belle Meade near Nashville, Tennessee. See D.A.B., IX, p. 561. **[209]** Fuller to Olney, January 30, 1895, Olney papers, Library of Congress. **[210]** Genet papers. The omitted portion of Jackson's letter of April 8, 1895 relates to Fuller's proposal to buy Jackson's home in Washington. Jackson did not think his house large enough for Fuller's family and recommended a house nearby. **[211]** The Nashville American, April 9, 1895, p. 3; The Morning News, Savannah, Georgia, April 9, 1895. **[212]** Genet papers. **[213]** Bancroft Davis papers, Library of Congress. Fuller noted in his opinion that the case was badly reported in 3 Dall.

A careless reporter might have omitted Marshall as counsel. He is shown as counsel for Hylton in another case (*Ware* v. *Hylton,* 3 Dall. 199) apparently argued at the same time. His co-counsel in that case was Campbell, who is shown by the Reporter as counsel in *Hylton* v. *U.S.,* 3 Dall. 171. *Pollock* v. *Farmers Loan & Trust Co.,* 1895, 158 U.S. 601. **[214]** Report of Wealth, Debt and Taxation at the Eleventh Census, 1890, Valuation and Taxation, p. 14, Table 3. **[215]** Quotation from Brown: 158 U.S. at pp. 688–89. The Nation, Vol. 60, pp. 417–18. **[216]** Field to Fuller, Genet papers. **[218]** Myers: History of the Supreme Court, p. 616, preface, pp. 5–9. **[219]** Corwin: Court Over Constitution, 1938, pp. 177–209; Ratner: American Taxation, 1942, pp. 193–214. **[220]** Corwin: Court Over Constitution, 1938, pp. 200–1. **[222]** Gray to Fuller, May 8, 1892, Genet papers. **[223]** Field to Fuller, March 25, May 9, 1896, Genet papers. Walter Wellman in Chicago Times-Herald, October 16, 1897. **[224]** Field to Fuller, March 8, 1896, Genet papers. Hughes: The Supreme Court of the United States, pp. 75–6. Chief Justice Hughes had this story from Justice Harlan. **[225]** Fuller to Field, May 4, 1897, draft with many interlineations, Genet papers. **[226]** Brewer to Fuller, August 21, 1897, Genet papers. Fuller to Mrs. Fuller, October 4, 1897, Genet papers. Field's farewell letter printed in 168 U.S. 713. **[227]** Harlan to Fuller, October 4, 1897, Genet papers. McDevitt: Joseph McKenna. **[228]** Judge Charles B. Bellinger to Fuller, September 11, 1897, Genet papers. **[229]** Judge C. H. Hanford to Fuller, October 7, 1897, Genet papers. John Addison Porter, Secretary to the

President, to Fuller, December 16, 1897, Genet papers. On McKenna see Pringle: The Life and Times of William Howard Taft, pp. 965, 971, 1059–60 for Chief Justice Taft's judgment that McKenna was a "weak" judge and Taft's difficulty in inducing McKenna to resign; Justice Felix Frankfurter said in a letter to the author, dated October 31, 1947: "Holmes, in common with other members of the Court felt a certain judicial inadequacy in McKenna. I remember how startled Holmes was when I ventured to say to him once before Brandeis came to the Court that, while McKenna's opinions were quixotic and undependable, he perceived the true nature of the Court's function in constitutional controversies arising under the Fourteenth Amendment more clearly perhaps than anyone on the Court with the exception of Holmes himself. (See for instance McKenna's dissent in *Connolly* v. *Union Sewer Pipe Company,* 184 U.S. 540 and his opinions in *German Alliance Ins. Co.* v. *Kansas,* 233 U.S. 389 and *Walls* v. *Midland Carbon Co.,* 254 U.S. 300.) And Holmes came to recognize these qualities in McKenna alongside his 'oscillations.' See Holmes-Pollock Letters, II, p. 129. Nor was Brandeis unappreciative of McKenna's qualities." On McKenna's votes with White see Klinkhamer: Edward Douglas White, p. 295, "Table of Justices' concurrences and dissents with White." See also the favorable but scholarly and objective biography of Justice McKenna by Brother Mathew McDevitt, 1946, Catholic University of America Press. **[230]** Fuller to Davis, April 15, 1891, February 28, 1896, Bancroft Davis papers, Library of Congress. **[231]** Davis to Fuller, March 9, 1900,

Genet papers. Head notes quoted: *Huntting Elevator Co.* v. *Bosworth,* 1899, 179 U.S. 415, *United States* v. *Morrison,* 1900, 179 U.S. 456. **[232]** 12 Harvard Law Review, 58, April, 1898. Fuller to Shepard, January 22, 1900, Shepard papers. Brewer to Fuller, July 20, 1902, Genet papers; "I . . . trust for the credit of the court that Davis has resigned"; Harlan to Fuller, September 18, 1902, Genet papers; "I am glad that Davis had resigned not only on his account but on account of the Court." Fuller to Davis, September 10, 1902, Genet papers. **[233]** Davis to Fuller, September 11, 1902, Genet papers. **[234]** Fuller to John Morris, February 23, April 9, May 6, June 2, 1896. **[235]** Fuller to John Morris, July 9, October 31, 1896, Morris papers. Fuller to Mrs. Fuller, March 30, 1898, Genet papers. **[236]** Miller in Slaughter-House cases, 1872, 16 Wall. 36, 73; Field in In re *Look Tin Sing,* 1884, 21 Fed. 905. **[237]** On relocation of the Japanese see: *Hirabayashi* v. *U.S.,* 1943, 320 U.S. 81; *Ex Parte Endo,* 1944, 323 U.S. 283. **[238]** George F. Edmunds to Gray, May 15, 1898; J. B. Thayer to Gray, April 8, 1898, Gray papers, Supreme Court Library. **[239]** 8 Harvard Law Review, 353. Jones: *Pollock* v. *Farmers' Loan and Trust Co.,* 9 Harvard Law Review, 198, 211. *Schollenberger* v. *Pennsylvania,* 1898, 171 U.S. 1; *Collins* v. *New Hampshire,* 1898, 171 U.S. 30. **[240]** See Cushman: The National Police Power Under the Commerce Clause of the Constitution, 1919, 3 Minn. Law Rev. 381, 405–6 (The Wilson Act was "emasculated"); Corwin: Congress's Power to Prohibit Commerce, 1933, 18 Cornell Law Quarterly, 477, 491 (The Wilson Act was "eviscerated"). *Austin* v. *Ten-*

nessee, 1900, 179 U.S. 343; a subsequent case involving the same facts (except that the packages of cigarettes were not in baskets) where the same division of the Court occurred, is *Cook* v. *Marshall County,* 1905, 196 U.S. 261. **[241]** Brewer to Fuller, August 7, 1900, Genet papers. Brewer's dissent (179 U.S. at pp. 364–88) is one of his best opinions and shows long and laborious effort. His arguments against the decision have been repeated with approval in the legal literature: See Trickett: The Original Package Ineptitude, 1906, 6 Columbia Law Review, 161, 170–73; Shenton: Interstate Commerce During the Silence of Congress, 1919, 23 Dickinson Law Review, 139, 145–47. White to Fuller, June 30, 1897, Genet papers. **[242]** White to Fuller, July 11, 1898, Genet papers. **[243]** Gray to Fuller, September 11, 1898, Genet papers. Brown to Fuller, May 3, 1901, Genet papers. **[244]** Brown to Fuller, May 6, 1901, Genet papers; Kent: Memoir of Henry Billings Brown, p. 31. Undated note Brown to Fuller, Genet papers. No. 303 is *Tucker* v. *Alexandroff,* 1902, 183 U.S. 424; see critical note on the decision in 15 Harvard Law Review, 657. **[245]** Harlan to Fuller, December 18, 1898, Genet papers. Davis to Fuller, January 15, 19, 1900, Genet papers. **[246]** Fuller to Mrs. Fuller, March 29, 1898, Genet papers; Fuller to Shepard, April 3, 1898, Shepard papers. Rear Admiral Arent Schuyler Crowninshield was Chief of Bureau of Navigation and John Davis Long, Secretary of the Navy; White to Fuller, July 11, 1898: "Your predictions as to the inferiority of the Spanish sea force have come true." Genet papers. McKinley to Fuller, August 18, 1898; Fuller to McKinley, August 18, 19,

1898, Genet papers. **[247]** Fuller to Shepard, September 17, 1898, Shepard papers. **[248]** *The Olinde Rodrigues,* 1899, 174 U.S. 510; *The Pedro,* 1899, 175 U.S. 354; *The Benito Estenger,* 1900, 176 U.S. 568; *The Carlos F. Roses,* 1900, 177 U.S. 655. Fuller to Shepard, February 20, 1900, Shepard papers. Fuller to Shepard, January 3, 1900, Shepard papers; the case referred to was *Tyler* v. *Judges,* 1900, 179 U.S. 405. **[250]** Cleveland: The Venezuelan Boundary Controversy; James: Richard Olney, pp. 96–192. **[251]** Report of the United States Commission on Boundary between Venezuela and British Guiana, Government Printing Office, 1897. The Secretary of the Commission was S. Mallet-Prevost, and among the experts who aided it were Dr. Justin Winsor of Harvard College, Prof. J. Franklin Jameson of Brown University, Prof. George L. Burr of Cornell University, Prof. James C. Hanson of the University of Wisconsin, and Dr. DeHaan of Johns Hopkins University. Holmes-Pollock Letters, 1941, I, pp. 68–9. And see Alverstone: Recollections of Bar and Bench, 1915, p. 237: "A most able memorandum of the British case had been prepared by Sir Frederick Pollock . . ."; Pauncefote to Fuller, April 3, 1896, Genet papers. Fuller's copy of this Blue Book is in the Fuller library at Bowdoin College. **[252]** Olney to Fuller, January 10, 1897, Genet papers. Crespo to Fuller, February 17, 1897, Genet papers. Olney to Fuller, April 24, 25, 1897, Genet papers; Fuller to Olney, April 25, May 2, 3, 1897, Olney papers; Fuller to Olney, May 2, 1897, Olney papers, Library of Congress. Andrade to Fuller, July 27, 1897; Brewer to Fuller, August 5, 1897; Fuller to Herschell and Col-

lins, August 7, 1897; Brewer to Fuller, August 11, 1897, Genet papers. **[253]** Brewer to Fuller, August 16, 1897, Genet papers. **[254]** Andrade to Fuller, September 6, 1897, Genet papers. On Martens: 10 *Journal* of *Comparative Legislation* (New Series) (1909), p. 9. Fuller to McKinley, August 19, 1898, Genet papers. Fuller to Lord Herschell, February 7, 1898, Genet papers. **[255]** Herschell responded: "It would be disastrous if you were to resign & another arbitrator had to be appointed. There is no saying to what complications it might give rise. We see no objection to the solution of the difficulty which you suggest." Herschell to Fuller, March 16, 1898. Fuller to Martens, February 7, 1898; Martens to Fuller, March 2, 1898, Genet papers. Thayer: John Hay, II, pp. 202–208; invitation and regrets in Putnam and Genet papers for Fuller's dinner for Herschell on February 6, 1899; on March 2, 1899 Fuller wrote to Mrs. Fuller: "You will be distressed at the news of the death of Lord Herschell. It was like a thunderbolt out of a clear sky. I sat with him for some time on Monday afternoon and was intending to call on him Wednesday on coming from court but he died that morning . . . I have written a few lines to Lady Herschell. . . . You might drop her a few lines. . . . I sent Lord Herschell the Memoirs of Henry Reeve & suppose the volumes will be returned. They had my name on them as presented 'by my dear wife.'" Genet papers. For Herschell Memorial see 173 U.S. 707. Fuller wrote his wife: "I enclose what I said [at the Memorial] though I said more and much better. Gray told me coming off that it was very fine. We could not pay him [Lord

Herschell] a greater compliment and it is the first time in the history of the court." Fuller to Mrs. Fuller, March 2, 1899, Genet papers. See also: The Late Lord Herschell, 12 Harvard Law Review, 557. Official notice of appointment of Lord Russell dated March 24, 1899, Genet papers. **[256–257]** The Edinburgh Review: The Venezuelan Arbitration, January 1900, CXCL, p. 123. **[258]** Alverstone: Recollections of Bar and Bench, pp. 235–40. Fuller to Shepard, July 30, 1899. "The case is interesting but the arguments are long and minute. . . . The weather is quite warm and from time to time hot. Should the heat continue it may drive us away. . . ." Shepard papers. Letter Uri Grannis of Chicago to the author under date of February 21, 1949. Mr. Grannis was a contemporary of the Chief Justice's son, Weston, and was a member of the party in Paris. Many dinner invitations are in the Genet papers. See Letters of Henry Adams, II, p. 241. **[259]** *Johnson* v. *McIntosh,* 1823, 8 Wheat. 543. Interview on August 22, 1947 with Roland Gray of Boston, who was Fuller's secretary at the Arbitration. **[260]** Award is printed in British and Foreign State Papers, 1899–1900, Vol. XCII, pp. 160–2. Biographies of Richard Everhard Webster and Robert Threshie Reid in D.N.B., 1912–1921 and 1922–1930 Supplements; The Times, London, December 12, 1899. The Venezuelan Arbitration, The Edinburgh Review, Vol. CXCL, p. 123, at p. 130. Interview with R. D. Weston of Boston on August 1, 1945. **[261]** Russell to Fuller, June 28, 1900; Collins to Fuller, August 25, 1900; James C. Carter to Fuller, December 21, 1900; Martens to Fuller, September 7, 1901; Acceptances and

Regrets for dinner on October 19, 1901 in Genet papers; many letters from Alverstone and Collins are in the Genet papers. Loreburn to Fuller, July 28, 1907. First edition of *The River War* in Fuller library at Bowdoin College. **[262]** Foraker Act: Act of April 12, 1900, 31 Stat. 77, c. 191. For a history of its passage see Latané: America as a World Power, pp. 140–1. For the author's explanation of the Act, see Foraker: Notes of a Busy Life, II, pp. 70–82. Randolph: Constitutional Aspects of Annexation, 12 Harvard Law Review, 291, December, 1898; Baldwin: Constitutional Questions Incident to the Annexation and Government by the United States of Island Territory, 12 Harvard Law Review, 393, January, 1899. **[263]** *Loughborough* v. *Blake,* 1820, 5 Wheat. 317, 319. Langdell: Status of Our New Territories, 12 Harvard Law Review, 365; Judson: Our Federal Constitution and the Government of Tropical Territories, XIX The American Monthly Review of Reviews, 67. **[264]** Lowell: Status of Our New Possessions, 13 Harvard Law Review, 155, November, 1899. Records, Briefs and Arguments of Counsel in the Insular Cases published by the Government Printing Office pursuant to H.R. Cong. Res. No. 72, 56th Congress. One of these briefs was filed on behalf of undisclosed "Industrial interests." Another was filed on behalf of the New England Tobacco Growers Association. The record of this filing was defective and the Reporter refused to comply with the Chief Justice's request to show it as filed in the official reports. Charles A. Gardiner to Fuller, June 6, 1901; Davis to Fuller, June 29, 1901; Fuller to Gardiner, July 8, 1901, Genet papers. **[266]**

War tariff case is *Dooley* v. *United States*, 1901, 182 U.S. 222. Lowell's principal reliance was on a dictum of Taney's in the case of *Fleming* v. *Page*, 1850, 9 Howard, 603. Brown said (182 U.S. 192, 4) that this dictum was wrong in fact and was "practically overruled" in *Cross* v. *Harrison*, 1853, 16 Howard 164. Randolph: The Insular Cases, 1 Columbia Law Review, 436; Littlefield: The Insular Cases, 15 Harvard Law Review, pp. 169, 281; Whitney: The Insular Decisions of December, 1901, 2 Columbia Law Review, 79. [268] Tree to Fuller, July 2, 1901; Jewett to Fuller, May 25, 1901, Genet papers. [269] Brewer wrote to Fuller, June 13, 1901: "I send you a copy of the New York Journal with Mr. Dooley's comments on our recent decision. I thought you would enjoy it." Genet papers. Doubtless Brewer, Fuller and the other dissenters took more pleasure in the Dooley version of the cases than did Brown or White. Oberholtzer: A History of the United States since the Civil War, V, 672; Rhodes: History of the United States, IX, 206; Beard: The Rise of American Civilization, II, 488; Sullivan: Our Times, I, pp. 544–53. [270] Klinkhamer: Edward Douglas White, pp. 38–39. Contemporary professional comment: Thayer: Insular Tariff Cases in the Supreme Court, 15 Harvard Law Review, 164, 165; Randolph: The Insular Cases, 1 Columbia Law Review, 436, 446–47. Harlan to Fuller, July 8, 1901, August 16, 1902; Brewer to Fuller, September 10, 1905, Genet papers. [271] Harlan to Fuller, July 8, 1901, Genet papers. [272] Harlan to Fuller, August 6, 1901, Genet papers. Fuller also submitted the draft opinion to Peckham and secured his approval of it. Peckham

to Fuller, September 5, 1901, Genet papers. Brown to Fuller, August 27, 1901, Genet papers. It was White's habit to take a very pessimistic view of the consequences of any decision with which he disagreed. See Klinkhamer: Edward Douglas White, p. 65, on his habitual use of the sentence: "It will ruin the court." Probably Brown had some figures on the small amount of trade between the date of cession and the passage of the tariff act. [273] *Fourteen Diamond Rings* v. *United States*, 1901, 183 U.S. 176. Harlan to Fuller, September 2, 1901, Genet papers; *Dooley* v. *United States,* 1901, 183 U.S. 151. [274] Fuller to Morris, December 5, 1901, Morris papers. No. 207 is *Dooley* v. *United States*, 1901, 183 U.S. 151 opinion delivered December 2, 1901. *Hawaii* v. *Mankichi*, 1903, 190 U.S. 197. [275] *Rassmussen* v. *United States*, 1905, 197 U.S. 516. [276] Butler: A Century at the Bar of the Supreme Court of the United States, pp. 92–94. See White in *Public Utility Commrs.* v. *Ynchausti Co.,* 1920, 251 U.S. 401, 426. Quotation from Taft: *Balzac* v. *Porto Rico,* 1921, 258 U.S. 298, 305. Case on tariffs drawn by Taft: *Lincoln* v. *United States,* 1905, 197 U.S. 419, on rehearing 202 U.S. 484; *United States* v. *Heinszen & Co.,* 1907, 206 U.S. 370. [277] Taft: Our Chief Magistrate and His Powers, 1916, pp. 99–103. [278] Fuller to Putnam, March 19, 1902, Putnam papers; Fuller to Morris, June 15, 1902. Selections from Correspondence of Theodore Roosevelt and Henry Cabot Lodge, I, pp. 515, 516. Chicago Legal News, October 25, 1902, Vol. XXXV, p. 149. [279] On July 24, 1902, Gray wrote to Fuller: "I am perfectly well except the local trouble [he had suffered a stroke] which is improving but very slowly. In that state of things and my doctors advising me that I could not undertake the work of another term without seriously endangering my health, I have sent to the President my resignation to take effect on the appointment of my successor. I have not told any one else but my immediate family. But as it had to be done I felt that the President ought to know presently." Gray to Fuller, July 24, 1902, Genet papers. Gray died on September 15, 1902, and Fuller attended with deep grief his funeral in Boston. Fuller to Mrs. Fuller, September 18, 1902, Genet papers. Roosevelt to Lodge, July 10, 1902, Selections from the Correspondence of Theodore Roosevelt and Henry Cabot Lodge, I, pp. 517–19. **[280]** 1886 Speech by Holmes, Speeches, pp. 24–25. Holmes-Pollock Letters, II, p. 72. Holmes' Journal shows offer made on July 24, 1902; Holmes to Lady Pollock, September 6, 1902, Holmes-Pollock Letters, I, p. 105. **[281]** 6 American Law Review, p. 570. That no such pledge was actually made see supra, pp. **130–131.** Lodge to Roosevelt, August 17, 1902, Selections from The Correspondence of Theodore Roosevelt and Henry Cabot Lodge, I, p. 526; Holmes to Pollock, August 13, September 23, 1902, Holmes-Pollock Letters, I, pp. 103–4, 106. "It makes one sick when he has broken his heart trying to make every word living and real. . . ." Fuller to Morris, November 8, 1897, Morris papers; Fuller to Holmes, August 12, 1902, Holmes papers. Speech of Holmes in Chicago on October 20, 1902 reporting his two prior visits to Chicago: "The other time was in the course of a journey across the continent when our beloved friend Huntington Jack-

son showed me the courts and introduced me to Mr. Fuller then just nominated by the President for Chief Justice of the United States." Chicago Legal News, October 25, 1902, Vol. XXXV, p. 153; Fuller to Holmes, April 15, 1904, stating that he had heard a speech of Holmes in June, 1895, Holmes papers. **[282]** Holmes to Lady Pollock, October 24, 1902, Holmes-Pollock Letters, I, p. 108; Fuller to Morris, October 16, 1902, Vol. XXXV, p. 141. The case was *The Winkfield,* L.R.P.D., 1902, 42. Fuller to Morris, October 16, 1902, Morris papers. **[283]** On Knowlton appointment: Holmes-Pollock Letters, II, p. 161; Lodge to Roosevelt, August 20, 1902, Selections from the Correspondence of Theodore Roosevelt and Henry Cabot Lodge, I, p. 527. **[284]** Roosevelt to Lodge, August 11, 1902, *ibid.,* p. 525: "I have had a very nice letter from Hoar and shall announce Judge Holmes' appointment today." Holmes to Fuller, October 14, 1902, Genet papers. Hoar to Fuller, November 5, 1902, Genet papers. **[285]** Holmes to Fuller, November 21, 1902, Genet papers. **[286]** Roosevelt to Fuller, November 25, 1902, Genet papers. Lodge to Fuller, December 2, 1902, Genet papers. Butler: A Century at the Bar of the Supreme Court of the United States, pp. 65–66. **[287]** Interview with R. D. Weston, Esq., Boston, August 1, 1945. On criticism of Holmes's opinions see Holmes-Pollock Letters, I, p. 258; II, pp. 58, 132, 175. **[288]** Volume of speeches in Fuller Library, Bowdoin College, with original letter dated April 15, 1904 laid in. Fuller to Holmes, April 15, 1904, Holmes papers. Speech at dinner of Harvard Law School in honor of Professor C. C. Langdell in June, 1895, Speeches

of Oliver Wendell Holmes, p. 69.
[289] Holmes to Pollock, December
28, 1902, Holmes-Pollock Letters, II,
p. 109. Holmes to Fuller, December
28, 1902, Genet papers. [290] See
supra, page 270. Interviews Mr. Justice Felix Frankfurter to whom
Holmes told the story; Cullom: Fifty
Years of Public Service, p. 241.
[291] Genet papers. Fuller to Peckham and endorsement by Peckham,
February 10, 1903, Genet papers. No.
121 is *Home Life Ins. Co.* v. *Fisher*,
1903, 188 U.S. 726. Suit on life insurance policy. Unanimous opinion by
Holmes. Fuller to Mrs. Fuller, February 18, 1903, Genet papers. The
Lottery case, *Champion* v. *Ames*,
1903, 188 U.S. 321; See 16 Harvard
Law Review, 508 and the excellent
discussion of this case by Cushman,
3 Minnesota Law Review, 381. [292]
Shiras to Fuller, February 13, 1903,
Genet papers; Pollock wrote to
Holmes, March 25, 1903: "I perceive
that the New York Sun . . . is very
angry with the decision of the Supreme Court [in the Lottery case]
and also thinks it is in some way
peculiarly wicked of you to be one
of the majority." Holmes-Pollock
Letters, I, p. 112. States' rights have
always been the particular concern of
the party out of power but the *Snyder*
case was the only case in the last
eighteen years of Fuller's regime
where a constitutional decision was
on strict party lines. Reeder: Chief
Justice Fuller, 59 University of Pennsylvania Law Review and American
Law Register, pp. 12–14. [294] Langdell: The Northern Securities Case
and the Sherman Anti-Trust Act, 16
Harvard Law Review, 536, 17 Harvard
Law Review, 41; Humes: The Power
of Congress over Combinations affecting Interstate Commerce, 17 Har-

vard Law Review, 83; Pollock: The
Merger Case and Restraint of Trade,
17 Harvard Law Review, 151; Cham-
berlain: The Northern Securities
Case, A Reply to Professor Langdell,
13 Yale Law Journal, 57. Fuller to
Holmes, February 16, 1904, Holmes
papers. [296] Fuller to Mrs. Fuller,
March 15, 1904, Genet papers. Interview, August, 1946, with Colley Bell,
of New York, a former secretary of
the Chief Justice. [297] Holmes to
Pollock, February 9, 1931, Holmes-
Pollock Letters, II, pp. 63–4. Butler:
A Century at the Bar of the Supreme
Court of the United States, pp. 170–2.
The Justice who changed his mind
could not have been Brewer, Peckham or Fuller. They had dissented
in the prior case of *Atkin* v. *Kansas*,
1903, 191 U.S. 207 (8 hour law for
state contracts held valid) and Brewer
and Peckham had dissented in *Holden*
v. *Hardy*, 1898, 169 U.S. 366 (8 hour
law for miners held valid). So the
Justice who switched must have been
either Brown or McKenna, or both.
[298] Utah miners case: *Holden* v.
Hardy, 1898, 169 U.S. 366. The opinion was by Justice Brown with only
Brewer and Peckham dissenting.
Brown was a member of the majority
in the *Lochner* case. Quotation, "I
loathe" etc., Howe: Touched with
Fire, Civil War Letters and Diary of
Oliver Wendell Holmes, Jr., p. 71.
[299] Frankfurter: Mr. Justice
Holmes and the Supreme Court, appendix, pp. 100–104. The dissents of
all the Justices in such cases in that
period are as follows: Fuller, 8; Harlan, 4; Brewer, 2; Brown, 0; White,
1; Peckham, 0; McKenna, 5; Holmes,
6; Day, 3; Moody, 1. Most of these
cases were, of course, tax cases.
Holmes to Fuller, August 18, 1904,
Genet papers. The Chief Justice re-

ceived an immense number of letters of condolence, including letters from Grover Cleveland, Theodore Roosevelt, William H. Taft and all of the Justices of the Court. **[300]** Letter dated "Sorrento, Aug. 26/04," Holmes papers. The quotation "of course her husband does & 'Praiseth her'" is from the Old Testament: Proverbs XXXI, 28. The Church of the Redeemer at Sorrento, Maine, contains a plaque, doubtless put there by the Chief Justice, which bears the same quotation. It reads:

For
Many Years
made happy by
her loving care
Mary E
and Melville W. Fuller
with their children
worshipped here together
Born Burlington, Iowa
August 19, 1845
and married Chicago, Illinois,
May 30, 1866
her tender and valiant soul
took flight
Sorrento, August 17, 1904,
Her children arise up
And call her blessed
Her husband also
And he praiseth her.

[301] Fuller to Holmes, September 16, 1905, Holmes papers. **[302]** Pringle: Life & Times of William Howard Taft, I, pp. 152–53, 217, 248. Roosevelt to Taft, October 26, 1902; Taft to Roosevelt, October 27, 1902; Roosevelt to Taft, November 26, 1902. **[303]** Taft to Roosevelt, January 8, 1903, quoted in Pringle: Taft, I, pp. 240–45. Washington Star, January 14, 1903. Chicago Tribune, February 6, 1903; Chicago Chronicle, February 8, 1903. Holmes-Pollock Letters, II, p. 161. John Spalding Flannery to the author, January 3, 1949. Flannery was MacVeagh's law partner and had the story from him. **[304]** McLean: William Rufus Day, the Johns Hopkins Political Studies in Historical and Political Science, Series LXIV, No. 3, 1946, p. 54; Fuller to Day, February 6, 1903; Day to Fuller, February 9, 1903; Acceptances and Regrets for Dinner on March 9, 1903, Genet papers. Butler: A Century at the Bar of the Supreme Court of the United States, pp. 164–66. Cleveland to Putnam, March 6, 1903, original in possession of William P. Thompson, Esq. of Boston; 47 Harpers Weekly, p. 462, March 21, 1903; Putnam to Fuller, April 6, 1903, Genet papers. **[305]** Interview R. D. Weston, Esq. of Boston on August 1, 1945. Cleveland to Fuller, April 12, 1903, Wallace papers. Report of the Eighteenth Annual Meeting of the Harvard Law School Association at Cambridge, published by the Association, 1904, p. 65. **[306]** McLean: William Rufus Day. **[307]** Stephen A. Day served as the Chief Justice's Secretary in 1906–7. Taft to Mrs. Taft, July 10, 1905, quoted Pringle: Taft, I, p. 311 and see pp. 313, 264–65, 314–17. Fuller to Holmes, March 20, 1906, Holmes papers. Gregory to Fuller, November 30, 1906, Gregory letter books. **[308]** Cleveland to Fuller, March 24, 1907, Genet papers. Shiras to Fuller, March 5, 1908, Genet papers; Root to Willard Bartlett, June 16, 1908, quoted in Jessup: Elihu Root, II, p. 126. Wiener: The Life & Judicial Career of William Henry Moody, Manuscript thesis, Harvard Law School, 1930. **[309]** Fuller to S. S. Gregory, December 5, 1906, Gregory papers; Holmes-Pollock Letters, I, p. 137. Interview R. D. Weston, Esq. of Boston on August 23, 1947; Holmes to Putnam, July 12, 1910, Putnam papers. Pringle: Taft, II, p. 966; Taft to Lurton, May 22, 1909, quoted in Pringle: Taft, I, pp. 529–30. Klinkhamer: Edward Douglas White, p. 46; White to Taft, July 16, 23, 1910, Taft papers, Library of Congress. [310] White to Fuller, undated, Genet papers. Holmes to Baroness Moncheur, July 14, 1910, Holmes papers. For Fuller's opinions in 1910 see *Williams* v. *Arkansas*, 1910, 217 U.S. 79; *Hutchinson, Pierce & Co.* v. *Loewy*, 1910, 217 U.S. 457; *Ex Parte Gruetter*, 1910, 217 U.S. 586. [311] The Globe and Commercial Advertiser, New York, March 19, 1909, p. 10. Printed copy of speech in Gregory papers. [312] Fuller to S. S. Gregory, March 11, 1909, Gregory papers. [314] Holmes-Pollock Letters, II, p. 138; Dicey's Conflicts of Law, 5th ed., p. 772. Holmes to Fuller, undated, Genet papers. [315] Holmes to Fuller, September 27, 1905, Genet papers. *The Eliza Lines,* 1905, 199 U.S. 119. See comment on the case in 19 Harvard Law Review, 200. Holmes cited *Roehm* v. *Horst,* 1900, 178 U.S. 1, the leading case (opinion by Fuller) on anticipatory breach of contract. [316] Holmes to Fuller, February 23, 1909, Genet papers. Fuller to Harlan, November 23, 1908, Harlan papers, University of Louisville. [317] Holmes to Fuller, February 6, 1905, Genet papers. [318] Butler: A Century at the Bar of the Supreme Court of the United States, pp. 126–29. Holmes to Fuller, March 30, 1904, Genet papers. [319] Holmes to Fuller, April 20, 1907, Genet papers. Holmes to Fuller, February 10, 1908, February 9, 1909, Genet papers. Holmes-Pollock Letters, I, p. 127;

see also I, p. 163, II, pp. 207–8. Holmes to Fuller, May 18, 1906, Genet papers. The case was *Vicksburg* v. *Waterworks Co.,* 1906, 202 U.S. 453. The former opinion of the Court was *Vicksburg Waterworks Co.* v. *Vicksburg,* 1902, 185 U.S. 65. Fuller to Holmes, September 26, 1905, Holmes papers. [320] Holmes to Fuller, September 27, 1905, Genet papers. Dent's article appears in 61 Central Law Journal, p. 123. Holmes' decision which is criticised is *Hardin* v. *Shedd,* 1903, 190 U.S. 508 and the prior decision of Bradley which Holmes followed is *Hardin* v. *Jordan,* 1891, 140 U.S. 371. Fuller to Holmes, March 20, 1906, Holmes papers. [322] On *Selliger* case: Holmes to Fuller, March 26, 29, 1909, Genet papers. [324] Fuller to all Justices, March 20, 1906, Holmes papers. Undated note in Genet papers from Moody to Fuller submitting draft of the information before it was filed. [325] Holmes opinion *United States* v. *Shipp,* 1906, 203 U.S. 563. Holmes to Fuller, March 16, 1909, Genet papers. [327] Holmes to Fuller, May 13, 1909, Genet papers. Imposition of punishments reported in *United States* v. *Shipp,* 1909, 215 U.S. 580. [328] Fuller to Mrs. Fuller, March 15, 1897, Genet papers. [329] Holmes to Putnam, July 12, 1910, Putnam papers. RESPECT AND CONFIDENCE: *Landmark,* Norfolk, Virginia, July 5, 1910. "Enjoyed the respect and confidence of the country to an extent not surpassed by even the greatest of his predecessors"; *Banner,* Nashville, Tennessee, July 4, 1910, "No other chief justice has . . . commanded more fully the esteem and respect of the whole country"; *Evening Globe,* New York City, July 4, 1910, "He had the respect and confidence of his associates, the bar and the country, and as time has gone on admiration has developed into reverence"; *Chronicle,* Houston, Texas, July 4, 1910, "His character was such that he earned the respect of everyone"; *News-Press,* St. Joseph, Missouri, July 4, 1910, "He maintained the position of reserve that commands public veneration of the supreme court"; *Times,* Washington, D. C., July 4, 1910, "There never has been a moment when the respect accorded the office was not accorded in equal or greater measure to the man"; *Tribune,* New York City, July 5, 1910, "He soon won the respect and esteem of the country which has long thought of him as worthily maintaining the best traditions of the chief justiceship"; *American,* Baltimore, Maryland, July 5, 1910, "By his associates, by his country, he will be revered and no deed of honor will be too high to pay him"; *Eastern Argus,* Portland, Maine, July 5, 1910, "Chief Justice Fuller filled this great position with an ability and dignity worthy of his illustrious predecessors, commanding the respect and confidence of the country"; *Herald Republican,* Salt Lake City, Utah, July 5, 1910, "Possessed the love, confidence and esteem of his countrymen"; *Observer,* Utica, New York, July 5, 1910, "Established himself firmly in the respect of his associates and the admiration of the country"; *Kennebec Journal,* Augusta, Maine, July 6, 1910, "Had grown into the respect and veneration of the public, as well as the ranks of his profession"; *Inter Ocean,* Chicago, Illinois, July 6, 1910, "His name was mentioned by no decent American save with respect and confidence"; *Daily Press,* Portland, Maine, July 6, 1910,

"None enjoyed the respect and confidence of men of all political beliefs more than did he"; *Press,* Utica, New York, July 5, 1910, "Won the respect of the profession and the people"; *Despatch,* Columbus, Ohio, July 5, 1910, "Retained the esteem and confidence of the people"; *Union Advertiser,* Rochester, New York, July 5, 1910, "President Taft will not easily find a man in all respects so perfectly fitted for the office. . . . He will find none who will more completely possess the respect and confidence of the country." Most Beloved: *Current Literature,* New York City, August, 1910, "Has been called 'the most beloved of all the country's Chief Justices' "; *Herald,* New York City, July 5, 1910, "He was widely beloved as a man"; *Daily Eagle,* Brooklyn, New York, July 5, 1910, "His associates loved him for his personal qualities and the bar . . . regarded him with affection and respect"; *Dispatch,* Pittsburgh, Pennsylvania, July 5, 1910, "His countrymen . . . had learned to venerate the lovable and picturesque figure"; *Republic,* St. Louis, Missouri, July 5, 1910, "Lovable of mind and heart"; *Republican,* Springfield, Massachusetts, July 5, 1910, "His unselfish devotion to duty, his gentle manners, his wealth of quiet humor endeared him to all with whom he came in contact"; *Post,* Worcester, Massachusetts, July 5, 1910, "His 'sweet and lovable nature' as President Taft well describes it . . . [has] been recognized by all men"; *Kennebec Journal,* Augusta, Maine, July 6, 1910, "Probably no . . . chief justice has been so widely known . . . And being known he has been loved and venerated"; *National Tribune,* Washington, D.C., July 7,

1910, "Held in the highest love and admiration"; *Green Bag,* New York City, August, 1910, "It is believed that no one of our Chief Justices was ever so loved by his associates and so honored by the American Bar"; *Daily Press,* Portland, Maine, July 6, 1910, quoting Judge William L. Putnam: "I do not believe there ever has been a justice of the Supreme bench of the United States who was more loved." ROOSEVELT'S HOSTILITY: Letter B. A. G. Fuller to the author, December 18, 1948. Theodore Roosevelt said to Dr. Fuller: "Your cousin [the Chief Justice] and I did not like each other one little bit." And see *Herald,* Louisville, Kentucky, July 5, 1910, "He was not loved by former President Roosevelt." APPEARANCE: *Outlook,* July 16, 1910; *Sun,* Baltimore, Maryland, July 5, 1910; *American,* Baltimore, Maryland, July 5, 1910; *News,* Denver, Colorado, July 5, 1910; *Times Dispatch,* Richmond, Virginia, July 5, 1910; *Union,* Springfield, Massachusetts, July 5, 1910; *Herald-Transcript,* Peoria, Illinois, July 6, 1910; *Republican,* Binghamton, New York, July 9, 1910. [330] DIGNITY: *Telegraph,* Philadelphia, Pennsylvania, July 5, 1910; *Times,* Brooklyn, New York, July 5, 1910; *News,* Buffalo, New York, July 5, 1910; *Journal,* Kansas City, Missouri, July 5, 1910; *Chieftain,* Pueblo, Colorado, July 6, 1910; *Gazette,* St. Joseph, Missouri, July 7, 1910; *Republican,* Binghamton, New York, July 9, 1910; *Bulletin,* Pittsburgh, Pennsylvania, July 9, 1910; *Journal,* Milwaukee, Wisconsin, July 5, 1910; *Gazette Times,* Pittsburgh, Pennsylvania, July 5, 1910. HUMOR: *Sun,* Baltimore, Maryland, July 5, 1910; *Republican,* Springfield, Massachusetts, July 5, 1910; *Daily Commercial,*

Bangor, Maine, July 5, 1910; *Daily Press,* Portland, Maine, July 6, 1910. Fuller to Morris, December 13, 1891, Morris papers; Fuller to Mrs. Fuller, March 27, 1876, Genet papers. COURAGE AND INDEPENDENCE: *Outlook,* July 16, 1910; *News,* Indianapolis, Indiana, July 4, 1910; *Post,* Boston, Massachusetts, July 5, 1910; *News,* Buffalo, New York, July 5, 1910; *Journal,* Milwaukee, Wisconsin, July 5, 1910; *Post,* Worcester, Massachusetts, July 5, 1910; *Law Journal,* New York City, New York, July 6, 1910; *Times Leader,* New Haven, Connecticut, July 7, 1910; *Outlook,* New York City, New York, July 16, 1910; Detroit *Free Press,* quoted, July 5, 1910. [331] IMPARTIALITY AND NONPARTISANSHIP: Philadelphia *Public Ledger,* July 5, 1910; Boston *Globe,* July 5, 1910; *Times,* New York City, July 5, 1910, "His impartiality and open mindedness were heartily conceded and admired by even the most pronounced opponents of his party"; *Times,* Brooklyn, New York, July 5, 1910, "Never permitted his political opinions to influence him in the slightest degree"; *Sentinel,* Ansonia, Connecticut, July 5, 1910, "Strictly non-partisan in his rulings"; *American,* Baltimore, Maryland, July 5, 1910, "Absolute judicial impartiality"; *Tribune,* Providence, Rhode Island, July 5, 1910, "Met his duties with open mindedness and discharged them with impartiality"; *Republic,* St. Louis, Missouri, July 5, 1910, "Never . . . was his long and honorable term as Chief Justice ever tainted by the smirch of partisan prejudice"; *Commercial,* New York City, July 5, 1910, "Never a partisan"; *Evening Globe,* New York City, July 5, 1910, "His lucid language is spread out in hundreds of decisions, yet industry can hardly find a trace of bias in them . . . It is difficult for a layman to understand how a jurist is thus able to rid himself of personal prejudices yet such capacity to be loyal to the law . . . is the very heart of the judicial faculty"; *Commercial,* Bangor, Maine, July 5, 1910, "There has never been even a whisper of partisanship in connection with his conduct of his high office"; *Gazette,* Burlington, Iowa, July 5, 1910, "He was above partisanship"; *Record-Herald,* Chicago, Illinois, July 5, 1910, "His career . . . was not that of a vicious partisan, but of an intelligent, conscientious and upright judge"; *Star Independence,* Harrisburg, Pennsylvania, July 5, 1910, "As Chief Justice he sank partisanship and personality and was only the impartial . . . head of a great court"; *Wisconsin,* Milwaukee, Wisconsin, July 5, 1910, "In politics Chief Justice Fuller was a Democrat, but he has never been accused of partisanship in his decisions"; *Star,* Newark, New Jersey, July 5, 1910, "In all his acts on the bench there was not the least color of political partisanship"; *Express,* Portland, Maine, July 5, 1910, "Chief Justice Fuller was great enough to forget the political affiliations of a lifetime and to serve for all these years at the head of the Supreme Court of the United States without once invoking a criticism of partisanship"; *Herald Republican,* Salt Lake City, Utah, July 5, 1910, "The decisions of Chief Justice Fuller were never clouded by his political views"; *Law Journal,* New York City, July 6, 1910, "He has been free from political bigotry"; *Statesman,* Austin, Texas, July 6, 1910, "There is nothing in his long service . . . that indicated a political bias in his decisions";

Globe, Fall River, Massachusetts, July 6, 1910, "No question was ever entertained regarding the sincerity of his convictions or that his judgment was swayed or influenced by personal bias or partisan prejudice"; *Post,* Jamestown, New York, July 6, 1910, "Although a Democrat of the old school Chief Justice Fuller never allowed partisanship to interfere with his decisions"; *Herald,* Rochester, New York, July 6, 1910, "No one whose opinion is worth listening to has ever accused the dead jurist of being unduly biased"; *Republic,* Boston, Massachusetts, July 9, 1910, "The most hide bound Republican admitted and respected Fuller's honesty and courage"; *Evening Globe,* New York City, July 4, 1910, "Deaf to clamor, deaf also to prejudice or self interest, this great judge has held the balance true"; *Telegraph,* Philadelphia, Pennsylvania, July 5, 1910, "He has at no time been swayed by public opinion or the clamor of the multitude"; *Commercial,* Bangor, Maine, July 5, 1910, "The highest court of our land under his administration has been indeed a court of justice where even-handed equity was meted out fearlessly and impartially to the high and the low, the rich and the poor, the powerful and the powerless." SCHOLARSHIP: *Commercial,* Bangor, Maine, July 5, 1910, "Chief Justice Fuller was distinguished even among scholars for his scholarship which was so wide in range as to excite amazement among his colleagues"; *Gazette Times,* Pittsburgh, Pennsylvania, July 5, 1910, "He was noted . . . for his erudition and profound mastery of the law"; *Dispatch,* Pittsburgh, Pennsylvania, July 5, 1910, "He brought to his exalted station . . . the experience and knowledge of law gained in a practice covering the span of a generation, a scholarly love of literature and learning that humanized the dryest text"; *News,* Savannah, Georgia, July 5, 1910, "He was remarkable for the extent of his information bearing upon the cases that came before the court, his memory being of the most retentive kind"; *Republican,* Springfield, Massachusetts, July 5, 1910, "He was broadly grounded in the law, clear in his understanding, simple in his judicial expositions"; *Times,* Troy, New York, July 5, 1910, "He possessed an intellect of extraordinary acuteness, a knowledge of law that was far reaching and a capacity for statement that made the opinions written by him worthy of the Supreme Court"; *Outlook,* New York City, July 16, 1910, "he was . . . a lover of the classics, the possessor of a fine . . . style, a scholar of culture"; *Observer,* Utica, New York, July 5, 1910, "Of an exceptionally agreeable personality and with intellectual attainments universally recognized"; *Press,* Utica, New York, July 5, 1910, "In character and habit he was an ideal judge, giving much time to the study of law and literature . . . Possessed of exceptional literary learning . . . his opinions were always well written"; *Herald,* Washington, D. C., July, 5, 1910, "His incumbency . . . was marked . . . by ripe scholarship"; *Kennebec Journal,* Augusta, Maine, July 6, 1910, "His ripe scholarship and personal worth has added luster and dignity to the highest judicial body in the world"; *News Tribune,* Duluth, Minnesota, July 6, 1910, "Justice Fuller was a fine example of the scholar at the bar. He was a man who loved the law, but added to it, wove into it and made to supplement it,

a wide knowledge of literature, of history and the kindred subjects written in books"; *Star,* Peoria, Illinois, July 6, 1910, "He was a scholar, a jurist profoundly versed in all the history and theory of the law"; *Chieftain,* Pueblo, Colorado, July 6, 1910, "He was a profound scholar of English and his opinions reflected his great research into literature"; *Times,* Rochester, New York, July 6, 1910, "During his long career . . . no one ever questioned his absolute honesty of purpose or his deep and thorough knowledge of the law"; *Post Intelligencer,* Seattle, Washington, July 6, 1910, "He has been a leader of great light, of profound erudition, of lofty national ideals and keen judicial conceptions"; *American Review of Reviews,* New York City, August, 1910, "Mr. Fuller was a man of scholarly mind"; *Despatch,* St. Paul, Minnesota, July 4, 1910, "A service noted for its wealth of research and its scholarly reasoning"; *Times,* Washington, D.C., July 4, 1910, "He was the delving, searching, student type. Into his cases he threw the best there was in him"; *Record-Herald,* Chicago, Illinois, July 5, 1910, "He was a persistent and close student of law, politics and literature, a wide reader and an industrious one"; *Journal,* Detroit, Michigan, July 5, 1910, "He had been successful in private practice and had shown enormous power of research"; *Journal,* Portland, Oregon, July 5, 1910, "On every case that came before the tribunal he was possessed of profound information that had an important bearing on the issues. He was an exhaustive student of constitutional law . . . and much of his vacations were devoted to study and reflection"; *Times Dispatch,* Richmond, Virginia, July 5, 1910,

"Rugged, impressive and with a marvelous capacity for work, he gave to the Court a standing and a prestige it enjoyed in other days when the great names of Marshall or Taney headed the roll of the Justices"; *Republic,* St. Louis, Missouri, July 5, 1910, He left "memories of those native endowments and rare acquirements which established his intellectual greatness. Both scholar and jurist, he became in his high station a successor whose worthiness to don the mantle of the illustrious line which preceded him . . . never was assailed . . . Throughout a span of life which nearly had attained fourscore years,—he remained a diligent student, an omnivorous reader, a thoughtful, earnest, untiring seeker for added knowledge. The extent of his general learning was deemed by his associates in our highest court as prodigious"; *Herald Transcript,* Peoria, Illinois, July 6, 1910, "Few men have devoted themselves to their work with such assiduity and concentration. To Mr. Fuller, the Supreme Court was indeed a cloister"; *Bulletin,* Pittsburgh, Pennsylvania, July 9, 1910, "Indefatigable in his research, sound in his arguments, clear in his elucidation, he made a name that will stand always among the highest in the law"; *Sentinel,* Milwaukee, Wisconsin, July 5, 1910, "To wide and profound professional learning he added literary tastes and a bent for writing that found vent in pleasant and scholarly excursions into the critical bypaths of literature before he was called to . . . the Supreme Court." **[332]** OPINIONS: *Times,* Troy, New York, July 5, 1910; *Press,* Utica, New York, July 5, 1910; *Republican,* Springfield, Massachusetts, July 5, 1910; *Law Journal,* New

York City, New York, July 6, 1910; *News,* Dayton, Ohio, July 6, 1910; *Daily Press,* Portland, Maine, July 6, 1910; *Law Notes,* Northport, New York, August, 1910. GENTLENESS AND COMPASSION : See Supra pp. **138, 183–184, 313–314;** *Times,* Washington, D.C., July 4, 1910; *Evening Mail,* New York City, New York, July 5, 1910; *Republic,* St. Louis, Missouri, July 5, 1910. MODESTY: *Evening Mail,* New York City, New York, July 5, 1910; *Press,* Philadelphia, Pennsylvania, July 5, 1910; *Sun,* Pittsburgh, Pennsylvania, July 5, 1910; *Republican,* Springfield, Massachusetts, July 5, 1910; *Democrat Chronicle,* Rochester, New York, July 6, 1910; *State Gazette,* Trenton, New Jersey, July 6, 1910. **[333]** Quotations from: *Press,* Philadelphia, Pennsylvania, July 5, 1910; *Republican,* Springfield, Massachusetts, July 5, 1910; *Herald Transcript,* Peoria, Illinois, July 6, 1910. In McLaughlin: A Constitutional History of the United States, 1936, out of a total of 355 cases cited in the book, 87 were decisions of the Supreme Court in Fuller's period. He wrote the opinions in only 8 of these cases. **[334]** See Frankfurter & Landis: The Business of the Supreme Court, Plates I and II, pp. 296–7 on his improvement of the Court's calendar. Quotations from Pittsburgh *Sun,* Pittsburgh, Pennsylvania, July 5, 1910. Draft of letter to Stephen A. Day in Holmes' papers, 1930. Holmes to Putnam, July 12, 1910, Putnam papers. **[335]** COMPARISON WITH MARSHALL AND TANEY: *That he did not rank with Marshall or Taney: News,* Indianapolis, Indiana, July 4, 1910, "We doubt whether Mr. Fuller will rank as one of the great judges of the nation"; *Tribune,* New York City, July 5, 1910, "It would be extravagant to rank him with Marshall or Taney as a moulder of the court's policy"; *Evening Mail,* New York City, July 5, 1910, "The late chief justice did not rank, in the importance or the lightning-flash luminousness of his decisions with Marshall and Story or their breed"; *Daily Eagle,* Brooklyn, New York, July 5, 1910, "He was . . . not in the class of Taney nor of Marshall"; *Age Herald,* Birmingham, Alabama, July 5, 1910, "History may not give him a place alongside either Taney or Marshall"; *Tribune,* Chicago, Illinois, July 5, 1910, "Justice Fuller will not go down in the history of the Supreme Court as one of its great judges"; *Star,* Indianapolis, Indiana, July 5, 1910, "He was not so great a genius in constructive jurisprudence as John Marshall"; *Journal,* Kansas City, Missouri, July 5, 1910, "The name of Chief Justice Fuller has not been associated with enough memorable decisions to place him with the historic chief justices of the past"; *News,* Savannah, Georgia, July 5, 1910, "He will rank high as a chief justice but hardly with the greatest of his predecessors"; *Post,* Pittsburgh, Pennsylvania, July 5, 1910, "He was never a Marshall or a Taney"; *Sun,* Pittsburgh, Pennsylvania, July 5, 1910, "Possibly not in the class with some of his most noted predecessors but worthy of being associated with them"; *Tribune,* Providence, Rhode Island, July 5, 1910, "To rank him with Marshall or Taney as a moulder of national political life or even of the Supreme Court's policy would be extravagant indeed"; *Republican,* Springfield, Massachusetts, July 5, 1910, "Unlike Marshall he was never disposed to make himself the overshadowing figure among his colleagues

and few of the great opinions of the court in the past 22 years are of his writing, whether for the court or for the minority. . . . He lacked Marshall's robustness of intellect and was perhaps happily wanting in the aggressive mentality of Taney"; *Post Standard,* Syracuse, New York, July 5, 1910, "His services as chief justice excelled that of all others in office save only John Marshall and Roger B. Taney"; *Post,* Worcester, Massachusetts, July 5, 1910, "He did not equal, and no man has, the wonderful luminosity and constructive genius that out of rugged common sense made the former's [Marshall's] judicial career epochal, while the profound acumen of Taney is still unmatched"; *Republican,* Binghamton, New York, July 6, 1910, "His work will not attach to his name the prominence attained by Chief Justices Marshall, Taney or Waite"; *Inquirer,* Philadelphia, Pennsylvania, July 6, 1910, "Possibly Fuller will never rank with Marshall and Story"; *Press,* Pittsburgh, Pennsylvania, July 6, 1910, "History will probably not accord him equal rank with Chief Justice John Marshall . . . or with Chief Justice Taney"; *Post Intelligencer,* Seattle, Washington, July 6, 1910, "Probably in the nature of our history Chief Justice Fuller will never be rated as the equal of Jay, of Marshall, of Chase or of Taney"; *Herald,* Rochester, New York, July 6, 1910, "He was not a Marshall, but he succeeded in winning the respect of all his colleagues, and, we think, of the bar and bench of the entire country"; *News,* Dallas, Texas, July 7, 1910, "Chief Justice Fuller did not impress himself on the imagination of the country to the degree that several of his predecessors did. . . . It was due perhaps quite as much to a disparity of occasion or opportunity. When Marshall and Taney sat . . . the Constitution was in a much more plastic state"; *Star Gazette*, Trenton, New Jersey, July 6, 1910, "He was never rated as a great jurist, but his fairness in reaching the decisions that he rendered won for him the highest regard among the best lawyers of the country"; *Financial Chronicle*, New York City, July 9, 1910, "While he perhaps did not win the very highest place in the history of American jurists, he was always a sound, careful and honored member of the Court"; *Index*, Pittsburgh, Pennsylvania, July 9, 1910, "The late jurist did not rank as the greatest chief justice the country has known. More important decisions were rendered by Chief Justice Marshall." *That he was comparable to Marshall or Taney: Banner*, Nashville, Tennessee, July 4, 1910, "No other chief justice has ranked higher than Chief Justice Fuller"; *Despatch*, St. Paul, Minnesota, July 4, 1910, "He will be classed by the discriminating historian as worthily occupying a place among the best who have sat upon the highest bench of the land"; *Evening Globe*, New York City, July 5, 1910, "For 22 years he sat on the bench and performed a volume of work far exceeding that done by either Marshall or Taney, although the years of their service were more numerous"; *Enquirer*, Cincinnati, Ohio, July 5, 1910, "The luster lent to the exalted position by a distinguished line of predecessors was in no wise diminished during the incumbency of Justice Fuller"; *Journal*, Milwaukee, Wisconsin, July 5, 1910, "Without the brilliancy or originality of some Chief Justice Fuller is entitled to high rank with the best of the chief justices of

the United States"; *Register*, New Haven, Connecticut, July 5, 1910, "There may have been greater heads of this great court; there never was a better one"; *Bee*, Omaha, Nebraska, July 5, 1910, "The final decision must give him high rank with other men who have held that exalted position"; *Public Ledger*, Philadelphia, Pennsylvania, July 5, 1910, "No man since Marshall has had to guide the Supreme Court through so intricate a maze of legal development. . . . This has been the more difficult for Fuller because he has presided over a rapidly changing court. . . . It may be that if Fuller had possessed the dominating personality of Marshall, these changes [on the Court] would have been less apparent; but his has been the constantly unifying influence that has held the court steady to its chart among all the personal variations of its members. No man has ever more completely realized the impartial impersonal integrity and dignity of the court in its splendid aloofness from prejudice and passion"; *Oregonian*, Portland, Oregon, July 5, 1910, "Few Chief Justices of the Supreme Court have lived during times when more weighty questions were up for decision, and probably the verdict of history will be that none have met their problems with more adequate wisdom"; *Telegraph*, Philadelphia, Pennsylvania, July 5, 1910, "It is no disparagement to the Marshalls and the Taneys and the Jays and the Rutledges and other worthies who have filled this exalted station to say that none of them has been superior in training, in honesty or in dignity"; *Gazette Times*, Pittsburgh, Pennsylvania, July 5, 1910, "He will rank in history as one of the great chief justices both in length and quality of service"; *Times Dispatch,* Richmond, Virginia, July 5, 1910, "He gave to the Court a standing and a prestige it enjoyed in other days when the great names of Marshall or Taney headed the roll of the justices"; *Herald,* Newport, Rhode Island, July 6, 1910, "While he will not rank with some of the giants among his predecessors, he will occupy a distinguished place in the annals of the tribunal"; *Post Intelligencer,* Seattle, Washington, July 6, 1910, "Just Americans will give him a place among America's great jurists"; *Financier,* New York City, July 9, 1910, "The death of Chief Justice Fuller removes from the Supreme Court bench a man admittedly the peer of any of his illustrious predecessors"; *Bulletin,* Pittsburgh, Pennsylvania, July 9, 1910, "He made a name that will stand always among the highest in the law. . . . Others will fill the place, probably as well, but none better." *That only the future can tell his rank: Evening Post,* Chicago, Illinois, July 5, 1910, "The generation which witnesses the activities of a public man is not the one best fitted to pass judgment on his abilities nor is it the one to fix the place he will have in history"; *News,* Denver, Colorado, July 5, 1910; *Dispatch,* Pittsburgh, Pennsylvania, July 5, 1910; *Post,* Worcester, Massachusetts, July 5, 1910; *Post,* Washington, D.C., July 5, 1910; *Republican,* Binghamton, New York, July 9, 1910. Quotation from Holmes and Miller, supra, p. 290; Holmes to Putnam, July 12, 1910, Putnam papers. Quotation from *Philadelphia Press,* July 5, 1910. And see *Sentinel,* Ansonia, Connecticut, July 5, 1910, "He greatly strengthened the Supreme bench by his influence"; *Times Dispatch,* Richmond, Virginia, July 5, 1910, "He gave to the Court a standing and a prestige it had enjoyed in other days when the great names of Marshall or Taney headed the roll of the Justices." **[336]** *Chicago Evening Post,* July 5, 1910.

INDEX

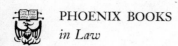
PHOENIX BOOKS
in Law

PHOENIX BOOKS
in Political Science